Mary Ann Creadon

BEGINNINGS

BEGINNINGS

Intention and Method

EDWARD W. SAID

Basic Books, Inc., Publishers / New York

Library of Congress Cataloging in Publication Data

Said, Edward W.
  Beginnings : intention and method.

  Includes bibliographical references.
  1. Literature—History and criticism—Theory, etc.
I. Title.
PN441.S3   809   74-78306
ISBN 0-465-00580-2

For Mariam

Wadie

Najla

Doctrines must take their beginning from that of the matters of which they treat.

Vico, *The New Science*

CONTENTS

PREFACE

WHAT is a beginning? What must one do in order to begin? What is special about beginning as an activity or a moment or a place? Can one begin whenever one pleases? What kind of attitude, or frame of mind is necessary for beginning? Historically, is there one sort of moment most propitious for beginning, one sort of individual for whom beginning is the most important of activities? For the work of literature, how important is the beginning? Are such questions about beginning worth raising? And if so, can they be treated or answered concretely, intelligibly, informatively?

For this book these are the beginning questions. Yet once they are taken up a process of delimitation occurs—mercifully, since otherwise they are almost impossibly complex questions to discuss. I have concentrated on beginnings both as something one does and as something one thinks about. The two sometimes go together, but they are always necessarily connected when language is being used. Thus there is a particular vocabulary employed— terms like *beginning* and *starting out, origins* and *originality, initiation, inauguration, revolution, authority, point of departure, radicalism,* and so on—when a beginning is being either described or pointed out. Similarly, when one actually begins to write, a complex set of circumstances obtains that characterizes the beginning enterprise. In language, therefore, writing or thinking *about* beginning is tied to writing or thinking *a* beginning. A verbal beginning is consequently both a creative and a critical activity, just as at the moment one begins to use language in a disciplined way, the orthodox distinction between critical and creative thought begins to break down.

Beginning is not only a kind of action; it is also a frame of mind, a kind of work, an attitude, a consciousness. It is pragmatic—as when we read a difficult text and wonder where to begin in order to understand it, or where the author began the work and why. And it is theoretic—as when we ask whether there is any peculiar epistemological trait or performance unique to beginnings in general. For any writer to begin is to embark upon something connected to a designated point of departure. Even when it is repressed, the beginning is always a first step from which (except on rare occasions) something follows. So beginnings play a role, if not always a very clearly understood one. Certainly they are formally useful: middles and ends, continuity, development—all these imply beginnings before them. A complex form, however, has a logic of its own. Does a beginning?

If we assume the presence of beginnings here and there for the reflective artist, reflective critic, philosopher, politician, historian, and psychoanalytic investigator, a study of beginnings can all too easily become a catalog of infinite cases. My task in this book is precisely to avoid compiling such a catalog (even while being aware of its possibility) and to take up instead the question of beginnings in an interesting, fairly detailed, practical, and theoretical way. I not only try to show what sort of language is used and what sort of thought takes place either as one begins or as one thinks and writes about beginning, but also I wish to show how forms like the novel and how concepts like *text* are forms of beginning and being in the world. Moreover, those changes that occur from one cultural period to the next can be studied as shifts in the notion of what a beginning is or ought to be. When one practices criticism today, for example, a highly circumstantial awareness of beginning to write criticism is in operation; we are less likely now than before to think that a writer's life has an absolute prior privilege when it comes to understanding his work. Why is this so, and what should we now begin with as we study a writer's work? What *are* the privileged terms and the principal aspects of critical awareness today?

Any work that pretends to deal with such questions risks being embarrassed not only by its beginning but also by its continuity, its choice of subjects, its vocabulary. The potential for such embarrassment with this particular book is something I have not underestimated. My own critical terms (*transitive* and *intransitive beginnings, authority, intention, method, beginning*—as distinguished from *origin—text, structure*) are built upon associations of ideas which, as will become fairly evident, gather in a rather wide range of interests. Each of the book's six chapters, or episodes, has an internal coherence that depends on some aspect of beginning; each covers a historical pattern (the development of the novel, for example) that does not stray very far from the core subject of beginnings, although paradoxically I find it possible in one chapter

(Chapter 3) to discuss both the early *and* the late phases of the European novel. Altogether, these six episodes constitute a structure for studying beginnings, though not in a linear fashion. Perhaps my decision to quote Vico in the epigraph and to make his work the subject of my conclusion makes my (circular) point best—namely, that beginnings are first and important but not always evident, that beginning is basically an activity which ultimately implies return and repetition rather than simple linear accomplishment, that beginning and beginning-again are historical whereas origins are divine, that a beginning not only creates but is its own method because it has intention. In short, beginning is *making* or *producing difference;* but—and here is the great fascination in the subject—difference which is the result of combining the already-familiar with the fertile novelty of human work in language. Each of my chapters builds on this interplay between the new and the customary without which (*ex nihilo nihil fit*) a beginning cannot really take place. The underlying interest of an essay such as this book is its true theme: the community of language and history—*from* the beginning, *despite* any one beginning. To say this *at* the beginning is hopefully thereafter to avoid the conservative safety of language without history, and vice versa. Thus beginnings confirm, rather than discourage, a radical severity and verify evidence of at least some innovation—of *having begun.*

ACKNOWLEDGMENTS

Dorem URING some of the time I have spent working on this book I have benefited from the generosity of the John Simon Guggenheim Memorial Foundation. In other ways, chiefly intellectual, I have incurred a great debt to my colleagues and students in the Department of English and Comparative Literature at Columbia College; it would be difficult to describe, or for that matter to thank, the extraordinary ambience of intelligence and friendship so often present on the fourth floor of Hamilton Hall. For the sympathetic reception of ideas, for the readiness to grant learning and speculation a high place, for the seriousness and wit of intellectual discussion there, I have found the collegiate atmosphere of Columbia inimitable. Friends and colleagues in other places have been kind in similar, and similarly valuable, ways: it is a special pleasure to mention Sadek el-Azm, Monroe Engel, Angus Fletcher, and Richard Macksey. For help in the preparation of the manuscript I am grateful to Louise Yelin, Lydia Dittler and Massimo Bacigalupo. Jamelia Saied of Basic Books helped immeasurably in putting the manuscript through the travail of editorial process and production. I was the undeserving beneficiary of freely given typing aid from Joan Ramos, Mona Iskandar, and Mariam Said. My wife's affectionate understanding, in particular, sustained me during this very long beginning.

PERMISSIONS

A NOTE ON TRANSLATIONS

I N ALL CASES any work from which I quote whose original language is not English is cited in an English translation. Although I do this both for the sake of consistency and because I would like the reader to have direct access to everything in this book, I must explain my policy on translation. Every text not in English (with the exception of those in Russian) I have studied in the original language. Wherever possible, however, I quote from an already published English translation, which I have checked against the original. In instances where there is no translation available or where the translation in my opinion is inadequate, I have made my own (sometimes mainly literal) translation. The reader is therefore to understand that unless otherwise indicated translations are my own; bad as some of these may be, I have preferred at least to make do with translations, done amateurishly, that render exactly those notions from the original in a way I can control, than to use aberrant versions done by someone else. Doubtless my translations are not especially elegant. Nevertheless, I have often parenthetically included short passages in the original language for the reader's benefit; also, I have always indicated sources for my translation in the original, non-English texts.

CHAPTER

ONE

_____

Beginning Ideas

I

THE problem of beginnings is one of those problems that, if allowed to, will confront one with equal intensity on a practical and on a theoretical level. Every writer knows that the choice of a beginning for what he will write is crucial not only because it determines much of what follows but also because a work's beginning is, practically speaking, the main entrance to what it offers. Moreover, in retrospect we can regard a beginnning as the point at which, in a given work, the writer departs from all other works; a beginning immediately establishes relationships with works already existing, relationships of either continuity or antagonism or some mixture of both. But the moment we start to detail the features of a beginning—a moment likely to occur in examining many sorts of writers—we necessarily make certain special distinctions. Is a beginning the same as an origin? Is the beginning of a given work its real beginning, or is there some other, secret point that more authentically starts the work off? To what extent is a beginning ultimately a physical exigency and nothing more than that? Of what value, for critical or methodological or even historical analysis, is "the beginning"? By what sort of approach, with what kind of language, with what sort of instruments does a beginning offer itself up as a subject for study?

The size of the present book is evidence enough that these are engrossing questions—at least to me. Yet I feel that what keeps the book from being merely a record of preliminary curiosities is that in subject matter, approach, and methodology this study of beginnings aims to contribute, however modestly, to contemporary criticism. It soon will become evident that by the term *criticism* I intend something rather unlike literary history, or *explication de texte,* or cultural generality; in this sense of its own

3

difference, therefore, this book begins by explicitly venturing a particular ambition for itself, an ambition that finally becomes intelligible only in the book's unfolding and not through first advancing some ideal type which it then seeks to fulfill. It must be added that this manner of criticism cannot claim any ultimate novelty, for its obvious reliance upon many other writers immediately invalidates the claim. But in seeking first to isolate a problem—that of the beginning which appears more abstract than problems dealt with in most criticism—in seeking then to make a selection of issues, examples, and evidence uniquely relevant to the problem, in seeking to work in discursive and conceptual language suited to the problem, in seeking to set the problem in as spacious and yet as pertinent a frame of modern reference as possible, and finally in seeking to learn from itself, to adjust to and change itself in progress: in all these ways this book aims to contribute to contemporary criticism. And since it would take many more pages to round out my prescriptive definition of *criticism,* I shall instead enumerate the questions, circumstances, and conditions that form this study and that influence its trajectory.

II

In each of the following relatively innocuous statements the sense derives prominently from a common sense understanding of the concept of "beginnings": "Conrad began his career with *Almayer's Folly*"; "*Pride and Prejudice* begins with the following sentence"; "Pope began to write at an early age"; "Before he began to write Hemingway would sharpen a dozen pencils"; "*This* is what one ought to do at the beginning"; "Civilization can be said to have begun in the Near East"; "As soon as he began to know Odette better Swann started to suspect her"; "From beginning to end Flaubert was ever the artist." Of quite another order of meaning are such statements as "In the beginning was the Word" or "In my beginning is my end." In both sets of statements, however, variations of the concept "beginning" designate a moment in time, a place, a principle, or an action. Just as obviously, these designations are verbal constructions employing variations of the term *beginning* in a relatively well-defined way: thus, the concept "beginning" is associated in each case with an idea of precedence and/or priority. Finally and most important, in each case a "beginning" is designated in order to indicate, clarify, or define a *later* time, place, or action. In short, the designation of a beginning generally involves also the designation of a consequent *intention*. We might not actually say as much every time, but when we point to the beginning of a novel, for example, we mean that from *that* beginning in principle follows *this* novel. Or, we see that the beginning is the first point (in time, space, or action) of an accomplishment or process that has duration and meaning. *The beginning, then, is the first step in the intentional production of meaning.*

In Chapters 1 and 2 I describe the conditions that pertain to the designation and the intention of beginnings: in what settings and by what instruments beginnings are formed, for what purposes different kinds of beginnings are designated, and what kind of mind and what kind of work tend to insist upon the importance of beginnings. In describing these I introduce a second sort of beginning, what I call the pure or intransitive beginning, one that has no intention other than simply to be a beginning in the sense of being first. In the major part of the book (Chapters 3, 4, and 5), I develop the consequences of those early adumbrations: how an interest in beginnings entails a certain sort of writing, thought, and meaning, how beginnings relate generally and specifically to different continuities, and how, paradoxically, an interest in beginnings is often the corollary result of not believing that any beginning can be located. All of this depends—importantly, I think—on the following generalization: whether an interest in beginnings is practical or highly theoretical, there is an imperative connection to be observed between the idea of a beginning and an aboriginal human need to point to or locate a beginning.

But all of these general projects of the book can only have at this stage a somewhat rarified significance for the reader. Therefore, it becomes necessary for me first to discuss the circumstances of this study: why such a study proposed itself to its author, why it is pursued in this way in particular, and how a rationale for such a study is arrived at.

III

As a problem for study, "beginnings" are attractive, first of all, because while one can isolate *a* beginning analytically, the notion of beginning itself is practically tied up in a whole complex of relations. Thus between the word *beginning* and the word *origin* lies a constantly changing system of meanings, most of them of course making first one then the other word convey greater priority, importance, explanatory power.* As consistently as possible I use *beginning* as having the more active meaning, and *origin* the more passive one: thus "X *is the origin of* Y," while "The beginning A *leads to* B." In due course I hope to show, however, how ideas about origins, because of their passivity, are put to uses I believe ought to be avoided.

But even this distinction seems relatively crude when one considers how many words and ideas in current thought and writing hover about the concept of "beginnings": *innovation, novelty, originality, revolution, change, convention, tradition, period, authority, influence,* to name but a few. Altogether they describe the rather broad field in which the present study is located—which should not be surprising, since most writing has kept these notions in mind. I am centrally concerned, however, with what takes place when one consciously sets out to experience or define what a beginning entails, especially with regard to the meaning produced as a result of a given beginning.

When I first became interested in beginnings several years ago, some of the problems struck me as essentially constituting the professional dilemma of the writer interested in "literary criticism": How should he begin to write? I then discovered that this question conceals at least four others: (1) After what training does one begin to write? (2) With what subject in mind does one begin to write? (3) What is the point of departure for writing—a new direction or one continuing from old ones? (4) Is there a privileged beginning for a literary study—that is, an especially suitable or important beginning—that is wholly different from a historical, psychological, or cultural one? Every one of these questions impinges upon the writer today, and what they represent, it is now clear to me, is by no means exclusively a "professional" issue. Rather, each of these questions involves theoretical and practical issues in equal measure.

Consider the general education brought to literary criticism by an individual today. Whatever else he may have been trained in, it was almost certainly not in classical philology, the one discipline in Europe and America that was practically *de rigeur* for the literary scholar until World War II. For studying literature in the

---

*As for example, in the "*origins* of Greek tragedy," the "*beginning* of consciousness," and so on ad infinitum.

university was considered a privilege to be earned by a scholar once he had mastered classical philology in some detail, as well as principles of textual study that were codified by years of practice and therefore not open to subjective "interpretation." The published reminiscences of such scholars as Leo Spitzer, Erwin Panofsky, Erich Auerbach, Ernst Robert Curtius, the volume of work produced by C. S. Lewis, Amerigo Castro, Ferdinand Baldensperger, Theophil Spoerri, and others like them, tell a rather humbling story about the researcher today, who can barely read another language (and certainly not Latin) and who thinks a "text" is one of a paperback series. Spitzer was able in his later years to write hundreds of pages on the meaning of words like *milieu* and *race* as they appeared in a half-dozen languages and literatures over four or five centuries—fully because he was *taught* by Meyer-Lubke "to find etymologies."[1] And for all his metaphysical interest in Man, Spitzer in his authoritative essays brings forth great masses of exact information obviously learned first from a teacher who, says Spitzer, "in reference to a given French form . . . would quote Old Portuguese, Modern Bergamesque and Macedo-Rumanian, German, Celtic and Paleo-Latin forms."[2] What is impressive here is not only the kind of information possessed by scholars like Spitzer, but also the fact that it was received information, handed down from generation to generation.

There is not much use in speculating why most people no longer regard education as adding links to a historical dynasty. We expect the student trained in literature to have a smattering of "humanities"—in translation—but an urgent sense of other knowledge, paraknowledge, that he assumes lies naturally alongside literature and in some way bears upon it. He will know a lot about Freudian psychology, about Marxism in some form, about Marcuse, Norman O. Brown, Laing, and so forth. This should not be taken simply as an attack upon either the contemporary student or his sense of relevance. In fact, *our* fate as scholars today is precisely that of our students, for how many of us can do classical philology? At best, we learned Greek or German to pass reading exams, and for most of us Romance philology was something we read about while we took courses in the accelerated reading of French or Italian. The bookstore, with its rack upon rack of translated works (Freud, Nietzsche, Proust, Hesse, Baudelaire), brings us closer and faster to the world of knowledge than any other means readily available. Certainly few students today can move, as Panofsky did, from one university to another, to listen to eminent scholars, whereas anyone can move very quickly from one book to another, from the study of one period or culture to another.[3]

One way of mitigating this change and even of enhancing the fact that it has taken place, is to argue that literature itself has gone through the same change. A medieval or Renaissance poet is likely to have been more learned than William Carlos Williams; and in general a Chaucer scholar probably knows Latin and Old English, whereas a D. H. Lawrence specialist need not and probably does not. Yet I am less interested in such generalities than in the fact that if a modern writer like Joyce was less formally learned than Richard Hooker, the former was almost surely equipped with more knowledge, arranged very differently. The problem we face today when we study Joyce, or when, untrained in classics or religion, we read Hooker, or when we deploy psychology in the study of a literary text, is a problem of irregularity, of discontinuity. That is, less background, less formal training, less prescribed and systematic information, is assumed before one begins to read, write, or work. Thus when one begins to write today one is necessarily more of an autodidact, gathering or making up the knowledge one needs in the course of creating. The influence of the past appears less useful and, as two recent critics, W. J. Bate and Harold Bloom, have argued, more likely to produce anxiety.[4] Therefore, Roland Barthes, paraphrasing Bachelard, has said that the study and the production of literature today is the study and the production of de-formation.[5] To read Joyce we must follow these de-formations, just as Joyce's reading de-formed the traditional curriculum.

It is less permissible today to imagine oneself as writing within a tradition when one writes literary criticism. This is not to say, however, that every critic is now a revolutionist destroying the canon in order to replace it with his own. A better image is that of a wanderer, going from place to place for his material, but remaining a man essentially *between* homes.[6] In the process, what is taken from a place ultimately violates its habitual way of being: there is constant transposition, just as when we read an imitation by Pound or by Lowell we read the redistribution of an Anglo-Saxon or Italian original that occupies a wider, less well-charted, and less predictable exterior space than the original.

It is worth pursuing a little further such notions as "exteriority" and "in-betweenness." They do not refer to a sort of fellow-traveling critical eclecticism. Rather, they describe a transformation that has taken place in the working reality of the self-conscious writer. He can no longer easily accept—for many reasons, spiritual or sociological—a place in a continuity that formerly stretched forward and backward in time. Already Eliot had understood that "tradition" was an achievement for the few, not the possession of all. Perhaps, also, today's writer is less comfortable with the unadorned fact of precedence—as opposed to Dante, for example, who had been comfortable with Virgil—and perhaps he can no longer know what it means to stand in a direct line of descent. History and tradition seem less communicable in sequential narrative because, as Foucault says, history appears to us now to comprise very large units of endeavor (the evolution of trade patterns, demographic alterations, slow shifts in agricultural or intellectual habits, and so on) that scant the individual life span.[7] Knowledge, therefore, is less formally embodied, whether in a subject like philology, a teacher like Meyer-Lubke, or in a traditional plot of unfolding like that of a Dickens novel.

Furthermore, exteriority and in-betweenness in the modern writer are the inevitable results of lacking either faith in or capacity for limited (discrete) but wholly integrated work. The modern writer often feels the urge instead to create new totalities, to cultivate random appetites, to deny forward movement altogether. The historic contest between Wilamowitz and Nietzsche after the publication of the latter's *Birth of Tragedy* in 1872 perfectly symbolizes the distinction I am drawing.[8] At bottom, their conflict centered around the idea of a "classical text": Was it one in a series to be revered, cultivated, emended, and described in the best scholarly tradition? Or was it rather, as Nietzsche believed (though not at all so simply as stated here), a text upon which, as upon a writing tablet, was inscribed a constellation of forces (instincts, urges, desires, wills) still present in the modern era and still as unseemly in their power to engage and intoxicate? In short, for Wilamowitz a text was a system of boundaries and inner constraints held intact by successive generations (a heritage passed on in time); while for Nietzsche it was an invitation to unforeseen estrangements from the habitual, an occasion for unconditional voyages into what Conrad so aptly called the "heart of darkness." The weight, in quantity alone, of most canonical modernist writing testifies to Nietzsche's victory.

As there is no shortage of criticism proclaiming the triumph, there is no need here to rehearse such themes in modern writing as nihilism, anguish, emptiness, or silence. I am interested, however, in noting how these themes reflect the critic's impasse, not the literature's difficulty. By using a vocabulary of high spiritual drama to describe what in fact are textual novelties, a great deal of modern criticism has lost the opportunity to rival its subject matter in inventiveness and in the redistribution of textual space. I mean to say that one of the chief characteristics that Joyce, Yeats, Conrad, Freud, Mann, Nietzsche, and all the others share in common has been a necessity *at the beginning* for them to see their work as making reference, first, to other works, but also to reality and to the reader, by adjacency, not sequentially or dynastically. The true relationship is by adjacency, while the dynastic relationship is almost always the one treated ironically, the one scoffed at, toyed with, or rejected. Therefore, the production of meaning within a work has had to proceed in entirely different ways from before, if only because the text itself stands to the side of, next to, or between the bulk of all other works—not in a line with them, nor in a line of descent from them.

A great many illustrations come immediately to mind, all of them combining surface energy and discontinuity with an improbable interest in precedence, in the past. Joyce's choice of the *Odyssey,* for example, does not say, "Look what has happened to the noble Greek idea when it descends to Dublin 1904," but rather, "Odysseus is like Bloom, Telemachus like Daedalus, Ithaca like Eccles Street, Chapter 18 like Chapter 1, and so on." Or take Freud's unconscious: banned from consciousness at the outset, it exerts an influence upon dreams and everyday life by means of distortions, exaggerations, mistakes which do not even deliver the unconscious whole; indeed, the whole of our conscious life is discontinuous with our unconscious principles of order, which in turn repeat and vary that initial rupture ad infinitum. Eliot's *Wasteland* complete with notes, to take a third example, is a collection of voices repeating and varying and mimicking one another and literature generally. Another way of conveying this idea of adjacency is to say that a text can neither be effectively read as commentary nor described by commentary. A text has no central point or central trajectory: it imitates no spatial or temporal object; and its "voice" is more likely to be a doodling pen rather than a narrating persona. From the point of view of the writer, a text is likely to be ink on a page, or folds in a paper, or what Mallarmé called "un espacement de la lecture,"[9] or a never-ending ambition to be a text; a text is something of a pure sign that the author's career went into making it. From the critic's point of view, a text is a challenge to provide proof that what he reads there cannot possibly imitate life. Nearly every consciously innovative major writer since Oscar Wilde has repeatedly denied (or even denounced) the mimetic ambitions of writing. A text, then, seems more essentially just itself—a text, with its own highly specialized problematics—than a representation of anything else.

So the critic faces irregularity on all sides. Because he cannot have direct recourse to tradition in solving the problems of writers like Joyce, and because his (and Joyce's) references are to *other* makeshift formalities of knowledge, the critic is aptly characterized in Lukacs's epithet for the novel as being transcendentally homeless.[10] He begins each work as if it were a new occasion. His beginning, as much as any modern writer's beginning, takes up a subject in order to begin it, keep it going, create it. As the beginning is related to what immediately follows it, so too are the parts of his writing to one another—irregularly, assertively, eccentrically. But these relationships, while consequent in a very literal sense, are not consequent in any simply causal sense. Such relationships cannot be plotted, any more than the succession of voices in *The Wasteland* can be plotted; neither are they symmetrically subordinate to any fixed central point, just as *Heart of Darkness* makes a deliberate havoc of any simple scheme based on the Quest. Indeed, I shall be arguing later that the order proceeding from beginnings as I have described them cannot be grasped adequately by any *image* at all. While the process of writing a classical novel and the course of its plot may be comprehensible within an image of time unfolding, as a family unfolds and generations are linked, in reading *The Wasteland* or the *Cantos* the critic cannot find, let alone create, an image according to which the writer or his subject can be understood. I shall argue that the composition of modern writing turns away from, conflicts with, any such patterns of imagery, rejecting them as having nothing to do with writing. The same process occurs in the career of the modern writer.

There is a reasonable danger that I will be misunderstood to be saying that no image means, by analogy, no definite intention or purpose. I am saying exactly the opposite. Intention, largely but never exclusively designated by a beginning, is a way of confining a work to one element: writing. With the discrediting of mimetic representation a work enters a realm of gentile history, to use Vico's phrase for secular history, where extraordinary possibilities of variety and diversity are open to it but where it will not be referred back docilely to an idea that stands above it and explains it.[11] In other words, there is only *one* order of reality for writing (not two—idea/image and writing) that includes the production of meaning, the method of composition, the distribution of emphasis, as well as the tendency to produce mistakes, inconsistencies, and so on. That is, we consider literature as an order of repetition, not of originality—but an eccentric order of repetition, not one of sameness[12] —where the term *repetition* is used in order to avoid such dualities as "the original versus the derivative," or "the idea and its realization," or "model/paradigm versus example"; and where *eccentric* is used in order to emphasize the possibilities for difference within repetition and to signify that while authors, works, periods, and influences are notions that pertain to writing in specific cases, they are really terms used to describe irregularities of varying degrees and qualities within writing as a whole. As Foucault has shown, the notion "author" admits of such various irregular formations of writing as *The Tatler,* or "Rabelais and rabelaisian," or "Freud" and "Marx."[13] In some cases the term *author* denotes a structure, a kind of work, a style, a kind of language, an attitude, or a collection of miscellaneous writing; this term is an excellent example of repetition and eccentricity.

An intention, therefore, is a notion that includes everything that later develops out of it, no matter how eccentric the development or inconsistent the result. I do not mean, on the other hand, that *intention* is a more precise equivalent of *totality.* (Rather, they are, like the pair of terms *model* and *paradigm,* about as exactly grasped for practical literary use as a cloud. We must, however, try to be precise.) By *intention* I mean an appetite at the beginning intellectually to do something in a characteristic way—either consciously or unconsciously, but at any rate in a language that always (or nearly always) shows signs of the beginning intention in some form and is always engaged purposefully in the production of meaning. With regard to a given work or body of work, a beginning intention is really nothing more than the created *inclusiveness* within which the work develops.

Stuart Hampshire describes this quirky business as follows: "The significance of a writer, whether poet or philosopher or historian, and that which makes him worthy of study now, commonly does not reside principally in the conscious intention behind his work, but rather in the precise nature, as we can now see it, of the conflicts and the imaginative inconsistencies in his work."[14] I agree completely with Hampshire so far as he goes; but

12

I somewhat differ with him insofar as he is unwilling to apply intention to conflicts and inconsistencies as well. Moreover, I would add that intention, despite its conscious formulations, is never inconsistent with method, although conscious intention—when is it ever exclusively conscious?—is frequently at odds with method.

Now it is Paul de Man's thesis that in criticism the very blindness of a theory with regard to certain aspects of literature makes possible that theory's discovery of the most valuable insights.[15] Intention, then, in my sense of the term, is the interplay between such blindness and such insight. In other words, intention is the link between idiosyncratic view and the communal concern.

IV

I have so far tried to show that when the modern literary critic begins to write he cannot sustain himself at all well in a dynastic tradition. For not only is this tradition foreign to him by training and circumstance, but its repudiation is also the intention, the subject matter, and the method of most modern literature. He must therefore undertake his work with initiative. He, too, must seek a more suitable point of departure, a different *topos,* for his study. I have been hinting very broadly that such a *topos* is the "beginning" or "beginnings," which presents a problem at once more precise and more exigent than does the "New." Beginnings inaugurate a deliberately *other* production of meaning—a gentile (as opposed to a sacred) one. It is "other" because, in writing, this gentile production claims a status *alongside* other works: it is *another* work, rather than one in a line of descent from X or Y. Beginnings, as I treat them, intend this difference, they are its first instance: they make a way along the road.

A beginning, therefore, is a problem to be studied, as well as a position taken by any writer. For the critic a novel begins, as it does for the novelist who wrote it, with the intention to write a novel and not a play or a poem. As a problem, beginnings seem to have a sort of detachable abstraction, but unlike an idea about which one thinks at some distance from it, a beginning is already a project under way. Two examples to which I shall refer periodically are *Tristram Shandy* and *The Prelude:* each at the outset is only a beginning, each is preparatory to something else, and yet each amasses a good deal of substance *before* it gets past the beginning. How does this happen? Or more precisely: if the critic is studying beginnings, how does he go about bringing together material "for" his study? How is his material arranged? Where does it begin?

In the case of this book I have apparently begun with the present chapter, which anatomizes and intends what is to follow. But in fact my first formal step is taken in Chapter 2, "A Meditation on Beginnings," about which I should like to speak briefly here. After the problem of beginnings first suggested itself to me it became fairly clear that my reading and teaching were increasingly addressing the question, sometimes directly and sometimes obliquely, but always in terms of auxiliary questions. I then sought a way to treat these auxiliary questions in and of themselves, as matters confronted in the practice of criticism. I also looked for a way of connecting them to the principal issues to which they are related. For example, every student of literature necessarily deals with originality and with the related subject of influences and sources; yet very few critics have systematically tried to examine originality in secular, as opposed to magical, language. I then found that critics like Paul Valéry, for whom the imaginative abstraction or the speculative generality was not an obstacle to thought but rather an enhancement and a provider of thought, suggested a kind of writing I might learn from directly. Valéry's critical prose, for all its sophistication, is virtually free of cynicism. It never resists purity as a subject, and yet it never refrains from submitting purity to a web of circumstances, most of them culled by Valéry from the immediate pressures upon him. In his relationships to Leonardo and to Mallarmé we can see how the weight of philosophical and personal intellectual pressures, respectively, bore down upon him. As a poet indebted to and friendly with Mallarmé, Valéry was compelled to assess originality and derivation in a way that said something about a relationship between two poets that could not be reduced to a simple formula. As the actual circumstances were rich, so too had to be the attitude. Here is an example from the "Letter About Mallarmé":

> No word comes easier or oftener to the critic's pen than the word *influence,* and no vaguer notion can be found among all the vague notions that compose the phantom armory of aesthetics. Yet there is nothing in the critical field that should be of greater philosophical interest or prove more rewarding to analysis than the progressive modification of one mind by the work of another.

It often happens that the work acquires a singular value in the other mind, leading to active consequences that are impossible to foresee and in many cases will never be possible to ascertain. What we do know is that this derived activity is essential to intellectual production of all types. Whether in science or the arts, if we look for the source of an achievement we can observe that *what a man does* either repeats or refutes *what someone else has done*—repeats it in other tones, refines or amplifies or simplifies it, loads or overloads it with meaning; or else rebuts, overturns, destroys and denies it, but thereby assumes it and has invisibly used it. Opposites are born from opposites.

We say that an author is *original* when we cannot trace the hidden transformations that others underwent in his mind; we mean to say that the dependence of *what he does* on *what others have done* is excessively complex and irregular. There are works in the likeness of others, and works that are the reverse of others, but there are also works of which the relation with earlier productions is so intricate that we become confused and attribute them to the direct intervention of the gods.[16]

Valéry converts "influence" from a crude idea of the weight of one writer coming down in the work of another into a universal principle of what he calls "derived achievement." He then connects this concept with a complex process of repetition that illustrates it by multiplying instances; this has the effect of providing a sort of wide intellectual space, a type of discursiveness in which to examine influence. Repetition, refinement, amplification, loading, overloading, rebuttal, overturning, destruction, denial, invisible use—such concepts completely modify a linear (vulgar) idea of "influence" into an open field of possibility. Valéry is careful to admit that chance and ignorance play important roles in this field: what we cannot see or find, as well as what we cannot predict, he says, produce excessive irregularity and complexity. Thus the limits of the field of investigation are set by examples whose nonconforming, overflowing energy begins to carry them out of the field. This is an extremely important refinement in Valéry's writing. For even as his writing holds in the wide system of variously dispersed relationships connecting writers with one another, he also shows how at its limits the field gives forth other relations that are hard to describe from within the field.

Learning what I could from Valéry, I embarked on what I called a meditation on beginnings. Because the *topos* is neither a traditional nor a usual one, I could not geometrically define it beforehand. I undertook, however, to let it make possible a system of relationships, a field or constellation of significance in which my writing moved in order to gather in both the grosser and the

15

more rarefied thoughts, images, and instances that crowd around beginnings. The logic of exposition I follow is not precursive; that is, my exposition follows no course determined in advance by convention, imitation, consecution, or thematics. The form of writing I chose was the meditative essay—first, because I believe myself to be trying to form a unity as I write; and second, because I want to let beginnings generate in my mind the type of relationships and figures most suitable to them.

Let me be more explicit. Every sort of writing establishes explicit and implicit rules of pertinence for itself: certain things are admissible, certain others not. I call these rules of pertinence *authority*—both in the sense of explicit law and guiding force (what we usually mean by the term) and in the sense of that implicit power to generate another word that will *belong to* the writing as a whole (Vico's etymology is *auctor: autos: suis ipsius: propsius: property*). The job of an initial meditation is to sketch this authority with regard to "beginnings" by allowing it to be set forth as clearly and in as much detail as possible. To do this as freely as possible, while preserving the necessary formalities of clarity, I did not confine myself to "the novel" or to "poetry." I make no claims of startling originality, and so far as possible I concern myself with works and figures of fairly wide currency. But it is no use looking in these pages for evidence arranged or amassed in familiar ways.

Since every beginning is different, and since there is no hope of dealing with every one, I arrange examples in *series* whose internal rule of coherence is neither a logic of simple consecutiveness nor random analogy. Rather, I adopt a principle of *association* that works, in a sense, *against* simple consecution and chance. For a subject like beginnings is more a structure than a history, but this structure cannot be immediately seen, named, or grasped. Moreover, as Roland Barthes has said of structure: "Tout concourt en effet à innocenter les structures que l'on recherche, à les absenter: le dévidement du discours, la naturalité des phrases, l'egalité apparente du signifiant et de l'insignifiant, les préjugés scolaires (ceux du "plan," du "personnage," du "style"), la simultanéité des sens, la disparition et la résurgence capricieuses de certain filons thematiques."*[17] As I have said, there is no

---

*"Everything conspires to make the structures one looks for appear either innocent or absent: the unwinding of the discourse, the naturalness of the sentences, the apparent equivalence of signifier and signified, scholarly prejudices (those of *composition, character,* or *style*), the simultaneity of meanings, the capricious disappearances and re-appearances of certain thematic strands."

precursive model to follow. Most important, since the whole field of possibilities for a beginning is so vast and detailed—so irrational—and since I am basing my study upon what is rationally apprehensible, the links between steps in the argument are struck according to what is allowable—according to what the subject of "beginnings" *authorizes.*

Much of this authorization is provisional, and even seems fortuitous in the meditation. But its value can be gradually established in the chapters that follow, chapters in which I will go on to make the association of ideas firmer. I want to insist that this is not a question of *proving* the meditation concretely, and still less of allowing the meditation to act as a "paradigm" for empirical study—unless by *paradigm* one very loosely adopts Thomas Kuhn's definition of the term as a "research consensus."[18] For me it is rather a question of letting the structure multiply itself into more branches, into projects that I believe it makes especially interesting (and that in some cases even makes possible): fiction, the making of texts, and the criticism, analysis, and characterization of knowledge and language.

V

As mentioned earlier, the inaugural meditative essay (Chapter 2) sets forth an intellectual and analytic structure for beginnings, a structure that moreover enables and *intends* a particular philosophical and methodological attitude toward writing. In the three chapters following Chapter 2 I investigate the importance of beginnings—as laid forth in the meditation—to prose fiction, to the historical and modern problems of producing and determining a (primarily) literary text, and to criticism broadly considered. In each of these three chapters there is an equal emphasis upon *what* the work in question begins and *how* that beginning implies, on the critic's part, a particular methodology for understanding that kind of work.

To ascertain what constitutes a beginning is very much to intend a particular course. Why and how a beginning is determined—intention and method—comprise a complex act of knowledge, experience, and art. Chapter 3 examines how the classical novel formalized, in textual form, a peculiarly social, historical, and psychological vision of beginnings: the novel is the major attempt in Western literary culture to give beginnings an authorizing, institutional, and specialized role in art, experience, and knowledge. Chapter 3 deals with beginning and continuity in the novel up to the time of Freud's discoveries, whereas Chapter 4 treats beginnings as aspects of the function of what we may call the postnovelistic text. Here we shall see how the text, which is a principal locus for either finding or putting beginnings, began undergoing a special process in modern writing once writers felt that the biographical form demanded (and exhausted in a way) by the novel no longer deserved their exertions. Initially the outcome of knowledge and art in writing, the text has become the beginning of an effort to achieve knowledge and art through writing of a violently transgressive sort.

Finally, Chapter 5 takes up the beginning in one of its most explicit contemporary forms, as a problem of discursivity. That is, as the problem of how one locates or designates a beginning *about* or *for* critical knowledge, knowledge of a kind that comes after the texts described in Chapter 4.

Chapters 3, 4, and 5 therefore comprise a unit that progresses more or less chronologically; Chapter 3 very roughly covering the eighteenth and nineteenth centuries, Chapter 4, the late nineteenth and early twentieth century, and Chapter 5, the mid-twentieth century. Such a unit aims to consider beginnings as a subject for study by seeing how their meaning and form have been intentionally and methodically worked out and transformed in time.

Despite the appearance of range and variety in these three long chapters, it is obvious that their focus excludes sustained analyses of the sociopolitical circumstances that bear upon fiction, criticism, and texts in general. Indeed, as linguists from Humboldt to Marcel Cohen have so convincingly shown, these circumstances bear intimately upon language itself. Foregoing an examination of these circumstances is, the reader may be assured, a sacrifice, not an act of laziness or of caprice. In common discourse, mention of a *beginning* (as well as *beginnings* in general) immediately suggests pinning down a single date or event, an exercise which, considering the kind of enthusiastic interest in beginnings I have, is too restricting. This is not to say that I have placed myself beyond the pale of concreteness and objectivity and embraced vagueness or airy speculation. Rather, beginning is a creature with its own special life, a life neither fully explained by analyses of its historical-political circumstances nor confinable to a given date in time called "*the* beginning."

18

Beginning is an activity, and like all other activities there are associated with it a field of play, habits of mind, conditions to be fulfilled. That these associations are set in time and society—that in a larger sense they "take place in" time and society—is of course something to be continually reaffirmed. Yet since a study of beginnings is, for better or for worse, mainly about the language used by anyone who begins (or talks of beginning), the intimate yet apprehensible circumstances of a beginning are verbal. While these circumstances cannot be detached from sociohistorical time in the widest sense, they do have a coherence and even a history of their own. It is this history and coherence of beginnings that I am concerned with here—specifically, *the history and coherence of beginnings as a fact of written language.* Such a setting of beginnings, as opposed to the history and coherence of social reality, is rather more internal; for as I discuss the activity, beginning is doing—intending—a whole set of particular things primarily *in writing* or *because of writing.* Thought, emotion, perception are functions of the beginning act of writing.

Is such a position too rarefied, too scanting of "larger" concerns? For most of my generation, *mind, culture, history, tradition,* and *the humanities,* both as words and as ideas, carry an authentic ring of truth, even if for one or another reason they do not lie easily within our grasp. I have no desire to have done with them, if only because as words and ideas they still seem partially to anchor the world we inhabit, if only because they also are still objects of our regard—and also because, to adapt a phrase coined by I. A. Richards, they are machines to think with. Temperamentally, I have an equal amount of intolerance, on the one hand, for manifestos of delight in the culture, history, and tradition of a given society, and, on the other hand, for vehement attacks on culture, history, and tradition as instruments of outright repression. Both these moods—and they are scarcely more than that—are irresponsible; worse, they are uninteresting. Occasionally they are useful as reminders—of the fact that the tradition somehow continues to exist, and that it can sometimes also be repressive. More often, however, it is better not to treat such attitudes simply as objects of praise or blame at all—in order, as Merleau-Ponty says of a verbal phrase, *to hear what they say.*[19] This approach is not a matter of passive receptivity but of active endeavor. As Merleau-Ponty explains: "Acquired ideas are themselves caught up in something like a second life [when they are heard] and perception."[20] Thus I use the word *writing* to indicate

19

sometimes the first but more often the second life, and *beginning* as the act that joins them irregularly. Rilke's description of "the fundamental element" of Rodin's art captures the essence of my ideas regarding writing and beginning at just that point where they come together: "This differently great surface variedly accentuated, accurately measured, out of which everything must rise."[21]

VI

Hugh Kenner's book *The Stoic Comedians* identifies a recurring motif in the work of Flaubert, Joyce, and Beckett: the bookishness of books.[22] The extent to which the writer's imagination is engaged by his particular medium of expression is not to be underestimated, and in one way or another the medium is a kind of practical spur for the writer, or at least an Aristotelian *material cause* in the most direct sense. Not only Flaubert, Joyce, and Beckett but also Dante, Shakespeare, Yeats, Goethe, and many others are enlivened in their imagination by other writing—*as writing*—that moves them to various responses, also in writing. I am not sure that this type of specialized interaction between writings, which is admittedly perhaps somewhat restricted, has ever been studied as a general phenomenon, although obviously E. R. Curtius's *European Literature and the Latin Middle Ages* studies the problem during a specified period with matchless erudition.[23] Both Kenner and Curtius give one an excellent account of the extent to which the writer's energies are caught up in writing over, rewriting, writing about, or writing to other writing. The polar extremes of writing's cosmology are writing-as-mere-writing (to which belong the images of the Book ridiculed and the Book glorified—by Beckett and Mallarmé, respectively), and writing-as-permitting, writing-as-making-possible, writing-as-beginning other forms of human perception and behavior (Keats's "On First Looking into Chapman's Homer" is an example). In between exists the whole field of other possible relationships between writings, which Borges, among modern authors, has exploited the most insistently in his clever *bibliofables.*

If we preferred to use a less literary or less sentimental vocabulary to describe the processes involved in such relationships, we could say that writing is a ceaselessly changing triangle of encipherment, decipherment, and dissemination. Yet this makes what I think is a fascinating, turbulent, and thick business sound like a bloodless mechanism. One has only to read Harold Bloom's "interchapter" on antithetical criticism to remark how deeply and interestingly influential can be the notion of writing against writing.[24] Some of the more egregious examples of what I am discussing can be noted here. The narrator/author of Swift's *Tale of a Tub,* perhaps the most thoroughly imagined bibliomyth ever produced, explains his career as a writer in very uncharitable terms. When he says that he "cannot imagine why we should be at Expence to furnish wit for succeeding Ages, when the former have made no sort of Provision for our own," he speaks as a true modern who is literally prevented from finding a place for his writing by the accumulation of past writing.[25] Just as the modern writers in *The Battel of the Books* precipitate a quarrel with the Ancients because the latter block their view, so too does the hungry Grub Street scribe wish to write in order to prevent other writing from first occupying the space he hopes to find for his own. Every bit of writing is imagined as mass which occupies scarce space. It is the duty of writing, therefore, to admit no other writing, to keep all other writing out.

Opposed to this attitude is the spaciousness of Coleridge's writing, which in a poem of welcome like "To William Wordsworth" recreates the recital of another's "long sustainéd Song" in the verse. "The truly great," says Coleridge,

> Have all one age, and from one visible space
> Shed influence! They, both in power and act,
> Are permanent, and Time is not with them,
> Save as it worketh for them, they in it.
> Nor less a sacred Roll, than those of old,
> And to be placed, as they, with gradual fame
> Among the archives of mankind, thy work
> Makes audible a linkéd lay of Truth,
> Of Truth profound a sweet continuous lay,
> Not learnt, but native, her own natural notes![26]

Greatness obliterates both the sequence and the displacements of time. Great poetry is its own continuous place and time that incorporates—blends "in one thought"—other writing. For Swift's Grub Street scribe, existing writing occupies the rightful place of other, newer writing and selfishly defends itself against the latter; while for Coleridge, writing is capable of evoking the spoken voice, it revives life in all its complexity (love, fear, knowledge, pain, and so on), it permits the illusion of living presence ("yet thou thyself/Wert still before my eyes, and round us both/That happy vision of belovéd faces").[27] Whereas Swift's author/narrator ends up writing about "Nothing," Coleridge finds himself somewhere between deep self-concentration and prayer, emerging, we may surmise, a better, fuller person for the experience of another's poetry.

Both Coleridge and Swift are extraordinarily addicted to quotation, as if to illustrate the literally unsettling effect—whether welcomed or not—that other writing has on their own. Throughout the whole range of experience of writing—that is, between and including the two extremes mentioned above—quotation is a constant reminder that writing is a form of displacement. For although quotation can take many forms, in every one the quoted passage symbolizes other writing as encroachment, as a disturbing force moving potentially to take over what is presently being written. As a rhetorical device, quotation can serve to accommodate, to incorporate, to falsify (when wrongly or even rightly paraphrased), to accumulate, to defend, or to conquer—but always, even when in the form of a passing allusion, it is a reminder that other writing serves to displace present writing, to a greater or lesser extent, from its absolute, central, proper place. Using a different vocabulary, Bate describes the burdensome effect of other writing upon romantic and postromantic artists—that it gave a neurotic cast to the problems of originality and sincerity.[28] Practically speaking, "originality" and "sincerity" signify the threats confronting a writer when he quotes others or is quoted by them: Will his writing appear less his, more derivative, than Homer's, or Milton's, or Dryden's?

The greater the anxiety, the more writing appears to be quotation, the more writing thinks of itself as, in some cases even proclaims itself, rewriting. The utterance sounds like—perhaps even is—a borrowing from someone else. Prophecy is a type of language around which this issue of originality perpetually lurks in many forms: Is the prophecy absolutely authentic and original? Does it speak *to* all men at a common level, or only *for* one, too original (i.e., alienated) man (the "prophet")? Yet *understanding* other writing prophetically is quite another matter for the writer, although most of us would not call understanding writing a prophetic enterprise. When, however, the writer's aim is an "orderly and systematic understanding of fixed and relatively permanent expressions of life," then the writings of previous eras become "those residues of human reality preserved in written form." And so system, understanding, and human reality together form an extraordinary prophetic whole. Dilthey then puts it this way: "The ultimate goal of the hermeneutic process is to understand an author better than he understood himself."[29] Thus the fear of being unoriginal is superseded by an ambition to be, in a sense, more original and more prophetic than even the first man who ever wrote.

Wherein, then, lies the *authority* of writing? How does one get hold of the principles that authorize writing? Does it reside in the man who existentially wrote? Or in the one who existentially writes? Or in neither, but in some common principle shared by both, but spoken only by one? The critic's role has traditionally been to pose these questions and to make these differences lively ones. Nevertheless, as with the Nietzsche-Wilamovitz dispute, such questions make sense only if the writing in question is considered stable and documentary. Once writing-as-text is thought of as energy on the one hand, or as a monument belonging to a specific series of like monuments on the other, authority cannot reside simply in the speaker's anterior privilege. Either authority is, as Foucault has been trying tirelessly to demonstrate, a property of discourse and not of writing (that is, writing conforms to the rule of discursive formation), or authority is an analytic concept and not an actual, available object. In either case authority is nomadic: it is never in the same place, it is never always at the center, nor is it a sort of ontological capacity for originating every instance of sense. What all this discussion of authority means is that we do not possess a manageable existential category for writing—whether that of an "author," a "mind," or a *"Zeitgeist"*—strong enough on the basis of what happened or existed *before* the present writing to explain what is happening in the present writing or where it begins. Our experience of writing is so varied and complex as to beggar any integral explanation of, for example, why and how *Vanity Fair* was produced as a novel and not as a musical score or a play.

I think that writers have thought and still do think of writing as a type of cosmos precisely because within the discontinuous system of quotation, reference, duplication, parallel, and allusion which makes up writing, authority—or the specific power of a specific act of writing—can be thought of as something whole and as something invented—as something inclusive and made up, if you like, for the occasion.[30] Anterior authority or any rationale based on the prior existence of something else, is thus minimized. It can never be eliminated entirely, for certainly one's childhood, one's present social circumstances, and the historical period in which one lives make their pressures felt regardless. The *beginning* of writing, however, is not something to be pushed further and further back until a set of forces is identified as having determined that beginning. "A book," said Conrad in a late essay, "is a deed, . . . [and]the writing of it is an enterprise." We need not take this mainly as still another reminder of writing-as-*ascesis* (denial) in the Flaubert-Joyce tradition. Rather, it is more positively an assertion of writing-as-action, albeit action of a fundamentally particular sort. To begin to write, therefore, is to work a set of instruments, to invent a field of play for them, to enable performance. "Every art then and every work of art has its own play or performance," wrote Hopkins in 1885 to his brother.[31]

If writers today do not explicitly invoke the Muse at the outset, they are nevertheless still perfectly aware that some force other than physiological causation usually impels them to write. Writing is not a fact of nature, just as reading is a highly sophisticated skill acquired only with difficulty. Writing has its own kind of action, its own dreams, its own restrictions—all doubtless acquired, all doubtless intimately connected to a psychological, social, and historical context. The same is true of reading. But to begin to write—and this is equally true for the novelist and for the "critic"—the old Muse is still necessary, in order to signify and dedicate the redirection of human energy from "the world" to the page—perhaps also, if Genet is to be believed, to signify the birth of a different sort of pleasure, the pleasure of writing in order to read oneself.[32] From then on, however, *free* writing—that is, as Barthes has said, words conceived aside from any demands made upon them, demands for form, meaning, experience[33] —is only a dream that is scarcely realizable. As I try to show, the classical novel was at once an attempt to dream the dream as embodied in the novelistic hero and a deliberate instrument for "molesting" or prodding the dream away from its privacy and freedom. In the movement from a dream of pure authority to a jolting molestation that brings writing back to its existence as a text, there is invention.

It is probably too much to say that the classical novel goes on today in the form of the critic's enterprise. Yet this is not so far off. For is not the invention of a "field" of study (English, the novel, the Faust theme), the invention of methods of study (historical, archetypal, Freudian), the invention of goals and conventions—are not all these inventions of the kind that permit visions within them of pure continuity, progress, activity, and even achievement? Furthermore, the critic today is molested in actuality as the fictional hero was. He is harried by the counterknowledges of psychology and linguistics, by the wideness and the detail of contemporary pressure, and most of all, as writer, by the library, that special monster of his working reality that tells him of other writers, which secludes writing and thus, in that partial seclusion from violence and disease, stands, at bottom, for writing only.[34] Hence:

L'écriture est précisément ce qui excède la parole, c'est un supplément où s'inscrit, non pas un autre inconscient (il n'y en a pax deux) mais un autre rapport du locuteur (ou de l'écouteur) à l'inconscient.

Donc la parole ne peut rien ajouter à l'écriture. Ce dont j'ai écrit m'est dès lors *interdit la parole*: que dirais-je de plus ou du mieux? Il faut bien se persuader que la parole est toujours *en arrière* de l'écriture (et donc de la "vie privée," qui n'est que le déploiement d'une parole: "je" suis toujours, par statu, plus bête, plus naïf, etc., que ce que j'écris: je ne suis pas *comme* j'ècris). Le seul genre d'entretien que l'on pourrait à la rigueur défendre, serait celui où l'auteur serait sollicité d'énoncer ce qu'*il ne peut pas écrire.* *[35]

The presentation of these "beginning ideas" about beginnings, the subject of this book, has been the means of setting forth upon the essay by writing. For me, probably as much as for the vigilant reader, what I write says what I am about and reminds us both of what I have not been able to write.

Conrad and his Marlow so beautifully catch the writer's predicament. A man *speaks* to other men, in their presence. The writer declares his ambition to make the reader see. What is spoken of takes time and many words: Jim and Kurtz are no clearer objects of vision than are the meanings of the words used to describe them. A printed record—a novel, a short story, some pages—is the locus of this paradox in which speech writes and where words remain to commemorate what was not, after all, said. The poignancy of beginnings:

*"Writing is precisely that which exceeds speech; it is a supplementary space where what is inscribed is not another unconscious (two do not exist) but another relationship between the speaker (or hearer) and the Unconscious. Therefore speech can add nothing to writing. What I write, from the moment I write, *forbids my speech* from existing: what can I say more or better than what I have written? One should persuade oneself that speech always *lags behind* writing (and therefore behind "private life," which is no more than the deployment of a sort of speech: 'I' am always, by definition, more stupid, more naive, etc., than what I write: I am not *like* what I write). The only sort of interview that one could, if forced to, defend would be where the author is asked to articulate what he *cannot* write."

BEGINNINGS

And later on, many times, in distant parts of the world, Marlow showed himself willing to remember Jim, to remember him at length, in detail and audibly.

Perhaps it would be after dinner, on a veranda draped in motionless foliage and crowned with flowers, in the deep dusk speckled by fiery cigar-ends. The elongated bulk of each cane-chair harboured a silent listener. Now and then a small red glow would move abruptly, and expanding light up the fingers of a languid hand, part of a face in profound repose, or flash a crimson gleam into a pair of pensive eyes overshadowed by a fragment of an unruffled forehead; and with the very first word uttered Marlow's body, extended at rest in the seat, would become very still, as though his spirit had winged its way back from the past.[36]

CHAPTER

TWO

A Meditation on Beginnings

I

WHERE, or when, or what is a beginning? If I have begun to write, for example, and a line has started its way across the page, is that all that has taken place? Clearly not. For in the act of asking a question about the meaning of a beginning, I seem to have discerned vague outlines of significance where very little had been suspected. Claude Lévi-Strauss suggests that the mind's logic is such that "the principle underlying a classification can never be postulated in advance. It can only be discovered *a posteriori*." Moreover, language, which seems to be man's most influential instrument of classification, is, according to Lévi-Strauss, "an unreflecting totalization [of] . . . human reason which has its reason and of which man knows nothing."[1] To identify a point as a beginning is to classify it after the fact—even if, as I shall try to show, this need not also mean that because one uses language to study beginnings one is condemned to a useless exercise. Yet a beginning is often that which is left behind; in speculating about beginnings we sometimes resemble Molière's M. Jourdain, acquiring retrospective respect for what we have always done in the regular course of things. Only now, as we ask about beginnings, classifying something as a beginning seems to matter more than before. We find ourselves retorting that we know now and always have known how to begin—whether in terms of speaking, feeling, thinking, or acting in one way rather than in another—and that we will continue to know and to do so. If that is beginning, then that is what we do. When? Where? How? At the beginning.

Constructing the tautology that says one begins at the beginning depends on the ability of both mind and language to reverse themselves, and thus to move from present to past and back again, from a complex situation to an anterior simplicity and back again, or from one point to another as if in a circle. It is the ability to do these things that makes thought both intelligible and verging on obscurity at the same time. We clearly know what it means to begin; then why question our certainty by reminding ourselves that in the realm of thought, beginning is not really a beginner's game. We deride the naïve thinker who, having discovered that thought can reverse itself, proceeds to claim that the order of things can also be summarily reversed; yet at other times we affirm such reversibility ourselves in order to make a point or move in a new direction. A revolutionary like Lenin is especially sensitive to left-wing communism because he knows reversibility as power and as limit, not simply as unconditional desire or phrase making. Swift is another intellect for whom language and politics are reversible processes—and like Lenin, Swift feels entitled to judge when a specific reversal is either realistic or not. The projectors in Book 3 of *Gulliver's Travels* who build houses beginning with the roof live a fantasy of reversibility; but in his political writings who more than Swift the hard-nosed pamphleteer wanted readers to see things clearly from the beginning—meaning that he wanted to reverse the ruinous trend of European war policy and the cancerous growth in the English language of neologism and cant?

The particular merit of *Gulliver's Travels* from the standpoint of beginnings and reversibility is that Swift seems to have designed the book as a set of experiments in changing directions. He did this as if asking himself what would follow from, say, switching a man's dimensions from normal to tiny, or from tiny to gigantic, or from human to animal. Most utopias are content with one switch, one new beginning, one reversal; but not the *Travels,* and this is its special interest for us here.[2] The third voyage is not about *changed* directions (as are places like Lilliput, Brobdingnag, and Houyhnhnmland), but about *changing* directions all the time, as a way of life. Hence the peculiarly chastening effect on Gulliver of seeing the Struldbrugs, those creatures whose immortality reverses the mortal goal of human life forever by canceling it entirely, thereby extending life into a kind of perpetual beginning. But it is mainly in the Academy of Lagado that Swift places the most irrepressible attempts at reversing processes:

The first Man I saw was of a meagre Aspect, with sooty Hands and Face, his Hair and Beard long, ragged and singed in several Places. His Clothes, Shirt, and Skin were all of the same colour. He had been Eight Years upon a Project for extracting Sun-Beans out of Cucumbers, which were to be put into Vials hermetically sealed, and let out to warm the Air in raw inclement Summers. . . .

I went into another Chamber, but was ready to hasten back, being almost overcome with a horrible Stink. My Conductor pressed me forward, conjuring in a Whisper to give no Offense. . . . The Projector of this Cell was the most ancient Student of the Academy. . . . His Employment from his first coming into the Academy, was an Operation to reduce human Excrement to its original Food, by separating the several Parts, removing the Tincture which it receives from the Gall, making the Odour exhale, and scumming off the Saliva.[3]

Despite Gulliver's timid silence on the scientific worth of these experiments, no reader of Book 3 can ever doubt that Swift felt for them disgusted scorn. With regard to the ongoing War of Spanish Succession, however, Swift's partisan attitude in 1711 (as a pamphleteer engaged by the incumbent Tory government to attack the former Whig ministry) was equally scornful. Except that there, in his writing of this period, fifteen years before *Gulliver's Travels,* Swift could argue against the war as a piece of rank fantasy, even though it had already cost millions in treasure and thousands of lives over the course of ten years, and for an immediate peace with France, as if to deny entirely the goals which had hitherto motivated the war against France. His major work of this period is called "The Conduct of the Allies and of the Late Ministry in Beginning and Carrying on the Present War"; here is a sentence from its conclusion: "Is it therefore our Interest to toil on in a ruinous War, for an impracticable End, . . . or to get under shelter before the Storm?"[4] But no less resistant a fact than an actual war is the spoken language. For this too Swift desired a reversal, which, had it appeared in *Gulliver's Travels,* we would have called "projection." In 1712 he addressed to the Earl of Oxford "A Proposal for Correcting, Improving, and Ascertaining the English Tongue." Decrying "the infusion of Enthusiastick Jargon," the "Manglings and Abbreviations," the constant "lapses into Barbarity" everywhere afflicting English, Swift proposed electing a group of persons who "should assemble at some appointed Time and Place, and fix on Rules by which . . . some Method should be thought on for *Ascertaining* and *Fixing* our language forever." All this despite actuality, and because Swift wishes a reversion to "that *Simplicity,* which is one of the Greatest Perfections in any language."[5]

Like many other writers, Swift generally ascribes a special privilege to simplicity, a concept with which the ideas of antecedence, novelty, and foundation continue to be commonly associated. Classicism and neoclassicism are phenomena of simplicity. What matters in classicism and in the type of reflection of which it is a part (an interest in antiquity, giving special value to "primitive terms") is, I think, that the simple is usually accorded eminence because it came first, because it began that which has persisted and endured. And thus what is first, because it *is* first, because it *begins,* is eminent. Most utopian models derive their force from this logic. The beginning as first point in a given continuity has exemplary strength equally in history, in politics, and in intellectual discipline—and perhaps each of these domains preserves the myth of a beginning utopia of some kind as a sign of its distinct identity.[6] To have begun means to be the first to have done something, the first to have initiated a course discontinuous with other courses. Consider the founders of dynasties, empires, nations (Aeneas, Cyrus, Washington), creators of traditions, realms of inquiry, methods of study (Moses, Luther, Newton, Bacon), explorers and discoverers of every kind from Archimedes to Scott, the instigators and achievers of revolution (Copernicus, Lenin, Freud). Related to such figures are the originals or eccentrics, like Dr. Johnson, who, while remembered for doing something in a characteristically eccentric way, nevertheless have not totally altered the framework of life in so decisive a manner.

To identify a beginning—particularly that of a historical movement or a realm of thought—with an individual is of course an act of historical understanding. More than that, however, it is what may be called an *intentional act*—that is, an act in which designating individual X as founder of continuity Y (a movement, say) implies that X has value in having *intended* Y. Although there are other ways of identifying beginnings, this one avoids the passivity of "origins" by substituting the intentional beginning act of an individual for the more purely circumstantial existence of "conditions."[7] I suspect that the reason for the enduring attractiveness of legends like those of Hercules is that, in dealing with a distant past, the mind prefers contemplating a strong seminal figure to sifting through reams of explanation. Not that a beginning-individual like Aeneas or Luther is simply a hypostasis. Indeed, he must fulfill the requirements of an exacting and, as it were, inaugural logic in which the creation of *authority* is paramount—first, in the requisite feat of having done something for the first time, an original achievement that gains in worth, paradoxically, precisely because it is so often repeated thereafter.

For example, while criticizing the Russian Revolution, Rosa Luxemburg nevertheless can conclude:

> It is not a matter of this or that secondary question of tactics, but of the capacity for action of the proletariat, the strength to act, the will to power of socialism as such. In this, Lenin and Trotsky and their friends were the *first*, those who went ahead as an example to the proletariat of the world; they are still the *only ones* up to now who can cry with Huttern: "I have dared!"
>
> This is the essential and *enduring* in Bolshevik policy. In *this* sense theirs is the immortal historical service of having marched at the head of the international proletariat with the conquest of political power and the practical placing of the problem of the realization of socialism.[8]

Luxemburg's argument implies that "immortality" and "uniqueness" together enable an enduring value. The necessary creation of authority for a beginning is also reflected in the act of achieving discontinuity and transfer: while in this act a clear break with the past is discernible, it must also connect the new direction not so much with a wholly unique venture but with the established authority of a parallel venture.[9] Erik Erikson's commemorative essay on Freud, "The First Psychoanalyst," describes precisely this phenomenon in much of its fascinating complexity. While Erikson portrays Freud in terms of the "dimensions of lonely discovery," he reminds us that Freud was forever the physician:

> It appears to be part of a creative man's beginnings that he may change his field and yet maintain the manner of work which became part of his first identity as a worker. Freud had investigated the nature of brain lesions by slicing the brains of young animals and foeti. He now investigated memories as representative cross sections of a patient's emotional condition. . . . Thus, the search for traumatic events in the individual's forgotten prehistory, his early childhood, replaced the search for lesions in early development.[10]

Noting that the idea of a search is preserved, Erikson goes on to describe an accompanying shift in the idea itself. Thus the beginning of a new science gains some of its authority when it points toward—intends—a continuity forged from what Erikson calls *coordinates*. Psychoanalysis redeploys old elements, arranging them discontinuously with, yet *parallel to,* the traditional manner. Note Erikson's italics in what follows—each of the coordinate phrases has meaning in law and architecture, as well as in conventional psychology:

> The dimensions of Freud's discovery, then, are contained in a triad which, in a variety of ways, remains basic to the practice of psychoanalysis, but also to its applications. It is the triad of *therapeutic contract,* a *conceptual design*, and *systematic self-analysis.*[11]

Erikson concludes by recollecting Freud's early interest in law as a profession and his late concern with Moses:

> With grim pride he had chosen the role of one who opens perspectives on fertile fields to be cultivated by others. As we look back to the beginnings of his work, and forward to its implications, we may well venture to say: Freud the physician in finding a method of healing himself in the very practice of emotional cure has given a new, a psychological rationale for man's laws. He has made the decisive step toward a true interpenetration of the psychological with the technological and the political in the human order.[12]

Freud's lonely discoveries originate what Foucault calls a discursivity—that is, the possibility of, as well as the rule of formation for, subsequent texts.[13] It is this authority in Freud's beginnings that interests Erikson, as indeed it interests any student of modern thought. Let us then formulate this general definition for any beginning that involves reversal, change of direction, the institution of a durable movement that increasingly engages our interest: such a beginning *authorizes;* it constitutes an authorization for what follows from it. With regard to what precedes it, a beginning represents, as I have said, a discontinuity (whether or not decisively enforced). In the case of a tract like the *Poetics,* the text authorizes much of what we call literary criticism. And yet we cannot forget that the authority limits as much as it enables. Certain concepts are inexpressible "according to Freud" (or to Aristotle), for instance, just as the discursivity we call Freudian or Aristotelian is not simply the repetition of a few ideas but the construction of thoughts, continuities, and words in a manner authorized (discursively) by Freud and Aristotle, respectively.

Thus one beginning is permissible; another one like it, at a different time or place, is not permissible. What are the conditions that allow us to call something a beginning? First of all, there must be the desire, the will, and the true freedom to reverse oneself, to accept thereby the risks of rupture and discontinuity; for whether one looks to see where and when he began, or whether he looks in order to begin now, he cannot continue as he is. It is, however, very difficult to begin with a wholly new start. Too many old habits, loyalties, and pressures inhibit the substitution of a novel enterprise for an established one. When the Old Testament God chooses to begin the world again he does it with Noah; things have been going very badly, and since it is his prerogative, God wishes a new beginning. Yet it is interesting that God himself does not begin completely from nothing. Noah and the ark comprise a piece of the old world initiating the new world. As if obliquely commenting on the special status of beginnings, Descartes observes in *Rules for the Direction of Mind:* "For the human mind has in it something that we may call divine, wherein are scattered the first germs of useful modes of thought. Consequently, it often happens that however much neglected and choked by interfering studies they bear fruit of their own accord."[14] Every human being is a version of the divine, Descartes seems to be saying, and thus what seems spontaneous in man is in fact due to the resumption of man's beginning connection with God. To begin is to reverse the course of human progress for the sake of divine fruits. Vico's understanding of "divine" always veers eccentrically toward divination, to which he would connect fabulation or poetization; for indeed there is something irreducibly poetic about new beginnings: "In the beginning was the Word."

A beginning must *be thought* possible, it must *be taken to be possible,* before it can be one, especially at the formal or designated opening of a literary work; by contrast, the "trouble" with *A Tale of a Tub* is that its alleged author does not really believe that he can get started. The mind's work, in order to be done, occasionally requires the possibility of freedom, of a new cleanness, of prospective achievement, of special and novel appropriation. No one today is likely to undertake so synoptic and original a task as Herbert Spencer did in *First Principles* (1862), yet his confidence in the possibility of some fresh movement, if not its scope or object, still retains its force. The mind must have this confidence in the course of its continuing enterprises—historical, sociological, scientific, psychological, or poetic. In other words, it must be *possible* to obey Paul's injunction to the Romans, "Be ye transformed by the renewing of your mind," or, to agree with Marx's correction of previous materialists, "The point . . . is to change the world."

Finally, and almost inevitably, for the writer, the historian, or the philosopher the beginning will emerge reflectively and, perhaps, unhappily, already engaging him in an awareness of its difficulty. This is true whether one thinks of beginnings in the past, in the present, or even in the future. Thus at a very practical level Erikson wonders where to begin in writing the biography of a great man: "How does one take a great man 'for what he was?' The very adjective seems to imply that something about him is too big, too awe-ful, too shiny to be encompassed."[15] Johan Huizinga, acknowledging that history in some way deals with "facts," still wants to know how to begin to distinguish a "fact":

35

To what extent may one isolate from the eternal flux of disparate units, specific, consistent groups as entity, as phenomena, and subject them to the intellect? In other words, in the historical world, where the simplest thing is always endlessly complex, what are the units, the self-contained wholes (to give the German *Ganzheiten* an English equivalent)?[16]

Erich Auerbach sadly acknowledges that even a "lifetime seems too short to create even the preliminaries" for what he calls a work of literary and historical synthesis, for no absolutely single-minded narrowness can accomplish the task:

The scholar who does not consistently limit himself to a narrow field of specialization and to a world of concepts held in common with a small circle of like-minded colleagues, lives in the midst of a tumult of impressions and claims on him: for the scholar to do justice to these is almost impossible. Still, it is becoming increasingly unsatisfactory to limit oneself to only one field of specialization. To be a Provençal specialist in our day and age, for example, and to command only the immediately relevant linguistic, paleological, and historical facts is hardly enough to be a good specialist. On the other hand, there are fields of specialization that have become so widely various that their mastery has become the task of a lifetime.[17]

Ferdinand de Saussure's predicament in trying to find a beginning for the scientific study of language is exemplary for me:

What is both the integral and concrete object of linguistics? The question is especially difficult. . . .

Other sciences work with objects that can be considered from different viewpoints; but not linguistics. . . . Far from its being the object that antedates the viewpoint, [in linguistics] it would seem that it is the viewpoint that creates the object; besides, nothing tells us in advance that one way of considering the fact in question takes precedence over the others or is in any other way superior to them. . . . We are left inside the vicious circle.

From whatever direction we approach the question, nowhere do we find the integral object of linguistics.[18]

To begin is first of all to know with what to begin. Language is both the medium of study and—since *beginning* has a meaning primarily in and regarding language—its object. Any worker in discursive language (novelist, philosopher, critic, or historian) must use language to delimit the linguistic object he studies and deals with. During this primary delimitation the object is created and its future extension in meaningful discourse is assumed. The process of delimitation is what Saussure calls establishing a *viewpoint*. But what keeps the viewpoint from being either a return to the vicious circle of uncertainty or a sort of *deus ex machine*? Saussure writes: "As I see it, there is only one solution to all the foregoing difficulties: *from the very outset we must put both feet on the ground of language and use language as the norm of all other manifestations of speech.* Actually, among so many dualities, language alone seems to lend itself to independent definition and provide a fulcrum that satisfies the mind."[19] This observation made, our problems do not thereby end: they only become more immediately apprehensible and epistemologically clearer than before.

But if Saussure's reflections on a beginning for the study of language are exemplary, then next to them we must place Nietzsche's equally exemplary propaedeutic philosophy, first adumbrated in the notes collected under the title *Das Philosophenbuch* contemporary with and immediately following *The Birth of Tragedy* (1872, 1873, 1875).

All the laws of nature are no more than *relationships* between an X, a Y, a Z. We define the laws of nature as the relationships between a set made up of X, Y, and Z, each set of which consequently is known to us in relation to other sets of X, Y, and Z.

Strictly speaking knowledge is only a form of tautology and as such *is empty.* Any knowledge that is an advancement is really an *identification of the not-similar* with the similar, which is to say, something essentially illogical.

It is only by such methods that we acquire a concept, as if, for instance, the concept "man" was really something actual, whereas such a concept is our creation, made by sacrificing individual characteristics of men to a general concept. We theorize that nature proceeds according to such concepts: here, however, first nature then the concept are anthropomorphisms. The *omission (das Übersehen)* of what is individual about men gives us the concept, and our knowledge begins with the concept: this knowledge begins by *standardization (im Rubrizieren)* and by the establishment of *general groupings (im Aufstellung von Gattungen).* But the essence of things does not correspond to such arrangements, which are processes of knowledge and have nothing to do with actual things. Numerous individual characteristics determine a thing for us, not all possible characteristics: the coherence of these traits brings about knowledge of a thing subordinated to a concept.

We manufacture things insofar as they are *bearers of qualities* and we produce abstractions insofar as they are causes of these qualities. If a unity, for example a tree, appears to us to be a plurality of qualities and of relationships, then it is doubly anthropomorphic: first because the delimited unity "tree" (*diese abgegrenzte Einheit "Baum"*) does not exist, and it is therefore arbitrary to isolate an object according to sight or to form; [second] such a relationship is not the real absolute relationship (*die wahre absolute Relation*) but is tainted once again with anthropomorphism.[20]

The ideas presented here form a sequential mini-genealogy of continuity, differentiation, conceptualization, and knowledge. All these, says Nietzsche, are products of the kind of beginning reflection we saw being performed by Saussure; and while

Nietzsche calls this kind of thinking "illogical anthropomorphism," he nevertheless acknowledges that it inaugurates knowledge. In his later works, Nietzsche studies in a more polemical mode the relations between mind and the pitfalls of language, drawing attention to only two principal features of this relationship. One, language is principally a means for and an instrument of differentiation. Thus man uses language to establish continuity, as well as to formulate concepts, by exploiting the ability of language to indicate (actually, to assert) the existence of continuity and concept alongside dispersion and particularity. A word like *beginning,* for instance, is a created general object whose function conforms as much to the individual user of language as it does to the universal laws of language. Two, both language and the particular use of it project human needs and instincts onto knowledge, which then proceeds dialectically to hold man in its grip. Furthermore, language as differentiation and as knowledge bears no necessary correspondence to reality. Saussure was later to describe this curious state of affairs as the arbitrary relationship in the sign between signifier (*signifiant*) and signified (*signifié*). Nietzsche is more insistent in maintaining that language *begins* the denominating function of knowledge by *omitting* many individual traits of objects; only after this does language *admit* concepts for what they can do to create unities or multiplicities (*Einheiten, Eigenschaften*), and even these are never unities held together internally by bonds of necessity (*die wahre absolute Relation*). All this is what Nietzsche means by *anthropomorphism.*

Nietzsche's thesis regarding anthropomorphism is explicated more fully elsewhere in the *Philosophenbuch,* notably in numerous passages on the crucial importance to man of *das Wollen* (will) and *das Tun* (action). The first is associated with need (*Not*), the second with the verb *schaffen,* to create. The job of the philosopher, Nietzsche says, is to recognize what feeling, what lack, what suffering or pain (*Leid*) causes universal Need; the artist's task is to create this feeling, to give it form. Whether as artist or as philosopher, man ultimately builds his world in that lacuna: "Er baut seine Welt in diese Lücke hinein."[21] Art in its highest manifestation for Nietzsche is pre-eminently poetry or music, those noniconic languages that do not represent but rather create a special other world. Therefore, "truth" is described by Nietzsche as a verbal stream fashioning itself into a sort of canonical unity:

What, then, is truth? A mobile army of metaphors, metonyms, and anthropomorphisms—in short, a sum of human relations, which have been enhanced, transposed, and embellished poetically and rhetorically, and which after long use seem firm, canonical, and obligatory to a people: truths are illusions about which one has forgotten that this is what they are; metaphors which are worn out and without sensuous power; coins which have lost their pictures and now matter only as metal, no longer as coins.[22]

What this says for our purposes is that language—and, by inclusion, a word such as *beginning*—is a necessary contingency, albeit one usually confused with "absolute truth" and "objectivity." This stance is relativistic, yes, but it is not the kind of manic hopelessness it is often taken to be. Nietzsche must not be interpreted, here or elsewhere, as a puerile, nay-saying nihilist. On the contrary, his interest in the difficult cohesion that makes up thought or culture includes, and appropriates, the subjective underside, or the charlatanry, of reason[23] —those faculties of reason that remind us how earthbound are even its highest flights. Earthbound, but rational nonetheless.

Such considerations are forced upon the contemporary mind by the wish to grasp fully whether one's activity has either begun or will begin; Saussure and especially Nietzsche epitomize the importance to this wish of language, including its attendant molestations. Attempting such a grasp always compels the mind into a rational severity and asceticism, an understanding of which is a major goal of this book. In this chapter, therefore, I intend first to draw attention to—perhaps even to exacerbate, as Nietzsche does—the problem we face when we begin an intellectual task. My view is that an intensified, even irritated, awareness of what really goes on when we begin—that is, when we are conscious of beginning—actually projects the task in a very particular way. For this projection inaugurates the presence of an enterprise by signifying an intention to produce meaning. This is not at all to say, however, that a beginning either forecasts or causes meaning, or determines or envisions it—any more than a beginning predicts specific inconsistency, error, or detail. Second, I should like to arrive at an understanding, however tentative, of what sorts of beginnings really exist. The word *beginning* itself is and will remain a general term covering a large variety of scattered occasions; like a pronoun, it has specific roles to play, at different points in the discourse.[24] These roles, however, are as much in the control of reasonable convention and rule as they are in the control of reasonable assertion. I should like to examine all this as it bears on the possible kinds of beginnings available to us. Lastly, I should like to record a part of the rational activity generated within us in the act of dealing with a beginning (where "rational activity," it will become clear, includes rational sentiment, passion, and urgency).

The best descriptive characterization of these enlivened ideas of rational activity that I know of is found in Bachelard's 1936 essay "Le Surrationalisme" (which also happens to be an indirect commentary on Bachelard's own rationalism). The essay rejects a rationalism based on dry-as-dust traditionalism, memory, and scholastic rigidity. Bachelard says: "*One must return to human rationality its function as a force for turbulence and aggression.* In this way sur-rationalism (*un surrationalisme*) will be established, and this will multiply the occasions for thought."[25] To use reason as a means of setting tasks, to generate thought in order to activate itself beyond the bounds and limits set by the mere historical conventions of reason—this experimental type of reason is to reality what for Tristan Tzara, the experimental surrealist, dream was to poetic liberty:

> Where then is the duty of sur-rationalism? It is to regain hold of those forms, altogether purified and made economically functional by logicians, and fill them psychologically, put them back into life and motion. . . .
> What must be sacrificed? Our crude pragmatic security or our own new aleatory and useless discoveries? No hesitation: one has to choose the side where one can experiment the most artificially, where ideas are at least fluid, where reason likes being in danger. *If, during an experiment one does not risk one's reason, then that experiment is not worth the attempt* . . . . Each real discovery determines a new method and ruins a pre-existing one. *In other words, in the realm of thought imprudence is a method.*[26]

The "forms" of which Bachelard speaks include such a one as "Beginnings." In what follows, therefore, I shall be treating beginnings as psychologically and vitally "filled" with the concerns of the mind. As for the sacrifices and the achievements of such a treatment, I can say only that Bachelard's claims strike me as worth making, although I cannot of course claim to have lived up to them.

II

The beginning as primordial asceticism has an obsessive persistence in the mind, which seems very often engaged in a retrospective examination of itself. We all like to believe we can always begin again, that a clean start will always be possible. This is true despite the mind's luxuriance in a wealth of knowledge about ongoing reality, about what Edmund Husserl calls *lebendige Gegenwart* (the living present). Significant attention is paid by the mind to an ostensible point in the past from which the present might have evolved; there is as well a nervous solemnity—when the question is thought of—in the choice of a point of departure for a specific project. Indeed, in the case of the great modern rethinkers, the beginning is a way of grasping the whole project. Marx, to consider only one example, attacks Proudhon not only because of the latter's uncritically good intentions, but because of his misplaced priorities. "For M. Proudhon," Marx writes in *The Poverty of Philosophy*, "the circulation of the blood must be a consequence of the theory of Harvey."[27] As Georg Lukacs surmised in *History and Class Consciousness*, it was Marx's job to show first that the apparently immutable and objectlike beginnings hitherto accepted by the forms of bourgeois thought contributed to, rather than lessened, the separation between man and his nature. Then Marx went on to demonstrate that, as Vico had demonstrated before him, man is in fact the beginning of all study—but man for whom "the *social* reality of nature, and *human* natural science, or the *natural science about man*, are identical terms."[28] Clearly this signals a radical displacement of traditional thought, for in order to see man as the true origin of social change a new fusion between man and his activity must be considered possible and thereby rethought in man's mind. The very act of beginning must no longer set man apart from his end, but must immediately suggest significant connections between it and man. Marx thus tied his own interpretive activity to human activity in general at a common revolutionary point of departure.

Formally, the mind wants to conceive a point in either time or space that marks the beginning of all things (or at least of a limited set of central things), but like Oedipus the mind risks discovering, at that point, where all things will end as well. Underlying this formal quest is an imaginative and emotional need for unity, a need to apprehend an otherwise dispersed number of circumstances and to put them in some sort of telling order, sequential, moral, or logical.[29] Very frequently, especially when the search for a beginning is pursued within a moral and imaginative framework, the beginning implies the end—or, rather, implicates it; this is the observation around which Aristotle builds the *Poetics*. If the search is more modest, less urgent, than the tragic one, the mind will look for a possibility in the past and will consequently look to the present and the future for a reflection of it, the result being three varieties or stages of possibility linked in continuous sequence. This sequence, however, seems to be "there," at a distance from me, whereas my own problematical situation is "here" and "now." For one rarely searches for beginnings unless the present matters a great deal; this is as true of comedy as of tragedy. It is my present urgency, the here and now, that will enable me to establish the sequence of beginning-middle-end and to transform it from a distant object—located "there"—into the subject of my reasoning. So conceived and fashioned, time and space yield a sequence authorized by a wish for either immanent or surface significance. Nietzsche states that the principal human faculty is the ability to perceive form (*Gestalt*); time and space, he adds, are but things measured according to a rhythm ("Raum und Zeit sind nur *gemessene,* an einem Rhythms gemessene Dinge").[30] Ever the dialectician, Lukacs writes that "since consciousness here is not knowledge of an opposed object [there], the act of being conscious overturns *the objective form of its object.*"[31]

While these verbal problems are very acute, they are nevertheless of crucial significance. A beginning suggests either (*a*) a time, (*b*) a place, (*c*) an object, (*d*) a principle, or (*e*) an act—in short, detachment of the sort that establishes distance and difference between either *a, b, c, d,* or *e* on the one hand and what came before it on the other. "All knowledge originates because of separation, delimitation, restriction; there is no absolute knowledge of a whole!" (Alles Wissen ensteht durch Separation, Abgrenzung, Beschränkung; kein absolutes Wissen eines Ganzen!).[32] *My* beginning specializes still more, but the moment I unconditionally speak of *the* beginning, knowledge is theologized, as Kenneth Burke very cogently argues in *The Rhetoric of Religion.*[33] Once made the focus of attention, the beginning occupies the foreground and is no longer a beginning but has the status of an actuality; and when it cedes its place to that which it has aimed to produce or to give rise to, it can exist in the mind as virtuality. In all this, "beginning" alternates in the mind's discriminations between thought that is beginning and thought about beginning—that is, between the status of subject and object. Paraphrasing both Hegel and Vico, we can say that formally the problem of beginning is the beginning of the problem. A beginning is a moment when the mind can start to allude to itself and to its products as a formal doctrine.

In language we must resign our thoughts to what in *Beyond Good and Evil* Nietzsche saw as "something [that] impels them in a definite order, one after the other—to wit, the innate systematic structure and relationship of their concepts."[34] Fifteen years earlier he had considered as a subject of interest "the philosopher caught in the nets of language."[35] Then later he spoke of "the unconscious domination and guidance by similar grammatical functions,"[36] of which language conceived as a system of concepts or of words is only a strong disguise; such a system merely gives the mind the right to a notion of formal beginnings. Language, as we perceive it in its universal use, has no beginning; and its origins are as marvelous as they are imagined—but they can only be imagined. Profoundly temporal in its manifestations, language nevertheless provides utopian space and time, the extrachronological and extrapositional functions over which its systematic determinism does not immediately seem to hold firm sway. Thus "the beginning," belonging as often to myth as to logic, conceived of as a place in time, and treated as a root as well as an objective, remains a kind of gift inside language. I shall be returning to this notion a little later. Heidegger and Merleau-Ponty have effectively argued for the equivalence of temporality and significance, yet philosophically and linguistically their view requires us, I think, additionally to acknowledge the mind as providing self-concerned glosses on itself over time, the mind as comprising its own philosophical anthropology.

What sort of action, therefore, transpires at the beginning? How can we, while necessarily submitting to the incessant flux of experience, insert (as we do) our reflections on beginning(s) into that flux? Is the beginning simply an artifice, a disguise that defies the perpetual trap of forced continuity? Or does it admit of a meaning and a possibility that are genuinely capable of realization?

III

Literature is full of the lore of beginnings despite the tyranny of starting a work *in medias res,* a convention that burdens the beginning with the pretense that it is not one. Two obvious, wide-ranging categories of literary starting point are the hysterically deliberate (and hence the funnier of the two) and the solemn-dedicated, the impressive and noble. The former category includes *Tristram Shandy* and *A Tale of a Tub,* two works that despite their existence cannot seem to get started; in each the beginning is postponed with a kind of encyclopedic, meaningful playfulness which, like Panurge taking stock of marriage before falling into the water, delays one sort of action for the sake of undertaking another.

The latter category includes *Paradise Lost,* a prelude to portraying existence after the Fall, and *The Prelude,* which was to ready its author "for entering upon the arduous labour which he had proposed to himself." In both instances what was initially intended to be the beginning became the work itself. Although vastly different, both of these great English epics perform similar intellectual and psychological tasks. It is no accident, I think, that both poems are beginning poems—in the sense that each prepares for something more important to follow—and that both are therefore ways of delimiting, defining, and circumscribing human freedom. Of course, Milton and Wordsworth employ very distinctive frames of reference for understanding freedom; basically, however, each poet uses his poem to begin to *put* man in the world, to situate him. Thus in each case man at the outset faces, not an unlimited range of possibilities, but a highly conditioned set of circumstances in which his existence (that of Milton, Wordsworth, Adam, or *The Prelude's* narrator) is properly inaugurated. Both poems are radical in that they imagine human life as having a "beginning"; and in both an investigation of that beginning is the subject of the poem. Both poems open with several images of creatures in a free state—that is, unconstrained, wandering, extraterritorial. Compare Wordsworth's image of how he

> escaped
> From the vast city, where I long had pined
> A discontented sojourner: now free,
> Free, a bird to settle where I will,[37]

in Book 1 of *The Prelude* with Milton's Satan:

> Here at least
> We shall be free: th'Almighty hath not built
> Here for his envy, will not drive us hence:
> Here we may reign secure, and in my choyce
> To reign is worth ambition though in Hell:
> Better to reign in Hell, than serve in Heav'n.[38]

In due course each poem develops correctives to such unrestrained sentiments. Wordsworth's are tied directly to the choice of a theme for the poem (this occurs at the end of Book 1), which in turn is associated with the decision to employ a vague, unbounded freedom for determinate ends:

> One end at least hath been attained; my mind
> Hath been revived, and if this genial mood
> Desert me not, forthwith shall be brought down
> Through later years the story of my life.
> The road lies plain before me;—'t is a theme
> Single and of determined bounds; and hence
> I choose it rather at this time, than work
> Of ampler and more varied argument,
> Where I might be discomfited and lost. . . . [39]

The choice of an autobiographical theme of course serves to evoke various phases and events in the poet's life. That this theme arises from a delimitation imposed at and for the sake of the beginning, however, accounts for the special type of vision which Wordsworth finally arrives at. I am referring not only to what he calls "the discipline/And consummation of a Poet's mind" (that is, of one who will now be able to go on after such a prelude), but also the scene on Mount Snowdon and the commentary upon it in the fourteenth book. This vision of "mutual domination" is "the express resemblance" of Imagination,

> that glorious faculty
> That higher minds bear with them as their own.
> This is the very spirit in which they deal
> With the whole compass of the universe:
> They from their native selves can send abroad
> Kindred mutations; for themselves create
> A like existence. . . . [40]

As a poem of beginning, *The Prelude* sheds its unconditional early liberty for the purpose of forging the beginning—as distinguished from a narrator's mere initial enthusiasm. By the time we come to Book 14 and the lines quoted above, we recognize that Wordsworth's mind is capable of intention, production, determination—albeit with a sense of the loss of youthful, animal instincts thereby incurred. The "glorious faculty" is the power to begin poetry, which is itself not mere effusion but a meaning that is embedded in human circumstances. Together, these circumstances and imagination begin the fruitful, mutual domination of self and reality, of time and vision, that when articulated in language is poetry.

Milton's scheme is more complicated, but its resemblance with *The Prelude* is striking nevertheless. Milton is anxious to represent gradations of freedom in a continuum—God, His Son, the Angels, Adam, Eve—through which like a nomadic zero moves Satan, archangel and archfriend. Satan is the beginning—the cause of "Mans First Disobedience"—the *arché* in response to which the continuities of human history and destiny are arranged. Before the onset of Satan's machinations, Adam's earliest life had been a mystery to him:

> For Man to tell how human Life began
> Is hard: for who himself beginning knew?[41]

Poised against this ignorance is, of course, Gabriel's knowledge, God's, Satan's, and Milton's. The whole of the poem in a sense is devoted to making intelligible to man his historical beginning after Paradise is lost and like Wordsworth's narrator (the "I" in *The Prelude*), "Man" in *Paradise Lost* discovers the commencement of history even as he loses the relatively untrammeled freedom of innocence. Milton's more heroic vision unashamedly weaves in the sexual drama, which more than any other image conveys the novelty, as well as the nexus of intention, circumstance, and force, that always characterizes the beginning. As Adam tells Michael, after the latter has explained Christ to him:

> O Prophet of glad tidings, finisher
> Of utmost hope! now clear I understand
> What oft my steddiest thoughts have searcht in vain,
> Why own great expectation should be call'd
> The seed of Woman: Virgin Mother, Haile,
> High in the love of Heav'n, yet from my Loynes
> Thou shalt proceed, and from thy Womb the Son
> Of God most High; So God with man unites.[42]

It is from such radical investigations as *Paradise Lost* and *The Prelude* that the pun in the title of Beckett's play *Comment c'est* (*How It Is*)—a homonym of *commencez* (the command "Begin!")—acquires its value. Yet not many writers would willingly combine the idea of a sort of universal beginning with the work's actuality; by the same token, in few works is the beginning so highly charged as in the two discussed here.

When a literary work does not dwell so self-consciously on its beginning as do the works just discussed, its actual start, as an intelligible unit, is usually deliberately formal or concessive. (I must put aside the question of whether it is really possible to begin unselfconsciously, though I am convinced that is not. The issue is one of degrees of self-consciousness: *Tristram Shandy* is uniquely sensitive about getting under way.) Specifying points of departure grew increasingly problematical during the eighteenth century, however, a trend as eloquently reflected by the titles of two modern works dealing with that period—Frank Manuel's *The Eighteenth Century Confronts the Gods* and W. J. Bate's *The Burden of the Past and the English Poet*—as by their contents.[43]

The search for such points not only is reflected in language, but is carried out in language and, as became evident to eighteenth-century thinkers like Vico, is necessary *because of* language. Polytechnical unlike any other human activity, language was discovered to be a suitable vehicle for posing questions of origin for purely linguistic as well as social, moral, or political reasons. Vico, miserable in his obscure position at Naples, sees the whole world of nations developing out of poetry; and Rousseau, for whom experience is clarified by words feels he is entitled to use them simply because he is a man of sentiments and a member of the *tiérs état*:[44] these are two prominent examples. Kant's *Prolegomenon to Any Future Metaphysics,* to speak now of a beginning that really aims to strip away the accretions of academic philosophy, undertakes a description of those radical conditions which must be understood before philosophy can be practiced. Nevertheless, Kant's *Prolegomenon* fully anticipates his *Metaphysics of Ethics* and *Critique of Practical Reason*—it is coterminous with them—as well as the critical method with which he refashioned European philosophy. And Coleridge, in his essay "On Method" (in *The Friend*), echoes Descartes in taking up the theme as follows: Method, which reflects the noteworthy mind in its work, its discipline, its sustained intellectual energy and vigilance, requires an "initiative," without which things appear "distant, disjointed and impertinent to each other and to any common purpose." Together, initiative and the method that follows from it "will become natural to the mind which has been accustomed to contemplate not *things* only, or for their own sake alone, but likewise and chiefly the relations of things, either their relations to each other, or to the observer, or to the state, and apprehensions of the reader."[45]

All such investigations have in common what Wordsworth calls "a cheerful confidence in things to come,"[46] which is another way of describing what I have been calling *intention*. What is really anterior to a search for a method, to a search for a temporal beginning, is not merely an initiative, but a necessary certainty, a genetic optimism, that continuity is possible *as intended by* the act of beginning. Stretching from start to finish is a fillable space, or time, pretty much there but, like a foundling, awaiting an author or a speaker to father it, to authorize its being. Consciousness of a starting point, from the vantage point of the continuity that succeeds it, is seen to be consciousness of a direction in which it is humanly possible to move (as well as a trust in continuity). Valéry's intellectual portrait of Leonardo divulges the secret that Leonardo, like Napoleon, was forced to find the law of continuity between things whose connection with each other escapes very nearly all of us.[47] Any point in Leonardo's thought will lead to another, for, Valéry says in a later essay, when thinking of an abyss Leonardo thought also of a bridge across it.[48] Consciousness, whether as pure universality, insurmountable generality, or eternal actuality, has the character of an imperial ego; in this view, the argument *cogito ergo sum* was for Valéry "like a clarion sounded by Descartes to summon up the powers of his ego."[49] The starting point is the reflexive action of the mind attending to itself, allowing itself to effect (or dream) a construction of a world whose seed totally implicates its offspring. It is Wagner hearing an E-flat chord out of which *The Ring* (and the Rhine) will rush, or Nietzsche giving birth to tragedy and morals by ascending a ladder of inner genealogy, or Husserl asserting the radical originality of consciousness which will support "the whole storied edifice of universal knowledge."[50]

Husserl merits special attention because the nearly excessive purity of his whole philosophic project makes him, I think, the epitome of modern mind in search of absolute beginnings; he has rightly been called the perpetual *Anfänger* (beginner). The course of Husserl's development is, in the main, too controversial, too technical a subject to warrant extended analysis here. Yet the meaning of his philosophical work is that he accepted "the infinite goals of reason" while at the same time seeking to ground understanding of these goals in human experience. Interpretation, a major task in both Husserl's and Heidegger's enterprises, is thus commited to a radical undermining of itself, and not only because its goals are pushed further and further forward. For also its point of departure, no longer accepted as "naïve"—that is, as merely given, or "there"—stands revealed to the scrutiny of consciousness;

as a result, the point of departure assumes a unique place as philosophy itself, "essentially a science of true beginnings, . . . *rizomata panton*," as well as an example of the science in action.[51] Putting this differently: Husserl tries to seize the beginning proposing itself *to* the beginning *as* a beginning *in* the beginning. Pierre Thevenaz describes it perfectly:

> In Husserl we see a circular movement which revolves around its point of departure, radicalizes it progressively without ever truly leaving it. This movement, by displaying itself simultaneously as reduction and intentionality, digs ever deeper, and in its exhausting "struggle for the beginning," for a beginning which is an end "situated at infinity," is consumed by a coming and going which Husserl himself characterized as zig-zag . . . . Obviously, it is inaccessible in fact and can only be aimed at . . . . The point of departure thus cannot be a *hold in being*.[52]

What emerges precisely is the sentiment of beginning, purged of any doubt, fully convinced of itself, intransitive, and yet, from the standpoint of lay knowledge—which Husserl acknowledges to be "an unbearable spiritual need"[53] —thoroughly aloof, because always at a distance, and thus almost incomprehensible. This kind of purely conceptual beginning is curiously reminiscent of the following lines from Wallace Stevens' "Of Mere Being," in which Being is that which cannot be held:

> The palm at the end of the mind,
> Beyond the last thought, rises
> In the bronze distance,
>
> A gold-feathered bird
> Sings in the palm, without human meaning,
> Without human feeling, a foreign song.

It is to Husserl that Valéry's phrase "a specialist of the universal" is best applied.[54]

What is important to modern ascetic radicalism of the kind that Husserl carries to an extreme is the insistence on a rationalized beginning even as beginnings are shown to be at best polemical assertions, at worst scarcely thinkable fantasies. Valéry's Leonardo is a construction, after all, and Husserl's phenomenological reduction temporarily "brackets" brute reality. The beginning—or the ending, for that matter—is what Hans Vaihinger calls a "summational fiction,"[55] whether it is a temporal or a conceptual beginning. But I want to shift Frank Kermode's emphasis in *The Sense of an Ending* by stressing the primordial need for certainty at the beginning over the usually later sense of an ending.[56] Without at least a sense of a beginning, nothing can really be done, much less ended. This is as true for the literary critic as it is for the philosopher, the scientist, or the novelist. And the more crowded and confused a field appears, the more a beginning, fictional or not, seems imperative. A beginning gives us the chance to do work that compensates us for the tumbling disorder of brute reality that will not settle down.

IV

Having gone so far as to imply that a beginning might as well be a necessary fiction, and since I consider this an important idea, I shall take the time here to examine the idea, and its place in thought, in schematic detail. In briefly surveying the lore of beginnings in the preceding sections I have been making two related distinctions with regard to my chief concern hereafter, which is the production of either artistic work or knowledge. The first of these distinctions is between an intransitive, "pure" beginning and a transitive, problem- or project-directed beginning. The second distinction—with which I shall be primarily occupied now—is that between a "real" transitive beginning and a "fictional" transitive one. In following chapters I shall be discussing this latter distinction as a uniquely modern problem, as a problem that was formulated and dealt with only after a period of some historical development: here, however, I want to outline the nature of the problem.

A transitive beginning assumes the following circumstance: an individual mind wishes to intervene in a field of rational activity. The historian is a ready example: he wants to write a history of X and therefore he must rationally find a suitable point at which to start his formal work. This is by no means a simple proposition, since in choosing a beginning he confers upon it a certain status based on its ability to intend the whole of what follows from it. The specific, characteristically modern pressures affecting anyone making such a choice are, first, his awareness that any such choice is in large part arbitrary (since a real—i.e., empirical, verifiable, concrete—beginning cannot be truly ascertained without either faith or Archimedean instruments, both of which are inapplicable or irrelevant); and secondly, his awareness that his field—whether history, sociology, linguistics, literature, philosophy, the sciences—is disposed, or laid out and ordered, not by calendars but according to structures ordered internally by rules, sets, impersonal groupings.[57] These two pressures are different sides of the same coin. Together, they conspire to discourage beginnings. They constantly remind the individual worker that gone are the days when knowledge or artistic production could be considered essentially the outgrowth of specific events, beginning on a certain date, emanating from a particular person.

This is not entirely a qualitative observation, since it is quite possible to argue that the proliferation of information (and what is still more remarkable, a proliferation of the hardware for disseminating and preserving this information) has hopelessly diminished the role apparently played by the individual. The analyses of the knowledge revolution and of the scientific revolution by Michel Foucault and Thomas Kuhn, respectively, assigns greater importance in transmitting and recording information to impersonal orders, the *epistémé* and the paradigm.[58] Nevertheless, for reasons that seem to be inherent in man's biology—that is, "instinctual" necessities—the notion of beginning persists. Those modern thinkers (we most profitably think of them now as a sort of group) who are most responsible for banishing beginnings by reshaping knowledge into vast, impersonal unities and discontinuities were also passionate radicals, minds bent on discovering beginnings. Think of Darwin's *Origin of Species,* Nietzsche's *Birth of Tragedy* and *Genealogy of Morals;* think also of the metaphors involving the concept of "depth" and of the disputatious radicalism in Marx and Freud.[59] What is interesting here is a transformation that takes place in the conception of beginnings, and this transformation is congruent with the change taking place throughout the creative disciplines. Satisfying the appetite for beginnings now requires, not beginning as event, but beginning as either *type* or *force*—for example, the unconscious, Dionysus, class and capital, or natural selection. These beginnings perform the task of differentiating material *at the start:* they are *principles* of differentiation which make possible the same characteristic histories, structures, and knowledges that they intend.

Of these beginning principles it is impossible, by definition, to have any direct, actual, unmediated experience; such beginnings challenge our ability to characterize them, since our perception of their form and function is always indirect. On the one hand, there is a vast body of particular "events" that are given meaning, however complex and diffuse, by specifically inaugural principles;

51

on the other hand, there are inaugural principles whose own beginning is permanently hidden from view. Each side of this dichotomy produces its own complex set of problems. Each corresponding set of problems is a response to the other, a way of dealing with the basic question the other set poses; both sets are all about beginnings. I shall now spell out these problems as simply as possible, and then go on to discuss and illustrate them.

A. If a field of knowledge comprises a wide-ranging array of "events" governed by impersonal rules; if this field cannot be rationally understood in terms of the genetic concepts formerly exemplified by heroes, founding fathers, continuous temporal narratives, and divine ordinance; and if nevertheless the field is universal, that is, if it involves the individual human regardless of will, by means of applying such notions as class, mind, pattern, structure, history, or evolution—if all these, then what power is left to the individual freely to act, to intervene, to motivate, when he wishes to effect a rational beginning for a course or project in that field?

B. If it is found that the individual as existential explanatory concept, as originating and organizing *cogito,* as a principle of sufficient anteriority, or as authoritative subject does not possess the power wholly to appear as mover, founder, or origin of a field of knowledge—if all this, then what particular beginning concept has displaced the individual by virtue of transforming the beginning in terms of intention and method?

This pair of problem sets, then, underlies the following:

—the emergence of a particular sort of problem for the contemporary understanding—for example, the problem of the notion of beginning as construction, or as fictional construct.

—revived attention to past thinkers and systems of thought which have recently acquired new and intense relevance—the work of Marx and Freud, for example.

—the adoption of a particular attitude toward knowledge which regards it, not as fixed and immutable, but as performing an enabling function, serving as a threshold to further discoveries and knowledge.

—the introduction of methodological initiatives of a kind that restore to the individual researcher the capacity for redefining, regaining and rethinking his position, and thus which give his position rational, active, even revolutionary status.

These innovations are most interestingly observed in an extended account of the problem sets, A and B, to which I now return.

A. The Individual Versus the System. Prior to his *Course in General Linguistics* (1910-11) Saussure was engaged in research on methods of Latin verse composition. Although the research was never published, it has recently been made the subject of a book by Jean Starobinski, *Les Mots sous les mots: Les Anagrammes de Ferdinand de Saussure.*[60] As he was to be in the *Course,* Saussure was concerned here with the relationships in linguistic performance between individual motive and initiative, on one side, and systematic involuntary behavior on the other. In having discovered, he believed, a peculiar habit of repetition in Latin verses, Saussure tried to determine the extent to which this habit was consciously practiced. The problem first engaged him during his attempts to determine how the meanings of legends became defined. He found that meaning is produced in the process of discourse itself—because of discourse; thus there is no such thing as preexisting meaning that merely becomes solidified or confirmed by force of practice. Since legends are verbal objects diffused phonemically, he then tackled the problem of the production of meaning. In the Saturnians, which is poetry governed by systems of regularity, he found that certain lines concealed hypograms—that is, rhythmically important letters, distributed along the length of the line, which when taken together and rearranged yielded a message, or what Saussure called a *word-theme* (*mot-thème*). Here are two examples:

> Taurasia Cisaunia Samnio cepit
>   ci   io pi

—an anagram of *Scipio*

From a Delphic oracle reported in Livy:
>   AD   MEA   TEMPLA   PORTATO
>   A   A   PL   PO   O

—an anagram of APOLLO[61]

From small examples of this sort Saussure extended his investigation to longer and larger units of composition; he studied Virgil and Lucretius this way, then Latin verse composed in eighteenth-century England. According to Starobinski, at no point did Saussure ever mystically assume the word-theme to be a sort of magical quantity that obscurely yielded the poetry. For

Saussure never said that the full-developed text pre-existed in the theme-word (*le mot-thème*); the text constructs itself *upon* the theme-word, and that is something altogether different. The theme-word at the same time *opens* and *limits* the field of possibility of the developed verse. It is the poet's instrument and not a vital seed out of which the poem grows: the poet is compelled to re-use the theme-word's phonic materials, if possible in their normal sequence. For the rest, the poet acts as he pleases, distributing words and phonemes in such a way as to satisfy the other rules of versification and intelligibility. The theme-word certainly antecedes discourse; yet nowhere does Saussure let us believe that by mysterious privilege the theme-word already *contains*, in concentrated form, the discourse reposing upon it. What the theme-word does is lend itself to the play of composition: after having had the density of a complete word, it unlocks its phonic links in order to become a canvas. [62]

Yet the prevalence of this phenomenon in Latin verse assured Saussure that no Latin poet could produce a text without the use of a word-theme. What stands immediately and practically behind any example of Latin verse, then, is not a creative subject-author, but rather a certain verse-engendering word; therefore, every Latin poet must have utilized a pre-text before and while producing his finished text. Starobinski rightly remarks that all of these studies raise the question of whether in first isolating and then studying this habit of composition, and finding it everywhere, Saussure was not also, or instead, *constructing* the anagrammatic method to suit his disposition to find it everywhere. Having raised this question, Starobinski goes on usefully to observe that the more valuable thing is to determine the relevance of Saussure's discoveries (i.e., the isolated anagrammatic word-themes). While he fails to pursue this question very far beyond Saussure's own predilections for understanding the internal constraints operating upon every user of language, Starobinski's observation has itself a general bearing upon some nontrivial issues.

Saussure's search for a method takes it for granted that language in use makes sense at the level of performance, not through prior ordination. The rules of composition are "present" because they are being employed, although Saussure was unable to find explicit reference to them in any Roman manuals of verse technique. This could mean either that the Latin poets were only unconsciously aware of what they were doing (even though the techniques they used to achieve anagrammatic statements seem highly sophisticated), or that this technique had been assimilated into poetic practice as thoroughly as grammatical rules had been into verbal performance. In either case, as Starobinski puts it, Saussure had before him a phenomenon whose beginning was obscure, but whose influence was strong enough as to have *regularized* poetic composition. Saussure's studies are therefore directly tied to a long tradition, in the West and elsewhere, of seeking to demonstrate that productions of the mind, most notably language, follow wholly compelling, universal patterns of behavior. This tradition, moreover, stands polemically opposed to a more liberal one that argues for the innovative powers of individuals to change these patterns, to inaugurate new patterns by setting individual precedents.[63]

Varro's *De Lingua Latina* regards the thesis underlying the first of these two traditions natural insofar as the study of language is concerned: words in a language are derived by analogy from consensually held paradigms of regular order. The view of the opposing tradition he calls "voluntary": words in a language are (to a greater or lesser extent, of course) anomalous, "the product of the individual person's volition, directing itself apart from control by others." Varro's own position, predictably enough, is a combination of both views.[64] Lest this be considered a perfectly natural compromise, however, it is worth mentioning here the very fierce debate between the schools of Kufa and Basra during the Islamic Middle Ages. The former were known as the anomalists, the latter the analogists.[65] To take yet another example, Vico's *New Science* is in part directed against those who argue that language and custom move from place to place in history by anomalous derivation and borrowing; Vico maintains, in opposition to this view, that language, and by extension all verbal production, follow regular patterns that are drawn from the individual's unconscious mental dictionary that are analogous in history from nation to nation.[66]

That all this is by no means an academic or purely philological question will be demonstrated, I trust, in the last chapter of this book. Yet I should still note here how the conflict between the partisans of analogy/regularity/universality and the partisans of anomaly/irregularity/locality has taken many forms and has invaded many fields. The battle between the ancients and the moderns in neoclassical France and England and the romantic debate over originality and tradition, are two literary manifestations of the argument. There has been great interest recently (see, for example, *The Art of Memory* by Frances A. Yates and *Religion and the Decline of Magic* by Keith Thomas)[67] in the quasi-encyclopedic and esoteric organization of popular knowledge in medieval and Renaissance society; here, too, regular and total formations of knowledge are seen as dominating the mentality of an era. Karl Polanyi describes in *The Great*

Transformation the difference in political economy between what he calls the radical illusion within a marketview of society—"there is nothing in human society that is not derived from the volition of individuals"—and the opposing contention that "power and economic value are a paradigm of social reality."[68] Lévi-Strauss goes into lengthy detail in the four volumes of *Mythologies* in seeking to show how mind's "seemingly un-controlled inventiveness" nevertheless reveals that "the human mind appears determined even in the realm of mythology, [and] *a fortiori*: it must also be determined in all its spheres of activity." This by virtue of "the existence of laws operating at a deeper level" than that of surface behavior.[69]

The interplay between these "deeper" laws and individual creativity, which according to Noam Chomsky, for example, combine and recombine "given" elements, is the aspect of this debate most relevant to contemporary understanding, and more specifically to contemporary rationalism.[70] One need only mention philosophies as wolly disparate as those of Freud, Chomsky, and Foucault to document the problem's compelling interest. Fundamentally, we can generalize fairly by saying that the issue now seems to be focused on the position of differentiation in human reality: Do the significant or systematic differences that individuate the various activities and productions of mind really begin at the level of self, or are they located more basically (or transcendentally) at a general epistemic level, a transindividual level? As Nietzche put the question presciently with regard to Homer one hundred years ago: "Was the person created out of a conception, or the conception out of a person?"[71]

B. The New Beginning-as-Construct. As was frequently the case with his predecessors in the eighteenth century, Nietzsche's interest in the creative personality revolved around the "Homeric question." Was Homer the author of both poems? Was he a person? Was this person "Homer?" Or was "Homer" a generic, functional name of some sort? Nietzsche's conclusion, in a passage which I shall quote in a moment, shows a curious hesitation. What seems to unsettle Nietzsche is the conception of an individual person, whose use he finds essential in assigning the epics not to an "idea" or "a people" but to a person, yet from which he backs away when it comes to confining the author of the poems to a single name. He resolves the dilemma by raising an author's creative authority to the level of an "aesthetic judgement" made by later poets, readers, or critics, and at the same time he maintains the validity of the particular idea of a person (as opposed to general ideas like "a movement" or "a people" or "an age") as author.

Homer, the poet of the *Iliad* and the *Odyssey,* is an aesthetic judgement. It is, however, by no means affirmed against the poet of these epics that he was merely the imaginary being of an aesthetic impossibility, which can be the opinion of only very few philologists indeed. The majority contend that a single individual was responsible for the general design of a poem such as the Iliad, and further that this individual was Homer. The first part of this contention may be admitted; but, in accordance with what I have said, the latter part must be denied. And I very much doubt whether the majority of those who have adopted the first part of the contention have taken the following considerations into account.

The design of an epic such as the *Iliad* is not an entire *whole,* not an organism; but a number of pieces strung together, a collection of reflections arranged in accordance with aesthetic rules. . . . But that stringing together of some pieces as the manifestations of a grasp of art which was not yet highly developed, still less thoroughly comprehended and generally esteemed, cannot have been the real Homeric deed, the real Homeric epoch-making event. On the contrary, this design is a later product, far later than Homer's celebrity. Those, therefore, who look for the "original and perfect design" are looking for a mere phantom. . . .

We believe in a great poet as the author of the *Iliad* and the *Odyssey—but not that Homer was this poet.*[72]

Nor is this peculiar conclusion the end of Nietzsche's remarks. He goes on to ascribe such investigations as his to philology, a science "enclosed and surrounded by a philosophical view of things, in which everything individual and isolated is evaporated as something detestable, and in which great homogenous views alone remain."[73] As an example of things "individual and isolated" Nietzsche cites the questions of a learned man about Homer: "Where does the good man live? Why did he remain so long incognito? A propos, can't you get me a silhouette of him?"[74] Faced with aesthetic events of such magnitude as the epic, Nietzsche finds the existential concept of "person" too comically weak to explain them. The event is anomalous, yet its domestication, its confinement to texts and organic wholes—at a later date—takes place nevertheless. On that later date a process of refinement occurs to make the anomalous event conform by analogy to regular formations we call "epic poems." There are thus two Homers: Homer One, gone forever, exhausted in the burst of inexplicable creativity that results in "an infinite profusion of images and incidents"; and Homer Two, with us today, an aesthetic judgement on the former, a fictional construction associated by later generations with Homer One and with two whole poems.

Nietzsche's division of Homer into two components bears resemblance to Oscar Wilde's fascination with the aesthetic powers of criticism to provide accurately inaccurate interpretations of creative energy.[75] What we need to emphasize is the extent to which the construction of such explanatory notions for artistic production relies paradoxically upon both an idea of energy—the synthetic power presumed to bring together creative work and give it form—and an individualized type which has some of the attributes of a person but not an existential identity. Precisely this sort of construction characterizes Freud's Moses, for example, or Nietzsche's Dionysus or his Zarathustra. Hans Vaihinger's *Philosophy of As-If* occupies the space between construction and actuality, more or less doing for philosophy what narrative fiction in the eighteenth century did for narrative history. The Marxist or para-Marxist use of such constructions as world-view, ideology, paradigm, or class as analytic instruments indicates no disregard of reality, but rather an acknowledgement that individuality per se fails to include transindividual experiences like economic or social development. Lucien Goldmann's schema of "potential consciousness," however much it may differ from Freud's Moses, comes from the same sort of insight into the communal reality of men and from the same certainty that that reality cannot be comprehended anecdotally or biographically.[76]

I do not wish this list of illustrations—for it is only a list at bottom—to stand for a rigorous methodological critique: that is not what I am doing. I am really circling around a very acute problem faced by any researcher whose primary evidence is textual. The problem can now be put in the following ways: To what extent is a text itself not something passively attributable, as effect is to cause, to a person? To what extent is a text so discontinuous a series of subtexts or pre-texts or paratexts or surtexts as to beggar the idea of an author as simple producer? If the text as unitary document is more properly judged as a transindividual field of dispersion, and if—as Darwin, Marx, and Freud respectively read natural history, economic history, and psychological history as textual fields of dispersion—this field stands as the *locus princeps* of research, where does it begin if not in a "creative" or "producing" individuality?[77]

No one can doubt that there is an original (in the vague,

somewhat passive sense of that word) if not a beginning connection between text and individual author, yet to readers, as even to a writing author, a text is not whole, but distorted. For writing is not coterminous with nature, and therefore it deforms its subjects (life, liberty, happiness) more than it forms them.[78] Reading and writing have this in common: they are particular distortions of general realities. There is violence in texts, which is answered by the reconstructions of the examining critic. Here is Freud:

> Thus almost everywhere noticeable gaps, disturbing repetitions and obvious contradictions have come about—indications which reveal things to us which it was not intended to communicate. In its implications the distortions of a text resemble a murder: the difficulty is not in perpetrating the deed, but in getting rid of its traces. We might well lend the word "*Entstellung*" [distortion] the double meaning to which it has a claim but of which today it makes no use. It should mean not only "to change the appearance of something" but also "to put something in another place, to displace." Accordingly, in many instances of textual distortion, we may nevertheless count upon finding what has been suppressed and disavowed hidden away somewhere else, though changed and torn from its context. Only it will not always be easy to recognize it.[79]

Freud is speaking of the Hexateuch, a more than ordinary text; yet as a general characterization of texts we can let it stand until Chapter 4. To begin to apprehend a text is to begin to find intention and method in it—not, in other words, to reduce a text to a continuous stream of words emanating from a disembodied causal voice, but rather to construct the field of its play, its dispersion, its distortion. But this subject is discussed in detail in a later chapter.

Insofar as a text, for reader or writer, cannot supply, no matter how much it says it is supplying, its whole field or even its intention in advance, it can properly be said to begin, therefore, with a large supposition. This is: herewith meaning is to be produced in writing, meaning more rather than less vague, but meaning intended in writing as opposed equally to no-meaning intended, or to meaning intended in painting, sculpture, music, and so forth. From then on, from that beginning, which to the extent of its generality and dreamy ill-defined ambition is a fictional construct, more precise meaning is gradually approached during the course of the work. Wordsworth's freedom at the opening of *The Prelude* and Milton's (or Satan's, his surrogate) at the opening of *Paradise Lost* are illustrations of the large intention "I am free, therefore I *intend* now to put it to use to mean written work, form, or achievement, which in turn puts my freedom into the world as something more than just an assertion." This beginning intention to mean is, I have said, a construct, or at least fictional, insofar as it says or avows much more *at* the beginning than it in fact is. Satan's declaration of freedom ignores the circumstances of his ejection from Heaven, his secondary status in the order of being, and so on, and Milton purposely leaves this in suspense until hundreds of lines later. Perhaps it was precisely because Satan luxuriates so freely in the beginning that Blake guessed Milton to be of the devil's party. For indeed the one kernel of *Paradise Lost* that still puzzles readers, Christian or not, is Lucifer's beginning on his own to move away from God even before the poem opens: there can be no more irreducible beginning than that. So, too, writing moves away from speech, or from music.

Supposition, construction, fiction: how can we justify connecting them not simply with a portmanteau word like *beginning* but with intention and method? Fortunately there is a series of works that programmatically dramatizes precisely these connections: Valéry's essays on Leonardo, of which the first (1894) is aptly enough entitled "Introduction to the Method of Leonardo da Vinci."[80] In all three essays Valéry disavows any biographical aim; his Leonardo, he says, is a construction made to fit the image of a mind whose universally diverse activities and "infinitely keen perception of the difference of things" were conducted with absolute rigor.[81] "Whoever pictures a tree must also picture a sky or background from which the tree stands forth; in this there is a sort of logic that is almost intangible and yet almost unknown. The figure [Leonardo] I am presenting can be reduced to an inference from this type."[82] This Leonardo (who prefigures Monsieur Teste) is a mind imagined by another mind that wishes to comprehend the invariable logic of variations, the continuity between discontinuous objects, the homogeneity of heterogeneity. Thirty-five years later, in his third return to "Leonardo" (each treatment philosophized more than the previous one), Valéry saw in that mind "some indefinable inner attitude for effecting continual interchanges between the *arbitrary* and the *necessary*."[83] An "indefinable inner attitude" and an "almost intangible" and yet "almost unknown" logic for dealing with the surprises of reality consequently suggest to Valéry an intelligence conceived neither as cause, nor as effect, nor as image. Each of those alternatives is an expression of method without force. To avoid what he calls the "automatism" of such hypotheses for Leonardo, as well as their anecdotal humbuggery—this is the problem.

Inevitably, method is a law of continuity found "among things of which we cannot grasp the law of continuity."[84] Valéry's construction of Leonardo is an attempt to articulate such a method imagined as intentional power for connecting things. As Valéry will use the word therefore, a *construction* is equivalent to an intention: the unity of a construction/intention is its method. The peculiar quality of Leonardo's method, already hinted at through the many negatives Valéry uses to describe it, is that it cannot be known outright, nor can it be experienced directly. Always in flux, this force is "at once the *source* of energy, the *engineer,* and the *restraints.*"[85] Valéry therefore puts himself at exactly the point where this force is located during the construction of *its* projects. "Constructing takes place between a project or a particular vision and the materials one has chosen."[86] Thus Valéry constructs a Leonardo who is himself constructing. "The truth may be that we cannot form a clear conception of anything unless we might also have invented it."[87] If an image is not the aim of such construction, what is? One aim is to experience the human joys of "the conscious act of constructing," that power of mind to "expand any of its conceptions to the point at which they are no longer conceivable."[88] Another aim is to experience knowledge as discovery; Valéry sees this aim as similar to "the tremendous undertaking of philosophy, . . . *an effort to transmute everything we know into what we should like to know.*"[89] Most important is the aim of dealing successfully with voids, rifts, lacunae, discontinuities in the world to which thought turns itself.

> We have arrived at the conception that parts of the world let themselves be reduced, here and there, to intelligible elements. Sometimes our senses suffice for the task; sometimes the most ingenious methods must be employed; but always there are voids. The attempts always remain lacunary. It is here that we find the kingdom of our hero. He has an extraordinary sense of symmetry that makes him regard everything as a problem. Wherever the understanding breaks off he introduces the productions of his mind. . . .
>
> This *symbolic* mind held an immense collection of forms, an ever lucid treasury of the dispositions of nature, a potentiality always ready to be translated into action and growing with the extension of its domain. A host of concepts, a throng of possible memories, the power to recognize an extraordinary number of distinct things in the world at large and arrange them in a thousand fashions: this constituted Leonardo.[90]

Marginally, Valéry notes that this process entails the abandonment of "images and the whole notion of visual and motor representation." Leonardo is the despair of modern specialized man, whose virtue is the absence of thought; Leonardo "must circulate through barriers and partitions. His function is to disregard them."[91]

Leonardo's language is formal. Valéry's description of Leonardo, however, is discursive. In attempting to reconcile the two modes in the last essay, Valéry faces the problem of how the mind articulates itself in language without recourse to either sheer privacy or complete banality. How can the mind's *hostinato rigore* be rendered intelligibly? Through common speech (*le language commun*)—which often wears out the philosopher who tries either to make his thought speak or to transmit his inner reality. Common speech, writes Valéry,

will doubtless continue to serve as the initial and general instrument for establishing relations between external and internal life; it will always be the means of teaching us the other languages that have been consciously created; it will adjust these potent and accurate mechanisms to the use of still unspecialized minds. But gradually, by contrast, it is coming to be regarded as a first crude means of approximation.[92]

Approximation to what? To "aberrant modes of existence":

But they are monsters full of lessons, these monsters of the understanding, these transitory states—gaps in which the known laws of continuity, connection and movement have been alerted; domains where light is associated with pain; fields of force in which we follow strange circuits between the poles of fear and desire; matter composed of time; abysses literally of horror, love, or quietude, regions bizarrely welded to themselves; non-Archimedean realms that defy movement; perpetual sites in a lightning flash; surfaces that cave in as they couple with our nausea, bend with our slightest intentions . . . . The wonder is not that things are, but that they are what they are.[93]

Common speech, then, is the beginning, but it is very complex. Valéry's reading of Leonardo is a construction precisely because it begins with what Leonardo himself began: a demotic or vernacular language. For Valéry as critic, for Leonardo as a construction being constructed, common speech leads to other, less ordinary structures than those delivered by pictorial representation. We must emphasize Valéry's own insistence on the abandonment of images that occurs when common speech (that is, discursive language) is accepted as the initial mode of expression, a point of departure for further expression. What Leonardo is able to do *from* common speech is to arrive at a realm ("the paradise of the sciences") comparable to that attained by the richest thought when it has become assimilated to itself, and recognized, consummated in a little group of words and symbols .... He exists ... almost without images.[94]

Words *are* the abandonment of images. Yet Valéry insists that Leonardo's art was really architecture, albeit architecture defined (by Valéry) as a sort of extraordinary poetic language. Here is an example of what he has in mind:

Architecture is commonly misunderstood. Our notion of it varies from stage setting to that of an investment in housing. I suggest we refer to the idea of the City in order to appreciate its universality, and that we should come to know its complex charm by recalling the multiplicity of its aspects. For a building to be motionless is the exception; our pleasure comes from moving about it so as to make the building move in turn, while we enjoy all the combinations of its parts, as they vary: the column turns, depths recede, galleries glide; a thousand visions escape from the monument, a thousand harmonies .... The architectural structure interprets space, and leads to hypotheses on the nature of space, in a quite special manner.[95]

Even architecture, which disposes of the most solid materials, is a hypothesis about space, in much the same sense that words on a page do not produce meaning directly but first divide the page—and consequently thought and poetry—into significance. Printed words constitute a hypothesis about verbal meaning that is formulated in different ways by writer and reader.

The willed relationship between material and setting is another way of defining intention and construction; construction begins on the level of physical experience (words on a page, stone in space, trees against a background), and proceeds thereafter to the composition of a multiplicity of meanings. Mallarmé's preface to "Un Coup de dés jamais n'abolira le hasard" probably confirmed, if not actually originated, the practice of exaggerating the physical and spatial aspects of written language. Mallarmé explained to readers that the asequential spaces on the page were to cause *un espacement de la lecture;* as for the white spaces next to the letters, they

assument l'importance, frappent d'abord; la versification en exigea, comme silence alentour, ordinairement, au point qu'un morceau, lyrique ou de peu de pieds, occupe au milieu, le tiers environ du feuillet: je ne transgresse cette mesure, seulement la disperse .... Il ne s'agit pas, ainsi que toujours, de traits sonores réguliers ou vers—plutôt, de subdivisions prismatiques de l'Idée .... Tout se passe, par raccourci, en hypothèse; on évite le récit.*[96]

---

*"take on importance, after having first struck one; versification demands this, as a surrounding silence, ordinarily, to the point that a piece, either lyrical or having few feet, takes up in the middle, about a third of the page: I do not transgress this rule, I only disperse it. ... This is not a matter, thus as always, of regular sonorous features or lines of verse—rather, it is a matter of prismatic subdivisions of the Idea .... Everything occurs, in an abridged fashion, hypothetically; one avoids narrative."

To compose as writer or as reader, echoed Valéry, does not consist of "trying to picture, with the help of document, the hero of the novel."[97] Everything Mallarmé and Valéry say of composition, construction, or intentional language means, I think, that they assert the difference between a set composed of linear sequence, pictorial representation, and biological generation on the one hand, and, on the other hand, a set comprising words dispersed in space, verbal presentation, and the transformations of which language is capable. To begin in (or with) language, therefore, is to abandon the first set for the second. What is hypothetical (or fictional) here is that such composition has no immediately observable equivalent in reality; the hero of a novel, however, *represents* or *embodies* such an equivalence. Nevertheless, both Mallarmé and Valéry misread novels polemically, I think, in order to clarify the difference between language and visual reality (or visual reality's visual representation).

If this long excursus into Valéry's Leonardo seems to substitute rarefied indulgence for reasonable speculation, then one can bring out the tendentiousness of Valéry's thought by juxtaposing it to that of Freud, his contemporary. For Freud the material of mental life is analyzable through language, since only words can engage the unconscious skillfully enough for them to bear its stresses. Dreams are not simply images that tell, for rather it is the interpretation of dreams by words—the dreamer's words, the analyst's interpreting words—that tells about dreams. Among many other negative characteristics of the unconscious, the absence of pictures fairly describes it, according to Freud. Despite his frequent comparisons between psychoanalysis and archeology, Freud carefully distinguished material phenomena like rock, temples, and statues from psychological energy. He said that mental life is apprehended by psychoanalysis from three standpoints—dynamic, economic, and topographical—each of which deliberately resists visual analogy. When, very late in life, Freud assessed the role of construction made by the analyst during analysis, there, too, he steered clear of pictures. The analyst's task, Freud writes, "is to make out what has been forgotten from the traces which it has left behind or, more correctly, to *construct it*."[98] Yet two things weigh against the analyst in the task—"that psychical objects are incomparably more complicated than the excavator's material ones and [that] we have insufficient knowledge of what we may expect to find." Therefore, "for analysis the construction is only a preliminary labour."[99]

Immediately thereafter Freud considers the problem of accuracy, especially as the patient's affirmation or denial of the analyst's hypotheses is a sign only of unconscious pressure on the patient, not of the analyst's perspicacity. Thus at any given point or in any section of the construction, accuracy cannot be determined. The principal reason is that there can be no direct correspondence between a mental construction—whether made by the patient, the analyst, or both together—and actual events. Writes Freud:

> The "upward drive" of the repressed, stirred into activity by the putting forward of the construction, has striven to carry the important memory-traces into consciousness; but a resistance has succeeded—not, it is true, in *stopping* that movement—but in *displacing* it on to adjacent objects of minor significance.[100]

The result of displacement is distortion or, to use Freud's word, delusion. So curiously methodical is this process of distortion in the attempt verbally and analytically to construct anything in words that Freud remarks, for example, how an event of importance to the patient may remain forgotten while details surrounding it are recalled with amazing clarity. To convince a patient that his recollection of these details is part of a delusion is fruitless. "On the contrary, the recognition in these details of a kernel of truth [buried in or distorted by auxiliary details] would afford common ground upon which the therapeutic process could develop." Freud's most complex insight now comes forward:

> But none the less I have not been able to resist the seduction of an analogy. The delusions of patients appear to me to be the equivalents of the constructions which we build up in the course of an analytic treatment—attempts at explanation and cure, though it is true that these, under the conditions of a psychosis, can do no more than replace the fragment of reality that is being disavowed in the present by another fragment that had already been disavowed in the remote past. . . . If we consider mankind as a whole and substitute it for the single human individual, we discover that it too has developed delusions which are inaccessible to logical criticism and which contradict reality.[101]

Both sorts of delusions, the patient's and the analyst's, build up around a kernel of historical truth that by definition appears exclusively in verbal subsitutions for the truth, or as an *already repudiated* experience. Words, therefore, stand at the beginning, *are* the beginning, of a series of substitutions. Words signify a movement away from and around the fragment of reality. This is another way of characterizing the human capacity for language.

To use words is to substitute them for something else—call it reality, historical truth, or a kernel of actuality. For Freud and Valéry—as for Mallarmé, Nietzshe, Conrad, and others whose project is a radical one—language is the beginning of *another* enterprise which, despite its seeming irrationality, has method. The difficulty of this method is that it does not imitate nature, but rather displaces it. This method does not center about a *cogito,* nor does it issue from the *cogito;* in fact, the individual subject has little more than a provisional authority to construct hypotheses (substitutions) bearing a perhaps distressing, perhaps seductive resemblance to delusions. Finally, the logic of this method is not to be found in biological succession—that is, filiation—but as in the Oedipus complex, in departures and divergences from it or entanglements of it.

The net result is to understand language as an intentional structure signifying a series of displacements. Words are the beginning sign of a method that replaces another method. The series being replaced is the set of relationships linked together by familial analogy: father and son, the image, the process of genesis, a story. In their place stands: the brother, discontinuous concepts, paragenesis, construction. The first of these series is dynastic, bound to sources and origins, mimetic. The relationships holding in the second series are complementarity and adjacency; instead of a source we have the intentional beginning, instead of a story a construction. I take this shift to be of great importance in twentieth-century writing. Indeed, a principal argument of this book is that a strong rationalist tradition in modern writing has for too long been hidden behind a facade of gloomy, irrational nihilism linked to a dynastic ideology. The progressive advance of knowledge, to which this shift belongs, displaces the burden of responsibility from origin to beginning.

What this means is that one can understand the history of the novel—as we shall be doing in Chapter 3—as a development from ideas of originality to their bankruptcy. In a certain kind of twentieth-century criticism, the crucial importance assigned to structure represents the beginning of purposive movement away from the automatic causality hitherto underlying the traditional life-and-work schema. Language and mind consequently play a redefined role in discourse—linguistic and psychological—about language and mind. Most important, the text is transformed from an original object into produced and producing structure whose laws are dynamic not static, whose materiality is textual not genetic, and whose effect is to multiply meaning not to fix it. To grasp a beginning within these changes is in effect to have recognized the ending of one mode of thought and to have begun anew. With what type of consciousness this occurs is depicted in the final paragraph of Mallarmé's "Le Démon de l'analogie":

> Mais où s'installe l'irrécusable intervention du surnaturel, et le commencement de l'angoisse sous laquelle agonise mon ésprit naguère seigneur c'est quand je vis, levant les yeux, dans la rue des antiquaires instinctivement suivie, que j'étais devant la boutique d'un luthier vendeur de vieux instruments pendus au mur, et, à terre, des palmes jaunes et les ailes enfouiés en l'ombre, d'oiseaux anciens. Je m'enfuis, bizarre, personne condamnée à porter probablement le deuil de l'inexplicable Pénultième.*[102]

The narrator begins by asking about a phrase ("La Pénultième est morte") whose meaning eludes him, yet which sounds as if it has been said before, or as if it is one in a series capable of explanation. One syllable from this phrase (*nul*) recalls a lute's tone; the narrator himself feels like a wing sliding over the instrument. As he walks out of his apartment and then into the street he sees his hand reflected in a shop window caressing something; as he repeats the phrase he remarks with horror that he is only repeating himself: "Je sentis que j'avais . . . la voix même (la premiére, qui indubitablement avait été unique)."[103] At that moment he stands at the beginning, surrounded by analogies—the shop window exhibiting dispersed lutes and wings, a recollection of the discomposed Muse now no longer the origin of poetry—facing the prospects of language he himself speaks. This language has no source or meaning other than in his efforts both to begin again and to make meaning. The preceding sounds and meanings are only that—what has gone before. If they have meaning, it is the meaning of whatever has ended, so that a beginning may begin. Analogy is not exact correspondence, but a similarity between units (the word, the lute, the wing) that the writer must himself assemble. Finally, the structure he must make now is fictional in that it cannot imitate what is, but must be a new structure of meaning. The methods of the old Muse are insufficient, and so too is the modern writer, for he is no Muse-inspired seer. He must take his place in the community of

---

*"But where the irrecusable intervention of the supernatural and the beginning of that agony under whose sway my formerly sovereign mind now agonizes—where this lodges itself is when I saw, lifting my eyes, in the instinctively followed street of antique-dealers, that I stood before a lute shop that sold old instruments hung on the wall, and, on the ground, yellow palms and wings, buried in the shadow, of former birds. I ran away, strange, a person condemned to mourn the inexplicable Penultimate."

writing produced as writing, not as original speech (i.e., speech bound to one origin). This new mode is one of intentional, methodical repetition.

V

Auerbach's retrospective analysis of his own work as a critic reactivates many of these arguments with reference to literary scholarship. In his essay "Philologie der Weltliteratur"[104] he at first rejects the possibility of imposing continuity on all literary production merely by endless fact-gathering; the immediate richness of literature is too great for that. He proceeds, however, to the description of a synthesis performed by the critic, one that depends on the choice of an appropriate *Ansatzpunkt* (point of departure). I think that Auerbach's use of *Ansatzpunkt* (and not *Anfang,* "beginning") is deliberate; thus the constitutive, or contructive, sense of beginning could be stressed. Neither "myth" nor "the baroque," Auerbach stipulates, "can be suitable points of departure for they are concepts as slippery as they are foreign to true literary thought";[105] rather a phrase like, say, *la cour et la ville,* fully embedded in the verbal reality of a historical period, will present itself to the researcher's mind (since it is a phrase common in seventeenth-century writings and not an entirely manufactured one) and will thereby link itself to the regulating inner movement of the period being studied. What is essential to Auerbach's meditations is the critic's willingness to begin with the proper instrument of discovery, forged from the language of the period being studied.

Auerbach felt the *Ansatzpunkt* to be a term in the mind's operation. It appears at first as a simple, single digit: he uses the word *figura,* for instance, because it is found to have a special place in many Latin texts. Detached from history and problematized because of an insistence that attracts the researcher's puzzled attention, key words like *figura* seem suited for a new addition to our knowledge; they play a role similar to Saussure's *mot-thème.* Yet a mechanical arithmetic is avoided when the *Ansatzpunkt* is revealed as a symbol in a formidable algebra. A point of departure is intelligible, just as X is intelligible in an algebraic function or *figura* is intelligible in Cicero's orations; yet its value is also unknown until it is seen in repeated encounters with other terms in the set and with other, parallel functions or texts. Thus the importance of a word like *figura* or of the phrase *la cour et la ville*: in the research, both emerge from a mere list of their repeated occurrences to enter history, which Auerbach construes as ready in his scholarly work to incarnate them—ready, that is, to change them and be changed by them. No longer mere words or unknown symbols, in Auerbach's writing they enact the combination of past and future woven into the historical fabric of language. A mute term, relatively anonymous, has given rise to a special condition of mind and has evoked the poignancy of time. The beginning is an effort made on behalf of discursive continuity; thus a term is converted into reconstructed history, a unit into a synthesis.

At first a recurrence among other sentences, Auerbach's *Ansatzpunkt* turns into a problem that asks the reason for its persistence. *Nihil est sine ratione.* And persistence will give the critic the opportunity to view a literature, or a so-called period, as information amenable to study, as information in need of interrogation. The extraordinary success of *Mimesis* is considerably the result of the questions Auerbach asks of the text. His chapter 1 is not the result of an empty chore—"compare and contrast Homer and the Old Testament"; rather, Auerbach seems to have asked himself why Homer's text wanders verbally in a way that Exodus does not. Such interrogation *creates* notable effects, of which one is the adumbration of hypotheses already contained in the question. Thus the disparities between texts by Racine, Corneille, Vaugelas, and Molière are regularized by an overriding code of significance—embodied in a repeated phrase, like *la cour et la ville*, to which these texts seem directed—that links them all and makes each of them intelligible despite the great differences among them. Both Auerbach and Spitzer describe their evidence as philological. Spitzer writes: "The philological character of the discipline of literary history . . . is concerned with ideas couched in linguistic and literary form, not with ideas in themselves (this is the field of the history of philosophy) or with ideas as informing action (this is the field of history and the social sciences)."[106]

Elsewhere Auerbach commends Zola for his daring, not to say for his undertaking a hopeless task, in attempting to deal novelistically with the tremendous complexity of the modern world; this same world philosophically considered offers a panorama of warring "facts," and is the one faced with trepidation by a literary scholar of Auerbach's learning, or considered philosophically by a philosopher of Husserl's radical energy. In his

Cartesian Meditations Husserl charges that "instead of a unitary living philosophy, we have a philosophical literature growing beyond all bounds and almost without coherence. Instead of a serious discussion among conflicting theories that, in their very conflict, demonstrate the intimacy with which they belong together, the commonness of their underlying convictions, and an unswerving belief in a true philosophy, we have a pseudo-reporting and a pseudo-criticizing, a mere semblance of philosophizing seriously with and for one another."[107] Yet only through the voluntary imagining and the radical asceticism of a formal willingness to undertake the bolus synoptically can the researcher, whether novelist, critic, or philosopher, even begin his task.

I use *formal* in two interrelated senses. First, *formal* means differentiated coherently and integrally. For example, when Spitzer speaks of philological evidence, he differentiates that from philosophical evidence. This may seem unclear to a scholar not of Spitzer's generation, so we can say that differentiation is sometimes the specialized function of a received tradition, of a discipline, of an institution—in this case, of philology. Second and more important, *formal* means differentiated by virtue of constitutive function. For Spitzer not to have spoken mechanically of philology there had to have been training and practice in putting together evidence, which seemed as a result to cohere, whose function is ultimately to articulate further the field of philology. In both senses of *formal*, therefore, the beginning of an enterprise is a hypothesis projected; it is subsequently to be tested and confirmed. This is very far indeed from a sort of ritualized program to be followed automatically by the would-be philologist. In his preface to *Les Mots anglais* Mallarmé described a formal willingness to do philology as a particular kind of *intention,* "a double effort of memory and of intellect." This following description applies well enough to any study of words whose number and strangeness require methodical handling:

L'étude, véritable d'un idiome étranger, ébauchée petit, doit être continuée par vous, grand ou grandissant. Tout un dictionnaire s'offre, immense, effrayant: le posséder, voilà la tentative, la lecture de livres aidant et une fois sus les rudiments de la grammaire.... Un pareil fouillis de vocables rangé dans les colonnes d'un lexique, sera-t-il appelé là arbitrairement et par quelque hasard malin: point; chacun de ces termes arrive de loin, à travers les contrées ou les siècles, à sa place exacte, isolé celui-ci et cet autre mêlé à toute une compagnie.... Tant d'actes, complexes et bien oubliés, recommançant avec docilité, pour vous seul, attentif à leur histoire: but des plus nobles et tout philosophique.... Le don suffit; mais la méthode aussi: et elle relève de qui a fait ou va faire ses "humanités." Toute une espece de réminiscences, vague ou adventureuses, le cédera à la vraie Mémoire, faculté qui se juxtapose à des notions ou à des faits: et le meilleur moyen pour savoir, reste la Science.*[108]

Beginnings and continuities conceived in this spirit are an appetite and a courage capable of taking in much of what is ordinarily indigestible. Sheer mass, for example, is compelled into a sentence or series of sentences. Books, names, ideas, passages, quotations—like the ones I have used—adjust to a system of relationships formally postulated for them; this is why Swift's "Modest Proposal" is so perfectly illustrative both of itself as a cannibalist tract as well as of the operations of criticism as formal rethinking. For the obduracy of Irish peasant bodies that are coerced into a marvelously fluent prose not unlike the obduracy of books and ideas coexisting in something we call either verbal reality or verbal history. A literary critic, for example, who is fastened on a text is a critic who, in demonstrating his right to speak, makes the text something that is continuous with his own discourse; he does this first by discovering, then by rationalizing, a beginning. Thus the critic's prose, like Swift's as it mimics the cannibalism it propounds by showing how easily human bodies can be assimilated by an amiable prose appetite, swallows resisting works, passes them into passages that decorate its own course, because it has found a beginning that allows such an operation. In the cheerful optimism that it sometimes gives rise to, the beginning resembles a magical point that links critic and work criticized. The point is the meeting of critic and work and it coaxes the work into the critic's prose. In finding a point of departure invariably in the meeting of his criticism with the text criticized, is the critic merely refinding his vision, his biases, in another's work? Does this involve the hope that "prior" texts have

*"The true study of a foreign idiom, started as a small rough effort, must be continued by you, made large or enlarging. A noble dictionary presents itself, immense, frightening: to possess it, that is the effort to be made, the reading of books helping the process and also, once they are known, the rudiments of grammar.... Such a medley of vocables ranged in the columns of a lexicon will appear to be placed there arbitrarily by a malign chance: not at all; each of those terms arrives to its exact place from afar, across countries and centuries, this word isolated from all others, this one mixed in with a whole company .... So many [linguistic] actions, complex and well forgotten, beginning their movement docilely, especially for you, who are attentive to their history: one of the most noble of goals and one altogether philosophical. ... A gift suffices, but method also: and it rests with he who has done or who will do his 'humanities.' A whole genre of reminiscences, either vague or adventurous, will yield him up to real Memory, a faculty in justaposition with notions or facts: and the best way of knowing remains Science."

prepared one's validity or right to exist with foresight, as Borges says of Kafka's precursors? [109] That *Ansatzpunkt* exist with one's name on them? What, in fine, is the critic's freedom?

VI

These are difficult questions. Let us examine Auerbach a little more. His *Ansatzpunkt,* as I said above, is a sentence or phrase, once spoken or written in a distance we call the past but now mute: *la cour et la ville,* for instance. Yet the recognition of its wanting-to-speak, its importance in the present, transforms the *Ansatzpunkt* from an uninteresting recurring motto into an instrument for the critic's work; like Aeneas' moly, it guides the critic through previously unnegotiable pathways. There must of course be an act of endowment or assertion on the critic's part before an innocuous verbal "point" can turn into the privileged beginning of a critic's journey. The critic's belief, as well as his reflective examination of the point, together germinate into a criticism that is aware of what it is doing. Since a beginning of this sort projects a future for itself in cooperation with the protocols of critical prose—nowadays we speak of texts, meanings, and authors as coexisting in "literature"—the critic would like to devise a means of working with this set of conventions. He would also like to preserve what is unique and possibly strange in his own work. At the sheer level of the writing itself, the critic accepts the determination of linguistic and critical convention while hoping to retain the freedom of possibility: the former is governed by historical and social pressures, the latter by a point of departure that remains exposed to its contingent, and yet rational, status, one that encourages interrogation and retrospection. In the critic's work, therefore, a vigilant method and a record of that method's accomplishments are produced together. Valèry's invention of the *implex,* with its capacity for multiplication, its systematic variations, and its contingency is an ebullient rendering of this union. [110]

The point of departure, to return to it now, thus has two aspects that animate one another. One leads to the project being realized: this is the transitive aspect of the beginning—that is, beginning with (or for) an anticipated end, or at least expected continuity. The other aspect retains for the beginning its identity as *radical* starting point: the intransitive and conceptual aspect, that which has no object but its own constant clarification. It is this second side that so fascinated Husserl (I spoke earlier of a beginning *at* the beginning, *for* the beginning) and that has continued to engage Heidegger. These two sides of the starting point entail two styles of thought, and of imagination, one projective and descriptive, the other tautological and endlessly self-mimetic. The transitive mode is always hungering, like Lovelace perpetually chasing Clarissa, for an object it can never fully catch up with in either space or time. The intransitive, like Clarissa herself, can never have enough of itself—in short, expansion and concentration, or words in language, and the Word. The relationship between these two aspects of the starting point is given by Merleau-Ponty: "Whether it is mythical or utopian, there is a place where everything that is or will be is preparing, at the same time, to be spoken." ("Qu'il soit mythique ou intelligible, il y a un lieu où tout ce qui est ou qui sera, se prépare en même temps à être dit.")[111]

Mythical or utopian, this place of which Merleau-Ponty speaks is probably the realm of silence in which transitive and intransitive beginnings jostle one another. Silence is the way language might dream of a golden age, and words, R. P. Blackmur says, are sometimes "burdened with the very cry of silence," with their very opposite and negation.[112] Yet we do speak and we do write. We continue to use language, its burdens and confusions notwithstanding. The capabilities of language are not beggarly. For articulated language is also a way of apprehending, of alluding to, and even of dealing with what is unknown, or irrational, or foreign to it, whether we call the unknown a myth, a dream, utopia, or absolute silence. We never know, Eliot says, in any assertion just what or how much we are asserting. The unknown can even be called a beginning insofar as the beginning is a concept that resists the stream of language. Since in its use language is preeminently a reality, a presence, any reference to what precedes it and to what is quite different from it is an unknown. Says Valéry: "Creative Ignorance.... Why, yes; before the Word is before the Beginning. Before ... the Before!"[113] If, as I speak, I refer to a beginning, I am referring to what is not immediately present, unless I am referring to the transitive, useful beginning defined as present for the purpose of the discourse. The intransitive beginning is locked outside language: it is unknown, and so labeled, as in Foucault's magistral *Histoire de la folie à l'âge classique*, where he demonstrates the "madness" in post-Renaissance Europe. And yet I can and often must refer to "the beginning," as Husserl did, even though it seems perpetually to refuse me.

Let me try another way of explaining this. When I read a page I must keep in mind that the page was written, or somehow produced in an act of writing. Writing is the unknown, or the beginning from which reading imagines and from which it departs in what Sartre calls a method of guided invention.[114] But that is the reader's transitive point of view, which is forced to imagine a prior unknown that the reader calls writing. From the point of view of the writer, however, his writing—as he does it—is perpetually at the beginning. Like Rilke's Malte he is a beginner in his own circumstances.[115] He writes for no real reason other than his writing: he writes in order to write, or, as Sartre says of Genet, to write something that he can read.[116] What he has already written will always have a power over him. But it, too, while he writes, in the presence of his act of writing, is an unknown. It is felt but not present. The writer is the widow of an insight. As Eliot says:

> It seems to me that beyond the namable, classifiable emotions and motives of our conscious life when directed towards action—the part of life which prose drama is wholly adequate to express—there is a fringe of indefinite extent, of feeling which we can only detect, so to speak, out of the corner of the eye and can never completely focus; feeling of which we are only aware in a kind of temporary detachment from action.[117]

The unknown absence, felt by the mind, is represented by modern poets, critics, and novelists as an antecedent power that incriminates and is *refracted*—the word is Harry Levin's—in the present: its mode of being, whether as horizon or as force, is discontinuous with the present and partial in appearance.[118] The great prior reality—whether we call it history, the unconscious, Leonardo, God, or writing—is the Other (Milton's "great task-master's eye"), present before, which is crucial to our Now. The unknown is a metaphor for felt precedence that appears in glances backward, as an intimation of surrounding discomfort, as a threat of impending invasion, always ready to wreck our tenuously performed activity. It is Eliot's backward look, "the partial horror and ecstasy"; it is Conrad's darkness, seemingly at bay yet ever closer to springing forward and obliterating mind and light; it is Kafka's trial that never takes place but is planned before K can do anything, a trial endlessly circumvented but oppressively present in its very impingements; it is Borges' ruins that gradually reveal themselves as part of a terrible plan whose entirety one can never fully perceive, ruins always felt to be immortal. Or, in radical criticism, it is the deep anterior claim of the writing, sometimes willfully forgotten, sometimes deliberately attenuated, but always haunting the critic whose reading abuts the mountains and the caverns of another's, an author's, mind at work: such critics write critical poems imitating the behavior of the mind. At its best, radical criticism is exactly like all radical activity: full of its own changing, and haunted by its opposite, by the discontinuities of the dialectic of writing, which it must reenact and record. Thus, according to Blackmur, "criticism keeps the sound of . . . footsteps live in our reading, so that we understand both the fury in the words and the words themselves."[119]

Here, it seems to me, Freud's 1910 essay "The Antithetical Meaning of Primal Words" is very relevant. In the work of the philologist Karl Abel, Freud found linguistic and historical confirmation of his view that signs or words in a dream can mean their opposite or at least something radically different from their appearance. Words in ancient Egyptian, according to Abel, simultaneously imply their opposite and even their negation. "Man," he goes on, "was not in fact able to acquire his oldest and simplest concepts except as contraries to their contraries, and only learnt by degrees to separate the two sides of an antithesis and think of one without conscious comparison with the other."[120] Abel, unlike Freud, was a meliorist: Freud believed that words in fact continue to imply their opposite, the known carrying with it a considerable freight of the unknown. Reading thus involves us in a regressive movement away from the text to what the words drag along with them, whether that is the memory of the writing or some other, hidden, and perhaps subversive opposite.

Because we must deal with the unknown, whose nature is by definition speculative and outside the flowing chain of language, whatever we make of it will be no more than probability and no less than error. The awareness of possible error in speculation and of a continued speculation regardless of error is an event in the history of modern rationalism whose importance, I think, cannot be overemphasized: this is to some extent the subject of Frank Kermode's *Sense of an Ending,* a book whose justifiable bias is the connection between literature and the modes of fictional thought in a general sense. Nevertheless, the subject of how and when we become certain that what we are doing is quite possibly wrong *but at least a beginning* has to be studied in its full historical and intellectual richness. Such a study would, for instance, show us when and how a novelist felt what he was doing was *only* writing a novel and not an essay, how and when a critic attributed to his criticism the power to predict its own invalidation, and when a historian saw the past projecting itself in his work.

VII

Let me recapitulate some of the things I have been trying to describe. The choice of a beginning is important to any enterprise, even if, as is so often the case, a beginning is accepted as a beginning after we are long past beginning and after our apprenticeship is over. One of the special characteristics of thought ever since the eighteenth century is an obsession with beginnings that seems to infect and render exceedingly problematic the location of a beginning. Two kinds of beginning emerge, really two sides of the same coin. One, which I call temporal and transitive, foresees a continuity that flows from it. This kind of beginning is suited for work, for polemic, for discovery. It is what Emile Benveniste describes as the "axial moment which provides the zero point of the computation" that allows us to initiate, to direct, to measure time to construct work, to discover, to produce knowledge.[121]   Auerbach calls his *Ansatzpunkt* a handle by which to grasp literary history: we find it for a purpose and at a time that is crucial to us; but the act of finding it ought never to be all interrogation, examination, and reflection unless we are willing to forego work for preliminaries. A beginning is a formal appetite imposing a severe discipline on the mind that wants to think every turn of its thoughts from the start. Thoughts then appear related to one another in a meaningful series of constantly experienced moments.

There is always the danger of too much reflection upon beginnings. In a sense, what I have been doing in this meditation proves the hazards of such an undertaking. A single topic can become the *idée fixe* mockingly transformed by Valéry into an epidemic of limitless titles: "On Omnivalent Ideas"; "On Omni-valence as a Depressive Stimulus"; "On Omnivalence, and the Treatment of Abnormal Favorites"; "On Omnivalent, Anti-logical Hyperfavoritism"....[122]   In attempting to push oneself further and further back to what is only a beginning, a point that is stripped of every use but its categorization in the mind as beginning, one is caught in a tautological circuit of beginnings about to begin. This is the other kind of beginning, the one I called intransitive and conceptual. It is very much a creature of the mind, very much a bristling paradox, yet also very much a figure of thought that draws special attention to itself. Its existence cannot be doubted, yet its pertinence is wholly to itself. Because it cannot truly be known, because it belongs more to silence than it does to language, because it is what has always been left behind, and because it challenges continuities that go cheerfully forward with *their* beginnings obediently affixed—it is therefore something of a necessary fiction. It is perhaps our permanent concession as finite minds to an ungraspable absolute.

The absolute's felt absence has, I think, seemed particularly necessary to the modern mind, mainly because the modern mind finds it exceedingly difficult, perhaps impossible, to grasp presence immediately. To paraphrase A. D. in Malraux's *La Tentation de l'occident*: we lose the present twice—once when we make it, and again when we try to regain it.[123] Even in the midst of powerful impressions upon us we find ourselves resorting to using intervening techniques that deliver reality to us in palpable form. We are peripatetic converts to every mediation we learn, and learning, the process Vico described as autodidactic philology, then seems more and more to be a matter of submitting to various linguistic fatalisms. A critic, for instance, cannot take in literature directly; as Auerbach said, the field is too minutely specialized now, too vastly spread beyond our immediate ken. So we create sequences, periods, forms, and measurements that suit our perceptual needs. Once we have seen them, these orders are left alone: we assume that they go on ordering to time's end, and there is nothing we can do about it. These mediating orders are in their turn commanded and informed by one or another moderately intelligible force, whether we call it history, time, mind, or, as is the case today, language. In *Le Visible et l'invisible* Merleau-Ponty writes:

> If we dream of finding again the natural world or time through coincidence, of being identical to the 0-point which we see yonder, or to the pure memory which from the depths of ourselves governs our acts of recall, then language is a power for error, since it cuts the continuous tissue that joins us vitally to the things and to the past and is installed between ourselves and that tissue like a screen. The philosopher speaks, but this is a weakness in him, and an inexplicable weakness: he should keep silent, coincide in silence, and rejoin in Being a philosophy that is there ready-made. But yet everything comes to pass as though he wished to put into words a certain

silence he hearkens to within himself. His entire "work" is that absurd effort.[124]

Everything that is left after these orders of mediated presence are accepted we call unknown. But, as I have tried to show, the unknown remains with us to haunt us from its horizon even after we have consciously begun. Thus the two types of beginning I have been describing are separate in analysis, but not really altogether separate in practice. When, after we begin, we hint at the unknown we involuntarily borrow the words of our experience, using them to harken back to an aspect of our experience at the beginning. The archetypal unknown is the beginning, which is also the certification of what we presently do. Newman called such a beginning an economy of God, and Vaihinger called it a summational fiction. We might call it radical inauthenticity, or, looking as far back as Husserl and Stevens did, the tautology at the end of the mind, or with Freud, the primal word, literally, with an antithetical meaning: the beginning that is not *the* one. Such a beginning is the partially unknown event that makes us—and with us, our world—possible as a vessel of significance.

The most peculiar thing about such a partially unknown beginning—aside, that is, from its enduring shadow in our minds—is that we make and accept it at the same time that we realize that we are "wrong." Its wrongness, however, resides in its *difference* from the merely accidental. Properly considered, a beginning shows us how much language, with its perpetual memories of silence, can do to summon fiction and reality to an equal space in the mind. In this space certain fiction and certain reality come together as identity. Yet we can never be certain what part of identity is true, what part fictional. This will be true as long as part of the beginning eludes us, so long as we have language to help us and hinder us in finding it, and so long as language provides us with a word whose meaning must be *made* certain if it is not to be wholly obscure.

CHAPTER

THREE

The Novel as Beginning Intention

I

IN its fully developed form as the great classical novel, from Defoe to Dickens and Balzac, narrative prose fiction is by no means a type of literature common to all traditions. Even in those traditions of which it is a part, the novel has had a limited life. This, I think, is an important fact. It may not tell us what the novel is, but it can help us to understand what needs the novel has filled and what effects it has produced among readers, societies, and traditions in which the genre is significant. Let me limit myself to a brief example that illustrates some of what I mean. Modern Arabic literature includes novels, but they are almost entirely of this century. There is no tradition out of which these modern works developed; basically at some point writers in Arabic became aware of European novels and began to write works like them. Obviously it is not that simple; nevertheless, it is significant that the desire to create an alternative world, to modify or augment the real world through the act of writing (which is one motive underlying the novelistic tradition in the West) is inimical to the Islamic world-view. The Prophet is he who has *completed* a world-view; thus the word *heresy* in Arabic is synonymous with the verb "to innovate" or "to begin." Islam views the world as a plenum, capable of neither diminishment nor amplification. Consequently, stories like those in *The Arabian Nights* are ornamental, variations on the world, not completions of it; neither are they lessons, structures, extensions, or totalities designed to illustrate either the author's prowess in representation, the education of a character, or ways in which the world can be viewed and changed.

Thus even autobiography as a genre scarcely exists in Arabic literature. When it is to be found, the result is wholly special. One of the finest and most famous books in modern Arabic letters is Taha Hussein's three-part autobiography *Al-Ayam* (sometimes translated as *Stream of Days*), of which the first part (1929) is the most interesting. It describes the author's boyhood in an Egyptian village early in the century. At the time he wrote the book, Hussein was already a learned man of letters and ex-Azharite whose later European education wrought in him a unique fusion between the traditional Islamic and occidental cultures. Hussein's achievements as a scholar, however, do not explain a remarkable feature of *Al-Ayam*. For almost every childhood occurrence narrated by Hussein is in some way connected with the Koran—not as a body of doctrine, but as a presence or fact of everyday life. Thus the boy's greatest ambition is to memorize the Koran; his father is happy when he does his recitation well and angry when he does not; his friends are all fellow learners; and so on and on. The book's narrative style bears no resemblance to Koranic Arabic, so there is no question of imitation and hence of addition as in the Christian tradition. Rather one's impression is that life is mediated by the Koran, informed by it; a gesture or an episode or a feeling in the boy's life is inevitably reduced (always in an interesting way) back to a relationship to the Koran. In other words, no action can depart from the Koran; rather each action confirms the already completed presence of the Koran and, consequently, human existence.

Examples like this make it apparent that a central purpose of the Western novel is to enable the writer to represent characters and societies more or less freely in development. Characters and societies so represented grow and move in the novel because they mirror a process of engenderment or beginning and growth possible and permissible for the mind to imagine. Novels, therefore, are aesthetic objects that fill gaps in an incomplete world: they satisfy a human urge to add to reality by portraying (fictional) characters in which one can believe. Novels are much more than that, of course. Nevertheless, I should like now to consider the institution of narrative prose fiction as a kind of appetite that writers develop for modifying reality—as if from the beginning—as a desire to create a new or beginning fictional entity while accepting the consequences of that desire.

Every novel is at the same time a form of discovery and also a way of accommodating discovery, if not to a social norm, then to a specialized "novelistic" reading process. As Harry Levin has said, the novel is an institution, wholly differentiated from the more generalized idea of "fiction," to which even the most unusual and *novel* experiences are admitted as functions.[1] Every novelist has taken the genre as both an enabling condition and a restraint upon his inventiveness. Both these factors are time- and culture-bound, but how exactly they are bound has yet fully to be studied. My thesis is that invention and restraint—or as I shall call them, "authority" and "molestation," respectively—ultimately have *conserved* the novel because novelists have construed them together as *beginning* conditions, not as conditions for limitlessly expansive fictional invention. Thus the novel represents a beginning of a very precisely finite sort insofar as what may ensue from that beginning. In this respect the classical novel has been a far more conservative and more precisely constraining beginning than would otherwise be expected of a genre so explicitly committed to fabulation. Alain Robbe-Grillet makes this point in his polemic attacking outdated conceptions of the novel, "Sur quelques notions périmées" (1957),[2] an essay that accurately notes just how severe and timebound are critical constraints upon the form.

By my two terms, *authority* and *molestation,* I wish to indicate the kind of perspective I am now adopting. *Authority* suggests to me a constellation of linked meanings: not only, as the OED tells us, "a power to enforce obedience," or "a derived or delegated power," or "a power to influence action," or "a power to inspire belief," or "a person whose opinion is accepted"; not only those, but a connection as well with *author*—that is, a person who originates or gives existence to something, a begetter, beginner, father, or ancestor, a person also who sets forth written statements. There is still another cluster of meanings: *author* is tied to the past participle *auctus* of the verb *augere;* therefore *auctor,* according to Eric Partridge, is literally an increaser and thus a founder.[3] *Auctoritas* is production, invention, cause, in addition to meaning a right of possession. Finally, it means continuance, or a causing to continue. Taken together these meanings are all grounded in the following notions: (1) that of the power of an individual to initiate, institute, establish—in short, to begin; (2) that this power and its product are an increase over what had been there previously; (3) that the individual wielding this power controls its issue and what is derived therefrom; (4) that authority maintains the continuity of its course. All four of these abstractions can be used to describe the way in which narrative fiction asserts itself psychologically and aesthetically through the technical efforts of the novelist. Thus in the written statement, beginning or inauguration, augmentation by extension, possession and continuity stand for the word *authority*.

Now, *molestation* is a word I shall use to describe the bother and responsibility of all these powers and efforts. By that I mean that no novelist has ever been unaware that his authority, regardless of how complete, or the authority of a narrator, is a sham. Molestation, then, is a consciousness of one's duplicity, one's confinement to a fictive, scriptive realm, whether one is a character or a novelist. And molestation occurs when novelists and critics traditionally remind themselves of how the novel is always subject to a comparison with reality and thereby found to be illusion. Or again, molestation is central to a character's experience of disillusionment during the course of a novel. To speak of authority in narrative prose fiction is also inevitably to speak of the molestations that accompany it.

Authority and its molestations are at the root of the fictional process; at least this is the enabling relationship that most fiction itself renders. Later we shall examine some reasons why this is so. But the problematic of novelistic fiction from the early eighteenth century on is how narrative institutes, alongside the world of common discourse, another discourse whose beginning is im-portant—indeed, crucial—to it, located as it is in the responsibility taken for it by the begetting writer/speaker. Yet this fictional progenitor is bound by the fact that he is always at a remove from a truly fundamental role. It is no accident, I think, that James and Conrad, those exceptionally reflective autumnal craftsmen of fiction, made this tantalizing distance from a radical beginning the theme of much of their best work. *Heart of Darkness* explores beginnings paradoxically through a series of obscuring narrative frames; borne from one narrative level to another, Marlow's African adventure gains its power from the uniqueness, the strangeness, of its persistence in those levels, not unequivocally from the strangeness of the experience itself. The heart of the matter—Kurtz's experience—is posited outside Marlow's discourse, which leaves us to investigate, if we can, the speaker's authority. By the end of the tale we are aware of something that Marlow has given birth to that eludes empirical verification, even as it rests most securely upon the fact that Marlow has delivered it. Here, in most of its senses, authority is involved, except that we are required to accept that authority as never final. There is derivation, begetting, continuity, augmentation—and also a nagging, molesting awareness that beyond these there is something still more authentic, beside which fiction is secondary.

No writer before Freud and Nietzsche to my knowledge has so obsessively investigated some of these notions as Kierkegaard, whose meditations examine more than a century of fictional authority. To read *The Point of View for My Work as an Author* (written in 1848; published 1859) simply as commentary on his own work is to rob it of its most useful insights. For there Kierkegaard probes what is fundamental to all writing (preeminently fiction and personal discourse) in the center of which is the relationship between a focal character whose voice for the reader is authoritative and the nature of the authorship such a voice entails. It is of a kind with the relationship between Isabel Archer, for example, the movement of whose consciousness the reader attends to very carefully, and the type of writing James had to practice in order to produce her. Behind both is the generative authority that as secular critics we characterize as "imaginative," but which Kierkegaard the Christian called "divine governance" (*Styrelse*). The role of such governance is described only after Kierkegaard lays out the principles that have distinguished his work. He has been writing two sorts of books, he says: aesthetic and religious. The former sort seems to contradict the more obviously urgent religious works, but Kierkegaard wants it understood that the aesthetic books have been designed, in manner at least, to deal with serious questions in a mode suitable to the frivolity of his contemporaries. Taken alone, then, the aesthetic works would be confusing, not to say hopelessly lacking in seriousness. But viewed as necessary preparations for the directly religious works, his aesthetic writings become indirect, ironic communications of higher truths.

Here we have the characteristic Kierkegaardian figure of repetition. The aesthetic works are what he calls a dialectical reduplication of the truth: "For as a woman's coyness has a reference to the true lover and yields when he appears, so, too, dialectical reduplication has a reference to true seriousness."[4] There is a strict connection between aesthetic and religious, one that binds them together in bonds of necessity: the religious is a prior, more important truth given in secondary, ironic and dissembling forms. The aesthetic works do not occur in a void, even though it appears otherwise, so striking is the freedom of their expression. We must remember, therefore, that "there is a difference between writing on a blank sheet of paper and bringing to light by the application of a caustic fluid a text which is hidden under another text."[5] The aesthetic hides or signals the religious, just as Socrates' comic personality conceals the deepest seriousness. We accept the indirect mode, which seems to nullify the truth in order that the truth might emerge more fully later. This is, says Kierkegaard, a teleological suspension practiced so that the truth may become truer.

Kierkegaard's authorship is a deliberately composite one; and the patron of his enterprise is Socrates, to whom he devoted his master's thesis, *The Concept of Irony*. What always interests Kierkegaard is the difficulty of speaking directly to an unresponsive audience about matters for which silence is the most suitable expression. The difficulty, however, reflects as much on the author's weakness as it does on that of his audience. In an extremely long footnote to a phrase in chapter 3 of *The Point of View*, Kierkegaard argues that his total authorship is a superfluity only because he has depended on God and has been a weak human being; otherwise his work would have come to grips with the human situation and "would have been interrelated with the instant and the effective in the instant."[6] So in his aesthetic works Kierkegaard is the strong author whose mode conceals the true weakness vis-à-vis God which the religious author was at pains to reveal. The aesthetic, then, is an ironic double, a dialectical reduplication, of a religious truth. The human author augments and is strong, whereas with regard to the divine he is weak; the divine causes his work to stand apart and to appear to be superfluous to the here and now.

One aspect of authorship, then, is its contingent authority, its ability to initiate or build structures whose absolute authority is radically nil, but whose contingent authority is a quite satisfactory transitory alternative to the absolute truth. Therefore, the difference between Abraham's true authority in Kierkegaard's *Fear and Trembling* and the narrator's contingent authority is that Abraham is silent, whereas the narrator universalizes in language; the point is that any absolute truth cannot be expressed in words, for only diminished, flawed versions of the truth are available to language. This is as much as to say that *fiction alone speaks or is written*—for truth has no need of words—*and that all voices are assumed ones*. The importance of Kierkegaard's formulations is that he is particularly adept in describing the tactics of his authorship, with its recourse to revealing pseudonyms, and that he is more generally accurate in describing the tactics of writing that commit the author self-consciously to using an assumed voice. This voice sounds certain because it apparently (or in fact) *intentionally* determines its own way and validates its pronouncements by acceptable and sometimes dramatic means. Thus Kierkegaard, calling himself Johannes de Silentio in order ironically to remind us how far his words are from Abraham's silence and truth, writes the following mock disclaimer in *Fear and Trembling:*

> The present writer is nothing of a philosopher; he is, *poetice et eleganter,* an amateur writer who neither writes the System nor *promises* of the System, who neither subscribes to the System nor ascribes anything to it. He writes because for him it is a luxury which becomes the more agreeable and more evident, the fewer there are who buy and read what he writes.[7]

Yet the assumed voice's authority is a usurped one, for behind the voice is the truth, somehow and always unapprehendable, irreducible to words, and perhaps even unattractive, to which the voice remains subservient in an entirely interesting way. (It is perhaps worth suggesting here that the novel is the aesthetic form of servitude: no other genre so completely renders the meaning of *secondariness.*) Here again Kierkegaard is very subtle. The relationship between truth and its artistic version is dialectical, not strictly mimetic—by which I mean that Kierkegaard permits the aesthetic a maximum freedom without losing an awareness of the aesthetic's rewording of the religious, without forgetting its precarious status. In other words, we are to understand the dialectical connection as making ironic the convincing pretensions of the aesthetic.

Any novelistic narrative has for an immediate referent the act of speaking or writing: "I speak . . . ," or "It is spoken . . . ," or "He speaks . . . ." Beyond that, of course, the narrative is not obliged to be "real" except in the formal ways analyzed at great length in such works as Wayne Booth's *Rhetoric of Fiction.*[8] Kierkegaard's insistence upon the inventiveness and freedom of the aesthetic (i.e., the fictional) mode emphasizes how narratives do more than simply and generally repeat reality: they create another sense altogether by repeating, by making repetition itself the very form of novelty. Thus, as Gilles Deleuze has shown, such intentional repetition opposes the laws of nature and the moral law, goes beyond good and evil, and stands against the generality of habit and the particularity of memory. Moreover, such intentional repetition "appears as the *logos* of the solitary, the singular, the *logos* of the private thinker."[9] The actuality of the narrative process is repetition, it is true, but it is not the repetition of backward but of *forward* recollection. Kierkegaard links repetition with the essence of creation, not of slavish transcription:

> If God himself had not willed repetition, the world would never have come into existence. He would either have followed the light plans of hope, or He would have recalled it all and conserved it in recollection. This He did not do, therefore the world endures, and it endures for the fact that it is a repetition. Repetition is reality, and it is the seriousness of life.[10]

Kierkegaard everywhere insists on the individuality of the aesthetic repeating voice. It is neither abstract nor vaguely communal. In an important passage in *The Concept of Irony* he discusses the most distinctive feature of the ironic, aesthetic voice:

> But the outstanding feature of irony ... is the subjective freedom which at every moment has within its power the possibility of a beginning and is not generated from previous conditions. There is something seductive about every beginning because the subject is still free, and this is the satisfaction the ironist longs for. At such moments actuality loses its validity for him; he is free and above it.[11]

What the ironic voice goes on to create is a "usurped totality" of progression based on a seductive beginning. Insofar as an author begins to write at all he is ironic, since for him, too, there is a deceptive, subjective freedom at the outset. The distance that separates him from actuality is a function of his personality—which, Kierkegaard says, "is at least momentarily incommensurable with actuality"[12] —and, we might add, of his continuing, augmenting authority. But we must never forget the abiding truth, from which the author departs in search of his new fulfillment.

Kierkegaard's analysis of authorship exposes the uneasiness and vacillation with which narrative fiction begins and from which it develops. If we suspend for a moment our lifelong familiarity with fiction and try not to take the existence of novels for granted, we will see that the seminal beginning conception of narrative fiction depends simultaneously upon three special conditions. The first of these is that there must be some strong sense of doubt that the authority of any single voice, or group of voices, is sufficient unto itself. In the community formed among reader, author, and character, each desires the company of another voice. Each hears in the other the seductive beginning of a new life, an alternative to his own; and yet each grows progressively aware of an authenticity systematically betrayed during the course of the partnership—the novelistic character feels this most of all. Our interest in Dorothea Brooke in *Middlemarch* rests on our perception of her expectations of some life different from the one she presently leads; impelled by those expectations, she becomes another person in her marriage to Dr. Casaubon. What she leaves behind during that unhappy episode she later recovers in a form tempered by the experience of self-deception. Initially dissatisfied with herself, she doubles her life by adding a new one to it. She does this by the authority of her personality, yet her travails are no less the result of that molesting authority. So too for Eliot, who creates Dorothea in the enactment of her (Eliot's) will to be another. Similarly the reader, who allows Dorothea the benefit of his doubt about his isolated self.

The inaugural act of usurpation once performed—because of pleasure taken in a free beginning, because of a desire to reduplicate, to repeat life in a more accessible form—there follows consolidation of the initial gain by various means. One is by the accumulation of prerogatives. Notice how skillfully this is done by Huck Finn at the opening of his narrative, as he asserts his right to tell us *his* version of things:

> You don't know about me without you have read a book by the name of *Adventures of Tom Sawyer,* but that ain't no matter. That book was made by Mr. Mark Twain and he told the truth, mainly. There was things which he stretched, but mainly he told the truth. That is nothing. I never seen anybody but lied one time or another.[13]

Other means include strengthening one's belief in one's project, cultivating psychological arrangements, and placing useful as well as frightening things in convenient locations.

In the chapter in *Capital* entitled "The Secret of Primitive Accumulation," Marx traces the growth of capitalist society from the dissolution of feudal society in terms that deserve mention here: he claims that once the individual has "escaped from the regime of the guilds, their rules for apprenticeship and journeymen, and the impediments of their labour regulations," he becomes a free-seller of himself, and thereby a producer first-hand.[14] Of course, Marx adds, this is really just another form of enslavement, for man has been robbed of his personal means of production: he therefore creates others, alternative to his own, and then falls prey to the illusion that he has free labor power. The real power is elsewhere, but the illusion persists that the individual is in control of his life as he generates values and prerogatives suitable to his condition. This is perfectly consonant with what Pip does in *Great Expectations.* Self-created, he labors to be a free gentleman leading a gentleman's life while in fact he is enslaved by an outcast who has himself been victimized by society. By his schemes Pip grants himself the right to manners, thoughts, and actions that dispose of life with grand ease. It is with the exposure of the falseness of these schemes, as well as with the actual successes he manages, that the novel is concerned.

The systematic reinforcement of illusions, which Marx and Engels treated earlier in *The German Ideology,* underlies Pip's course in *Great Expectations.* His progress up the social scale is supported by every character in the novel, so committed is everyone (Joe Gargery included)—in thought, at least—to an ideology that equates money with privilege, morality, and worth. Although the novel itself licenses Pip's expectations, it also mercilessly undercuts them, mainly by showing that these expectations are inherently self-limiting. That is, Pip can neither hold expectations nor realize them without a patron who makes them possible. Thus Pip's freedom is dependent upon an unnamed patron who requires visits to Jaggers, who requires that no questions be asked, and so on. The more Pip believes he is acting on his own, the more tightly he is drawn into an intricate web of circumstances that weighs him down completely; the plot's progressive revelation of accidents connecting the principal characters is Dickens's method of countering Pip's ideology of free upward progress. For Marx, the equivalent of Dickens's plot is history, which progressively reveals how one or another "freedom" is in fact a function of class interest and alliances and not really freedom at all: hence the illusion of free labor-power that allows the worker to think he can do as he pleases, whereas in fact he dangles on strings pulled by others.

The second special condition for generating narrative fiction is that the truth—whatever that may be—can only be approached indirectly, by means of a mediation that, paradoxically, because of its falseness makes the truth truer. In this context, a truer truth is one arrived at by a process of elimination: alternatives similar to the truth are shed one by one. The elevation of truth-resembling fiction to preeminence becomes a habitual practice when fiction comes to be considered the trial of truth by error. In trying to account for this rationale we enter a realm of speculation to which the best guide is Vico. In *The New Science,* Vico focuses his inquiries on a point of original juncture of three primal elements: human identity, human history, and human language. Since these are also the components with which the novel must begin its work, each of which it in turn individualizes, the correspondence between Vico and the engenderment of a novel is worth examining. Let us keep in mind, first of all, that in the center of a novel is the character who, unlike his counterpart in the classical drama, is not conceded at the very outset to be a known figure. Tom Jones, Clarissa, Robinson Crusoe, Tristram Shandy, Ahab, Julien Sorel, Frederic Moreau, Stavrogin—all these are figures deliberately and specifically original, however much they are generally of one type or another; they are not Oedipus or Agamemnon, for whose portrayal the dramatist relies upon a common mythic past, or upon a community of socially invested values and symbols. A novel's protagonist may resemble a known character, but the filiation is an indirect one. Whatever we recognize in the novelistic character we do at another level of much less prominence—that is, at the level of private authority.

Authority, says Vico, comes from *auctor,* which "certainly comes from *autos (proprius* or *suus ipsius)*"; thus the word's original meaning is "property." Property is dependent upon human will and upon choice; therefore, it is axiomatic for Vico that "philology observes the authority of human choice, whence comes consciousness of the certain." So the study of language recovers the conscious choices by which man established his identity and his authority: language preserves the traces of these choices, which a philologist can then decipher. Opposed to philology is philosophy, "which contemplates reason, whence comes knowledge of the true."[15] Note the demarcation: on the one hand, language, authority, and certain identity, on the other hand, the true. Certainty pertains to poetic creation (and its understanding to philology), for creation does its work in three forms of authority: divine, human, and natural. By this Vico means that human history is made by man in three stages of mythologized power, three phases of locating human interests and forming agencies to maintain them. In the divine phase, the gods fix the giants by chaining the latter to earth (*terrore defixi*): whatever man fears he divides into a subduing and a subdued power. Thus Jove and the chained giants. In the second or human phase, the giants, who have been wandering the earth, learn to control their bodies, thereby exercising will. They inhabit caves, and settle there, domesticated. Finally, after a long period of settlement, they become lords of dominion, occupation, and possession. A third division occurs: there are *gentes majores,* or the founders and originators of families, on the one hand, and the people over whom they rule on the other hand.[16]

Vico's term for this succession of periods, "poetic history," designates not so much a "real" sequence as a retrospective construction. What the construction describes, however, is real enough, even if its figures are highly metaphorical. It is the institution of a humanized milieu, populated with beings and maintained by an authority that conserves itself while slowly being reduced from grandiose powers to more and more sharply differentiated functions—just as, for example, in *Mansfield Park* Fanny apprehensively enters the wealthy environment of her aunt's house, then slowly comes to understand and live with it enough to disapprove of her cousins' mistreatment of its spirit. The pivotal moment in Vico's sequence is the Flood, or great rupture, an event that separates man's history into two distinct types that thereafter flow concurrently: sacred history and gentile history. Of the first Vico has little to say, except that it is in a sort of permanent rapport with God. The second is mankind's, an alternative to the first: it is the "new" life sought by Julien Sorel, or the one created perforce by Crusoe. Like Kierkegaard, Vico sees things in a double perspective, aesthetic and religious. And like Kierkegaard's writing, his is more fluent, more at home in the former than in the latter. The important point is that both men see that the aesthetic (or poetic) requires a reconstructive *technique* (since it is an order of repetition), that it gives rise to a special manner of being and to a universe of distinctions, while always remaining conscious of its alternative status. What is most interesting about this alternative consciousness is that it is a valid and even necessary institution of life despite the relative subservience of its position, which we may call aesthetic and ironic with Kierkegaard, or poetic and fictional with Vico.

The third special condition for the generation of novelistic fiction is an extraordinary fear of the void that antedates private authority. This, I think, is one of the less well-noted themes of the novel which extends at least as far back as *Robinson Crusoe*. For in the shipwreck that casts him into his island wilderness, Crusoe is "born," with extinction always threatening afterward, and with his new-gained and constantly experienced authority over his domain providing the safeguard of his continuing existence. A whole range of principal characters in fiction are based upon the same premise: orphans, outcasts, parvenus, emanations, solitaries, and deranged types whose background is either rejected, mysterious, or unknown. Sterne's fascination with Tristram's birth toys with the seemingly limitless hovering between nullity and existence that is central to the novelistic conception of character and to its representation in language. Were it not for a rejection of the anonymous void, both Ishmael and Pip, for example, would be unthinkable. Ishmael pointedly tells us that his narrative of shipboard existence is a substitute for the philosophical flourish with which Cato threw himself upon his sword. And the bond between the character's novelistic life and the death from which he is stayed while he lasts before us is querulously summed up in *The Nigger of the Narcissus* by James Wait, who announces, "I must live till I die."

I said parenthetically above that the novel is a literary form of secondariness; here we can refine this generality to say that the novel makes, procreates, a certain secondary and alternative life possible for heroes who are otherwise lost in society. In a sense, the novel's attitude as a formal institution toward its *dramatis personae* is that of a chiding father who has endowed his children with a patrimony and an abode he himself cannot really ever relinquish. In being the author—and notice how this applies equally to the writer/author, the novel-father/author and the character/author—one engages oneself in a whole process of filiation not easily escaped. In this (as in so much else) *Don Quixote* is exemplary. There is the Cervantes-Sidi Hamete-Quixote relationship. There is the Amadis-Quixote relationship, there is the astonishingly fertile link between Quixote and Panza—now one, now the other rears his partner in the furthering and fathering forth of illusion; and there is, as every novelist and historian of the novel avers, *Don Quixote* itself as parent novel. James Wait's "I must live till I die" is an alternative way of saying that as a novelistic character he must live in that abode, in the family of men (the crew) which is taken by the novelist to be the stuff of fiction and which is, so far as the plot is concerned, inherited from life and from the life of novels, therefrom to be fashioned into a line of succession. This line and this sense of heritage, it seems to me, stands at the absolute center of the classical novel; and yet how interestingly secondary, how intentionally flawed and derived a line it is. I shall return to it presently.

In using Marx, Kierkegaard, and Vico to point up requisite conditions for fiction I have tried to parallel their thought with the novel's ground in human experience. Thus the philosopher or historian belongs in his work to a common mode of conceiving experience of which another version is the novel. I refer, of course, to such common themes as succession, sequence, derivation, portrayal, and alternation, to say nothing of authority itself. Here we may remark the similarities between thought that produces philosophical works, for instance, and thought that produces novels. Yet the difference is no less crucial. It is a difference in degree. The difference between Kierkegaard's anthropology of authority and, say, Pip's in *Great Expectations* is that Pip is *more* of an augmenter, continuer, and originator, both because Dickens willed it so and because that is Pip's essence as a character. As to the productive impulse that has such staying power that is not commonly diverted into either philosophy or history (Tolstoi is an exception), we can look ahead briefly to Freud for an explanation.

In any of the reconstructive techniques, whether history, philosophy, or personal narrative, the objective, according to Freud, is both to create alternatives to a confusing reality and to minimize the pain of experience. In other words, the project is an economic one. Yet insofar as it is also a repetitive procedure it has to do with instincts leading the mind over ground already traveled. Some instincts are life-promoting, others return one to the primal unity of death. The novelistic character gains his fictional authority, as we saw, in the desire to escape death; therefore, the narrative process endures so long as that essentially procreative will persists. Yet because a character's real beginning takes place in the avoidance of the anonymity of pure negation—and this is nowhere more beautifully described than in the first and last volumes of Proust's novel—there is a simultaneous pressure exerted upon him by that which he is always resisting. The demystification, the decreation or education, of illusions, which is the novel's central theme—and, paradoxically, its own alternate theme—is thus an enactment of the character's increasing molestation by a truer process pushing him to an ending that resembles his beginning in the midst of negation. The sheer length of the classical novel can almost be accounted for by the desire to initiate and promote a reduplication of life and, at the same time, to allow for a convincing portrayal of how that sort of life leads inevitably to the revelation of a merely borrowed authority. The element that contains as well as symbolizes the whole enterprise is, as recent critics have shown, the language of temporal duration.[17]

But whether we depict the narrative in temporal or strictly verbal terms, the important thing is that one must understand narrative as wholly qualified by the extremely complex authority of its presentation. Pip, Dorothea, and Isabel (in *The Portrait of a Lady*) are flawed by their illusions, by a skewing of their vision of themselves and of others. Yet all three of them *move:* out of them rises, from them *begins,* a sense of motion and of change that engages our serious interest as readers. For Pip's illusions there are, as an unforgettable counterpoise, Miss Havisham's solitary paralysis: whereas he generates a life for himself whose falseness is more and more manifest, she does next to nothing, memorialized in the sarcophagus of Satis House. Late in the novel he tells her accusingly, "You let me go on"; what is enough for her is only the beginning for Pip. And Dorothea's affections and aspirations contrast sharply with Dr. Casaubon's frigid personality, symbolized by his unfinished, locked-up manuscript. Lastly, James contrasts Isabel's flights with Osmond's perfect retreat at Roccanera, the one whose manner is that of a beautiful projector, the other the creature of a prison from which all humanity has been excluded. Within a novel, then, the principle of authority provides a motion always attempting to steer clear of obstacles that emerge to inhibit, maim, or destroy it utterly.

In historical novels of the early nineteenth century there are figures of authority to whom the protagonists are subordinate. Cardinal Borromeo in *I Promesi Sposi* and the King in *Quentin Durward,* to mention only two examples, each serves within the novel as a reminder of the limits to a character's secular power, limits that are vestiges of the "real," historical world, the truer realm, which persist into the fiction. Yet the function of each will become incorporated into the character's increasing self-consciousness of his weakness in the world, in the same way that the Marshalsea Prison in *Little Dorrit* is still more a psychological molestation of poor Mr. Dorrit when he is free than even it was in reality. The incorporation of reality into the great realistic novels of the mid-nineteenth century is performed by converting figures of secular authority into forms of sociomaterial resistance faced by the protagonists. If these forms are not imaginatively represented by cities—as in the Paris of Balzac and Flaubert, Dickens's London, and so forth—they are nevertheless felt by such figures as the Underground Man to be the generally hostile outer reality.

Such exterior circumstances exist at the level of plot. I want now to return to the authoritative character as the novel's conceptual matrix. Sometimes, as in Goethe's *Wahlverwandschaften* or Laclos's *Liaisons dangereuses,* the fiction is sustained by pairs whose destiny is always intertwined. Edward, Ottilie, and Charlotte produce Goethe's story through a complex series of partnerships whose permanence is practically ontological in terms of the novel's existence; similarly Valmont and Merteuil, whose schemes together are the veritable abstract without which the plot could not be. Richardson's Clarissa, in comparison, is an example of private authority resisting interventions, yet beseeching Lovelace's interventions by the deep attractiveness of her inviolate privacy. In the case of Pip—which I want to analyze in some detail—we have a remarkably economical individual character. From Pip, Dickens is able to derive a very diverse range of originating circumstances (circumstances that give rise to an entire world), which taken as a group provide a perfect example of the authoritative or authorizing fictional consciousness. The more remarkable is this economy when we realize that Dickens makes use of every traditional narrative device—development, climax, linear plot sequence, physical setting, realistic accuracy of detail—together with a thoroughly imaginative method of using them, in so complete a way that even James and Eliot cannot match him. *Great Expectations* reposes upon Dickens's portrayal of Pip as at once the novel's condition for being, the novel's action, and the character in it: this gives the notions of authority and molestation I have been discussing an archetypal form. The first-person narration adds to the purity of Dickens's achievement.

Pip's name, he tells us at the outset, is the sort of beginning sign for the identity he is left with after he mixes and shortens his given name Philip Pirrip, words no longer meaningful to him but inherited by him "on the authority" of his parents' tombstones and by his sister's command. He lives, then, as an alternative being: as an orphan without real parents and as a harassed surrogate son of a much older sister. Throughout the novel the initial division will be perpetuated. On the other hand, there is Pip's natural, true genealogy that is banished from the novel at the outset, but which makes its appearance fitfully through Joe, Biddy, and the new little Pip who springs up near the novel's end. The fact that Joe Gargery is like a father to him, though in fact being his brother-in-law, makes Pip's alienation from the family continuity all the more poignant. On the other hand, the second branch in the novel's order is a substitute family, which has its roots in the unpleasant household of Mrs. Joe. Once established by Dickens, this order recurs throughout, with Pip going from one incarnation of it to another. This is the novel's most insistent pattern of narrative organization: how Pip situates himself at and affiliates himself with the center of several family groups, families whose authority he challenges by trying to institute his own through the great expectations that finally destroy him. Each family is revealed successively to belong within the sphere of another, more dominant, prior one. Miss Havisham and Estella's circle later admits Jaggers, then Magwitch, then Molly and Compeyson. And after each revelation Pip finds himself a little more self-implicated and a little less central. Each discovery informs him that his beginning has been preceded by compromises that emerge, one after the other, to wound him.

In this sequence of discoveries Dickens allows Pip, even though he seems occasionally to be fortunate, to see how there is a necessary connection between himself and prison and crime. Those fearful things are real enough, as are, too, the harshness of his childhood, the schemes of Magwitch and Miss Havisham (his alternate parents), and the bankruptcy to which he arrives later on. Set against this theme is the motif of reassembling unpleasant fragments—for nothing is given whole to Pip, or to anyone else—into new, fabricated units. A brief sojourn at Miss Havisham's is transformed by Pip into an extraordinary adventure which, despite Joe's solemn warnings, he will repeat again and again. The ironical significance of Pip's constructions is accentuated by Wemmick's house, that fantastic melange of remnants fabricated into a mock-medieval castle by the man's irrepressible desire to create a better life at Falworth—and also by Wopsle's acting, for which Shakespeare is only a beginning excuse for a rather free improvisation. These, like Pip, are *bricoleurs,* who, "brought up by hand," by fits and starts, assert their authority over the threats of unpleasant dispersion.[18] The image of a fabricating hand and its cognates is carried over into almost every corner of the novel: for example, chains are filed through, a release effected, and the hands retied in a different manner. Pip is linked by strong hands with Magwitch's and with Miss Havisham's compensatory impulses and, through Estella, with Molly's exceptionally powerful hands. After his breakdown, Pip finds himself reposing like a baby in Joe's paternal arms.

The basic scheme I have been describing is the cycle of birth and death. Pip's origin as a novelistic character is rooted in the death of his parents. By his wish to make up for that long series of graves and tombstones he creates a way for himself; and yet, over the novel's duration, Pip finds one route after another blocked, only to force open another. Like Isabel and Dorothea, Pip as a character is conceived as excess, wanting more, trying to be more than in fact he is. The augmentations are finally all rooted in the death from which he springs, and to which he returns in the end. Only by then a new, more authentic dispensation has been bred, which finally yields up a new little Pip:

> For eleven years I had not seen Joe nor Biddy with my bodily eyes—though they had both been often before my fancy in the East—when, upon an evening in December, an hour or two after dark, I laid my hand softly on the latch of the old kitchen door. I touched it so softly that I was not heard, and I looked in unseen. There, smoking his pipe in the old place by the kitchen firelight, as hale and as strong as ever, though a little grey, sat Joe; and there, fenced into the corner with Joe's leg, and sitting on my own little stool looking at the fire, was—I again!
>
> "We giv' him the name of Pip for your sake, dear old chap," said Joe, delighted when I took another stool by the child's side (but I did *not* rumple his hair), "and we hoped he might grow a bit like you, and we think he do."[19]

Between them, the two Pips cover an expanse whose poles are true life, on the one hand, and novelistic life on the other. Both Dickens in *Great Expectations* and Flaubert in *Madame Bovary* use money to signify the protagonists' transitory power to shore up their authority to dream and even for a while to be something they cannot long remain being. Catherine, the aged farmworker, little Pip, Joe and Biddy—these are the inarticulate, abiding natures that money cannot touch nor illusion tempt.

Together little Pip and old Pip are Dickens's way of aligning the molestations of truth against an imperious authority badly in need of restraint. That Dickens makes the alignment explicitly only near the novel's end is a sign of how, relatively late in his novelistic career, he had come to see the problem of authority as rooted in the self and therefore to be checked primarily also by the self: hence little Pip appears only to *confirm* Pip's transgression, his subsequent education, and his irremediable alienation from the family of man. One indication of Dickens's later acute understanding of the self's way with itself is that in *Great Expectations* Pip undergoes the experiences of mystification and demystification on his own, *within himself;* whereas in *Martin Chuzzlewit* two estranged Martins, one young and one old, educate one another into a family embrace. In the later novel Dickens represents the harsher principles of authority—that at bottom the self wants its own way, unshared, and that its awakening to truth entails a still more unpleasant alienation from others—which in the earlier novel he had divided between a pair of misunderstanding, willful relatives. The self's authority splits apart again later in the century—for example, in *The Picture of Dorian Gray,* in *The Strange Case of Dr. Jekyll and Mr. Hyde,* and, later still, in "The Secret Sharer." In all three of these works, however, the alter ego is a hidden reminder of the primary self's unstable authority. Jekyll's sense of "the fortress of identity" includes as well a recognition that the fortress has hideous, molesting foundations. Dickens refused to embody these recognitions *outside* the individual, as would Wilde, Stevenson, and Conrad: it is imperative in Dickens's view that such an individual as Pip should become the architect equally of his expectations and of their destruction. Doubtless he saw Pip's predicament as one communally shared and even abetted. But nowhere is there any excuse for Pip—neither orphanhood, nor poverty, nor circumstance—that can reduce the deliberateness of his choices, his individual responsibility, and his often venal compromises with reality, all of which return finally to burden him:

> That I had a fever and was avoided, that I suffered greatly, that I often lost my reason, that the time seemed interminable, that I confounded impossible existences with my own identity; that I was a brick in the house wall, and yet entreating to be released from the giddy place where the builders had set me; that I was a steel beam of a vast engine, clashing and whirling over a gulf, and yet that I implored in my own person to have the engine stopped, and my part in it hammered off; that I passed through these phases of disease, I know of my own remembrance, and did in some sort know at the time.[20]

Here the severe repetitiveness of his realizations and their insistent parallelism appear to Pip as the actual material of a reality from which he has hitherto hidden himself. After such knowledge he can only be "a weak helpless creature" and thankful for the Gargery family's solicitude; but he remains an orphan.

Yet Pip's history begins with the loss of a family and—no less important—with a favor performed out of fear. Pip's act of terrified charity is the germ of his later experience; so far as the plot is concerned, it is the author of his history and, of course, of his troubles. One might be perhaps too rash to say that in its bases at least, Pip's act, with its extended consequences, is an aesthetic dialectical reduplication, even an ironic one, of the charity we associate with Christ's ministry and agony. And yet, directly or not, novels too reflect the ethos of the Christian West. The original instance of divine errancy, the Incarnation, transformed God into man, an alternative being—the record of that mystery is given in language that only approximates the deed.

So, we might say, novels represent that process and its record at many removes, and after many secular transformations. The beginning attribution of authority to a character by a writer; the implementation of that authority in a narrative form, and the burdens and difficulties admitted as a result—all these are ways by which the almost numinous communal institutions of language accept and conserve the imprint of an individual force. This is why the novel is an institutionalization of the intention to begin. If in the end this institution chastens the individual, it is because he needs to be reminded that private authority is part of an integral truth that it nevertheless cannot fully imitate. The authority of any single piece of fiction repeats that insight, for invariably the central consciousness of a novel is found wanting in the wholeness which we normally associate with truth. Each piece of fiction, therefore, excludes a larger truth than it contains, even though it is the novelist's task to make his readers see active relationships among various orders of reality or truth both inside and outside the text. In few major novels does this activity dominate the author's concern more fully than in *Nostromo,* and so it is to a detailed examination of that work that we must now turn.

II

Despite its extravagant range of national and social origins, the cast of Conrad's *Nostromo*—the most massive of his works—is bound together by two inner affinities. The first is that everyone in the novel has an unflagging interest in the fortunes of Costaguana, for the most part in the form of a private vision of personal advantage. Charles Gould, for example, considers the good of Costaguana synonymous with the good of his work in the San Tomé mine. The second affinity is that nearly everyone seems extremely anxious about both keeping and leaving a personal "record" of his thoughts and action. This anxiety seems to be based upon an extraordinary preoccupation with the past, as if the past, left to itself, given only ordinary attention and no official recording, were somehow unthinkable and without sufficient authority.

After a few pages of impersonal geography and history, the

reader is led into Costaguana along the way cleared by Captain Mitchell, the English sea captain who has led a life of rather unthinking courage. For Mitchell, life in Costaguana has been a series of adventurous episodes, which he proudly dubs "historical events." When he later informs his audience that, like a much-lived much-traveled Aeneas, he too was a part of these events (*quarum magna pars fui*), the sizable distance separating his ingenuous record from the reality appears even wider. His loquacious and insistent recollection of the past takes for its theme the high adventure of life in Costaguana, though the dominant variation on that theme is the inherent rascality of the "foreign" mind. Mitchell's unfortunate run-in with the sanguine Sotillo—in which Mitchell clearly emerges as the victor—emphasizes the disparity between "colonial" and native, a disparity that removes Mitchell's recitation of his activities even further from the truth. In short, Mitchell has little sense of the complexity with which his artless narrative has been coping.

In no characterization does Mitchell's narrative miss the mark so widely as in his portrait of Nostromo. But in this Mitchell is only as wrong as everyone else. That the admirable *capataz de cargadores* has sacrificed his honor to a desire for a spotless, enviable reputation is a matter known only to Nostromo. Only Nostromo understands the meaning of his remark to Dr. Monygham in a moment of passionate irritation with the *hombres finos* who have apparently robbed him of his enviable reputation. He will later find out that he still has the reputation and, with it, an immensely onerous burden.) "The capataz is . . . destroyed." he says at this point; "there is no capataz" (p. 487).[21] As the town, the republic, of Sulaco grows in prestige and wealth many years later, so also does Nostromo grow in eminence within the new republic. Yet he lives *outside* his fame, which to our eyes seems a thing apart from him, as if a great public reputation possessed its own authority. The man and his reputation have become completely distinct; to Sulaco, though, Nostromo's carefully engineered record of heroism *is* Nostromo, and Sulacoan independence is attributed to his efforts.

The more modern and civilized citizens of Costaguana are no less sanguine about the records they want left. Their subtle intelligences allow them, however, a scarcely more accurate sense of history. More nervous, more sophisticated and introspective, their "records"—kept by them in various ways—are hardly more than poignant abstractions for which there is little evident use.

Martin Decoud, the originator if not the executor of Sulacoan independence, finds time in the midst of a fierce bombardment to write his sister a letter that may never reach her.

> In the most sceptical heart there lurks at such moments when the chances of existence are involved, a desire to leave a correct impression of the feelings, by which the action may be seen when personality is gone, gone where no light of investigation can ever reach the truth which every death takes out of the world. Therefore, instead of looking for something to eat or trying to snatch an hour or so of sleep, Decoud was filling the pages of a large notebook with a letter to his sister. (p. 255)

No matter how urgently recorded and felt, feelings like this are regrettably private; counterbalancing them in the novel is Don José Avellanos's enduring record in which the country's elder statesman leaves a public narrative of Costaguanan political life. His book, *Fifty Years of Misrule,* is written out of disinterested political wisdom; Decoud's letter to his sister, and his subsequent activity on behalf of Sulacoan integrity, are motivated by his lover's illusion.

Neither, if judged by their practical effects on Costaguanan history, can compare with the record left by Charles Gould, writ large in the incredibly influential history of the San Tomé silver mine whose economic and moral authority overrides the country with ever-increasing strength. Holroyd, who thinks of himself as leaving a record of his Christian altruism; Sir John, the British railroad builder who crisscrosses the land with steel rails that signify progress and expansion; and Gould, their reticent minion in Sulaco—these three work for the mine together under the auspices of Costaguana's major *idée reçue*: material interests. In the minds of their agents, these interests give rise to so dehumanized a set of goals that spiritual life petrifies into a slavish round of work in the service of the mine. The record of this work is, of course, preserved in the history of the mine's grand success.[22]

To this maliciously successful record, Giorgio Viola's touching faith in "liberal" politics provides a sad and hopeless foil. His dedication to an irrelevant ideal—irrelevant because Costaguana is so thoroughly dominated by silver interests—makes him, in Sulaco, a relic to whose ponderous silence and majestic bearing the city is vaguely deferential. His one decisive act, the accidental murder of Nostromo, is a ceremony inspired by an ancestral record of "honor" and Garibaldean ethics. Inadvertently, Viola mars the record of Nostromo's perfection; this is the climax to what Douglas Hewitt calls Conrad's "deflating" of Nostromo.[23]

Conrad's account of the novel's composition in his introductory note written many years after *Nostromo*'s completion in
1904[24] is very much like all of his other "notes": engaging,
affable, and relaxed. In the phrase "the most anxiously meditated
of [my] longer novels" (p. 1), for example, one gets only a *sense*
of the trouble the novel caused him. Yet a random sampling of
letters to friends written by Conrad while composing the novel
reveals a struggle with difficulties of a sort that make "anxious
meditation" seem an innocuous euphemism. Early in 1903, some
weeks after he had begun the novel, he wrote H. G. Wells a letter
that concluded with the following remarks:

> I . . . am absolutely out of my mind with the worry and apprehension of
> my work. I go as one would cycle over a precipice along a 14-inch plank. If I
> falter I am lost.[25]

In May he wrote Edward Garnett, his "literary confessor,"[26] that
Nostromo was not yet one-quarter written: "I am indeed appalled
at myself when I think what rotten contemptible bosh it must and
shall be. By Jove I am too tired and with a heart worn too
threadbare to be honest."[27] Conrad's honesty with his friend A.
H. Davray was sufficient, on August 22, to describe a terrible state
of affairs produced by stupor of mind, a disgust of his pen, and a
terror of the inkpot. With half of the novel now written, he had
embarked upon a terrible journey from which he could expect no
relief: "Solitude is taking me over: it is absorbing me. I see
nothing, I read nothing. It is like being in a tomb which is at the
same time a hell where one must write, write, write."[28] On the
same day he described himself to John Galsworthy as "a mental
and moral outcast, . . . always deeper in the mire."[29] As the year
wore on, writing *Nostromo* became more and more of a physical
task. He wrote Wells on November 30 as if the book were
threatening him with a physical catastrophe:

> Things are bad with me—there's no disguising the fact. Not only is the
> scribbling awfully in arrears but there's no "spring" in me to grapple with it
> effectually. Formerly in my sea life, a difficulty nerved me to the effort: now
> I perceive it is not so. However, don't imagine I've given up, but there is an
> uncomfortable sense of losing my footing in deep waters. . . .
> I say so because for me, writing—the only possible writing—is just simply
> the conversion of nervous force into phrases. With you too, I am sure, tho' in
> your case it is the disciplined intelligence which gives the signal—the impulse.
> For me it is a matter of chance, stupid chance. But the fact remains that
> when the nervous force is exhausted the phrases don't come—and no tension
> of will can help.[30]

On December 5 he had reached page 567 of the novel, and at that moment, writing to A. K. Waliszewski, he felt it necessary to observe about himself that he had become "an Englishman . . . and a *homo duplex,* in more than one sense."[31] The letter was written at a time when Conrad knew that appeals to his publisher for sympathy for his overworked capacities and for his terrific spiritual problems with his work would neither earn pity nor gain an extension of deadlines. In 1902 he had weathered a severe crisis with William Blackwood, then his publisher.[32] Now, at work on the most troublesome project of all, Conrad realized that the shortest way to the world's affections was a show of cheer; he hoped that a stiff upper lip would make him more understandable to his adopted countrymen. The horrors of composition continued, of course, but he developed a rather mannered outward composure. He literally created a genial, outward Conrad, his *persona,* to whom struggles with work were unknown except as manifestations of an underground second-self over whom he had no control.[33] As Conrad continued in later years to please his successfully won-over public, the underground man disappeared; the evasive and charming author of the introductory notes remained instead. So amiable and authoritative a personage could not discuss such embarassments as, for example, the loss of spiritual footing; molestations like that were better left in an ignorant, hidden past. Thus the personal record the author presented to his public was as different from the realities that the record concealed as Captain Mitchell's "historical events" are different from real events. (Mitchell, of course, *is* ignorant of what really happened; Conrad was not, obviously.) The *"homo duplex* in more than one sense" that Conrad spoke of to Waliszewski refers, I think, to the consciously authored doubleness of his life at the time that he was working on *Nostromo.* If for no other reason than a desire to forget what was extremely unpleasant to him, he postured outwardly as if everything was fine, and—because he seemed to have little choice—he continued his hellish efforts to finish his novel.

By the early part of 1904 he was again writing Wells, this time assuring him that "no one's position is too absurd to be argued with. An enlightened egoism is as valid as an enlightened altruism—neither more nor less."[34] The meaning of this assertion is that Conrad had arrived at a point where two opposing positions, or realities, seemed to have equal validity. Was this not another way of saying that his real struggles with *Nostromo* on the one hand, and his public image on the other, were each making acute claims on him? Each demanded from him a sort of ultimate recognition. Two equally articulate individualities fighting within the same single existence led him to the brink of madness: on April 5, 1904, he wrote to David Meldrum that he was "verging on insanity."[35] That he managed to go on with what he used to call "that dread thing" is, I think, something of a miracle. He suffered many bouts of debilitating illness, his wife was also frequently ill, and, as his letters to William Rothenstein show, he was almost continually in financial straits. Writing Rothenstein on June 27, he said:

> I dare do nothing. Either my soul or my liver is very sick. If it is the liver then the cold shall make it worse. Even here I go about shuddering when a cloud passes over the sun. And I am tired, tired, as if I had lived a hundred years. Reverting to the matter of that salvage you are conducting to preserve a rather rotten old hulk (but full of the best intentions)—I think. . . . [Here follows some detailed advice and requests about some money Rothenstein was arranging to get for Conrad.] It is late—and tomorrow is another dread day. G. Graham has been here for the Sunday and we talked much of you. He is in very good form and very friendly but the episode of his visit has not refreshed me as much as I expected. I am not myself and shall not be myself till I am born again, until after Nostromo is finished.[36]

The agony was terminated a short time later: *Nostromo* was finished on August 30, 1904. Eight years later he wrote André Gide of the novel in terms that expressed a combination of incredulity and alienation, for by 1912 the composition of *Nostromo* had become a problematic experience he could no longer stand to recollect in detail: "It's a black oven [*un four noir*], you know. I, I have a kind of tenderness for that enormous machine. But it doesn't work; that is true. There is something that prevents it from working. I don't know what. All in all, even with all my tenderness, I myself cannot stand to read it."[37] Because Gide was one of Conrad's closer friends, the letter has none of that impersonal whimsy of which Conrad was capable in his introductory notes. Nevertheless, it is quite apparent that a disengagement has occurred in Conrad's mind between the actual process of composing the novel and his manner of recalling the experience some years later. Perhaps the manner of the later recollection was only a convenient way of narrating a messy affair; after all, who inclines to specific details when details—unpleasant ones with neither shape nor focus—are all that one remembers?

There is an interesting parallel to be drawn between the characters of *Nostromo* and Conrad himself. In each case the individual has performed or witnessed problematic, jumbled action from which a descriptive record is distilled and then authorized for public consumption. So restless is this action, so engrossing its complications, that, at the time it occurs, the individual is totally immersed in it. When the action is later recalled, it has become "history," which in the novel at least is usually a comparatively thin record whose author is a known figure: his work appears as a summary definition of the past. In their recollection of the past, the characters of *Nostromo* are also affected by their idealism, which, to judge by its force, borders on vanity. Nostromo's ideal of what a brave man should be forces him to hide the secret of his scandalous theft; among his fellow citizens he pretends that the silver has sunk to the bottom of the Golfo Placido so that they may continue to believe that his "record" of behavior is still unimpeachable. There is little doubt that his interest in the silver is quite subordinate to his concern about his reputation. But the novel's task is to represent the actuality, the record of it by an individual, and the individual himself in the act of being an author as he mediates between actuality and record. All three of these things add up to *Nostromo's* dense fabric.

So strong a plan of representation derives, I think, from Conrad's habit of viewing his life as an uneasy compromise between two conflicting modes of existence. Because it reflects Conrad's radical uncertainty about himself and also the tension he so often felt between opposed positions on any given matter, it is a complex habit. The first mode is to experience reality as an unfolding process, as action-being-made, as always "becoming." To experience all of this is to feel oneself in the midst of reality. The second mode is to feel reality as a hard quantity, very much "there" and definable. To experience this is to view reality retrospectively, since only in looking back upon what has already occurred can one master the unceasing movement of action-being-made. In other words, the first mode is that of the actor, the second that of the author. Yet because mastery inevitably means control, the retrospective view modifies, and even contradicts, the richly complex dynamics of a specific action. In *Nostromo* the two modes are of course the conflict between immersion in action and the retrospective definition (record) of that action; and as readers, we are expected to note the often startling disparities between action and record that such a conflict produces.

We are also expected to ask whether a correspondence between the record and the action is ever to be hoped for.

Presumably such a correspondence is possible for most people in some situations, yet it is never even momentarily allowed in *Nostromo*—except, as we shall see in a moment, in Emelia Gould's mind. The rest of the time the characters who carry out the retrospection distort reality almost beyond recognition. This is one of the novel's peculiarities—that each character is portrayed as the author of a record in conflict with several other records. That is why nearly every character seems curiously myopic about Costaguanan politics. No one wants to see the whole of what is really happening. Instead everyone sees what he likes to *believe* happened. The result of this myopia in Costaguana gives *Nostromo* one of its principle subjects.

The reconciliation between action and record is performed by Mrs. Gould, the only character in the novel with really accurate vision. She has the capacity both for understanding action as it happens and for being aware of the psychological traps men create for themselves as they cast a congratulatory glance back over their activity and plan new action. It is, after all, because the retrospective inaccuracy of a personal record breeds inaccurate, wrongheaded self-assessments that Charles Gould is so pathetic a figure in the novel. A lifelong education in the pathetic mis-management of a life comes to Emelia during the course of her marriage to Charles. She watches him slowly drawn away from her by the attractive personal challenge he finds in the mine. The more successfully he copes with the challenge, the more he is claimed by material interests. For his success is measured in the enlarging scope of his material interests: he is Charles Gould first, and then he becomes *el rey de Sulaco*. But Emelia can admire the king at the same time that she knows the other Charles, a poor slave who sacrifices himself to the delusion that silver, his silver, can be humane. The more he is a king, the less able he is to know what a slave really is.

Emelia's ability to see accurately and at the same time charitably to accept people for what they are is so unique in the novel that every one of the men is attracted to her. Dr. Monygham sees her as a good fairy seated in a charmed circle at the Casa Gould. Decoud quite naturally gravitates toward her quiet house and honors her even as he loves Antonia Avellanos. It is left to Nostromo—perhaps because he has dared the most—to pay her the supreme compliment, which is to reveal his dishonoring secret to her. During that wonderfully described, hushed moment toward the end of the novel, the uncomfortable vacillation between what

Nostromo is and what he has made others believe about himself—the authorized version—is revealed to Mrs. Gould. The spell he has cast on Sulaco is broken, and he is exposed as a thief. Because the Republic of Sulaco owes its independence to his daring ride over the mountains for royalist help ("He carried all our lives in his hands," p. 539), it also is exposed as a state based on a sham reputation. Here is a portion of the scene:

> "Nostromo," Mrs. Gould whispered, bending very low, "I, too, have hated the idea of that silver from the bottom of my heart."
>
> "Marvellous!—that one of you should hate the wealth that you know so well how to take from the hands of the poor. The world rests upon the poor, as old Giorgio says. You have been always good to the poor. But there is something accursed in wealth. Señora, shall I tell you where the treasure is? To you alone. . . . Shining! Incorruptible!"
>
> A pained voluntary reluctance lingered in his tone, in his eyes, plain to the woman with the genius of sympathetic intuition. She averted her glance from the miserable subjection of the dying man, appalled, wishing to hear no more of the silver.
>
> "No, capataz," she said. "No one misses it now. Let it be lost forever."
> (pp. 624-25)

The intense poignancy of the scene is all the more effective when we remember the agonies of Conrad's creative life. It is not difficult to imagine him wishing for some relief from the deception of the pose he was forced to assume. Nevertheless, he must have known that his entire creative existence could remain viable only so long as he maintained his masquerade as a cheery writer of tough adventure yarns. He could never confess himself to anyone, but he could do it vicariously in nearly every one of his stories. For all of his heroes hide some shameful secret, and each of them dreams of the day when he can be cleared before those he loves best. Yet Conrad's severity of vision enables Mrs. Gould to express understanding and assurance without granting either one or the other to anyone else in the novel. Busy Sulaco has become so prosperous that its shabby past can no longer embarass it. It stands above its complicated history, secure in the unambiguous record of its rags-to-riches adventure. Only Mrs. Gould knows Sulaco for what it is, but she can never make her knowledge effective. Her moment of greatest understanding and illumination is also her moment of least practical influence. Yet she knows that it is possible for the integrity and courage of one person to sustain the life of a nation. So, as Nostromo once saved Sulaco with his daring ride (although he had already by then dishonored himself), now she preserves Sulaco's record by withholding a secret certain to dishonor the country. Here, the refusal to be an author is a quality worthy of admiration. The tragic fact, of course, is that her courageous act is nugatory by the standards of modern politics; of what use is it to possess a morally harmful secret about a whole country? From what sort of real, tangible threat has she saved Sulaco? The magnificence of the moment does not entirely depend upon our admiration for Mrs. Gould, but also upon Conrad's justly cynical depiction of her as a frail, politically powerless woman, childless, a parent without offspring as much as a good fairy without good deeds. One can picture her proclaiming her secret in order to arouse the conscience of Sulaco—and being diplomatically hushed by Don Juste, the elegant parliamentarian.

* * * * * * * *

As in so many of his other works, in *Nostromo* Conrad pits the sea against the land as if they represented opposing values; unlike most of his "typical" works, however, *Nostromo* concerns itself mainly with land affairs. Yet the sea is very much a power of which Costaguana is aware: it defines the republic's coast, a vast, inexpressibly strong and unchanging desert, very different in its eternal brooding from the petty self-seeking of land life. The sea swallows up Martin Decoud with huge indifference to his human littleness; in his final yielding to it, Decoud seems drawn to its unlimited power like a man seeking union with the infinite.

Decoud's death very convincingly dramatizes the difference between land and sea. The values of the land in *Nostromo* have been concentrated into silver, which, when put to the test of the open sea off Costaguana, fails Decoud miserably. The history of the land is begun when values, like those of the silver, are made the focal point of all subsequent life. Yet silver gradually assumes still greater influence in the lives of Costaguanans. By the end of the novel it has practically become the *raison d'être* of the independent Republic of Sulaco. Decoud goes as far as to call the silver-producing mine "the greatest fact in the whole of South America" (p. 237). The silver enslaves everyone in the novel except Mrs. Gould, for whom alone silver's valuable solidity and hardness is not an attraction. The trouble is that silver seems to provoke visions of concrete power and achievement in the minds of its devotees. Men want to model their lives into perfect, hard blocks of silver; yet they do not realize that such lives will be stunted and selfish. From its beginning, the craze for silver displaces normal human judgment so completely as to divert the broad course of human activity into a narrow stream that resembles molten silver flowing into an ingot mold. This prisonlike activity is the record of Costaguana suffering under the influence of "material interests," a general dementia of which silver fetishism is a particular branch.

To have put all of this into the book is not a simpleminded social novelist's trick to shock readers into an appreciation of the value of spiritual interests—or, for that matter, of "sea" interests. *Nostromo* has little to do with advocating other interests over material ones. It accepts material interests as a fact and not as a fantasy to be wished away. The novel does, however, use Costaguana's beginning passion for these interests in order to trace a pattern, ostensibly social, historical, and economical, which makes pertinent reference to human psychology and to a kind of inscape of Conrad's mind. Thus *Nostromo* is a novel about political history that is reduced, over the course of several hundred pages, to a condition of mind, an inner state. It is like a *trompe-l'oeil* painting of a city that upon closer inspection turns out to be an anatomical drawing of the brain.

Like all great novels, *Nostromo* has an almost inviolable objective impersonality; but unlike most great novels, *Nostromo* also has a very subjective personality of its own that criticizes and undermines the objective edifice. This point cannot be emphasized too strongly, for it has become customary to speak of *Nostromo* as belonging to the same class of fiction as *War and Peace,* in terms not only of size but also of manner and conception.[38] In sheer size, of course, the two novels are similar; but beyond that, comparing them is not valuable. *Nostromo* aspires to no authority on matters of history and sociology, and neither does it create a normative world that resembles our own. Rather, it is the result of a strangely idiomatic vision (something which *War and Peace* is able to conceal definitively) that obviously derives from the almost incredibly peculiar life and vision of its author. Finally, *Nostromo* is most assuredly not the product of a great established literature. Even though it is written in English, its author was not an Englishman but a Polish émigré who was educated in France. Because its origin as a novel is so devious, *Nostromo* bears little resemblance to novels in either French, English, or Russian. It is most profitable to compare the novel with novels written in the more insecure, individualistic, and nervous American tradition. *Nostromo's* closest counterpart anywhere—at least in strangeness of idiom and intention—is *Moby Dick.*

There are certain clues planted in *Nostromo* that incline one to view the novel as a solid, objective edifice undermined and haunted by a private vision; and since these clues need to be connected with one another and with what we have been saying about the silver, they require detailed description. The most immediate fact in the novel is Costaguana, somewhere on the coast of South America, a country whose history reflects the continent of which it is a part. The heritage of South America is, "as the great Liberator Bolivar had said in the bitterness of his spirit, [that] 'America is ungovernable. Those who worked for her independence have ploughed the sea' " (p. 206). In this struggle for independence the "ancestral Goulds," whose presence in Costaguana is so "indelible" (p. 52), participate very actively. They have been there for three generations, prospering as merchants, revolutionists, and liberators; they are well known and respected. Until the era of Charles Gould, however, no Gould could command the respect and influence that earns the mine's latest owner the title *el rey de Sulaco*. The background of this title is what, in the Gould chronicle, concerns the novel most.

Unlike his ancestors, Charles has come to Costaguana after many years of life abroad; in this he is similar to the majority of characters in the novel. Each of them has a period of expatriation from Costaguana—on the one hand because of exile, or, on the other, because of foreign birth. In the first group are Decoud, Montero, and Don José; in the second Nostromo, the Violas, Dr. Monygham, and Captain Mitchell. During the course of the novel each of these characters earns his citizenship in Costaguana either by an act or by a process of naturalization. Charles Gould's naturalization is accomplished under urgent pressures. He grows up as a homeless Englishman in Europe who is helplessly tied to a desperately angry father. Thousands of miles separate the boy and his father, and the boy grows into manhood with a need for attachment and purpose. Gould senior has been given the mine concession against his will as a payment for a loan, and since the mine is sterile he wastes his life in frustration. Charles, however, becomes more interested in the mine at the same time that his father is slowly being killed by it (p. 63). What for the father had been a bitter waste of effort is a challenge to the son's moral strength: not only will the mine vindicate his father's tenacity, but it will also be the instrument of Costaguana's betterment. At this point Charles cannot see that his own ambitions and the country's improvement are almost the same thing. In young Emelia he finds a worthy companion and steward of his hopes, and he marries her immediately after receiving news of his father's death. In the following passage Conrad characterizes them at the time of their marriage:

These two young people remembered the life which had ended wretchedly just when their own lives had come together in that splendor of hopeful love, which to the most sensible minds appears like a triumph of good over all the evils of the earth. A vague idea of rehabilitation entered the plan of their life. That it was so vague as to elude the support of argument made it only the stronger. It had presented itself to them at the instant when the woman's instinct of devotion and the man's instinct of activity receive from the strongest of illusions their most powerful impulse. The very prohibition imposed the necessity of success. It was as if they had been morally bound to make good their vigorous view of life against the unnatural error of weariness and despair. (pp. 81-82)

When transplanted from Europe to Costaguana, "a vigorous view of life" and an "idea of rehabilitation" become modern concepts that implicitly defy Bolivar's bitter maxim. Charles can be defiant because he is young; and as any reader of Conrad's "Youth" will remember, youth has a facility for romanticizing unpleasant realities. Charles also has a severe sense of rectitude; he is like an architect who sees that a building is "off" because of some defect in construction and cannot resist correcting it. Yet making a success of the mine represents more to him than the fulfillment of a moral imperative. Once he realizes that "the mine had been the cause of an absurd disaster" and that "its working must be made a serious and moral success" (p. 64), Charles begins to respond to the attractions of action considered for its own sake. He thinks that doing something is always better than doing nothing, particularly as his father's plight has taught him the unhappiness of inactivity. Charles's plan is to rebuild the mine, to rework it, and so to "plough the sea" to which Bolivar referred. Furthermore, the mine project is Charles's way of disproving his father—and God—neither of whom had seen anything of worth in Costaguana.

And he asked his wife whether she remembered a passage in one of his father's last letters where Mr. Gould had expressed the conviction that "God looked wrathfully at these countries, or else He would let some ray of hope fall through a rift in the appalling darkness of intrigue, bloodshed, and crime that hung over the Queen of Continents."

Mrs. Gould had not forgotten. "You read it to me, Charley," she murmured. "It was a striking pronouncement. How deeply your father must have felt its terrible sadness!"

"He did not like to be robbed. It exasperated him," said Charles Gould.

"But the image will serve well enough. What is wanted here is law, good faith, order, security. Any one can declaim about these things, but I pin my faith to material interests. Only let the material interests once get a firm footing, and they are bound to impose the conditions of which alone they can continue to exist. That's how your money-making is justified here in the face of lawlessness and disorder. It is justified because the security which it demands must be shared with an oppressed people. A better justice will come afterwards. That's your ray of hope." His arm pressed her slight form closer to his side for a moment. "And who knows whether in that sense even the San Tomé mine may not become the little rift in the darkness which poor father despaired of ever seeing?"

She glanced up at him with admiration. He was competent; he had given a vast shape to the vagueness of her unselfish ambitions. (pp. 92-93)

Charles embarks upon his mission, his mind preserving "its steady poise as if sheltered in the passionless stability of private and public decencies at home in Europe" (p. 53). He believes in work, in honesty, in self-possessed conduct, in steadfastness. Like the other characters in the novel, he believes that if he abides by his program (which he believes will be his record for the future) and acts according to it, then the results foreseen by the program will in fact be realized. The more he believes and then acts on his belief, the more tenaciously he clings to his beliefs—and the less capable he is of thinking critically about what he is doing and why. Man, Conrad reminds us, "is a desperately conservative creature" (p. 61). Gould's conservatism—as anyone's might be—is of the kind that banishes thought from his existence on the grounds that thought might produce ideas capable of damaging what is being conserved. In time, Charles falls victim to a vicious circle of activity as completely as his father was frustrated by the futility of South America. "Action is consolatory. It is the enemy of thought and the friend of flattering illusions. Only in the conduct of our actions can we find the sense of mastery of the Fates. For his action, the mine was obviously the only field" (p. 72).

It seems to Gould that life—instead of being, as Marlow had put it eloquently and somewhat evasively in *Heart of Darkness,* "a mysterious arrangement of merciless logic for a futile purpose"[39] —is the satisfactory realization of an easily understandable logic. Take for your beginning the most chaotic place on earth, believe something strongly enough, apply it to that place, and you are able to author a new beginning whose intention is to make order out of chaos, because underneath everything there is a benign continuity. The discernment of that order, however, is subject to the burdens—indeed, to the molestations—of all individually authored schemes; but no one seems aware of so disastrous a snag. Even as wise a man as Don José Avellanos believes in benign impersonal continuity. The title of his book reminds us that for all of those fifty years of misrule there could have been a right rule. Old Giorgio Viola intuits the right rules merely by looking at his treasured portrait of Garibaldi; Decoud at first lives his life according to the rules of a boulevardier; and Captain Mitchell stubbornly applies the ramrod-stiff code of the imperialist English gentleman among the "natives." Each of them insists that his view of the world is the right one. It is a familiar rationale. More than likely, Conrad may have discovered its abstract pattern in Schopenhauer, who, as Galsworthy informs us, had been a great favorite of Conrad's.[40] For what is an uncritical, sustained belief in order but egoism based on the assumption that "the world is my idea"? The purpose of this egoism is a sense of mastery over life, and its true beginning perhaps the fear that life may not be worth living after all, or that without a decreed beginning life cannot have method.

As always, Emelia Gould is different from the others; or, if she is not different at bottom, her character is less overtly venal. As a young girl she seems to have been so sure of her competency in living as to expect an equal competency in anyone she would love. "Charles had struck her imagination from the first by his unsentimentalism, by that very quietude of mind which she had erected in her thought for a sign of perfect competency in the business of living" (p. 54). When she becomes the first lady of Sulaco, "gifted in the art of human intercourse" (p. 50), we are given superficial evidence of the competency in her; a more profound sign of that competency is her realization that it is only Charles who can give "a vast shape . . . to the vagueness of her unselfish ambitions" (p. 93). Another person, an incompetent one, might have stood in his way; but *she* dedicates herself—with *noblesse oblige*—to the furtherance of his ambitions. Society in Sulaco is hers; whereas her husband conquers the land financially and politically, she conquers it socially.

A woman with a masculine mind is not a being of superior efficiency; she is simply a phenomenon of imperfect differentiation—interestingly barren and without importance. Doña Emilia's intelligence being feminine led her to achieve the conquest of Sulaco, simply by lighting the way for her unselfishness and sympathy. She could converse charmingly, but she was not talkative. The wisdom of the heart having no concern with the erection or demolition of theories any more than with the defence of prejudices, has no random words at its command. The words it pronounces have the value of acts of integrity, tolerance, and compassion. A woman's true tenderness, like the true virility of man, is expressed in action of a conquering kind. (pp. 73-74)

Conrad leaves us in little doubt that the "action of a conquering kind" (which we shall discuss a little later) is undertaken by the Goulds because they have committed themselves from the beginning of their married life to the world they have created, the world in which their "unselfish ambitions" are given concreteness and form. At the moment that Emilia accepts her husband on that unhappy day in Italy many years ago, Conrad writes, "immediately the future hostess of all the Europeans in Sulaco had the physical experience of the earth falling away from under her. It vanished completely, even to the very sound of the bell" (p. 69). Charles's world becomes hers, and the history of their married life becomes the history of the mine (p. 73). The mere business of living is transformed by them into watching over a vested interest. It is their world and they become unthinkable without it: life turns into a perpetually renewed act of attachment. Their beginning provides their later existence with ceremony and continuity.

The norm of Charles's existence is the constant saving of the country from the savagery of its inhabitants (pp. 53-54). Every intellectual and spiritual value that usually complicates human life (scepticism and self-criticism, for example) is put aside. Instead, all values derive from the silver ingots that, standing for the beginning of life, have become life's goal. To the Goulds, and indeed to everyone in Costaguana, the silver is not merely the object of a simple concupiscence; if it were that, it would have been easy, as Conrad's predecessors among the Victorian sages had done, to rail at the obvious corruptions brought on by the cash-nexus. No, the silver has "a justificative conception, as though it were not a mere fact, but something far-reaching and impalpable, like the true expression of an emotion or the emergency of a principle" (p. 118). It follows that "the San Tomé mine was to become an institution, a rallying-point for everything in the province that needed order and stability to live. Security seemed to flow upon this land from the mountain-range" (p. 122).

With his "shoulders sustaining the whole weight of the *imperium in imperio*" (p. 164), Gould is to Costaguana as Shakespeare's Prospero is to his island. The management of the mine, his constant visits to it, and the dynamite he plants in it are evidence of his commanding executive spirit regarding the mine. He is able to radiate magical influence into every corner of Sulacoan life; the Casa Gould is Sulaco's version of Prospero's cave. But just as Prospero has sacrificed his own dukedom for the scholar's robes, so conversely has Gould sacrificed his proper estate, his humanity, for the mine. Emelia Gould is her husband's only concession to humanity, for, as he once tells her, the best of his feelings are in her keeping (p. 79). Such a remark makes it possible, I think, to speak of the death of Gould's soul, if we mean by *soul* that entity in man which is most concerned with human feeling and activity. The engrossing work that Gould performs for the mine's sake has claimed his attention so thoroughly (particularly as it is work requiring a minimum of human feeling) that his soul has become supererogatory and simply ceases to exist. As evidence of this death, one ought to consider, for example, that for a character so apparently powerful in Sulaco Gould radiates an extraordinary passivity, especially when he is compared with his wife and with the three energetic characters in the novel—Decoud, Nostromo, and Dr. Monygham—who also undergo a death of the soul.

Gould dies in the mine's service but is never reborn out of it. Rather than ennobling him, it debases him, and he "lives" on a purely mechanical level as a dehumanized organizer, the archforeman of an endless mechanical process. There is something of the same depressing effect of Gould's activity in Lawrence's description of Gerald Crich in *Women in Love,* who totally organizes his family's coal mine into what becomes, for Lawrence, a monument to death-in-life. Decoud's agony on the *Isabel* is that he suffers a death whose cause is the crushing of his soul by a solitude that he cannot resist. Even if Decoud's struggles against the overwhelming power of silent immensities do not save him, he has nevertheless remained vital right up to the end: his recollections of Antonia and his ironic musings on his predicament are proofs of his human activity, even though his beginning is an insubstantial sentiment. Gould of course survives human solitude only because he concedes his human problems and works uniquely for the sake of an inhuman process. Nostromo dies a metaphorical death on the Golfo Placido, but he is reborn a thief and a scoundrel. Monygham, too, has died when, under the torture devised by Guzman Bento, he betrays himself completely. Yet he later chooses a myth—Mrs. Gould—and begins to live again, using it to prop up his existence. Emelia, who is frequently described as a fairy, is something of a magic triumph for all that is best in humanity. Is it not magic, in so threatening and dehumanized a world, for her soul to retain its identity so that she is herself, alive and human, at every point in the novel?

Emelia's resilient consistency of character is remarkable because *Nostromo* is so concerned, even obsessed, with rapid change, with inaugurations of new states, with a cascade of beginnings that initiate novel visions, actions, and protagonists. There are constant changes from one political status to the next, from one emotional mood to another, from one personal confrontation to another. The paradox is that all these bewildering changes occur for one unchanging reason: the silver, the arch-beginning. In his own life, Gould typifies the change made for the silver's sake: while his feelings are in someone else's keeping, he has become the mine's wholly devoted steward. Since, in so becoming, he has given the country one firm, unimpeachable, unchanging value—the silver—and has himself become as constant as the mine, it remains for everyone else to adjust to these constant values. Each person believes himself to have made a perfect adjustment, and yet each of these adjustments provokes discord. The reason for this is quite apparent: to everyone, the best adjustment is the final possession of the mine. No wonder that immediately after the mine is established in Costaguana a whole series of revolutions takes place. Only when Gould decides to intervene on the side of the Blanco party is order restored; Gould and the Blancos bring Ribiera, who is "their own creature" (p. 41), to power.

The extent of "revolutions," of inaugurations into new states, in Sulaco is further complicated and enriched by Conrad's subtle, yet functional, adumbration of the South American setting. He shows, for example, the relationship between the atmosphere of the New World and the art of declamation (p. 91) which presses for continual changes in the emotional and political status quo. Also, he understands the effect of Old World Caesarism upon the emerging political mentality of the New World. The brilliantly accurate account of the Monterist revolt is a result of Conrad's grasp of this phenomenon. Most remarkably, he catches the climate of ungovernable excess that dominates life in Sulaco once there has occurred the critical break from the values that the silver has dislodged—a break for which the Goulds are perhaps responsible.

Conrad's representation of life in Sulaco is so consistently convincing in both its dramatic and social aspects that one tends to forget that he is depicting a world based upon unreality. The mine's service is extremely demanding, and it is long; but it is not, as one might think merely "normal": the illusion of normality is all the more remarkable when Conrad extends it to cover all phases of life in Costaguana. Yet to have considered the implications of the action of the novel, as we have done, is to see the entire foreground of the novel as undergoing a prolonged revelation of horror, a revelation initiated at the beginning of the mine's influence and ending with Nostromo's death. In order to make this a little clearer, it will be useful to review the distinction made in the first part of this discussion between action and record in *Nostromo*. To read *Nostromo* as if its intensely articulated surface were all there was to it (and, I hasten to add, the richly documented surface is designed to give the illusion of all the truth one needs to know) is to read a record very much like the ones created by the various characters in the novel. This is another way of saying that *Nostromo* is masquerading as an ordinary political or historical novel. The real action, on the other hand, is psychological and concerns man's overambitious intention to author his own world because the world as he finds it is somehow intolerable: this action underlies the historical and political events in *Nostromo*. The horror occurs in the gradual, prolonged discovery that the world created by one man is just as intolerable as the world he has superceded. Such a far-reaching conclusion needs political and historical substantiation; hence *Nostromo's* bias for connecting individuals to history, and history to the cruel designs of life.

The example of Charles Gould is instructive. In his decision to take up his father's work in the mine he is given very little real choice. Can one believe that he could have done anything else except return to Costaguana and make a moral success of the mine that had killed his father?

> Two big lamps with unpolished glass globes bathed in a soft and abundant light the four white walls of the room, with a glass case of arms, the brass hilt of Henry Gould's cavalry sabre on its square of velvet, and the water-color sketch of the San Tomé gorge. And Mrs. Gould, gazing at the last in its black wooden frame, sighed out:
>
> "Ah, if we had left it alone, Charles!"
>
> "No," Charles Gould said, moodily; "it was impossible to leave it alone."
>
> "Perhaps it was impossible," Mrs. Gould admitted slowly. (p. 231)

Because he is a man, and because life has placed him at an impasse ("Forget about the mine that has killed your father and do something else"), Gould must resort to action of a begetting kind. What begins for him as a sort of sophisticated vengeance in the name of his father turns, before he is aware of it, into a desire to master life, to make it subservient to him. Like many of Conrad's other protagonists, Gould is decoyed by life into an impossible course of action. The difference between Kurtz and Gould is that whereas Kurtz pronounces on the machinery of existence—"The horror, the horror"—Gould is silent: he goes on with the work he has begotten.

The major similarity between Kurtz's experience in Africa and Gould's in South America is to be found in the atmosphere, which, because it is conducive to extremes of thought and emotions (perhaps because it is "foreign"), stimulates the protagonist to further efforts at mastery. The so-called New World of South America is Conrad's metaphor for the whole modern world which, because of its addiction to extreme forms of action stemming from willful beginnings, persuades morally convinced people of the necessity for action of a mastering, conquering kind. The articulate Decoud muses on the character of the New World:

> There is a curse of futility upon our character: Don Quixote and Sancho Panza, chivalry and materialism, high-sounding sentiments and a supine morality, violent efforts for an ideal and a sullen acquiescence in every form of corruption. (p. 189)

Left to themselves, Quixote and Sancho might destroy each other in a crazed war. But, as Decoud says, behind this deeply divided character are "the natural treasures of Costaguana." They "are of importance to the progressive Europe represented by this youth" (p. 189). So Gould, the representative of progressive Europe, seeks to possess that treasure because it means revenge for his father, the imposition of order in the New World, and the chance to dominate.

Gould is convinced that what he does is right. Once again the prescient Decoud comments indirectly: "It seemed to [Decoud] that every conviction, as soon as it becomes effective, turned into the form of dementia the gods send upon those they wish to destroy" (p. 221). The real horror of this thought becomes apparent when one reflects on the impossibility of life without conviction. Life is authoritative action: action is based upon conviction: conviction is the molestation underlying dementia: therefore, life is dementia. Decoud himself proves this. Raillery to him is a way of life: he scoffs at everything and accepts nothing. Yet he leaves Sulaco on a crazy errand with the silver because he is a man capable of a lover's illusion (which is a form of conviction whose aim is domination). As he dies, the illusion becomes less and less applicable to the terrifying solitude that underlies the life without action to which he is committed on the *Isabel*. His more successful companion, Nostromo, is another example of the process repeated. Decoud dies, but Nostromo emerges from the darkness as a thoroughgoing cheat. In the end Nostromo is also destroyed, and we are left asking the same question about life that Conrad himself is asking: is there any other pattern, any other outcome for an intentional beginning, in life? In Sulaco there is an unreal prosperity based on Gould's mission and Nostromo's exploit. On the Golfo Placido, what is there but solitude and death?

After Nostromo returns from the sea, and after he rides over the mountains to save Sulaco, we are reintroduced to Sulaco, once again by Captain Mitchell. If his first guided tour of the city (which occupied the early part of the novel) was inaccurate, the second is nothing but well-intentioned propaganda. As if to underline the irony in Mitchell's views on Sulaco's new-found prosperity, Conrad has him take a hypothetical visitor on a tour of all the main "places of interest"; the point is that propagandistic descriptions of monuments, as Nietzsche once observed, provide one with the most insufficient and inaccurate sort of history. And so goes the chronicle of Sulaco. It flourishes in its monumental prosperity, with its silver exports reaching every corner of the world, and excludes, in the manner described by Foucault, everything inimical to it. In Foucault's terminology one can also say that Sulaco's archives contain rarefied versions of its history. "The most famous and desperate affair" (p. 582) of one man's life has thus produced the very richest rewards. The reader is caught up in the jocular warmth of a wealthy country, jealous of its prestige and power, a partner among civilized nations. No one in Sulaco (except for Mrs. Gould) has second thoughts about the origins of Sulaco's power and wealth: no one remembers Costaguana, no one really cares about Decoud's death, no one worries much about the meaning of Sulaco's independence. This, of course, is the way of political life, and Conrad portrays it realistically and "archeologically."

But we must remember that Sulaco is a newly created state and that as such it represents the triumph of Gould's work, which has been to create his own world, to rule it, to possess it completely. Just as the silver has come to symbolize an objectified, justificative value, so too does Sulaco represent the objectified wish of one man. In defying life's intractability, Gould has escaped into a world of his own making—a world, however, that finally makes a prisoner of him. Only his wife is able to articulate her awareness of the horrible perfection that this plan has achieved:

> She saw the San Tomé mountain hanging over the Campo, over the whole land, hated, wealthy, more soulless than any tyrant, more pitiless and autocratic than the worst government, ready to crush innumerable lives in the expansion of its greatness. He did not see it. He could not see it. It was not his fault. He was perfect, perfect. . . . But she saw clearly the San Tomé mine possessing, consuming, burning up the life of the last of the Costaguana Goulds; mastering the energetic spirit of the son as it had mastered the lamentable weakness of the father. A terrible success for the last of the Goulds. . . . An immense desolation, the dread of her own continued life, descended upon the first lady of Sulaco. With a prophetic vision she saw herself surviving alone the degradation of her young ideal of life, of love, of work—all alone in the Treasure House of the World. The profound, blind, suffering expression of a painful dream settled on her face with its closed eyes. In the indistinct voice of an unlucky sleeper, lying passive in the toils of a merciless nightmare, she stammered out aimlessly the words:
>
> "Material interests." (pp. 582-83)

Even though Emelia, like most of Conrad's female characters, is content to endure in virtual silence, it is necessary for the critic to discover what is common both to so eloquently expressed a sense of horror as hers and to Conrad's urgent passion to incarnate this horror so painstakingly in fiction. To this discovery—which is a discovery of Conrad's vision of life's beginning machinery—we must now turn.

*   *   *   *   *   *   *   *

In her comprehending silence at the end of the novel—which is ironically set off against Giorgio Viola's uncomprehending and murderous silence—Mrs. Gould achieves a balanced view of past, present, and future: "It had come into her mind that for life to be large and full it must contain the care of the past and of the future in every passing moment of the present" (p. 582). This is the wholeness of vision which *Nostromo*'s winding narrative stream has been seeking ever since the novel's murky, disorienting early pages. In the confusion of its uncertain focus, *Nostromo* resembles many of Conrad's other tales in which the course of the narrative stream is unclear; because of this we are never really certain about the novel's time scheme. Thus the present seems most reluctant to

121

take and hold center stage, unless dragged before us and kept there by a willing volunteer like Mitchell, the simpleminded type (and like Marlow in *Heart of Darkness*) whose purpose is to set things moving, perhaps because he feels himself "in the thick of history" (p. 150). Even Mitchell only starts his narrative and proceeds to add a few reflections, before he is pushed aside, almost dissatisfiedly, by a torrent of qualifying recollections. Within the first eighty-five pages in the novel we pass from a general description of Costaguana to Ribiera's rescue, to the Viola family, to Nostromo's part in the rescue, to the dinner party on the eve of the railroad's inauguration, to Sir John's trip, to Henry Gould's presidency under Bento, to tea at Don José's house, to the history of the mine, and then to the courtship of Charles and Emilia Gould—as a prelude to the story of the slow establishment of the mine in Sulaco, which is the burden of part 1 of *Nostromo*. Part 2 revolves around two long scenes: the one between Decoud and Antonia at the Casa Gould, and the rescue of the silver by Decoud and Nostromo. Finally, in part 3, the novel takes up the defeat of the Monterist revolt and the new era in Sulaco's history, during which period Nostromo is killed. Interspersed are the stories of Dr. Monygham, Hernandez, Father Corbelan, Hirsch, and Sotillo; there are also some important interludes provided by scenes between the Goulds and scenes at the new parliament. Yet all this unfolds without benefit of any linear chronological order.

This roundabout narrative approach, as opposed to a straightforward linear one, was of course promoted and practiced by both Conrad and Ford Madox Ford, Conrad's erstwhile collaborator.[41] Conrad and Ford argued that the approach allowed them the maximum in psychological realism, since, as in real life, one does not comprehend an event all at once; instead, knowledge of an event comes to the mind in small pieces and is only gradually pieced together. The concentrated, prepackaged "reality" presented by earlier novelists, they felt, cannot do justice to life's diffuse complexity. In *Nostromo,* however, the narrative's reluctance to pin down the present is perhaps the result of a more interesting and functional hesitation to begin, a hesitation seemingly induced by the "cool purity" of Higuerota, the tall mountain "which seemed to hold itself aloof from a hot earth" (p. 29) and from Sulaco at its foot, and which shames and humbles the inconsistent, weak, and wavering humanity below. Higuerota holds Sulaco in its gaze as if it, Higuerota, were the eye of God, turned away from the Golfo Placido and now brooding over Sulaco.

The mountain is a transcendant, constantly felt presence in the novel; awesome and monolithic, it represents an aspiration as unattainable by the novel's fragmented action as Mallarmé's *azur* is by his tortured soul. It may have been the contrast between Sulaco's atomized political life and Higuerota's solid, abiding presence that led Arnold Bennett, writing to Conrad concerning *Nostromo* in 1912, to maintain that "the said mountain [is] . . . the principal personage in the story."[42] While Bennett's remark of course is an exaggeration, the force of the mountain is nevertheless unmistakable. One can imagine Conrad feeling the grand, Olympian presence of the mountain in the narrative and, seeking a comparable human force in the panoramic action he is about to relate, hesitating, explaining, qualifying. Where to begin? From his own experience he knew that a master mariner, for example, commands the art of sailing with the same authoritative, consistent domination that Higuerota commands Sulaco. In Sulaco's political life there is no analogous dominant individual. Life is too untidy, man too weak. The narrative's meanderings comprise a search for such a superior man, a man who, like Nietzsche's Übermensch, compels history.

All of this is rather speculative. Is it not safer to remark that Higuerota's presence endows the novel with a sense of height and space and depth? There it stands, its solidity giving the novel a specific spatial perspective. Yet an examination of Conrad's many available letters to his closest personal friends reveals a desperate search in his personal life for Higuerota's positive qualities of consistency, power, and unity. The mixed elements of his life—his Polish birth, French cultivation, and English citizenship, and his double career as a sailor turned man of letters—gave him an acute sense of splintered individuality. In his letters to Marguerite Poradowska between 1890 and 1895, for example, he often appears in pursuit of a single workable identity. While these extremely self-conscious letters for the most part ramble on, when Conrad briefly finds himself he displays a lucid awareness of a persistently dual "selfhood": one is "afraid" of oneself, he writes,

of the inseparable being forever at your side—master and slave, victim and executioner—who suffers and causes suffering. That's how it is! One must drag the ball and chain of one's selfhood to the end. It is the price one pays for the devilish and divine privilege of thought; so that in this life it is only the elect who are convicts—a glorious band which comprehends and groans but which treads the earth amidst a multitude of phantoms with maniacal gestures, with idiotic grimaces. Which would you be: Idiot or convict?[43]

Later, to Edward Garnett, he laments the absence of starting points in his stories and attributes this absence to the fact that his life seemed to have had no clear starting point;[44] so confused was he about himself that his mind could seize upon no point in either time or place for the purpose of beginning to write. Perhaps his most pathetic lament is in an 1895 letter to Edward Noble, an apprentice writer: "[Yours] is an individuality," he writes, "that will stand wear and tear, that has resistance and power—while I shall be used up in a short and miserable sputter of dim flame."[45] Whenever he persevered in his hope that his individuality might achieve lasting strength, he worked himself into a rage at the folly of such a thought; individuality, he concluded, was a mere sham. He wrote Garnett of this in 1896:

> When one looks at life in its true aspect then everything loses much of its unpleasant importance and the atmosphere becomes cleared of what are only unimportant mists that drift past in imposing shapes. When once the truth is grasped that one's own personality is only a ridiculous and aimless masquerade of something hopelessly unknown the attainment of serenity is not very far off. Then there remains nothing but the surrender to one's impulses, the fidelity to passing emotions which is perhaps a nearer approach to truth than any other philosophy of life. And why not? If we are "ever becoming—never being" then I would be a fool if I tried to become this thing rather than that; for I know well that I never will be anything. I would rather grasp the solid satisfaction of my wrongheadedness and shake my fist at the idiotic mystery of Heaven.[46]

But to "grasp the solid satisfaction of [his] wrongheadedness" was not within Conrad's ability. He needed an inner security of mind and character to sustain him, even in wrongheadedness, that his lonely battles with his fiction made impossible. In describing the progress of his work to his friends, he wrote frequently of struggles in a black cave, of being in a terrible nightmare, of rowing across an ocean of ink without any goal in sight.[47] Thus he considered his portrayal of MacWhirr in *Typhoon* to be the portrayal of an unimaginative man single-mindedly standing up to nature's worst, as something of a counterbalance to his own lack of strength of character. In 1901 he wrote to William Blackwood about a book of naval experiences, written by an Admiral William Kennedy, which apparently contained much that Conrad considered reminiscent of *Typhoon:*

> Now a book of that sort *is* the man—the man disclosed absolutely; and the contact of such a genuine personality is like an invigorating bath for one's mind jaded by infinite effort after literary expression, wearied by all the unrealities of a writing life, discouraged by a sunless, starless sort of mental

solitude, having lost its reckoning in a grey sea of words, words, words; an unruly choppy sea running crosswise in all the endless shifts of thought . . . . A wrestle with wind and weather has a moral value like the primitive acts of faith on which may be built a doctrine of salvation and a rule of life.[48]

Having created in MacWhirr a character of consistency and strength, though, Conrad came to the unexpected conclusion that he should hold MacWhirr in emphatic disrespect, reasoning that the vitality of someone like MacWhirr failed to compensate for whatever desirable virtues (skepticism, for instance) were lost in achieving such a "consistent" character. Beneath this rather shrewd reasoning, as in his letter to Galsworthy later in 1901, is the obvious fact that Conrad's disrespect derived from his envy for what he personally lacked:

Say what you like, man lives in his eccentricities (so called) alone. They give vigour to his personality which mere consistency can never do. One must explore deep and believe the incredible to find the new particles of truth floating in an ocean of insignificance. And before all one must divest oneself of every particle of respect for one's character. You are really most profound and attain the greatest art in handling the people you do not respect.[49]

So curious an amalgam of attitudes accounts for such diverse types in Conrad's shorter fiction as Kurtz and MacWhirr. As consistent characters they are puzzling to the reader because of Conrad's shifting point of view toward them. Are either Kurtz or MacWhirr noble or admirable? The difficulties this question raises can be traced to the deathly inner emptiness in which lies, for better or for worse, the real individuality of these characters. Because of the extraordinary sense of inner lifelessness communicated by these apparently heroic figures, Conrad can be said to have a truly ambiguous conception of character. Although these characters are endowed with the consistency and courage that Conrad believed absent in himself, they also remind one of spectres. The same can be said of Charles Gould and Nostromo. Each in his own way rescues the action of the novel from aimlessness; each dominates it authoritatively and momentarily, just as Higuerota dominates Sulaco. Each such individual in a sense "authors" the action of a large part of the fiction. Conrad's habitual image for authority in his fiction is a rescue, usually one performed by an able man who is later revealed to be a sham. Thus in the first third of *Nostromo* there are two "rescues" of Costaguana's history: Nostromo's rescue of Ribiera and Gould's rescue of the San Tomé mine. Gould is figuratively captured by the mine at the outset: because of his servitude, rather than

125

despite it, he rises in political importance, and in so rising he matches Higuerota's eminence on a more mundane level. Yet his submission to the cause of silver is, as we said earlier, a sort of suicide. Perhaps this image is Conrad's way of forcing us to believe that the consistency of character gained by Gould (which is institutionalized in his royal title) is not worth the sacrifice of his human "eccentricities."

Nostromo is a different case. He is presented to the reader in the most flattering way as the dashing devil-may-care leader of Sulaco's dockhands. Yet from the beginning his personality is somewhat paradoxical, for he is, as Mitchell remarks, the leader of "an outcast lot of very mixed blood" (p. 15), *and* he is also Nostromo—literally bosun and "our man"—to all of Sulaco. The outcast and the man who is "one of us" remain the two aspects of his formidable character that hold our interest, even though the second, popular aspect will grow like a cancer to envelop the other, freer, outcast one. (There may even be an intended connection between his name, "our man," and the mine he serves in the later part of the book: the San Tomé silver can say confidently of him, he is *mine.*)

Nevertheless, in part 1 Nostromo is allowed an extraordinary moment of beautiful, unspoiled freedom. To my mind it is the most splendidly theatrical moment in all of Conrad's fiction, belonging, for the sheer excitement and immediacy of its effect, next to Hemingway's superb description of Maera, the proudest and the most tragic of matadors, in *Death in the Afternoon.* Maera's pride and his unparalleled manly carriage are quite equal to his bravery and skill with the bulls.[50] Like Maera, Nostromo has, during his moment of real glory, an inner, authentic nobility that matches his dazzling appearance. Resplendent in his uniform, the mounted capataz is confronted by Pasquita, his Sulacoan sweetheart; the lovers are surrounded by a crowd that is curious about Nostromo's every act. He is this crowd's man just as surely as the matador is the arena's man when he is fearless and free. The girl hurls a flower at Nostromo's face, and then she taunts him; he remains slow and careless. When she threatens to stab him for his indifference, he leans down and picks her up, asking at the same time for a dagger. He lets her cut off all his silver buttons, and then he is finished. "The circle had broken up, and the lordly capataz de cargadores, the indispensable man, the tried and trusty Nostromo, the Mediterranean sailor come ashore casually to try his luck in Costaguana, rode slowly towards the harbor" (p. 144).

Is it not right that a man with such "unapproachable style" and "finished splendor" (p. 138) command the destiny of Sulaco? Here is the complete hero for whom the novel has been searching.

The capataz's triumphs do not, however, go uncriticized. In the first place, Conrad heaps too many flattering phrases upon him. The relevant technique, which characterizes the style of the whole novel, is Conrad's excessive use of appositional phrases. Thus Nostromo is not just the capataz, but also "the indispensable man, the tried and trusty Nostromo"; Decoud is the "boulevardier," the "universal wit," the "lover"; Gould is the "king of Sulaco," the "hope of Costaguana," the "perfect man"—and so on. A source of constant ironic shocks, excessive in its jocularity and courtesy, the technique is Dickensian. Phrases of this sort used repeatedly cannot be developed; hence they serve to remind us of the character's beginning authority, of his initial desire to be a public institution or monument or record. Further criticism of Nostromo is furnished explicitly by Teresa Viola, who cannot resign herself to the successes he gains because she believes that he unashamedly kowtows to the English. Her constant objections to Nostromo's behavior are like mocking echoes of the adulation he receives from everyone else. For the most part, however, she succeeds in piercing his perfect camouflage of style and splendor to glimpse the equally perfect vanity that drives him. What enables her success in this is the "intimacy of antagonism as close in its way as the intimacy of accord and affection" (p. 280). Yet Nostromo tolerates her for her husband's sake. The old man has a "personal quality of conviction . . . his terribilitá" (p. 35) that Nostromo deeply respects. Not that Nostromo lacks an equally intense conviction; rather, Viola's is somehow more objective than Nostromo's completely subjective, degenerate self-conviction, a trait that perhaps renders him vulnerable to Teresa's attacks even though she does not understand that for all his vanity Nostromo is as amoral (rather than immoral) as any animal. It is not, as she believes, the "fine words," but the silver, that corrupts him: it makes him a slave to his own unthinking vanity and greed. The silver also makes his reputation a problem, for until his magnificent exploit in the Placido he had managed to blend the two aspects of his character (the popular and the outcast) into a free, profitable, and rather picaresque existence.

Because of his uninhibited vanity and faith in himself, Nostromo distrusts Decoud's skepticism. Decoud appears to be "an idle boulevardier" whose "cosmopolitanism [is] in reality a mere barren indifferentism posing as intellectual superiority" (p. 168). Worse yet, Decoud "had pushed the habit of universal raillery to a point where it blinded him to the genuine impulse of his own nature" (p. 169). Only when he submits to "that note of passion and sorrow unknown on the more refined stage of European politics" (p. 173) is Decoud able to accept himself and put a stop to the scoffing that alienates him from his inner self. Only when he becomes submerged in the rather attractive sentimentality of his love for Antonia Avellanos does Decoud begin to act like a rational patriot who welcomes the responsibility of serious action—which is based, paradoxically enough, on a lover's illusion.

All this time Gould is tenaciously committed to the mine he has rescued and rehabilitated. When part 2 begins, Sulaco has itself become involved in Gould's commitment, for Sulaco's civic existence is now completely dependent on the mine. Besides Gould, only Nostromo occupies a position of comparable (though not equal) power in the city. When a Monterist invasion threatens the city, the duty of tending the silver is divided, quite properly, between Gould and Nostromo: Gould will remain in Sulaco in control of a charge of dynamite buried in the mine, and Nostromo will take the silver ingots themselves out of the city. Decoud is chosen to go with Nostromo because it is generally believed that the educated, intelligent patriot is a necessary complement to the foreign man of action.

Together the two men leave Sulaco in the middle of a very dark night. The episode is described with a compelling tension, one far more controlled in tone and contour than the journey Marlow takes into the heart of darkness. (Interestingly, the presence of Hirsch, the cowardly stowaway, gives the scene something of the same macabre absurdity to which Marlow, in his description of the Congo voyage, insistently draws attention.) There is no masking narrative voice as there had been in *Heart of Darkness,* and so the distracting aspects of that voice—its breathless insistence, its ill-timed jocularity—are avoided. The greater effectiveness of the later passage, however, is due as much to the episode's relevance to Conrad's personal predicament as it is to his strengthened technical assurance. The setting of the difficult adventure could have been taken straight out of his anguished letters, perhaps even from this one written to Garnett in 1899:

The more I write the less substance do I see in my work. The scales are falling off my eyes. It is tolerably awful. And I face it, I face it but the fright

128

is growing on me. My fortitude is shaken by the view of the monster. It does not move; its eyes are baleful; it is as still as death—and it will devour me. Its share has eaten into my soul already deep, deep. I am alone with it in a chasm with perpendicular sides of black basalt. Never were sides so perpendicular and smooth, and high. Above your anxious head against a bit of sky peers down—in vain—in vain. There's no rope long enough for that rescue.[51]

As the two men row the lighter out from the harbor, each knows that the importance of the task is completely transforming his existence. Sulaco's material interests become irrelevant to Decoud, who is now "in the toils of an imaginative existence, and that strange work of pulling a lighter [which] seemed to belong naturally to the inception of a new state [now] acquired an ideal meaning from his love for Antonia" (p. 294). Yet in a short while he feels himself "on the verge of delirium" (p. 295) resulting from his overintensified exertions in an unreal cause. This immediately recalls Conrad's own sentiments as he worked on the novel. Conrad's letter to Edmund Gosse on March 23, 1905, contains the declaration that "I have often suffered in connection with my work from a sense of unreality, from intellectual doubt of the ground I stood upon."[52]

Nostromo has no sympathy with this sort of intellectual convolution. Because he is certain that only "sheer desperation will do for this affair" (p. 306), he is inspired to new extremes of vanity and bravery. Even Decoud, who has always known the extent of Nostromo's vanity, is surprised by his behavior: "The natural characteristic quietness of the man was gone. Something unsuspected by every one had come to the surface" (p. 313). This is Nostromo's bloodthirsty determination to live up to his reputation, a determination that sweeps aside all barriers of class between the two men and compels Decoud into his service.

During this absolutely central episode in the novel, the two men are intellectually and spiritually poles apart. Nostromo not only exults in the darkness but turns it into an advantage because he is so certain of himself; Decoud, on the other hand, suffers the immense handicap of self-doubt and feels himself in the grip of a growing sense of unreality. One man recoils when confronted with the beginning of a major exploit, the other welcomes the opportunity to author it. Yet Decoud gradually becomes accustomed to the oppressive darkness. "It was part of a living world, since, pervading it, failure and death could be felt at your elbow" (p. 314). Nostromo is the quintessential man of action who is working to secure his great reputation even more firmly; Decoud is a man of thought who suddenly discovers himself in a totally unfamiliar situation. Neither man is really working for himself, for in their efforts on behalf of the silver both recognize and serve a common master:

> Each of them was as if utterly alone with his task. It did not occur to them to speak. There was nothing in common between them but the knowledge that the damaged lighter must be slowly but surely sinking. In that knowledge, which was like the crucial test of their desires, they seemed to have become completely estranged, as if they had discovered in the very shock of the collision that the loss of the lighter would not mean the same thing to them both. This common danger brought their differences in aim, in view, in character, and in position into absolute prominence in the private vision of each. There was no bond of conviction, of common ideas; they were merely two adventurers pursuing each his own adventure, involved in the same imminence of deadly peril. Therefore they had nothing to say to each other. But this peril, this only incontrovertible truth in which they shared, seemed to act as an inspiration to their mental and bodily powers. (p. 328)

The authentic ring of this scene derives, I think, from Conrad's obsessive notions about himself. The two adventurers are the double strain in Conrad's life which, as we noted earlier, he had come to believe made him a *"homo duplex."* The atmosphere of deadly peril in which the two men find themselves uncongenial partners represents the nightmare world that Conrad inhabited as he worked on his fiction. The analogies between Conrad and the two men extend even into the past histories of Nostromo and Decoud. The Genoese adventurer is a sailor whose desertion of his ship is kept rather noticeably in the background; throughout his career Conrad was fascinated with the idea of desertion, a theme so recurrent that Gustave Morf, an early critic of Conrad, based his integral reading of Conrad's fiction on it.[53] Moreover, Nostromo is a thoroughgoing man of action who has successfully moved his profession from sea to land; if this is still Conrad talking about one of the two men he was, Nostromo is an idealization of the sailor-turned-landlubber that Conrad himself had become. Yet the capataz is also an opportunist and an adventurer, which is one of the unavoidable results of being a professional man of action. It is significant that Conrad rather defensively anticipated the danger of being called an opportunistic adventurer himself, perhaps because he felt that at some point in his sea career he had been one. Interestingly, he once wrote a correspondent a somewhat petulant reminder that he was not a simple adventurer.[54] Decoud is Conrad's portrayal of himself as the confused intellectual for whom the ground he walks on is subject to doubt, the author for whom even the simplest sentence was very hard to begin. Decoud's most serious moments (which occur during the long scene when he discusses his ideas with Antonia at the Casa Gould) echo the romantic, self-doubting tone of Conrad's letters to Marguerite Poradowska.

Before considering the real purpose of the mission undertaken by Nostromo and Decoud it is necessary to consider Conrad's reasons for bringing together the two men in the episode. If one recalls that *Nostromo* examines the problematical relationship between action and historical record, then the combination of Decoud and Nostromo represents the relationship on a human level. (It goes without saying that the two men are sufficiently realized as characters also to represent themselves more than adequately.) In terms of the novel's total concerns, the masterful scene on the Golfo Placido takes up the issues of a true intellectual knowledge of action versus the flattering distortions of a created record; of individuality that is realized in a problematical, difficult life in the world versus individuality that believes and makes others believe in itself; of a complicated inner dimension versus a strategically simplified exterior; of Decoud's complex and passionate understanding of the wholly difficult realities of his situation versus Nostromo's desire to make his reputation the dominant image in Sulaco's life—in short, of Conrad's authentic voice in his rich, confusing private writings versus the voice he created for his prefatory notes.

All these conflicting alternatives are forced to surface by the crisis in Sulaco's history, when, like an author about to begin his writing, characters must determine a starting point and with it, of necessity, a future course of action. What now happens to Sulaco is to be decided by the deportment of the two men. The analogy in Conrad's life to the "objective" historical crisis in the city is the personal and artistic crisis he had reached by 1902. He felt that he was not producing well enough, that he never had enough money, that his whole existence seemed to be in the most unimaginable disarray (a point his publishers were always willing to make); there seemed to be no alternative solution to his predicament except drastic action. Shortly after this crisis a new Conrad emerges, a Conrad who, as I have noted elsewhere, publicly replaces the tortured figure of the preceding twelve years.[55] This new person is mirrored in the success Nostromo achieves because of Decoud's timely death. A smiling public man emerges whose place in the new Sulaco is based on a deliberate fraud. If Nostromo is partly an idealized apology for a life of action, he is a shattering criticism of the public personality. *Nostromo* is the beginning of a new phase.

Gould's connection with all of this is interesting. His sustained immersion in his work at the mine typifies man's identification of life with work, or, as Conrad had put it in *Heart of Darkness,* with efficient devotion to an idea.[56] Nostromo and Decoud are irrevocably tied to this devotion, even though each thinks that he is acting for his own reasons. In the same way that Gould is "run" by Holroyd, Nostromo and Decoud are "run" by Gould. None of the three has any freedom; each is the sustainer of another's vanity—Decoud of Nostromo's, Nostromo of Gould's, and Gould of Holroyd's. After Decoud's death, Gould muses that

the only thing that was not changed was his position towards Mr. Holroyd. The head of the silver and steel interests had entered into Costaguana affairs with a sort of passion. Costaguana had become necessary to his existence; in the San Tomé mine he had found the imaginative satisfaction which other minds would get from drama, from art, or from a risky and fascinating sport. It was a special form of the great man's extravagance, sanctioned by a moral intention big enough to flatter his vanity. Even in this aberration of his genius he served the progress of the world. (p. 21)

In the immediate context of the work he does, each man, according to the novel, believes himself and is believed by others to be free, especially if he seems to have begun at the beginning; from the point of view afforded the reader by the total action of the novel, exactly the opposite becomes true. The king of Sulaco is as subjugated as the lowliest peon working in the mine. In what way, one wonders, is Gould different from the Indians to whom the mine is a fetish (p. 442)? If both the workers and their master are subservient to the mine, does the fact that the grand Englishman doesn't work with his hands mean that his spiritual slavery is any less degrading? True, Gould has position, but that is all he has. If Decoud and Nostromo on the Golfo Placido represent Conrad's double nature engaged in a struggle for freedom—and even though the victory is Nostromo's we are left in little doubt that it is a morally inferior one—then Gould, ever at his post with one finger on the detonator, embodies the ever-continuing process of life at its most disheartening, vainest level. It is the level at which man insists upon creating his own world and then seeks to preserve the values of that world at all costs. Better to destroy that world than change it: *he* might change, but *it* must not. The rescue of the silver brings both Nostromo and Decoud closer to Gould in this respect.

As the action sorts itself out in the Monterist revolt and in what follows the revolt, an extremely depressing truth becomes evident: once rid of confusion by such author-heroes as Gould and Nostromo, action, or history in the making, is clearly proceeding, beneath its seemingly chaotic surface, according to some inherent malignant plan, a sort of ultimate molestation which no one can escape. As this plan becomes apparent, a remarkable similarity emerges between the current of a person's life and the process of history. In a human life—Gould's, for example—it might appear possible to believe in the freedom of one's initiative or of one's action; at the same time, when such freedom is viewed from a more accurate perspective, the same activity is seen to be unfree. These mutually contradictory views also apply to the novel's total action: the action at the beginning of the novel seems to wind its confused way forward until a hero appears who can dominate it in order to give it intention and method, whereas it eventually becomes apparent that the action has merely been searching for a hero (Nostromo or Gould) to own, to use, to enslave.

It was no accident that Conrad so conceived the novel. The moral of such a conception is that the fabric of life is manufactured by some devilish process the purpose and logic of which is profoundly antihuman. Man is never the author, never the beginning, of what he does, no matter how willfully intended his program may be. The substance of this belief was expressed by Conrad in a powerful letter to Robert Cunninghame Graham:

> There is a,—let us say,—a machine. It evolved itself (I am severely scientific) out of a chaos of scraps of iron and behold!—it knits. I am horrified at the horrible work and stand appalled. I feel it ought to embroider,—but it goes on knitting. You come and say; "This is all right: it's only a question of the right kind of oil. Let us use this,—for instance,—celestial oil and the machine will embroider a most beautiful design in purple and gold." Will it? Alas, no? You cannot by any special lubrication make embroidery with a knitting machine. And the most withering thought is that the infamous thing has made itself: made itself without thought, without conscience, without foresight, without eyes, without heart. It is tragic accident—and it has happened. You can't even smash it. In virtue of that truth one and immortal which lurks in the force that made it spring into existence it is what it is—and it is indestructible!
>
> It knits us in and it knits us out. It has knitted time, space, pain, death, corruption, despair and all the illusions,—and nothing matters. I'll admit however that to look at the remorseless process is sometimes amusing.[57]

The idea is wholly despairing and eminently private. Authority, it asserts, permanently resides outside man. Every beginning, every record meticulously kept, every intention maintained is by definition secondary because antedated by a process that has no respect for man and his rationale. Such an idea, with its deceptive invitation to action and its destruction of hope, is reflected in *Nostromo* by the textual web of personal "records" held together by a "machine" that scants man and human action. All this endows *Nostromo* with what Henry James, Conrad's admiring colleague and friend, would have called "a deep-breathing economy and an organic form."[58] Conrad's remarkable achievement lies in his ability to project this esoteric vision of life into the public, solid, and real world of Costaguana. No wonder that writing the novel proved such a strain on Conrad; to have remained so fanatically true for so long to his extreme pessimistic view of human existence must have been painfully difficult. It is indeed possible to feel, as one reads the novel, the war going on between Conrad and his fiction.

Readings of *Nostromo* that overemphasize its political dimension detract from the novel's overall effect. The accession of Nostromo to the role of principal hero, for instance, is very disconcerting to strictly political interpretations. Why should so much time be given to Captain Fidanza's private life? With its political course charted anew, Sulaco ought to retain stage center instead of playing a supporting role in a semiconventional story of covert passion and mistaken death. The fact is that Nostromo has become, toward the end of the novel, a miserably haunted creature because he has attempted to live as if the machinery of existence did not exist. He has not attempted this by his own will but because a lucky accident has conferred great wealth upon him and forced him to become a sort of author in spite of himself. As he muddles on he remains sufficiently interesting to Conrad to warrant the continuing special attention that is so obvious in the famous passage describing Nostromo's "rebirth"—a passage that in fact reiterates his natural qualities, for it is these qualities that will enable him to go on alone. He understands that he is thrust into an existence beyond that of conventional society and that the treasure, which is suddenly his, is the cause. But his growing attachment to the silver and the suffering he endures for its sake make it plain that he is still the victim of life's antihuman machinery. Now he begins to feel a secret shame that intensifies his moral disgrace—the price exacted by life from one upon whom it has bestowed the status of "hero" or "father of his country." Consequently, the idea of the treasure and secrecy become connected in his mind (p. 551), and so when Viola is entrusted with keeping the new lighthouse, Nostromo sees this as a calamitous event:

He was struck with amazed dread at this turn of chance, that would kindle a far-reaching light upon the only secret spot of his life, whose very essence, value, reality, consisted in its reflection from the admiring eyes of men. All of it but that; and that was beyond common comprehension, something that stood between him and the power that hears and gives effect to the evil words of curses. It was dark. Not every man had such a darkness. And they were going to put a light there. A light. He saw it shining upon disgrace, poverty, contempt. Somebody was sure to . . . Perhaps somebody had already. . . (pp. 586-87)

Nostromo is nevertheless an unusual man. Only he and Mrs. Gould finally know all that there is to be known of life's horror, he by experience, she by the knowledge he gives her of it. Perhaps Dr. Monygham could also have shared this knowledge, but he is too much under Mrs. Gould's spell to know it for himself. No, it is Nostromo alone—like Kurtz and Lord Jim—who knows the dread secret and feels its shame; this, after all, is the purest beginning of all. Nostromo's tragedy—which has something farcical about it (p. 405)—is that his shame is for a colossal secret for which the world seems to have no use. Even in this, life, the machinery, has tricked him. He must bear the burden of slavery to the silver that also belongs to Sulaco, although he alone is selected to feel this burden. Society cuts him off from itself by making it impossible to reveal his secret to anyone.

When he dies, Sulaco has time only for its material interests; no one except Mrs. Gould has been made any wiser by his death. Those who care that Nostromo is dead, people like Viola and his wretched daughter, live in a silent world of immense, empty spaces across which floats an incoherent cry symbolizing mankind's inarticulate sadness for itself. The immobility that ends *Nostromo* is a sterile calm, as sterile as the future life of the childless Goulds, in which all action is finally concentrated into a cry of motionless despair. No better ending for the novel could have been written. Existence has worked its worst, and after that there is only an acceptance of what is everlastingly true and hence everlastingly novel; having shown that, the novelist's pen drops from an exhausted hand. The only relief now would be for one who no longer contemplated life's machinery. But because Conrad was a possessed realist, for him such relief was not possible; a short time after completing *Nostromo* he was to begin work on *The Secret Agent.*

* * * * * * * *

Since *Nostromo* contains a highly passionate, almost religious, vision of life, it is fitting that Father Roman—the one character in the novel who is schooled in the tradition of grand visions—express the outlines of the vision most convincingly:

> Political atrocities . . . seemed to him fatal and unavoidable in the life of a state. The workings of the usual public institutions presented itself to him most distinctly as a series of calamities overtaking private individuals and flowing logically from one another through hate, revenge, folly, and rapacity, as though they had been part of a divine dispensation. (p. 443)

Roman's interpretation is affected, of course, by his creed. Thus the divinity he mentions does not contradict Conrad's representation of a "divine" machinery in life, but it errs on the side of optimism by assuming the divine to have a benign purpose. Similarly, Roman envisions a logic to the complications caused by human weakness; but he does not, as Conrad does, see logic— equally relentless and disastrous—in the "divine dispensation," in the machinery that manufactures human life. The major qualification enjoined by *Nostromo* upon Roman's vision is that such weaknesses as hate, revenge, and folly do not alone carry calamity through time. For human courage, idealism, and hope, like human weakness, are also aspects of being human and being active as a human individual. Man's fault, in other words, is that he is alive, the very fact of his authority as a human being, for in being alive he nurtures and sustains weaknesses that turn into strengths and strengths that turn into weaknesses. Every moment of life is filled with activity, and that activity issues from human beings whose motives are invariably tarnished by their "humanity."

For Conrad the palpable harshness of the world and hence of life in that world is itself something that provokes one into attempting to master it and, failing at those attempts, into allowing it to incriminate itself in the very process of failure. Thus while Charles Gould, and indeed all of Sulaco, like the rest of mankind, have fallen in love with their own creations (p. 442), Conrad's precept, his example in the writing of *Nostromo,* was not to have fallen in love with *his* creation. The ultimate greatness of that novel is that life, through Conrad, authorizes it, but that Conrad, life's harried agent himself authored by life, had enough strength finally to withhold affirmative consent to it. The lesson is one of self-abnegation, and it has intimately to do with a general loss of faith in the ability of novelistic representation directly to reflect anything except the author's dilemmas, of which one is that he is both human and a writer. Conrad's position is that of a man wholly in life, yet a man decoyed into depicting a life process of which he is a part. Any attempt made to lead one's life as Nostromo does results in either silence or death.

This is a radical impasse arrived at through fiction by an author for whom writing is a form of exposure or investigation. Such an attitude in an author developed partly out of the institutional logic of novels, given the dynamic of molestation and authority I discussed earlier. Conrad's exceptional status thus lies in having produced a novel (and novels) *implicitly* critical of the beginning premises of all earlier novels. Instead of mimetically authoring a new world, *Nostromo* turns back to its beginning as a novel, to the fictional, illusory assumption of reality; in thus overturning the confident edifice that novels normally construct *Nostromo* reveals itself to be no more than a *record* of novelistic self-reflection. What had once been the novel's creative abundance becomes here regressive production: the metaphors, the method, and the attitudes have changed radically, as the beginning premise has become more problematic and more intrinsically a function of the novel's *textual* ontology. The greater significance of this will become apparent as we proceed to examine groundbreaking novels roughly contemporary with *Nostromo*. Whereas in the classical novel there had been both a desire to create or author an alternate life and to show (by molestation) this alternative to be at bottom an illusion with reference to "life," the later version of this desire was a revulsion from the novelist's whole procreative enterprise and an intensification of his *scriptive* fate. Not only does this reaction constitute a critique of the traditional theory of mimetic representation, it also radically transforms the idea of a text.

III

The discovery by Jude and Sue, at the scene of suicide and murder of their children, of a wretched note of explanation for the deed—"Done because we are too menny"—does nothing to attentuate their grief.[59] Ever since he so inopportunely enters their lives, Little Father Time is the emblem of their misgivings about life, and these misgivings are lamentably fulfilled in the premature deaths he causes. This scene in *Jude the Obscure* is almost too sad and despairing even for Thomas Hardy, but the pun in the last word of the child's suicide note should not pass without comment. For just as the superannuated boy himself sums up all the disasters heaped by time upon man in general and upon Jude in particular, so too the pun—a sort of distant echo of Nietzsche's cry "human, all too human," in withdrawal from the distressing quality and sheer weight of being human—itself sums up that which perhaps turned Hardy away from fiction after completing this novel. And that was the observation, which had become increasingly more explicit in one after another of his previous novels, that if fiction is to be narrative at all, it must necessarily be linked to and coeval with the very process of life itself; and furthermore, if narrative is to be mimetic as well as productive, it also must be able to repeat as well as record the "fathering-forth," "the over and overings" (the phrases are Gerard Manley Hopkins's) of human life, the essence and image of which are biological self-perpetuation and unfolding genealogy based on the pro-creative urge, marriage, and family.

Hardy's case in *Jude the Obscure* is, I believe, the recognition by a great artist that the dynastic principles of traditional narrative now seemed somehow inappropriate. Narrative was no longer, as before, first fashioned by the writer according to the sequential character of time, and thereafter given to the reader to be read, or possessed, along the printed line in which his eyes and mind repeated by miraculous multiplication the sense and direction of life. These principles, so far as Hardy was concerned, can be said to have terminated in an epitaph: "Done because we are too menny." For coinciding in these words are man, his death, and a futureless despair. *Jude the Obscure,* however, moves to its own distraught conclusion, one that would be adopted henceforward by Hardy as the crux of his purposefully short and compressed poetry.[60] That poetry depicts an impasse among things human, spiritual, divine, and inert, an impasse that is aesthetically useful to Hardy because it isolates things from one another and, mocking the sterility of time, proceeds to reassemble them in order to let them be destroyed. Time-bound narrative here cedes its spacious character and its familial coherence to crabbed, often destructive convergences in which time and purpose are emasculated at the moment of coincidence. One thinks in particular of Hardy's majestically ironic poem "The Convergence of the Twain," and of its final stanzas, with the scornful pun "intimate welding." The poet here is speaking of the ocean liner *Titanic* and the iceberg that destroyed it:

> Alien they seemed to be!
> No mortal eye could see
> The intimate welding of their later history,
>
> Or sign that they were bent
> By paths coincident
> On being anon twin halves of one august event,
>
> Till the Spinner of the Years
> Said "Now!" And each one hears
> And consummation comes, and jars two hemispheres.[61]

Both Little Father Time's name and his presence yield up further observations which, we may feel—as did the bishop who reportedly burned his copy of *Jude the Obscure*[62] —do great damage to the sacrament of ongoing human life. For the boy is neither really a son nor, of course, a father. He is an alteration in the course of life, a disruption of the archeology that links generations one to the other. His death is the affirmation, or realization, of this indisputable role that he plays, just as Jude's successive dreams—of scholarship, of architectural ambition, of patrimonial and matrimonial order—are realized in about equal measure in his tormented life with Sue Bridehead and in the gingerbread models of Christminster he is reduced to selling near the end of the novel. Three conditions of radical, or beginning, divorce are interconnected here: the divorce of man from his generative role either as man or as author; the divorce of man from time; and the divorce of man from his "natural" intentions.

This celibacy is gained at a very high price indeed; and we may look to George Gissing's parable of the narrative life, *New Grub Street,* to see the sacrifice made flesh. Every writer in this grim vision of the economics of narrative manuscript production is either sterile, blind, or celibate; otherwise he is not a writer but a manager. The books produced are a wilderness of mirrors that reflect the doomed effort to produce without originality, to originate without energy, and to fable without bread. For neither the nutrient of man nor of his work is given to the writer: it must be quarried from unyielding matter, either the word or the world, and thereafter wastefully enshrined in the tedious plots of three-volume society novels.

Gissing's unrelentingly naturalistic *New Grub Street* and Hardy's valedictory novel are both reflections of something like an event, near the end of the nineteenth century, in the life of the novel itself. And since the novel is alternative, fictional history bounded traditionally (as is history) between birth and death, we search in fiction, as when reading history, for configurations of sense, character, event, motive, and significance that link the absolute terminals of each to the names, forms, and identities we can discern. In fiction and in history, narrative, to borrow a phrase from Joyce, is the ineluctable modality of the legible. We must ask ourselves now: what is the significance of the moment in the life of fictional narrative exemplified by, among other events, Father Time's death in *Jude the Obscure* and Reardon's death in *New Grub Street*—deaths whose monuments are, respectively, a punning note and the terrifying vision of bookdom's graveyard, the Reading Room of the British Museum?

Modality no longer fruitful, but stopped short, brutally interrupted, pushed inward. A moment that will drive Bernard Shaw, the erstwhile novelist, into dramatic forms like that of *Major Barbara,* forms that energetically imitate not the new modes of hardheaded realism, socialism, and materialism which are lauded in the play's preface, but the "new" modes of Dionysiac celebration, dithyrambic irrationality, musical fluidity. For in rewriting *The Bacchae,* Shaw was noisily substituting the rebirth of bloodthirsty individualism, the gospel according to Undershaft-Dionysus, for the stultified rigor of decent bourgeois life, which—he asserted—the conventional novel took for its subject. A moment that will turn Samuel Butler's hero Ernest Pontifex into a symbol of rejection of family and, conversely, into a symbol of acceptance of a mysterious force independent—like his munificent Aunt Althea—of biological life itself. Yet Oscar Wilde deserves greater credit than do either Butler or Shaw for seeing that, for the artist, the natural continuity of things had been ruptured. In leaving life to servants, Wilde recognized that his capricious, though earnest, illusions were at least creative and worthy of bothering with, whereas life was neither one nor the other. Yet Wilde's artistic triumph made inevitable his personal tragedy: the happy narcissist on the page intended the pilloried defendant in court—a theme to which we shall return in Chapter 4.

Let me now integrate what I have been speaking about into an account of narrative itself. Fulfilling the special conditions (discussed in Section I of this chapter) for novels *in practice* requires basically that two things be available to the novelist: first, the technique of consecutive explanation, and second, the liberty to return to whatever he has already passed over in the narrative sequence. The fundamental example is the *Odyssey*. The ideal course of fiction can be characterized as including one or more instances of returning to a point of fertile beginning in the past from which the narrative subsequently unfolds and to which it can repeatedly return. The variations of which this rather simple scheme is capable are apparent not only in novels themselves, but also in such seminal works as Harry Levin's *Gates of Horn*, Georg Lukacs's *Theorie des Romans,* and René Girard's *Mensonge romantique et verité romanesque.*[63] Disparities of method and intention notwithstanding, such critical studies illustrate the way in which, to use I. A. Richard's phrase, the novel in particular and fiction generally are speculative instruments—that is, the way in which readers have used novels to engage their own narrative histories, or the way in which fiction participates historically in the most intimate actualities of human life.

As we saw, the primordial discovery of a novel is that of self—and *primordial* is intended here in a privileged way: the primordial as the preeminent, as the prior, as the first validating condition for intelligibility. In a novel such as *Tom Jones,* for example, the foundling is discovered immediately after birth, only to be rediscovered—and this is the function of the narrative—through a series of adventures that clarify the circumstances of that birth: he is given paternity. By extension (and I intend the sexual pun), Tom himself becomes capable of paternity, although this, also by extension, is to be fulfilled outside the novel. It is precisely the contours and the occasionally embarrassing intimacies of this process with which *Tristram Shandy* tampers. The eighteenth-century novel is like the eighteenth-century personality (one can think of Swift and Dr. Johnson as characters, together with Tom and Tristram), growing out of the initial, somewhat grudging acceptance of egoism, slowly transformed by time and unceasing activity into an irreducible character whose special virtue is that he welcomes and easily assimilates stories about him. Whether in a novel, or in Boswell's *Life of Johnson,* or in the ongoing sequence of Swift's work, narrative redefines ego so that it emerges as strong historical identity; as Meredith saw, the Book of Life and the Book of Egoism—the novel—gradually became synonymous.

An important qualification to this characterization of narrative and its novelistic version is the condition of secularity. If, regarding what I have been saying so far, the fundamental text is the *Odyssey,* then the fundamental antitext or antitype is the New

Testament, and especially, of course, the Fourth Gospel.[64] Fictional narrative is thus an *alternative* departure, a set of misadventures that *begins* away from the Origin (a term almost theological in that it must be understood in the strictest sense possible—as pure anteriority and, paradoxically, as pure genetic power). For that Origin, a unique miracle, cannot be duplicated or incarnated within the absolute boundaries of human life. The history of imitation in the West, as both Auerbach and Curtius have shown,[65] is the history of a gradual literary specialization of styles whereby the models of imitation slowly lose their exemplary force and their Originally divine reference. We might keep in mind, for instance, the distinction between Thomas à Kempis and *Don Quixote* and how it is that what I have referred to as the reflection of the Christian ethos nevertheless took place in two such different works. It is from an aberrant version of this ethos that the classical novel derives the unvarying temporal structure that Lukacs calls ironic.[66]

Thus the novel's mimetic ambitions are essentially secular, even though the hero's ambitions, as in the case of Don Quixote himself, could have timeless and noble religious antecedents. Religious narrative, Christ's biography, and what Vico called sacred history are founded upon and *originate* in the original mystery of a Virgin Birth that can never be wholly verified, but which demands recognition and unqualified acceptance; whereas secular narrative, our concern here, is based on—*begins* in—the common and indisputable fact of natural human birth—or, using more severe terms, in the natal banishment of man from immortality and in his initiation into an afflicted family, not one that is apostolic but is rather a problematical combination of repression and love. This, as Stephen Dedalus poignantly comes to recognize, has the profoundest implications for the verbal artist, since the words of the language he uses are lapsed recollections of the single Original Word. Narrative lives in the temporal, quotidian element, that element which commemorates the absence of timeless mystery.

In view of its mortal strictures, and insofar as it is centrally concerned with the lives of men and women, narrative also contains the seeds of its own aging and death. In order to be read, a life has to be discovered; to be discovered, a life must have begun; to begin is equivalent to having a beginning; and to have a beginning, a life must in some way be novel. While narrative in the great period of the European novel affirms each of these tautologies, it is the manner of the affirmation that is crucial: how does narrative affirm the beginning as time, place, quality, or deed? By methodically realizing the verbal intention to create—in short, by wedding a mimetic, verbal intention to time. Hence, for instance, the linear successive form of biography. But all happy families (and marriages), Tolstoi says in *Anna Karenina*, are the same, all unhappy families (and marriages) different. In order to be original and recognized as such, a life must be different and novel. And to be different is to sense most of the time that one's life has an uncommon, even unhappy, destiny. By the time the novel became a specialized institution in nineteenth-century bourgeois society, narrative had been subverted for an adulterous purpose: no longer a marriage between intention and time, narrative had become a private arrangement between an original character (Julien Sorel, for example) and that character's version of time. Such a character is hungry for the distinction of more and more originality. His time is no longer the property of the community, nor of the family man, but is rather an illicit dream of projected self-fulfillment whose highly subjective achievement by the novel's end has been radically undermined and molested by the refusals, sacrifices, renunciations, and selfishness on which it was based.[67] Such a life resembles orderly biography less than it does a series of collisions and compromises. The difficulties presented by realism derive from its ambiguous attitude toward these arrangements made between time and character, arrangements which seek to replace the bonds of community with the creative, subjective freedom of unfettered emotion. Yet this new private affair—especially in its compulsive form—tends to represent the substitution of irresponsible celibacy for fruitful marriage. This last observation, however, sometimes only reflects orthodox morality, for inasmuch as celibacy stands for irresponsible freedom, it also represents constraints or, as I have already noted, deliberate renunciation.

Hardy's Jude and Little Father Time are luckless epigones (for one can scarcely call them children) of the mid-nineteenth-century bachelor-protagonist: titans like Captain Ahab in *Moby Dick* and sorrowful orphans like Pip in *Great Expectations*. In figures like Ahab and Pip the realistic novelist depicts man's freedom of choice in determining his own fate by showing him, from his beginning, renouncing the common destiny for the sake of one that passes for an "original" one. What destroys both Pip and Ahab, who otherwise differ so much in temperament and energy, is that neither can simultaneously pursue the quest that defines his putative originality and participate in the generative processes of life. The austere realism pervading both novels results from the fact that the narrative of the hero's life is based upon a beginning (which in each case defines their character in and for the novel) that is deeply flawed. Pip is brought up "by hand" and lacking a true family; Ahab loses his family when he loses his leg. Neither character can have (Turgenev's Bazarov is another instance) a true biography. The more radical the flaw, the more symmetrical is the novel's structure of balance between authority and molestation— the more closely, that is, does the novel resemble a kind of dream edifice constructed of insubstantial hopes. A quest for what Ishmael calls the ungraspable essence of life—whether that essence be a phantom, a whale, the sea, or even the theory and practice of being a gentleman when one is merely a country lad—can be narrated only at the expense of *not* narrating life's ordinary generative process. Pip's great expectations depend on the generosity of some unknown person, whom he secretly believes to be Miss Havisham. He flatters himself by believing that she has turned back from the brink of marriage for the express purpose of being able to endow him with the benefits of a handsome will. Yet the will, in one sense, is his own; in a more literal sense, however, it belongs to a convict, who is banished from society and who compensates for his isolation by making a gentleman-son out of Pip.

One should not overemphasize the similarities between two such different, but so strangely celibate, novels as *Moby Dick* and *Great Expectations*. But what strikes one with great force in both works of will (and I use the word *will* in the sense of both "volition" *and* "inheritance") is how the main character in each discovers that he has substituted volition for inheritance. Both Pip and Ishmael stand to one side of life's generative processes, and yet each occupies the narrative center of his novel just as Fidanza occupies the center in the last part of *Nostromo*. In Pip's attempt to fill in the blank of his true origins with the wealth of fantasy, in Ishmael's attempt to embark upon a whaling voyage of instruction, in Ahab's demonic chase of Moby Dick—in each of these three linked analogies, the narrative of adventurous exploits is, first of all, a beginning that replaces the obscurity of ordinary life; second, a willed effort the character exerts thereafter to live exclusively in search of his projected aims; and third, a discovery that at the beginning of the quest there stands an unwelcome cipher, that the quest itself is an attempted impregnation of life by sterile self-will and by a written record, and that the end of the quest is decipherment, by which I mean the effacement of the cipher with its elucidation by death, spiritual, physical, or both. Near the end of each novel there is a poignant scene wherein a kind of alter-protagonist is collected into the bosom of a family. In *Great Expectations* this is the scene to which I have already referred, where Pip sees little Pip, Joe and Biddy's son. In *Moby Dick* Ishmael, no longer a *Pequod* "isolate," becomes a member of the *Rachel's* crew. The common pattern here is the initial rejection of natural paternity in the narrative, which then leads to a special procreative yet celibate enterprise, which in turn leads to death *and* a brief vision of what might have happened had the narrative and the initial act of self-isolation never been undertaken. All this illustrates how narrative returns to discover its beginnings in the act whereby the generative faculty was sacrificed to celibate individuality. In each case, therefore, the novelist has committed himself to producing a record of that celibacy.

Marx's discovery of the imaginative role played by money in mid-nineteenth-century Western society is analogous to the discovery made by the novelist's record of a celibate enterprise. What I have been calling the alternative life willed by a novel's protagonist Marx calls "the confounding and compounding of all natural and human qualities." Money is always in evidence during the course of the realistic novel. It seduces the protagonist from natural procreation to a "novelistic" enterprise, to living with great expectations. Much of Dickens, Balzac, Flaubert, Thackeray, James, and Gogol is contained in the following account by Marx of how money gives fiction its potency:

If I long for a particular dish or want to take the mail-coach because I am not strong enough to go by foot, money fetches me the dish and the mail-coach: that is, it converts my wishes from something in the realm of imagination, translates them from their mediated, imagined or willed existence into their *sensuous, actual* existence—from imagination to life, from imagined being into real being. In effecting this mediation, money is the *truly creative* power.

. . . Being the external, common *medium* and *faculty* for turning an image into reality and reality into a mere *image* (a faculty not springing from man as man or from human society as society), *money* transforms the *real essential powers of man and nature* into what are merely abstract conceits and therefore *imperfections*—into tormenting chimeras—just as it transforms *real imperfections and chimeras*—essential powers which are really impotent, which exist only in the imagination of the individual—into *real powers* and *faculties*.[68]

These observations are noteworthy for the (perhaps inadvertent) mixture of sexual, monetary, and literary metaphors. Marx apparently conceived of an intersection where material power, the verbal incarnation of reality, and sexual generation interact in ways "confounding and compounding"—and it is this very interaction that the realistic novel manipulates. The result, in that type of novel and in Marx, is the description of something that is unnatural even while being almost entirely effective—something, that is, capable of holding one's attention and enduring despite its eccentricity.

There is still a further stage in the narrative's developing consciousness of its (by now) peculiarly unnatural aims. The chief of these aims, as I said earlier, is to wed inaugural promise to time—to be, in other words, the course of such a marriage, the issue of which is discovery, explanation, genealogy. The narrative represents the generative process—literally in its mimetic representation of men and women in time, metaphorically in that by itself it generates succession and multiplication of events after the manner of human procreation; yet the history of the nineteenth-century novel documents the increasing awareness of a gap between the representations of fictional narrative and the fruitful, generative principle of human life. These are divergent paths that eventually become completely irrelevant to one another. The awareness, therefore, is that narrative cannot represent, cannot truly mime, marriage *and* be original fiction at the same time.

The purpose of Flaubert's lifelong struggle with the dull and the humdrum was to show that the novel could be made productive at exactly those points where life is not. The novelist's monstrous project is by means of fiction to make a desert bloom—into fiction. Emma Bovary's adultery enhances her beauty, which seems unconnected not only to the circumstances of her marriage, child, and husband, but—Flaubert here intensifies the eccentricity even further—in its terrible artificiality parallels and yet overcomes the failure of Charles's experiment to straighten Hyppolite's clubfoot. The subtlety of Emma's beauty escaped even from the folds of her gown and from the line of her foot. [69] Like the novel, she is a made object whose express intention is to spite her "natural" failure as a mother and wife. Note, in the following description, how Flaubert uses words to create an altogether nonvisual, and hence literary impression: Emma is a beautiful verbal object *because* she has overstepped the limits of

146

what is commonly expected of a bourgeois family woman, or even of a natural object.

> Never had Madame Bovary been so beautiful as at this period; she had that indefinable beauty that results from joy, from enthusiasm, from success, and that expresses the harmony between temperament and circumstances. Her cravings, her sorrows, her sensuous pleasures and her ever-young illusions had slowly brought her to full maturity, and she blossomed forth in the fullness of her being, like a flower feeding on manure, on rain, wind and sunshine. Her half-closed eyelids seemed perfectly shaped for the long languid glances that escaped from them; her breathing dilated the fine nostrils and raised the fleshy corners of her mouth, shaded in the light by a slight black down. Some artist skilled in corruption seemed to have devised the shape of her hair as it fell on her neck, coiled in a heavy mass, casually reassembled after being loosened daily in adultery.[70]

Such characters risk being dissolved into a shapless mass of fragments. What holds them together, as Lukacs has said of *L'Education sentimentale,* is time, which

> brings order into the chaos of men's lives and gives it the semblance of a spontaneously flowering, organic entity; characters having no apparent meaning appear, establish relations with one another, break them off, disappear again without any meaning having been revealed. But the characters are not simply dropped into that meaningless becoming and dissolving which preceded man and will outlast him. Beyond events, beyond psychology, time gives them the essential quality of their existence . . . . The life totality which carries all men here becomes a living and dynamic thing: the expanse of time which the novel covers, dividing men into generations and integrating their actions in a historico-social context, is not an abstract concept, not a unit conceptually constructed after the event, . . . but a thing existing in itself and for itself, a concrete and organic continuum. This totality is a true image of life in the sense that no value-system of ideas enters it except in a regulative function.[71]

Although Lukacs's celebrated description accurately emphasizes the importance that Flaubert ascribes to time, it fails to make the distinction between the peculiarly sterile time within the novel and the concrete and organic continuum "established by empiric time in the natural and social human community." And this distinction is crucial: even though it occurs most decisively and explicitly at the end of *L'Education sentimentale,* it is the novel's beginning premise. Our final glimpses of Frédéric are in two scenes, one with Marie and the other with Deslauriers. Both scenes are incidents of unconsummated sexual passion. Marie visits Frédéric in March of 1867 (all of the novel's main action takes place between 1840 and 1848); she is an old woman with white hair and wearing a black lace veil. They reminisce together,

Frédéric astonishing her with his memories of events many years ago. Yet he is disappointed, and to conceal his real feelings he falls to his knees before her; his speech is a patently false one, yet "she rapturously accepted these adorations for the woman she no longer was." When she leaves him a little later, it is forever; but her slightly ridiculous final moment is to snip off one of her white locks for him. "Et ce fut tout"—that was all.[72]

A few months later Frédéric and Deslauriers are together, going over their former lives. Neither has amounted to much. The novel closes as both think back to 1837 (three years *before* the novel opens) when as boys they paid a visit to the local brothel. Overcome by heat, apprehension, and the sudden sight of so many women at his disposal, Frédéric runs out without doing anything and, because he has no money, Deslauriers must follow. They agree that that period was the best time of their lives.[73] The two scenes have in common not only unconsummated passion, but also a place at the end of the novel where, in a sense, they reveal novelistic time entirely capable of unity and unnatural order. Insofar as both scenes reveal to us the novel's true beginnings—in Frédéric's addition to sentiments wholly inappropriate to reality (in one scene he is an old man playing the role of a lover twenty-seven years too late, in the other he ignores the lapse in his sexual experience in order to enjoy a suggestive memory of vaguely erotic good times)—at the *end* of the novel, they confirm the novel's structure and its plot, both of which reverse the order of nature. Like the 1848 events, the time of Moreau leads nowhere; but unlike those events, the novel has a compositional integrity which is ironically based upon sterility, celibacy, and eccentricity. Frédéric's authority as the novel's central character rests upon everything in him that has not developed naturally. Hence the winter-in-spring effect of the last scenes. So complete is the disparity between genealogical continuity and novelistic continuity that Flaubert, as if to be impudent, places these infinitely rich and suggestive primary scenes outside the main action of the novel—specifically, doubly defiant, at the end. Both scenes take place at moments of temporal detachment from the main body of events: one nineteen years *after* them, the other three years *before* them.

Dostoievsky in *The Possessed,* even more decisively than Flaubert in his novels, presents the disjunction between character as beginning authority and the character's actions in his time, on the one hand, and, on the other, the sequential order of time in genealogical succession. This discontinuity feeds our ever-increasing suspicion of a narrator anxious to make outrageous events conform to the seeming order of his narrative. Our suspicion is aroused from the novel's very opening, so strongly, in fact, that we soon consider the narrator himself as much a Quixote as we do Stepan Trofimovitch. For what is one to make of a reporter whose introductory account of a character is as full of purposeful vagueness as that character himself? Here are some instances of what I have in mind, taken almost at random from chapter 1 of the Garnett translation:

> Yet Stepan Trofimovitch was a most intelligent and gifted man, even so to say a man of science, though indeed in science, . . . well, in fact he had not done such great things in science. I believe indeed he had done nothing at all. . . .
>
> Later on—after [Trofimovitch] had lost his post as lecturer, however—he published (by way of revenge, so to say, and to show them what a man they had lost) in a progressive monthly review, which translated Dickens and advocated the views of George Sand, the beginning of a very profound investigation into the causes, I believe, of the extraordinary moral nobility of certain knights at a certain epoch or something of that nature.
>
> Some lofty and exceptionally noble idea was maintained in it, anyway. It was said afterwards that the progressive review had to suffer for having printed the first part. That may very well have been so, for what was not possible in those days? Though, in this case, it was more likely that there was nothing of the kind, and that the author himself was too lazy to conclude his essay. He cut short his lectures on the Arabs because, somehow and by some one (probably one of his reactionary enemies) a letter had been seized giving an account of certain circumstances, in consequence of which some one had demanded an explanation from him. I don't know if the story is true.[74]

The hedgings, the doubts, the second- and third-hand reports, the ambiguous passive constructions, the leaps in argument—all are part of a textual fabric badly concealing its radical internal discontinuity as well as its disjunctive relations with reality. Furthermore, every human relationship in the novel seems to lack connection and defy consummation: marriages, in other words, are either ended or unrecognized, whether in the legal state or outside it. Consequently the relations between men and women, as well as those between parents and children, are uniformly skewed. A catalog of the abuse heaped upon the state of marriage, the family, and the individual, which would be a long one indeed, would suggest the extent to which the novel tampers with the most intimate continuities. The principal actors in the book are as disruptive in their effects upon us as are Pyotr Stepanovitch Verhovensky's designs for chaos.

Stavrogin is one such actor. Having refused every burden and gift offered him, having affirmed and denied all ties to others, yet having tortured himself about them either in explanation, settlement, or acceptance, he gives his written confession to Father Tihon. So confounding are Stavrogin's actions in the novel—as son, student, friend, husband, lover, revolutionary, comrade—that his confession, in intention at least, is presented as an instrument for straightening things out. What the psychologist-saint Tihon does is to show Stavrogin how the confession is *representation*,[75] a chronicle whose intention is to narrate a portion of Stavrogin's life and its great sin, but which conceals the man who has lived it behind the façade of its almost ridiculous ugliness. Tihon volunteers an alternative to publishing the document: silence and secret withdrawal from the world. Otherwise, he fears, either Stavrogin's confession once published will be construed as attempting to provoke the public, or that just before publication Stavrogin will be found to have committed another terrible crime "solely to avoid the publication of these sheets."[76] One of the points of this difficult scene, I think, is that writing and psychology conspire to overwhelm any morality or ethic based upon a common sense understanding of consequence. Whereas such understanding stipulates that the consequence of a confessed crime is absolution for the believer as well as punishment, Tihon (whom Stavrogin calls a "cursed psychologist") argues that so complex are the mind and its refractions in writing that one cannot expect to find any consecutive sense in them at all. A confession therefore might result in being accused of yet another crime, instead of simply requiring repentance, forgiveness, and retribution. Words do not necessarily tell what happens, since they have a life of their own, discontinuous with and eccentric to the "real" world. The insufficiency of narrative—which is what Stavrogin has written—is once again revealed; Dostoievsky's technique is to make text, sequential time and understanding, the biological order of human genealogy all, in his novel, totally discontinuous elements.

In such circumstances, as Hardy was less richly to recognize in *Jude the Obscure*, a man like Stavrogin cannot survive, and so he chooses death by suicide. He stands enigmatically in the midst of four other characters who are first poised at the brink of, and then like him plunge into, the psychological void separating conscious withdrawal from their inauthentic habitual roles, on the one hand, and, on the other, an infinite chaos which neither the historical nor the natural senses can comprehend: Shatov is the victim of ritual murder, Stepan becomes the wandering oracle, Kirrilov elects self-conscious suicide, and Pyotr disappears into the interior of Russia. Stavrogin in a way represents their collective mystery. When he hangs himself, we feel—because Dostoievsky evidently wants us to feel it—that the narrative description of his death is now prodding the silent traces of death into a sort of supplementary verbal life.

Novels increasingly take the form of retrospective, puzzling adventure at the end of the nineteenth century and at the beginning of the twentieth. The attention paid to narrative technique by James, Conrad, and Ford is evidence of the way in which the novel abandons its quasi-paternal role in favor of an almost total supplementarity. An event is presumed to have occurred—as in *The Good Soldier* or *Heart of Darkness* or *What Maisie Knew*—which the novel attempts to reconstruct by means of investigation; yet the reconstruction is performed as a form of discursive retrospective supplement to the event-as-action. Character then becomes an instrument for the author and reader to use in composing this supplement. Often the mode of this supplement is utterance—a speaking voice—and its goal commemoration. Thus in *Ulysses*, Bloom, Molly, and Stephen commemoratively, and in spite of themselves, repeat Homer; their words and actions recite the *Odyssey*, the original narrative, in the midst of which they have been inserted all along. A father bereft of his son, a son casting off his usurping family: these characters are ironically, impossibly reconciled in an impersonal and unattractive Ithaca. The resident Penelope performs her wifely and maternal roles in the endlessly postponing form of a speaking dream.

The note of betrayal running so strongly throughout *Ulysses* is partly, of course, a Joycean obsession. Yet the reader would do well to see in this theme another meaning: Stephen's constant preoccupation is with the idea that he will always be considered an Irish artist, a secondary person twice over; thus his art, as Buck Mulligan puts it, is well-symbolized by the cracked looking-glass of a servant.[77] History and society seem to have forced upon the novel its supplementarity, to which the novelist's most effective answer is a very difficult art whose connections with reality are seldom obvious. This is the betrayal of art by society, according to Joyce, and the retaliation of art. Nevertheless, such a rationale does not exhaust the meaning of betrayal. The problem is the author-novelist himself, upon whom the pressure of the novel as institution weighs heavily. The novel's paternal role—to author, father, procreate a rival reality—appears to be increasingly a formal one. Authority gives way to repetition, as mimesis gives way to parody and innovation to rewriting.[78] Each new novel recapitulates not life but other novels. It is not much to say, I think, that the late-nineteenth-century phase of the novel I have been discussing can be characterized as one in which narrative loses the sense of beginnings with which it had commenced. And this because the author now considers himself as much a creation as his writing. This motif in the novel, present since *Tristram Shandy,* is one of the molestations of authority whose force never diminishes. If being "too menny" induces the author to stray too far away from authority, then he can no longer be the old father. Instead, as human subject, he finds himself a subject of interpretation in the course of his authorship; the provisional character of his power to authorize a fiction seems ever more accentuated.

"When one has grasped that the 'subject' is not something that creates effects, but only a fiction, much follows." Thus Nietzsche in 1887. If everything known can be reduced to the status of a fiction, and all truth to interpretation, then, according to Nietzsche the

> will to truth is a making firm, a making true and durable, an abolition of the false character of things, a reinterpretation of it into beings. "Truth" is therefore not something there, that might be found or discovered—but something that must be created and that gives a name to a process, or rather to a will to overcome that has in itself no end—introducing truth, as a *processus in infinitum,* an active determining—not a becoming—conscious of something that is in itself firm and determined. It is a word for the "will to power.". . .
>
> Man projects his drive to truth, his "goal" in a certain sense, outside himself as a world that has being, as a metaphysical world, as a "thing-in-itself," as a world already in existence. His needs as creator invent the world upon which he works, anticipate it; this anticipation (this "belief" in truth) is his support.[79]

This is as much as to say that a writer can take nothing for granted. Each invention is an act of overcoming flux, a way of temporarily forcing a created subject-object upon the world. The more powerful the will (to power or to belief), the more durable, and hence more convincing, the truth it seeks to promulgate. Nothing separates "truth" in this definition from "reinterpretation"; the latter is the will to truth of one interpretation—more durable, more strongly argued—over others. Yet since no one interpretation can be said to be more original than another (no interpretation is the first interpretation), to invent or to anticipate the world requires of the inventor a strong initial conviction of self. When, as in narrative, author and invention are tied temporally to the same beginning—the desire to narrate an event—the risk that author and invention will dissolve one into the other increases greatly.

The explicit results of such a dissolution are to be found, confirmed, and sustained in T. E. Lawrence's *Seven Pillars of Wisdom*.[80] A passage from its formerly suppressed opening chapter demonstrates the difficulty Lawrence had in making his "truth"—his invention, his creation, his interpretation—endure ("the old men" in the passage refers to the victory of other interpretations):

> In these pages the history is not of the Arab movement, but of me in it. It is a narrative of daily life, mean happenings, little people. Here are no lessons for the world, no disclosures to shock people. It is filled with trivial things, partly that no one mistake for history the bones from which some day a man may make history, and partly for the pleasure it gave me to recall the fellowship of the revolt. We were fond together, because of the sweep of the open places, the taste of wide winds, the sunlight, and the hopes in which we worked. The morning freshness of the world-to-be intoxicated us. We were wrought up with ideas inexpressible and vaporous, but to be fought for. We lived many lives in those whirling campaigns, never sparing ourselves; yet when we achieved and the new world dawned, the old men came out again and took our victory to re-make in the likeness of the former world they knew. Youth could win, but had not learned to keep: and was pitiably weak against age. We stammered that we had worked for a new heaven and a new earth, and they thanked us kindly and made their peace.[81]

In the rest of the book, however, every dream of glory from Western man's epic past is assembled by this scholar-adventurer-initiator-author-originator. The scene is a real war (World War I), the setting a real desert, given to Lawrence by history, in which to execute his perfect action, with beginning, middle, and end. The narrative rivals the titanic fictions of Dostoievsky and Melville by treating the realities of an accomplished desert campaign.[82] It was Lawrence alone who could pick his goal, his prophet, and his warriors for this utterly male campaign. He seeks out Féisal in the same way that a poet seeks out his theme: "I felt at first glance that this was the man I had come to Arabia to seek—the leader who would bring the Arab revolt to full glory."[83] And these chosen ambitions were to replace the vagaries of Arab existence and Muslim faith, which for too long had clung vaguely to Mecca and Medina, with an entire project, superimposed on the nomadic givens like a grand pattern for a great house.

Out of the chaos was to come a story, characters, purpose. Whereas the Arabs wanted quite naturally to recapture Mecca and Medina from the Turks in a series of fixed battles, Lawrence wanted instead to take Damascus by a more-or-less unconnected series of moving attacks. Early in the book, as Lawrence rides through Arabia toward Medina, he reflects: "My thoughts as we went were how this was the pilgrim road, down which for uncounted generations, the people of the north had come to visit the Holy City, bearing with them gifts of faith for the shrine; and it seemed that the Arab Revolt might be in a sense a return pilgrimage, to take back to the north, to Syria, an idea for an ideal, a belief in liberty for their past belief in a revelation."[84] Thus Lawrence's creative presence shifts and reinterprets the Arab revolt's whole direction, just as, for instance, Joyce shifts the triviality of a June day in Dublin into a pattern of eighteen episodes out of the *Odyssey*. Lawrence's will converts the East into the forms of the West: not Medina and Mecca, but Jerusalem and Damascus; not Muhammad and his sherifs, but Christ the prophet played by Feisal; not mere desert tribes, but a congregation of the faithful, a People, led by a warrior-zealot-Paul—Auda. Even the classicist in Lawrence could be satisfied. For here, too, were Troy, Agamemnon, Achilles, and the Greeks. If accomplished then, such a many-tiered plan would be a triumph indeed.

Everything in *The Seven Pillars* is heavily determined by Lawrence's interpretations, which while he writes is retrospection, but as he acts in the book is anticipation. The work's subtitle is "A triumph," a clear enough phrase as anticipation of the revolt's victory; this is how Lawrence's contemporaries, and many of the Arabs, saw it. Yet in the book itself the narrative drifts ever further from triumph and further from sequential progress. Lawrence goes to Arabia as a young and energetic man, yet at the end of *The Seven Pillars* he emerges a broken man. At the beginning, he says, "I wrote my will across the sky in stars," and further on in the book he details this a bit further: "The desert was held in a crazed communism by which Nature and the elements were for the free use of every known friendly person for his own purposes and no more."[85]

These purposes are defined by Lawrence in chapter 33, during an illness that has rendered him semidelirious. He realizes that the house of war, as he calls it, must be designed carefully; but since the plan for it is imaginative, the elements have to be treated as if they, too, are nonmaterial. This transvaluation of his army and mission makes Lawrence invent a new science—composed, he says, of an algebraic, a biological, and a psychological part: even the rubrics are rarefied. The whole is designed to transcend logical sequence in the average mind. This was to be a war of detachment, not of contact; there would be no central point to the campaign, just raids spread out as far as possible; no front, no army, no confrontation. The plan was based on irregularity and extreme articulation. From then on in the book the writing becomes increasingly more technically detailed and less readable, for the text and the plan of the book have been transvalued into a special mode of existence, creating an actor and created by the author—in both cases, Lawrence himself.[86]

A flaw, however, hinders the narrative. The flaw is the author himself, Lawrence, miming the Arab and yet acting the god, torn between his disguise as participant and his imperialistic will as unnatural father of the movement. The seven pillars are erected: Damascus is gained. Yet the gaps between the large blocks of the structure are signs of an origin betrayed in the very process of building. Thus in history the Arabs win, yet their original aim, a finished state, is withheld from them by historical necessity in the West. In the narrative, the book completes itself, yet its meaning resides almost wholly in the traduced aim and the violated integrity known only, and then very obscurely, to the author: "There seemed no straight walking for us leaders in this crooked lane of conduct, ring within ring of unknown, shamefaced motives cancelling or double-charging their precedents."[87] The text is a mausoleum commemorating a secret no longer remembered after Lawrence's postwar mind-suicide (the phrase was Lawrence's for his self-burial in the ranks of common soldiers); the secret resembles the mysterious initials, "S. A.," to whom the book is dedicated, and which provide the reader with a minimal clue—or a death without a corpse. Reduced to mere textuality, the book's virtue, as Lawrence wrote Lionel Curtis in 1923, was its secrecy; or, as he wrote to V. W. Richards in 1920, his narrative was to be "the-book-to-build-the-house."[88] Narrative has come to this, then: a house without women, without fulfillment, without family. Which is why Malraux says that "the Arab epic became in Lawrence's mind the medium for a grandiose expression of human emptiness."[89] In his more diffident yet more direct way, E. M. Forster wrote to Lawrence: "I find something not quite satisfactory in your presentation of the human race."[90]

IV

Both Malraux and Forster felt that Lawrence's portrayal of man was insufficiently "real" and solid. Forster's suggestion was to "put in more conversations," on the theory that since in real life men talk, they should also be seen talking in narratives. In conflict here, I believe, are the concepts of traditional novelistic man, whose portrayal relies exclusively on the conventions for depicting man institutionalized by the classical novel, and another sort of man—Lawrence's—whose presence in writing obeys only the exigencies of the writing—whatever those may be—rather than those prescribed by any existing genre. Lawrence had confessed that *The Seven Pillars* was an atypical mixture of confession and history, with the former almost always overriding the latter; Lawrence's own psychology was far from static, and thus the specific difficulties he encountered in rendering his hyperactive self-consciousness dictated not only his method of writing narrative history, but also his conceptions of history and change, of man in history, and of the kind of text that could deliver the fullest psychological account in the context of history. During the course of *The Seven Pillars,* Lawrence begins to become conscious of playing a part in events that he set in motion. He becomes thereafter an agent of what he has himself created among the Arabs, and from then on he turns into an unwilling transcriber of events. The text goes forward with himself in its very grip. When he is captured at Deraa, his masquerade as an Arab is exposed, and he is punished for it. As author, Lawrence becomes, during the last part of the book, a victim of his writing—a project that, like the Arab revolt, he must see through to completion despite his efforts to withdraw from it. Lawrence's failure to be sincere with the Arabs is balanced by his fanatical sincerity in rendering his hypocrisy. The revolt as a project is finally terminated, as is the book, but the result (as Lawrence well knew) was a shabby history of betrayal and manipulation, a shattered, unfinished monument. For Lawrence the book represented a perpetual confrontation with his personality, with his authority as a man in history: the authority of a writer, an adventurer, a famous personality whose inescapable fate was to write a story of irregular initiation, irregular campaign, and irregular triumph.

There is a stark contrast between the epic grandeur of *The Seven Pillars,* to which most admirers of Lawrence respond very easily, and its far more complex and interesting psychological and textual problems. In 1886 Nietzsche had written of the difference between "the old mendacious pomp, junk, and gold dust of unconscious human vanity"—which in Lawrence corresponds to his successes in the Arab revolt—and the "basic text of *homo natura.*"[91] A narrative history such as Lawrence's history of the Arab revolt only implicitly incorporates the "basic text," yet within that text the dynamic of molestation and authority that I discussed earlier is less well-disguised and nearer the surface than it is in the classical novel. Both Lawrence's overburdened privacy and the public nature of the Arab revolt obviously violate the novel's conventional restraints. Yet along with Conrad, Dostoievsky, and Hardy, Lawrence feels very strongly the human encroachments upon the practice of being an author. And along with theirs his work reconsiders the fundamental problem of how to make language in general and narrative in particular more responsive than before to the task of describing man's nature. My argument is that central to such a description is the difficulty of rendering the sequential order of man's life in time, especially since language and psychology seem to operate outside the exclusively linear rules of progress or meaning. As we saw, the classical novel contained the molestations of psychology and language in the pattern of procreation and generation found in the genealogically imagined plot, the family, and the self. But such a pattern cannot properly begin or order writing once the human subject is no longer given as capable of such procreation, once as a subject its major feature is not the author's faith in it but the fact that it, and its author, are fictions together being produced during the writing.

The value of Lawrence's narrative is that it can be studied more freely than the novel as a work exposing the psychological, textual, and conceptual strains to which the novel was susceptible. I suggested earlier that these problems result from the specific cultural role of novels in the West: novels represent as well as contain change; they add to reality and interpret it; they accept the burdens, as well as the pleasures, of such desires on the part of the author and the reader. Thus a novel *begins* in a particular way and moves according to a logic of development implicitly acknowledged by both author and reader. For the critic, however, this beginning and this development are not simply duplicated over and over during the course of the genre's history. Rather, the critic regards them as investigative instruments that not only contribute to the ideas of beginning and development but also change those ideas. The more those ideas change, the more radically (by definition) the novel can be seen as a reinterpretation of its own beginning and development, as well as those of man, the novel's protagonist. The attention I have paid to Conrad, Hardy, Flaubert, Dostoievsky, and Lawrence has had the purpose of characterizing a late stage in the changing conception of the novel as an enterprise for reflecting on beginning and development. Historically, this stage coincides with two other major efforts to deal with these issues on somewhat the same grounds as the novel does.

A very considerable part of what Nietzsche and Freud set out to do in their work is radically anthropological in the same sense as was the late-nineteenth-century novel. Each regarded the task of accurately describing man as fundamentally connected with three related problems. One is the problem of biography as embodied in genealogical sequence: to what extent is this sequence adequate for reflecting the ascertainable discontinuities in a man's life? Where in this sequence does one locate the beginning if, for instance, psychological knowledge is not based solely upon the fact of birth, but upon transpersonal, natural, and "prehistoric" forces like the unconscious or the will? The second problem is that of language in relation to human reality: how well does writing— how well *can* writing—incarnate this reality given that mimesis is scarcely a comprehensive technique? What sort of text is most faithful in rendering the complexities of human psychology? The third problem is that of dealing with man's fiction-making capabilities: if producing narrative is in some way a basic human tendency, how does one cognitively deal with fiction and image making in narrative? That is, is fiction utilitarian, or simply decorative?

It is fairly evident that all these questions are interrelated. But consider for a start Nietzsche's statement of the program of re-interpreting the three problems to which he, and presumably also Freud, would give assent:

> To translate man back into nature; to become master over the many vain and overly enthusiastic interpretations and connotations that have so far been scrawled and painted over that eternal basic text of *homo natura;* to see to it

that man henceforth stands before man as even today, hardened in the discipline of science, he stands before the *rest* of nature, with intrepid Oedipus eyes and sealed bird catchers who have been piping at him all too long, "you are more, you are higher, you are of a different origin!"—that may be a strange and insane task, but it is a *task*—who would deny that? Why did we choose this insane task? Or, putting it differently: "why have knowledge at all?"[92]

This passage's use of such metaphors and expressions as "translation," "interpretation," "basic text," and so forth to describe knowledge of man indicates how strongly Nietzsche feels to be the connection between man and language. Equally strongly, I think, he feels that all hitherto available and formal uses of language betray "the basic text of *homo natura.*" To restore that text Nietzsche calls for a combined Oedipus—strikingly prefiguring Freud—and Odysseus who would begin the task by radically making knowledge the intention of the text.

But why should that be so: why should knowledge be sought anyway? Nietzsche's answer is as follows:

Learning changes us; it does what all nourishment does which also does not merely "preserve"—as physiologists know. But at the bottom of us, really "deep down," there is, of course, something unteachable, some granite of spiritual *fatum,* of predetermined decision and answer to predetermined selected questions. Whenever a cardinal problem is at stake, there speaks an unchangeable "this is I": about man and woman, for example, a thinker cannot relearn but only finish learning—only discover ultimately how this is "settled in him." At times we find certain solutions of problems that inspire strong faith in *us;* some call them henceforth *their* "convictions." Later—we see them only as steps to self-knowledge, signposts to the problem we *are*—rather, to that great stupidity we are, to our spiritual *fatum,* to what is *unteachable* very "deep down."[93]

Intimations of Freud are present in this passage, too—not only in its use of imagery of depth to describe that which is unteachable, and presumably unconscious, in man, but also in its references to the dialectical learning process and—more important, I think—in its conception of man as problem. If, as the last sentence of Nietzsche's declaration seems to suggest, man's deepest reality is that he *is* a problem, then the insane task of gaining knowledge requires finding, first, a form of understanding that recognizes this truth, and second, a language and a text in which to contain, express, realize, fulfill, or incarnate this knowledge. Invoking ancient heroes like Oedipus and Odysseus concedes at the outset that the task is historically, fearfully, and perenially demanding. For such knowledge does not carry with it the ordinary rewards of human self-aggrandizement, nor does it simply identify man with nature. Rather, this knowledge imposes upon man responsibility for his mind as well as for his "unteachable" participation in the facts of nature. Comparable ambition in seeking knowledge is found, I think, in the last lines of W. B. Yeats's poem "The Tower." The poet charges himself "to study in a learned school" in order to render his soul capable of regarding with equanimity the wreckage of his entire physical, sensual world—body, friends, beauty. Decrepitude will appear to

> Seem but the clouds of the sky
> When the horizon fades,
> Or a bird's sleepy cry
> Among the deepening shades.[94]

Just as nature is a complex space in which events occur in temporal as well as spatial dimensions that are not uniformly linear or progressive, so man's knowledge of himself is (or ought to be considered) similarly complex. Yet "nature" cannot be grasped immediately; the very use of so general a rubric frequently disguises an enormous amount of ignorance, as Nietzsche himself most incisively observed. Rather, nature has to be interpreted, or read, just as man must be read and interpreted. This is a fundamental point which, in The Interpretation of Dreams, Freud was to make many times and in many different ways. Dreams, he says at some point, do not come into being with the intention of being understood: they simply are (and they are problematical), they unscrupulously yield to any method of granting visual representation to dream-thoughts, and their unity is simply an illusion. Therefore, like nature under the gaze of the scientist, dreams are hieroglyphics which can only be understood by schooling oneself in their peculiar mechanisms. Yet the most problematical thing about dreams is that everyone, even their interpreter, dreams them. How, then, does one separate the object of study from the object of experience—or from the experience tout court? The relatively simple answer to this question is appealing indeed, and Freud seems not to have evaded it: first one experiences the object, then one analyzes it. Or, as most writers would say, first one gets the material oneself, then one studies it as something whose method of acquisition is itself significant.

Yet as with any novelist or reader, Freud at the very beginning is faced with deciding how to deal with objects of experience and analysis whose primary, absolutely basic feature is their subjective

160

distortion of reality—objects of experience, moreover, that are admitted fictions whose mode of existence is *as* experience. For one can not only legitimately doubt the value of a dream, but also legitimately question its boundaries, its relation to life, its recollection. Given these difficulties, it is obviously very hard to gather material on dreams, and even harder to make fast distinctions between the "real" facts and illusory ones regarding them. The *Interpretation* deals as much with the nature of psychological reality as with the meaning of dreams, but the book's fascination lies in the fact that Freud does not choose between illusion and reality until the very end. His policy seems to have been to record everything possible about dreams and then to sift out the true from the counterfeit. The structure of the book is therefore intended to reflect the stages of an investigation, not just its results. Such a structure, I think, consciously minimizes what would have been an otherwise passive transcription of "scientific" findings. In a sense Freud wishes his text to be the stage, the locale, where dream interpretation takes place.[95]

However strong Freud's wish to make his investigations seem to be unfolding before the reader, he is too systematic a writer to deliver a slapdash text. Nevertheless, his text is ordered according to a planned dissociation, a dismemberment of image clusters (dreams) into fragments of thought—despite the fact that the claim to attention made by his objects of study is precisely their striking, if irrational and distorted, unity of composition. Such a strategy is of special interest to the student of literature. It is as if Freud were taking into account the impasse reached by so many late-nineteenth-century and early-twentieth-century novels—as reflected by their tendency to represent supplements to activity the writer cannot fully capture and by their disillusionment with mimetic attempts to represent man in language. In both instances novelists turned to techniques that compensated for deficiencies in the novel's traditional mimetic strength. Conrad's use of interlocking and qualifying "records," Flaubert's use of temporality, the images of victimizing and enigmatic texts in Dostoievsky and Lawrence—these, as we saw above, have their roots, technically at least, in the traditional novel's radical dynamic of authority and molestation. In Freud's case he deliberately avoids the instruments socially, culturally, and institutionally linked in the West to the practice of fiction, even as his material is—and remains throughout his career—firmly connected to that same practice. For *dreams* we can easily imagine substituting the word *fiction,* for *distortion* the

161

term *point of view,* for *regression* and *condensation* the term *biography,* for *parents* the novelistic *family,* and so on. When Freud in one place states the value of dream interpretation, he even reads like Henry James's description of fiction as a house with many windows: "The interpretation of dreams is like a window through which we can get a glimpse of the interior of that apparatus" (p. 219).[96]

Thus a further burden is imposed upon Freud. The *Interpretation* is not only an encyclopedia of dream interpretation, a theater for staging Freud's scientific investigations: it is also a text whose intention is to begin a discourse one of whose principal purposes is the conscious avoidance of certain specific textual conventions.[97] The first of these conventions is supplementarity, a defensive tactic used to separate the text temporally and spatially from the events it is describing. Thus the text comes after the event and its mode is verbal, whereas the events are taken to be "material." A second convention is the adoption of a logic of structure and argument based on temporal and spatial forward movement. Despite digressions and temporary regressions, the principal motion is sequential, a movement forward until, as the expression has it, a conclusion is reached. Third is the convention of adequacy, according to which the text is assumed to be fully equal to the task of conveying, incarnating, containing, realizing, or fulfilling its intention, its meaning, or both together. Most hermeneutics assumes this sort of adequacy, for the argument is that frequent "returns" to a text will yield up a meaning that is wholly knowable, and wholly embodied in the text—at least for the purposes of its adequate reading. Fourth is the convention of finality. Each portion of the text—each discrete unit, from the smallest to the whole of the text itself—is *in its place* more or less finally, by which I mean that neither what precedes each such unit nor what follows it is considered equal to it at that moment. A hierarchy is established in which the text or any subunit thereof fully and finally displaces every other text or unit at the moment of that text's appearance and/or reading. The fifth and final convention is that the unity, or integrity, of the text is maintained by a series of genealogical connections: author-text, beginning-middle-end, text-meaning, reader-interpretation, and so on. Underneath all these is the imagery of succession, of paternity, of hierarchy.

Some combination of these conventions is taken for granted, I think, in most writing before Freud and Nietzsche. My argument has been that the classical novel employs all of these in its plot, subject matter, and development for the specific reasons and in the characteristic ways discussed above. In a sense, then, the novel most explicitly realizes these conventions, gives them coherence and imaginative life by grounding them in a text whose beginning premise is, as we have said above, paternal. This is decidedly not the case with Freud's writing, and a great deal of what I shall be saying specifically about *The Interpretation of Dreams* applies not only to other texts of Freud but also to the general textual theories of Nietzsche. I shall leave till subsequent chapters the question of how these theories can be construed as having a bearing on the attitude of other modern writers toward the text. Certainly at first glance Freud's general theory of dreams and of the unconscious seems undeniably to have influenced the vocabulary of modern writing. Yet no less a pioneering effort is Freud's textual practice itself in *The Interpretation of Dreams*.

In studying this text it is important, I believe, to keep in mind the conventions referred to above, as well as Freud's lifelong fascination with the role of the father. Not only does the latter play a key role in Freud's discussion of the Oedipus complex, but it also returns later in Freud's historical essays, such as *Moses and Monotheism* and *Totem and Taboo*. There are strong echoes of paternity as well in his analyses of the superego, of culture and of religion. A general observation worth noting here is that Freud's displacement and qualification in his psychology of the father's role—a role which is always complex and, despite radical qualifications upon it, highly ambivalent—is accompanied by parallel displacements and qualifications made in those genealogical, hierarchical, and consecutive conventions to be found in the idea of a text. Perhaps it is too glib to see in this Freud's interest in substituting brothers for fathers, copresence for consecutiveness, temporal and spatial simultaneity for the (relative) finality of sequence. None of these displacements comes about by assertion, however; rather, each is concomitant with Freud's special sort of analytical reasoning, in which a healthy respect for what he calls the wisdom of the ancients is combined with a daring insolence in advancing novel hypotheses. Another simple way of stating this is to call Freud's writing an amalgam of scientific and "traditional" wisdom.

It is no accident that the protocol of *The Interpretation of Dreams* is not at all that of a conventional scientific text, but rather that of a narrative account of multifaceted experiences

163

related to a presumably educated reader—though not necessarily a professional one. The text is shot through with many personal asides, bits of anecdotal history, retractions and corrections of views previously forwarded by the author himself (sometimes earlier in the same chapter). Freud's favorite narrative image, of course, is that of a rambling walk during which prospects open up, are closed off, or ignored. The most celebrated sentence in the book—"The interpretation of dreams is the royal road [*via regia*] to a knowledge of the unconscious activities of the mind"—brilliantly transforms the pervasive image of a rambling walk into that of a highly purposeful and forceful journey toward a goal. Yet even in that very late statement in the book, Freud does not desert the possibilities of his earlier formulation: for when dealing with something so impervious to efforts at straightforward, final definition as the unconscious, it is fairly certain that yet again we will have to content ourselves with rambling toward it, even on the royal road.

At no point in the *Interpretation* does Freud scant the variety of his evidence—or, for that matter, the fact that most of it is inconclusive, contradictory, of doubtful origin, and even commonsensically useless. This is quite apart from the evidence of dreams themselves. As a writer, Freud says on numerous occasions, his job is to somehow make his prose adequate for extracting the useful from the dross. Yet his beginning principle is an extremely catholic one—is no less than the belief that all "psychical events are determined, [that] there is nothing arbitrary about them" (p. 514). A few pages later he says, "That is why in analysing a dream I insist that the whole scale of estimates of certainty shall be abandoned and that the faintest possibility that something of this or that sort may have occurred in the dream shall be treated as complete certainty" (p. 516). Therefore, all the evidence of (and on) dreams is interconnected, it is admissible, and it all works. How all the evidence is connected together and how and why it works is the problem. A still greater problem is presenting the evidence in language. Near the end of the book Freud indicates the scope of his difficulties:

> In venturing on an attempt to penetrate more deeply into the psychology of dream-processes, I have set myself a hard task, and one to which my powers of exposition are scarcely equal. Elements in this complicated whole which are in fact simultaneous can only be represented successively in my description of them, while, in putting forward each point,

I must avoid appearing to anticipate the grounds on which it is based: difficulties such as these it is beyond my strength to answer. In all this I am paying the penalty for the fact that in my account of dream-psychology I have been unable to follow the historical development of my own views. Though my own line of approach to the subject of dreams was determined by my previous work on the psychology of the neuroses, I had not intended to make use of the latter as a basis of reference in the present work. Nevertheless I am constantly being driven to do so, instead of proceeding as I should have wished, in the contrary direction and using dreams as a means of approach to the psychology of the neuroses. I am conscious of all the trouble in which my readers are thus involved, but I can see no means of avoiding it. (p. 588)

If his text is one result of these insufficiencies, Freud is admitting here that it cannot be regarded as the unequivocally happy realization of his plans for it. The available guides for prose construction were not adequate for his material. He says earlier that as he writes he has had to keep at bay all the ideas associated with a particular dream, then adds, "And in the meantime the 'meaning' of the dream was borne in upon me. I became aware of an intention which was carried into effect in the dream and which must have been my motive for dreaming it" (p. 118). A (disguised wish for) intention is present and it works to give the dream a meaning, but an evident subdivision has taken place between presence and the awareness of it. In other words, whereas an intention must have determined the dream itself, the intention does not immediately and prescriptively yield to analysis. Instead, associated thoughts appear to the analyst; they cling to the intention as clusters around a nucleus or, as Freud says later, as mushroomlike growths around a deep node (p. 525). Just as any dream is a palimpsest, sections of which remain vivid while others are almost invisible or partial, so the analysis has the same quality.

Two practical, textual consequences follow, one more obvious than the other. First, Freud's text is constructed like a palimpsest. Thanks to James Strachey's precise editing, we can see physical signs of how, in each of the eight German editions, Freud interpolated new or revised material, sometimes to make new or revised points, sometimes to clarify old ones. The palimpsest goes beyond this sort of intervention. Since Freud's subject matter and his attitude toward it can be grasped only in verbal fragments (whether of dreams or of language—i.e. sequential prose), they must be able to accommodate important changes. Usually the reason for these changes is that the fragment as first apprehended was necessarily incomplete—that is, its intention, while present,

165

was not visible. Therefore, none of Freud's sentences at a given point in the text is a final statement, not even in its immediate context. Here is a perfect example of what I mean:

> We shall be taking into account everything that has been brought to light by our analysis of unpleasurable dreams if we make the following modification in the formula in which we have sought to express the nature of dreams: *a dream is a (disguised) fulfillment of a (suppressed or repressed) wish.* (p. 160)[98]

The typographical devices—the italics and the parentheses—used here to indicate Freud's later changes, emphasize the proleptic as well as the recapitulatory aspects of the observation. In addition, the parentheses on the printed page represent the mechanisms of disguise and repression, not only by virtue of their presence, but also, paradoxically, by their delayed appearance.

The second textual consequence is immediately related to Freud's analytic method. Every dream has a "plot" of its own that has no corresponding parallel in reality. In a real sense, dream continuity is, like the novel's plot, an alternative way of perceiving a movement of images: such a continuity may seem arbitrary, but it has an undeniable logic and order that we tend to deprecate with the thought that "it's only a dream." It is the construction of the dream that is unfamiliar, for the images themselves are not created images, but rather familiar, mostly mnemonic images combined in self-protective and unfamiliar ways (pp. 418-19). Freud's analytic way with these combinatory puzzles is to dissociate them from one another by first writing them down or speaking them aloud in sentences and then grappling with the possible meaning of the sentences one by one. That is, his verbal interpretation of dreams operates at the sentence (or even phrase) level rather than at the paragraph level, even though the latter more closely parallels the overall organizational pattern of the dream. In the sequence of dream-images Freud discerns certain types of barriers—distortion, condensation, displacement, secondary revision—whose function is to safeguard, even seduce, the dominant consciousness from experiencing an unpleasant encounter with the unconscious. By sidestepping the sequential order that images follow in the dream, Freud therefore lets "thought" emerge as a result of the analysis; and during the analysis he also discovers that a dream-thought reaches representation in imagery through dream-work. The sequence of images then achieves order by effacing the traces of dream-work and dream-thought. Because the dream-plot also usually frees itself of the powerful emotions and desires that brought it into being, Freud likens the dream to corpses lying on a battlefield (p. 467). His interpretive task is thus to make the battlefield come alive again.

I have detailed these steps to show how methodic is Freud's decision not to let images and sequences, or plots made up of images, determine the order of his analysis. Similarly, in his text each image is dissected into its associated thoughts. Essential to this procedure is the transformation of the dream from images into words. The element of dreams is imagery (even though images in dreams sometimes "speak" using words); its logic, or plot, is the particular way that images can combine with one another. Once translated from images into interpretive language, the plot of the dream, and hence its image, loses its effective power to dominate one's attention. When the image becomes a sentence recorded as part of the interpretation, the "plot"—which Freud describes as using any means within its reach, "legitimate or illegitimate" (p. 411), illogical or contradictory (p. 318), to preserve its liberty—becomes a composition of "dream-thought," and the dream thus becomes amenable to analysis. The dream-image marks the beginning of an analysis whose method is consistently antivisual. Thus for Freud the beginning is when one departs from the dream-image, in the course of analysis, and enters the realm of language: here one sees the kernel of Freud's "speaking cure."[99]

Freud's text consequently does not *supplement* the dream; on the contrary, it *opposes* words to the dream and its images. In place of discrete images the text substitutes relatively untidy explanations in prose. Whereas the images properly begin in the dream-day, their interpretive endings "cannot, from the nature of things," be definite (p. 525). Every statement made about the dream proceeds according to "*unknown*—or, as we inaccurately say, unconscious—purposive ideas" (p. 528); by a logic of double negatives, however, the images are guided by a known intention—namely, the intention not to be understood (p. 341). Furthermore, images are the guardians of sleep. Not only do they often allay anxiety (p. 267), but their visual form is directly linked to censorship, which can be bypassed by the interpretation. Since the dream-images and dream-thoughts have different centers (p. 305), the same is true of the dream-plot on the one hand and, on the other, of the verbal interpretation. Formally, the dream-plot designates a specific period of time and place, while the verbal interpretation is far more diffuse. Therefore, the text of the interpretation inhabits a totally *verbal* dimension of time: in

167

effect, this means that each discursive statement made during the interpretation is radically incomplete, for it is capable of infinite associations, each of which will substantially alter its status as a statement.

Freud has various ways of demonstrating this. The simile of the entrepreneur and his capital (p. 561), for instance, corresponds to the relationship between the dream and the unconscious. The wealth of an image (its arresting visual qualities) is separated from the illusion and attached instead to a far more interesting polysemy in thought. A version of this technique is Flaubert's placing of the final scene in *L'Education sentimentale* outside the main temporal frame of the action. Even if the young men's memory is of an abortive episode, which is only a silent spectacle, in other ways it is extremely fertile and wealthy: it produces much of the novel's plot. And this despite the fact that the memory is of something not done, just as in Freud wealth arises from that which is by definition unknown. For a prose text like the *Interpretation* this means that meaning cannot be imagined as residing in a finished object like the dream; nor for that matter can meaning precede its verbal description. Rather, the meaning of the unknown (unconscious) is something always being produced; each segment of an analysis builds a more complex sense—until, however,

there is often a passage in even the most thoroughly interpreted dream which has to be left obscure; this is because we become aware during the work of interpretation that at that point there is a tangle of dream-thoughts which cannot be unravelled and which moreover adds nothing to our knowledge of the content of the dream. This is the dream's navel, the spot where it reaches down into the unknown. The dream-thoughts to which we are led by interpretation cannot, from the nature of things, have any definite endings; they are bound to branch out in every direction into the intricate network of our world of thought. It is at some point where this network is particularly close that the dream-wish grows up, like a mushroom out of its mycelium. (p. 525)

At first glance, this seems to be Freud's way of introducing the idea of antecedence, attributing to it ultimate priority, and then throwing it out. This is not the case. He is saying that any sequence of discursive explanations normally is reversible: a sequence of sentences A through M, for example, increases our understanding additively: at M we know more than we did at A, and conversely, at A we know less than we knew at M. Furthermore, according to Freud, dream interpretation does not work that way generally, although it does at particular moments. Instead of a linear progression from one end of the interpretation to the other (say, from A to M), the analyst encounters a "tangle" in the dream which either sends one to another sequence (A_1 to M_1) or stops one entirely. The new sequences of interpretation may either parallel the A-to-M set, intersect it, or contradict it altogether. In short, the interpretation as a whole cannot be visualized at all as having a linear trajectory from birth to maturity, or from ignorance to knowledge, or from absolute terminal to absolute terminal. Neither can one assume that the more antecedent a beginning point, the more certain and the greater the amount of sense. Interpretation is a field of understanding in which statements are dispersed but whose positions can be determined with regard only to certain (but not all) other statements. Not every statement is connected intelligibly with every other one. This is so because in the interpretation of dreams one is essentially dealing with a psychical locality (p. 536), not an anatomical one. Freud's description of regression, as an instance, employs topographical, formal, and temporal categories—all nonanatomical terms, just as his model of the "mental apparatus" is distinctly and explicitly structural, spatial, and temporal though not visual.

Let us return to the "tangles." Even if they do not add to our knowledge of the dream's content, they are nevertheless present. They stand for something there which the sequence of analysis hitherto adopted cannot affect. Yet these tangles are only barriers to an additive sort of knowledge; Freud nowhere says that they prohibit knowledge of a *different* kind. A way of breaking through the barrier is to be found, I think, in Freud's interpretation of the Oedipus story (pp. 261-64)—specifically, in a footnote that he added in 1914 and that was apparently the section of his text that provoked the most controversy. Freud himself found more value in the story as time went on: in 1919 he remarked the story's "undreamt-of" importance. In the myth, the hero is adept at solving a riddle, but is destroyed by the realization of his incestuous desires. The traditional lesson of Sophocles' play, says Freud, "is submission to the divine will and realization of [man's] impotence" (p. 262). More impressive is the fact that "the poet, as he unravels the past, brings to light the guilt of Oedipus, [and] he is at the same time compelling us to recognize our own inner minds, in which these same impulses, though suppressed, are still to be found" (p. 263). That which resists interpretation—the tangle of thoughts—can be unraveled by the poet, but not without sacrificing Oedipus and, indeed, our pride and ignorance.

Many things are involved here. Once again Freud draws attention to a type of knowledge so devastating as to be unbearable in one's sight, and only slightly more bearable as a subject of psychological interpretation. In essence, this knowledge is of incest, which can be very correctly described as a tangling-up of the family sequence. For instead of a father and mother reproducing the line of generation in a son, and the son in his turn doing the same thing, the son becomes another lover of the mother and killer of his father. Oedipus is not simply king, father, and husband, but also parricide, adulterous son, royal criminal, and national calamity. The tangle of roles resists ordinary sequential understanding, for the original author of the family line, the father, is murdered and his place usurped by the son. What overwhelms Oedipus is the burden of plural identities incapable of coexisting within one person. In such a case the image of a man conceals behind its facade multiple meanings and multiple determinations. What in the classical novel had been a family romance becomes, in Freud's interpretation of the Greek tragedy, an almost unbearably complex tangling of opposites.

The collapse of the one into the many, of the genealogical line into a plurality of "unnatural" relationship, of systematic linear analysis into a tangled skein of problems—all these leave sustained effects in consciousness. For the writer a major effect is that the authority of what he says is undermined by the possibility that, unconsciously, he either does not or cannot say what he means. When Vico said that man achieves rationality when he conceives the gods as chaining the titans (in a gesture he sees as paving the way for the historical, linear procession of human life, and also for a narrative account of that life), Freud's text, as he says, serves to release those repressed forces. They do not come forth unaided, but by virtue of a conscious wish. This contradictory union obscures the otherwise clear sequence of conscious process:

> My supposition is that a conscious wish can only become a dream-instigator if it succeeds in awakening an unconscious wish with the same tenor and in obtaining reinforcement from it. From indications derived from the psycho-analysis of the neurosis, I consider that these unconscious wishes are always on the alert, ready at any time to find their way to expression when an opportunity arises for allying themselves with an impulse from the conscious and for transferring their own great intensity on to the latter's lesser one. It will then *appear* as though the conscious alone had been realized

in the dream; only some peculiarity in the dream's configuration will serve as a finger-post to put us on the track of the powerful ally from the unconscious. These wishes in our unconscious, ever on the alert and, so to say, immortal, remind one of the legendary Titans, weighed down since primeval ages by the massive bulk of the mountains which were once hurled upon them by the victorious gods and which are still shaken from time to time by the convulsion of their limbs. (p. 553)

These convulsions are perceptible initially as a change in the form of a wish—or for that matter, in the form of a statement, image, or word. Verbal slips, dreams, and the like have in common with poetic form that they are *interventions* in the ongoing course of things, not additions to it. Where once stood a *pater familias,* or an unfolding plot, or a single image (like a Platonic idea of the father) that bred successive and genealogically related "children," we have instead a break in the sequence:[100] one image is then grasped as an inadequate summary of several thoughts; Oedipus is a king whose position in Thebes cannot exhaust his incestuous history; a text is not the sum of its words added together; an author—his scientific detachment and professional discretion notwith-standing—is not free of the unseemly implications of his writing.

Freud's words keep such ideas at bay. The text is not only not a supplement to them, it is a defense against them, an alternative way of dealing with them. For if such jumbles as can be produced by the incestuous, repressed unconscious are inexpressible in sequential discursive prose, they are nevertheless quite capable of suddenly breaking through the words. Beyond the reach of genealogy, and yet more devastating than any logically productive agency, these "presences" impart a new freedom of organization to words, children, ideas—all those pluralities freed from the domination of a single original cause, like the father or the image. This is a positive result. The text, for example, no longer need be confined to consecutive explanation, even as it remains scientific, rational, and realistic. Such is the case with Freud's discourse. On the other hand, the text is vulnerable: it will always appear to hedge its assertions; it can never be complete; it must constantly defend itself against the penetrations of the "tangled" obscure. Many years later, Freud's historical and anthropological researches led him to see these eventualities writ large in the story of the primal horde dislodging the father from his position of supremacy; the children all become brothers then, and the father is resacri-ficed and venerated in religious rites. Still later, in *Moses and Monotheism,* Freud averred how the idea of paternalism, before it became oppressive, signified an advance in thought over the matriarchal idea: "Maternity is proved by the evidence of the senses while paternity is a hypothesis, based on an inference and a premise." Freud connects this advance with the discovery and acceptance of "intellectual [*geistige*] forces . . . [that] cannot be apprehended by the senses, particularly by the sight, but which nonetheless produce undoubted, and indeed even extremely powerful effects."[101] That these effects may, like religion, comprise a higher, more spiritual illusion about *homo natura* does not controvert their strength.

In any case, Freud's repeated analysis of the ambivalent father throughout his career can be considered as confirming some general conclusions we can now put forward. In a material and legal way, the role of father for a text is taken by the author, whose ideas, argument, and conclusions are viewed as emerging sequentially in the writing, as being his offspring. As a scientist, of course, Freud had no wish to confine his text in this sort of enclosure. Yet his theory of infantile sexuality frankly acknowledges exactly this sort of regression, a determinism so severe that it literally spares no individual. Thus the text of the *Interpretation* can be traced back step by step to Freud's own self-analysis and the discovery of his own Oedipus complex; nevertheless, of this period he said, "Insight such as this falls to one's lot but once in a lifetime" (p. xxxii). An equally powerful motif in the book is its status as genuine interpretation whose value is at best illustrated— not validated—by its author's experience. What the prose keeps equally in abeyance is the formal disorder of unmethodical structure *and* the material disorder of private obsessions, problems, and experiences. It is much too fanciful to say that the *Interpretation* does away with, or kills, its author-father, Freud. But I think it is not too much to say that the book devises a textual solution for discussing what cannot be divorced from man's most intimate experience without concurrently becoming an impersonal recitation of laboratory results. Another way of expressing this is to say that the material determinism of a beginning is lifted from the writing, so that as a *text* it can be shown to have an effective, or theoretical, beginning.

Throughout the text there is something highly dramatic about the way Freud struggles to ground interpretation in something more theoretically distinguished as a starting point, or beginning, than his own experience. "Do as I do in remembrance of me" is *not* the kind of ritual celebration Freud expected of his readers.

Instead, I think, Freud willfully abandoned paternal originality in order to be able to erect in its place a structure of theoretical understanding. The key step in each of Freud's analyses in the book, as well as the structure's beginning, is the abandonment of quasi-natural continuity—continuity as paternal authority, as the dream's "plot," as Freud's narrative history of his experiences, as the "step-by-step" logic of consecutive explanation. Moreover, it was no small achievement to associate the abandonment of sequential continuity with the intentional shift to language, as well as with the bypassing of censorship:

> Nevertheless, what Schiller describes as a relaxation of the watch upon the gates of Reason, the adoption of an attitude of uncritical self-observation, is by no means difficult . . . . I myself can do so very completely, by the help of writing down my ideas as they occur to me. The amount of psychical energy by which it is possible to reduce critical activity and increase the intensity of self-observation varies considerably according to the subject on which one is trying to fix one's attention.
>
> Our first step in the employment of this procedure teaches us that what we must take as the object of our attention is not the dream as a whole but the separate portions of its content . . . . If . . . I put the dream before [a patient] cut up into pieces, he will give me a series of associations to each piece, which might be described as the "background thoughts" of that particular part of the dream. Thus the method of dream interpretation which I practise already differs in this first important respect from the popular, historic and legendary method of interpretation by means of symbolism and approximates to the second or "decoding" method. Like the latter, it employs interpretation *en détail* and not *en masse;* like the latter, it regards dreams from the very first as being of a composite character, as being conglomerates of psychical formations. (pp. 103-4)[102]

What enables one to decode these conglomerates is the existence of a force called "secondary revision," whose function is to perform a "transvaluation of all psychical values" (p. 507). This transvaluation obeys certain rules that any analyst can uncover by interpretation and that form the basis of the codes peculiar to the dream.

No dream, then, is the privileged creature of its author, for each dream obeys the dictates of a universal "dream-work," a transindividual faculty present in each human and whose purpose is to produce dreams at night and daydreams during wakefulness. Regarding the decoding of secondary revision, as with decoding the other characteristics of dreams, no one can achieve meaningful results except in the analytic situation. Underlying the *Interpretation* is the analytic relationship between dreamer and interpreter. It is this relationship, I believe, that replaces the author's univocity. Although the *Interpretation* is *by* Freud, it also marks the beginning—theoretical, formal, effective—of psychoanalysis, whose core condition of existence will thereafter become the analytic encounter, which corrects the distortions in the family tangles brought to light by interpretation. In several of his retrospective writings, Freud constantly emphasized that this relationship brings to light "an intense emotional" bond whose technical name is "*transference,* . . . a factor . . . which can claim, alike technically and theoretically, to be regarded as of the first importance." When "it is affectionate and moderate, . . . [transference] is neither more nor less than the mainspring of the joint work of analysis."[103] Insofar as interpretation is concerned, then, Freud sees analysis as a joint venture that makes possible a mutual discourse.

What keeps such a discourse from being hermetic—although it is hermetic in that it is mainly, though not exclusively, clinical—is that transference is of a part with "each person's relations to his human environment." In the evolving discursive relationship between patient and analyst, Freud prefigured and encapsulated a change very similar to the one that transformed the patriarchal primal horde into the brotherly clan. From being father, legislator, authority undisputed, the analyst becomes brother, interlocutor, discursive partner. Moreover, in Freud's autobiographical sketches the reader becomes accustomed to yet another parallel transformation of this kind—the one in which Freud, the lonely "wounder" of man, becomes one of a band of like-minded scientists. In each case, Freud's work accomplishes the institutionalization of its beginning intention, the effort to understand psychological reality as something essentially available only to interpretation, and yet available to neither direct representability (one cannot draw pictures of it, nor mimetically portray it in language) nor univocal statement. A beginning intention, therefore, is in constant need of reworking: it is not, like the "author" an origin to which, by virtue of precedence and unchanging being, everything can be referred for explanation. Above all, an intention in the psychoanalytic discourse is the immediate practical application of the mutuality between men which ensues when a repressive central authority is removed. Nietzsche's distinctions between *origin* and *purpose* in the passage that follows correspond to the distinctions I have been making between *author* (origin) and *beginning intention* (purpose and interpretation):

The cause of the origin of a thing and its eventual utility, its actual employment and place in a system of purposes, lie worlds apart; whatever exists, having somehow come into being, is again and again reinterpreted to new ends, taken over, transformed, and redirected by some power superior to it; all events in the organic world are a subduing, a *becoming master,* and all subduing and becoming master involves a fresh interpretation, an adaptation through which any previous "meaning" and "purpose" are necessarily obscured or even obliterated. . . .

Purposes and utilities are only *signs* that a will to power has become master of something less powerful and imposed upon it the character of a function; and the entire history of a "thing," an organ, a custom can in this way be a continuous sign-chain of ever new interpretations and adaptations whose causes do not even have to be related to one another but, on the contrary, in some cases succeed and alternate with one another in a purely chance fashion. The "evolution" of a thing, a custom, an organ is thus by no means its *progressus* towards a goal, even less a *progressus* by the shortest route and with the smallest expenditure of force—but a succession of more or less profound, more or less mutually independent processes of subduing, plus the resistances they encounter, the attempts at transformation for the purpose of defense and reaction, and the results of successful counteractions. The form is fluid, but the "meaning" is even more so.[104]

Nietzsche's emphatic concerns here include identifying the interpretive discourse as a function of those in power. This is candidly to assert that between analyst and patient, for example, there exists a power over life: life is no longer the natural sequence of events, but has instead turned into an interpreted series, a made *career,* a reconstructed chain of interpretations. Such a series can in turn become something to be protected and conserved, similar to what in his later writings (like *Beyond the Pleasure Principle*) Freud was to describe as the "will to repeat," its purpose and method. Nevertheless, the particular advantage of the analytic discourse lies in its ability to lay bare not only the system of resistance, inhibitions, complexes, and symptoms overlaying man's ambition to love and work, but also the specific complexes discovered (or invented) by psychoanalysis, such as excessive transference, dependency, resistance to the discovery of resistance, defensive mechanisms arising in the analyst himself, and so on. Much of Freud's metapsychological writing underscores this fertility. Because of it, psychoanalysis inspired new discoveries and made possible new revisions and interpolations; and not least of all, because of its fertility psychoanalysis evolved into an institutionalized form of discourse distinguished as much by its enemies as by its adherents, as much for the virtuosity of attacks upon it as for the ingenuity of its new formulations.

Of course, it is largely hindsight that allows us to associate this fertility with Freud's unhappiness with the *Interpretation* as a written textual object. He did in fact find fault with the book's lack of form, its involved sentences, its indirect phrases, its incomplete mastery of the material (see his letter to Fliess, September 21, 1899).[105] As we shall see in the next chapter, this sort of dissatisfaction also characterizes the modern writer whose work intentionally begins moving away from the traditional continuities of form and toward projects whose trajectory must be created, in Merleau-Ponty's phrase, as a constant experience, without distinctive form, without authorizing imagery, without a predetermined "*progressus* toward a goal." Such a text as Freud's sacrifices what I have called finality, and with it adequacy, for the sake of a type of indeterminacy which, in Freud's case, is necessarily congruent with a reality largely unknown (the unconscious) and always incompletely grasped by language. Just as the author's vocation is transformed into a career by constant reinterpretation—a theme I shall also examine in chapter 4—so too the text yields up its formal completeness to a constantly reforged discursivity or productivity. Such a text cannot, by definition, be confined, either theoretically or ethically, within the limits of its language genealogically considered. This is not simply because it is assumed that the reader treats the text with a sometime accurate, sometime inaccurate, but always imperious will. Rather, it is because the subject of the text constantly experiences imperfect, incomplete realization, for which psychoanalytic interpretive language is by definition, if not supplementary—which it never is—then another alternative.

As much as he seemed to disparage and disown the efforts of his disciples to make of psychoanalysis an explicit *Weltanschauung,* Freud could not but recognize that the psychoanalytic viewpoint was in fact just such an alternative available to the culture. Its role was not limited to rivaling other disciplines, however; it also served to complement them and, in the case of literature, prolong them. One speculates what the later Freud felt as he witnessed the books he had authored becoming the fundamental authorizing texts of a new science. Probably he felt a strange combination of pride, resignation, and jealousy. He cannot have been ignorant of the fact that his texts established not only a precedent but also a sustaining structure of language; and it was this language that determined the bounds of *what was psychoanalytically possible to say.* From these doxological bounds Freud himself was not exempt. To read his later revisionist works (*The*

Ego and the Id, for instance, or *Civilization and Its Discontents*) is to witness the structure of psychoanalytic theory refining the possibility of even its author's statement, refining itself, placing new limits on itself and on him. This is especially true of Freud's reclaiming for the unconscious some of the "territory" he had previously found occupied by consciousness, which, in his wish to school it in rationality, seemed after all more closely allied with repression.

These tendencies in the Freudian text are aspects of the "serious consequences" that Freud said were involved with "the raising of the thought-process . . . above perception."[106] *The Interpretation of Dreams* began the step by laying out a vocabulary for dealing with a reality that was "unconscious," unknown, indescribable, and yet present. The text of the book, in describing dream imagery by means of quasi-grammatical combinatorial rules of formation, is a record of accommodations made between ascertainable work (the presence of the unknown in a dream) and the ascertainable limits of knowledge (beyond which the unconscious is a blank). This sounds very much like Freud's definition of a dream as a compromise between the wishes of two systems, unconscious and preconscious, "in so far as they are compatible with each other" (p. 579). The text, such as it is, with all the problems and characteristics we have discussed, *is* that maximum compatibility Freud was able to achieve between alternating presence and absence.

One of the most challenging motifs pervading the text of the *Interpretation* takes us still further into the question of presence and absence: "The unconscious is the true psychical reality; *in its innermost nature it is as much unknown to us as the reality of the external world, and it is as incompletely presented by the data of consciousness as is the external world by the communications of our sense organs*" (p. 613). Reported and transcribed dreams are among the data of consciousness, data which gained in substance, if not in reality, once they were admitted into analytic language (from memory) for interpretation. A dream is always private, although "a thought . . . is objectified in the dream, [and] is represented as a scene, or, as it seems to us, is experienced" (p. 534).

This experience achieves a heightened reality, however, when it is reported and analyzed. The virtue of psychoanalytic interpretation is that it confers upon even the most absurd and trivial dream experiences the materiality of a scientific object. Words are the means of doing this, and it is the materiality of language that further objectifies dreams, draws them out from the recesses of subjectivity, where they guard sleep, and admits them into discourse. Freud's argument is that such a bringing to light, such a materialization, increases the analytic value of a dream by putting it into words; yet paradoxically, from the point of view of psychical reality, the verbal dream has lost still more of the reality which in the experienced dream took the form of distortion, displacement, and so on.

Carrying this logic a bit further, one can say that in analysis a further distortion takes place, since by translating the dream into words the original experiences are further removed from their first form. However, this does not seem to be in fact the case. A dream-image is itself a substitute for what Freud calls "the constrictions of thinking" (p. 344). "Each dream—whose distortions more or less closely expose the unconscious—therefore is a neater, more economic, more discrete device for bearing the pressures of the unconscious. Thus, for example, propinquity in subject-matter is expressed by the dream as propinquity in time": in just the same way, Freud adds, "if I write an '*a*' and a '*b*' in succession, they have to be pronounced as a single syllable '*ab*' " (p. 247). Were thought to express itself in the same amount of time as a single syllable, thinking—as opposed to the manipulation of imagery—would take up more space, become crowded together, and fail to find a way to express a wish. For the image to be decoded, it would have to be attacked as a single entity and decomposed into the thoughts which it had replaced. Thus the images of a dream, the interpretive verbal transcription of the dream, and the attendant analysis belong to different orders of substitution. While taking different forms, each bears a trace of the unconscious: the image as distortion, the transcription as pseudocontinuity or plot, the analysis as thoughts leading to a (supposed) wish.

Now certainly no one of these seemingly distinct orders can be entirely detached from the others within the entire period of interpretation. No one can occur without the other, just as conceptually, for Freud, each order necessarily implies the coexistence of the others. Yet I think it is correct to say that Freud's general scheme in the *Interpretation* is that the "original" reality, the unconscious, is for the purposes of analysis given as a nonpresent, not immediately apprehendable force. Each successive verbal version of a dream, beginning with the image, through the transcription, to a practically interminable analysis, does not so much make clear what the unconscious is as begin and continue the traces of the unconscious in language. The written text, because it is at least materially evident in print and on paper, is not the last effort to capture these traces; as part of a discourse presuming previous substitutions and assuming later ones (respectively, Freud's own self-analyses and his later writings) the text is part of an ongoing effort, a practically unending series of substitutions. In what direction and toward what sorts of either tentative or fixed conclusion the series may go cannot concern us here, although a remarkable indication of how profoundly and how dynamically Freud saw the process is given in his late paper "Analysis Terminable and Interminable."[107]

Because it has the merit of constituting a rare moment of insight at the beginning of Freud's career, *The Interpretation of Dreams* is an inaugural text. Nevertheless, theoretically and even materially its status as a beginning *includes* its superceding itself as beginning. In other words, because it is a substitute, because it comes between a before and an after, because as a whole it cannot claim to have gone unequivocally forward from one point to another, what is most true of the text is that it collects traces of the unconscious in varying forms of verbal behavior, with varying degrees of distortion, occupying varying amounts of interpretive space. Even though certain stages are reached and certain points made, the dynamic of interpretation precludes a fixed beginning, even an arbitrary one to which one can refer retrospectively. All this is true of the text considered as part of an institution we have called the psychoanalytic discourse. Yet in one absolutely crucial sense, the text as a whole retains a particular beginning *function.* As the physical location where dream-thoughts are verbally created for the purposes of analysis, the text is, as Freud implies, continuously novel. Previously, attempts to arrive at a dream's meaning worked directly on its manifest content. But

we are alone in taking something else into account. We have introduced a new class of psychical material between the manifest content of dreams and the conclusions of our enquiry: namely, their *latent* content, or, (as we say) the "dream-thoughts," arrived at by the means of our procedure. It is from these dream-thoughts and not from a dream's manifest content that we disentangle its meaning. We are thus presented with a new task which had no previous existence: the task, that is, of investigating the relations between the manifest content of dreams and the dream-thoughts, and of tracing out the processes by which the latter have been changed into the former. (p. 277)

The text's innovation is that as a body it intervenes between the dream-images (manifest content) and the dream's thought and meanings. The text allows—indeed, occasions, as Freud goes on to say—a comparison between the original dream-thoughts and their "translation" into the language of manifest dream-images. Lest this seem to make of the text a passive object, Freud indicates emphatically that the text is the producer and formulator of a new task; that is, the existence of the text as intervention between manifest content and meaning is coterminous with the task of showing the *connections* between manifest content and meaning. Another way of understanding Freud's meaning is to regard the text as coming into being whenever the task of connecting a dream's manifest content and the dream-thoughts is *intended*. Once this occurs, the dream can be regarded as a picture puzzle or rebus, and "each separate element [is replaced] . . . by a syllable or word that can be represented by that [pictorial] element in some way or other" (p. 278). So long as the replacement of one by the other continues, given individual particularities of style, culture, and historical circumstance, the text is being produced. The text of a specific book called *The Interpretation of Dreams* is the beginning of the text of other such interpretations, all of which, according to Foucault, we can consider as constituting the psychoanalytic discourse.[108]

One does the text a considerable disservice, however, by failing to take account of its subversive force—indeed, its power to remind the reader of unpleasant ideas without which Freud's work would seem pallid. Among these ideas Freud included his theories of resistance and transference, although he realized quite unmistakably that even these lacked the negative effect of his ideas on sexuality. The latter, of course, left its imprint on the *Interpretation,* but in circumstances that Freud was later to elucidate more fully and more interestingly. In his "History of the Psychoanalytic Movement" (1914) he tells how his fight for "a new original idea"—the determining role of sexuality in psychical life generally and in the etiology of the neuroses particularly—helped offset the hostility that his propagation of the idea generated. Yet one day his "memories grouped themselves in such a way as to disturb this satisfaction." He found that discovery of his idea in fact belonged to three other men—Breuer, Charcot, and Chrobak—whose timidity had caused them to draw back from their own conclusions. The difference between Freud and them was put this way by Freud:

I am well aware that it is one thing to give utterance to an idea once or twice in the form of a passing *aperçu,* and quite another to mean it seriously—to take it literally and pursue it in the face of every contradictory detail, and to win it a place among accepted truths. It is the difference between a casual flirtation and a legal marriage with all its duties and difficulties. "Epouser les idées de . . ." is not an uncommon figure of speech, at any rate in French.[109]

What they refused to do was commit themselves seriously to a problematical idea. Freud's way of doing his duty was, figuratively, to marry it, a course which he obviously identifies with public and theoretical profession of the idea. One offspring of the marriage is the *Interpretation,* a permanent written record of fidelity, winning its place—the metaphor fits very well with what we said of the text as doing what Nietzsche called reinterpreting, overcoming, and outstripping—among accepted truths. This is in contrast to the spoken but unwritten recognition of the idea by Freud's predecessors, who abandoned it as a rake would a passing flirt. That Freud would in this manner also reassert his paternal role as author rings quite beautifully true to his achievement, noted earlier, of ceding authorial paternalism in the *Interpretation* to a structure of theoretical understanding. For now in the "History" he shows that what the natural *father(s)* of the idea abandoned, he, as foster parent, legally adopted and nurtured. In other words, the idea of sexuality, which had been abandoned either to passing *aperçus* or to the casual obscenity, Freud *implanted* in scientific discourse. Or as he says on the same page in his "History": "I have not of course disclosed the illustrious parentage of this scandalous idea in order to saddle other people with the responsibility of it."

Thus the text constitutes responsibility to *old* subversive ideas, a haven for the wicked knowledge of the ancients, a place for cultivating what in the *Phaedrus* Socrates called "the living word of knowledge," which is different from words "tumbled out anywhere . . . [with] no parent to protect them" (p. 276). In short, the text as well as the author reinstate difficult knowledge by giving that knowledge a sort of human pedigree. Even though the ideas contained in the *Interpretation* make of Freud (who quotes Hebbel here) "a disturber of sleep," the ideas in the text, or perhaps the idea of the text, is restored to a human family that had disowned it. Because of the text, that is, dreams and other potentially disturbing manifestations of psychical life are shown to be connected genealogically *as knowledge* with previous kinds of knowledge whose unpleasantness, elusiveness, and universality

181

require the parental care and responsibility and solicitous courage of an author. What is distinctive about this knowledge is not that it needed someone to create it—for it is, after all, a timeless knowledge of "prehistoric" things—but that it needed a locale in which to be developed fully in order for it to become knowledge. Its "biography" is important only in that it has one (which proves that it is not the product of an alienated, celibate mind, but of a community), not because as such its genealogy can make it easier to understand or accept. For as one reads such a text, one is increasingly grateful for its ability to take physical responsibility for ideas whose direction is both out of sight and out of consciousness and, in a deeply troubling way, beyond the bounds of human biography.

When one thinks, for example, of Proust's attitudes toward the novel or of Kafka's use of fiction to respond textually to what is, among other things, certain and essentially elusive, Freud's researches as the maker of a text about dreams appreciate in critical value for the study of novels. Freud's frankness in admitting that his text haltingly transacts, as it were, between appearance and meaning, that its innovation resides in the fact of its beginning intervention between two fundamentally unending, unconfineable movements away from consciousness, that compared to it biography can be seen as either an aspect of interpretation or as evidence of transhuman problems, that the indeterminacy of its language is a sign of a radical compromise in order to deal with the present and the unknown, and, finally, that as a text its language and its textuality together comprise one element in a series leading further and further away from psychical reality even though nearer and nearer to discursive, institutional permanence—all these present the critic of novels with instruments for reading Mann's *Doctor Faustus,* of all great modern novels the most thoroughly imbued with the history of novels as an institution, the novel most conscious of how overripe it is late in that history, and the novel nearest to a kind of dizzying anarchism in which the text as beginning effort coincides with the end, or final unsuitability, of man as a subject that can be represented using the written language.

The physical text of *Doctor Faustus* is the result of Zeitblom's effort to preserve a portion of his own and his nation's history during a period of unprecedented civil convulsion. More than that, however, his chronicle of Leverkuhn purports to translate into "human letters" the facts of a life and an achievement whose central feature is a radical, antihumanistic divorce from the life of men. Thus music and an artist's constantly self-transcending career together comprise a total rejection of the premise that what is human is knowable, is verbally describable, is consecutively developing, is capable of subordination to "the human image." On the other hand, Zeitblom's life and time, as he writes, are in the grip of national changes in a Germany whose increasing irrationality eludes ordinary sense. The pages he produces therefore attempt a mediation (or intervention) between two parallel histories—one Germany's, a manifest outer history of increasing eccentricity, the other Leverkuhn's, an inner career of musical works whose principal thoughts and cultural importance *require* representation in either words or images. The position of Zeitblom's text between two such disparities strikingly reproduces the position of Freud's text between the manifest content of dreams and their meaning. Like *The Interpretation of Dreams*, Zeitblom's text allows for a comparative study between Adrian's life and music and its translation into German history.

An exigency of the novel's explicit textual project as I have described it, the Faustus-Devil story works in two principal ways. First, the text's structure is an unlimited parody consisting of innumerable parallelisms. At bottom, such a structure reminds the reader that, as Freud had said to his reader of dreams, there are no innocent details in the text: as in a dream, each detail or image in some way corresponds with one or more dream-thoughts. If one such correspondence is admitted, no matter how arbitrary either the connection or the image, there must be correspondence everywhere—this is the fundamental rule of dream interpretation.[110] In *Doctor Faustus* the "elements" of the text—characters, plot, motif, symbols, themes, and so forth—are themselves employed in the text as parallel elements. This technique supports Zeitblom's effort to parallel Adrian and Germany. Just as Johan Leverkuhn's speculating over elements shows how inorganic crystals mime and parallel organic nature, so too each element in the text mimes, sometimes parodies, another element. Thus, to list a few examples: Zeitblom and Adrian, the scholar and the artist, *haetera esmeralda* and the motifs based on it in Adrian's music, the structure of parallels in the novel and the tone-row principle of composition, Germany and Adrian, music and theology, Kaisersaschern and Pfeiffering, disease and genius, language and music, Adrian and Faust, parody and counterpoint—

and on and on. The point of all this is that nothing can exist *temporally* without corresponding with, standing in relation to, something else: because of such correspondence and the consequent engaging relationships (and not because of each "element" intrinsically), there is meaning. It is as theoreticians of this diacritical principle of meaning that Mann characterizes both the Devil and Adrian in their encounter. The result of that encounter is that every artistic achievement, moment, or gesture comes to appear as something that excludes every other one: this is itself a parallel of the Nietzschean idea of overcoming, in which the artist, by excluding everything except the aesthetic faculty, creates a "world." In reality, however, the artistic statement by ruthless exclusion *includes* (in the same way the excluded unconscious is included in the meaning of a dream) every other statement in order for it to make meaning: the opposition between aesthetic and nonaesthetic begins *aesthetic* meaning.

What the Devil reveals to Adrian is that in art there has been a turning against "the self-contained work." In music, for instance, the material

shrinks in time, it scorns extension in time, which is the dimensions of a musical work, and lets it stand empty. Not out of impotence, not out of incapacity to give form. Rather from a ruthless demand for compression, which taboos the superfluous, negates the phrase, shatters the ornament, stands opposed to any extension of time, which is the life-form of the work.[111]

In both language and music, time imparts to composition the authority of sustained creation, the temporal duration of a prolonged world exemplified by the classical novel and the symphony. The Devil's observation emphasizes how the parallelism between the time of an artistic composition and the dynastic continuities of nature tends historically to make the artist regard art as an unhealthy encroachment upon nature. This is the phase realized in *Jude the Obscure,* among other works, where *compression,* the collapse of time, is felt to be the more proper prerogative of art. The more compressed in his work an artist becomes, the Devil becomes, the more power he exercises, the further from miming nature and truths his art moves. Art becomes increasingly "untruth of a kind that enhances power [and] holds its own against any ineffectively virtuous truth."[112] The demonic artist is given (or takes) the right in his work to break through temporality, as well as the meaning that is based upon the mimesis of nature in art, in order to become "elemental." In breaking

184

through time, the artist grasps the absolute beginning, free of all natural, historical, and social restraints, and in so doing becomes doubly barbaric, both absolutely primitive and the representative of the absolute refinement of all history and art. The Faustian contract requires that in return for that power and, ironically, for the fulfillment of that total power to begin, Adrian must ultimately pay the price of damnation, hell, silence:

> Only it is not easy actually to speak thereof—that is, one can really not speak of it at all, because the actual is beyond what by word can be declared; many words may be used and fashioned, but all together they are but tokens, standing for names which do not and cannot make claim to describe what is never to be described and denounced in words. That is the secret delight and security of hell, that it is not to be informed on, that it is protected from speech, that it just is, but cannot be public in the newspaper, be brought by any word to critical knowledge, wherefore precisely the words "subterranean," "cellar," "thick walls," "soundlessness," "forgottenness," "hopelessness," are the poor, weak symbols. One must just be satisfied with symbolism, my good man, when one is speaking of hell, for there everything ends—not only the word that describes, but everything altogether. This is indeed the chiefest characteristic and what in most general terms is to be uttered about it: both that which the newcomer first experiences, and what at first with his as it were sound senses he cannot grasp, and will not understand, because his reason or what limitation soever of his understanding prevents him.[113]

Here the beginning and the end are finally one, since by demonic logic a radical element in its purity is an absolute presence basically resistant to time or development; hence the fact of its beginning is also its end.

If Zeitblom's text is, as we said above, a place where Leverkuhn's career can be compared with German history, then the included whole of Adrian's discussion with the Devil in Zeitblom's narrative shatters the compromise of the old scholar's text. For the "fiction" underlying Zeitblom's writing is that although Adrian and Germany are disparate entities, a written document can relate them to one another: Mann's use of parallelism is vindicated by the material text itself, which with all its own internal parallelism and correspondence places itself *between* the artist's career and the national story, using the former to understand the latter. Yet the Devil's visit disturbs the text's intervening position—and now we come to the second principal use of the Faust-Devil motif. Just as the regularity of the "natural" human order is disrupted by the appearance of the Devil, in Zeitblom's text the regular course of his narrative is disrupted in chapter 25 by "Adrian's secret record." For this is the only time in *Doctor Faustus* Adrian speaks directly to the reader. So anxious is Zeitblom to preserve the force of this "frightful and precious treasure" that he transcribes the words by hand from Adrian's music paper: not even the printer was to see the treasure. Moreover, Zeitblom must cease to speak in order that the new text can reach us. When the chapter ends, Zeitblom returns to his narrative "undisturbed" by the "unreasonable demands" that Adrian's text has made on the reader.

Yet Zeitblom seems aware, now as never before, that his text is a complex temporal object tied to "a threefold ordering of time"[114] —the reader's time, the chronicler's time, and historical time. Thus the text takes over, substitutes itself for Adrian's life, and redisposes that life into a text. Zeitblom reflects with an author's characteristic vanity:

> Certainly the time in which I write has vastly greater historical momentum than the time of which I write, Adrian's time, which brought him only to the threshold of our incredible epoch. I feel as though one should call out to him, as to all those who are no longer with us and were not with us when it began: "Lucky you!" and a fervent "Rest in peace!" Adrian is safe from the days we dwell in. The thought is dear to me, I prize it, and in exchange for that certainty I accept the terrors of the time in which I continue to live on. It is to me as though I stood here and lived for him, lived instead of him; as though I bore the burden his shoulders were spared, as though I showed my love by taking upon me living for him, living in his stead. The fancy, however illusory, does me good, it flatters the always cherished desire to serve, to help, to protect him—this desire which during the lifetime of my friend found so very little satisfaction.[115]

Regardless of Zeitblom's protestations, the rawness and density of Adrian's own direct speech is not obscured, either literally and figuratively, by the comparatively neat, consecutive, humane narrative that Zeitblom has produced for the composer. Like Adrian's music, which is "heard" in the novel only as a function of Zeitblom's narrative, and like the third movement of Beethoven's Opus 111 whose absence is explained in Kretschmar's lectures, language cannot match the void it tries to describe. Adrian's silence, as composer and as damned genius, exceeds the powers of narrative to contain it. Indeed, Adrian's encounter with the Devil symbolizes precisely what stands outside verbal temporality—a sort of speculative delirium uniting absolute radicality with the satanic discontinuity following a moment of indescribably final and inventive rationality. For if the text as an intervention between manifest appearance and (artistic) thought is an interpretive compromise between the two, then any intervention within the text overwhelms the compromise. Across written language there bursts proof of how a text is but one in a series of verbal substitutes for what cannot be put into words—substitutes leading to and from an "irrational" or unknown point.

The tendency of *Doctor Faustus* as a whole seems nonetheless to support the humanness of Zeitblom's effort to chronicle and historicize the elemental, the barbaric, and the nonverbal. The novel's cultural moment indicates as much, for in Mann's career it corresponds with a self-critical phase in which he came to terms with the question of German responsibility for the Second World War. Mann's feat as a novelist was to put into verbal and artistic form that which historically seemed either to negate or to transcend words and art. Thus Zeitblom's sense of duty coincides with Mann's: both recognize that in such circumstances as Germany's, even an act of narration is a moral act in which the narrator seeks, through the "humaneness" of narrative, to overcome the negation of narrative in German history. Because it is a temporal art of sustained duration, narrative also sets itself against the demonic thesis that the only serious art is "the very short, the highly consistent musical moment."[116] Moreover, the biographical mode of the narrative, announced on the title page, was intended to restore to narrative its capacity for formal "play and pretence," which conflicted with everything about Adrian's life, with its interest in knowledge, intensity, atemporality, and unmediated statement. Therefore, the frequent rhetorical excesses of Zeitblom's text constitute a kind of salutary balance to the dionysiac intensity of the composer's icy rationality.

These characteristics represent a tendency that is, I think, acceptable to most readers of the novel; there can be little doubt that Mann rather consciously placed them as close as possible to the novel's surface. Yet also near that same surface is the fact that both Zeitblom and Adrian are deliberate creatures of the pen—Zeitblom for moral reasons, Adrian for Zeitblom's reasons. They belong less to the mimetic, representable world of the classical novel than to the authorizing power of *writing,* the very fact which signifies something quite opposed to the novel as an institution. As writing, *Doctor Faustus* intervenes in reality so that writing as presence may stand before, may attempt to *precede,* a total flight from the responsibilities of history. In writing, Zeitblom hopes to begin a restoration of Germany and of Adrian in the form of a text of some sort, for otherwise Adrian's tragedy as well as Germany's would have to remain locked within the wordless cry of that last collapse: "I might compare his absentness to an abyss, into which one's feeling towards him dropped soundless and without a trace."[117] The text is an effort, therefore, "to coordinate language and passion"[118] within a formal structure.

But writing that not only is a beginning, but itself begins by introducing the notion of a formal structure existing outside ("not as framework but as houses") its material, plays with theoretical complexities that cannot be ignored. To what extent is the text like the paralyzed composer in 1939?—"he that was once Adrian Leverkuhn, whose immortal part is now so called .... What a mocking game Nature here [i.e., in his physical appearance] played, one might say: presenting a picture of the utmost spirituality, just there whence the spirit had fled!"[119] What is there to prevent writing from spinning out a clever surface, an "inaccessible communication" part ornament, part illiterate symbol? From being the form of secondary communication, with its mimetic authority derived genealogically from an "original" reality, the novel now deliberately draws the reader to its textuality. As with other great modern texts, *Doctor Faustus* on the one hand presents itself as the text of an artistic career while, on the other, its surface virtuosity and ambiguous rationale call attention to its career as a text in relation to which even its "author" is a subordinate function. The novel thus undergoes transformations peculiar to its institutional history; at the same time, it has become involved in a dynamic affecting all literature in the modern period—the specific problematic of a text. We must begin there now.

CHAPTER

FOUR

Beginning with a Text

I

IN his 1968 survey of structuralism, Jean Piaget broadly defined a *structure* as (1) a system of transformations, (2) a totality, (3) something capable of self-regulation (*autoréglage*).[1] These three characterizations of structure are obviously interconnected—though obviously different emphases are possible within the various disciplines influenced by structuralist thought. In his own analysis, Piaget applies his considerable experience as a psychological empiricist and theoretician. For him the central problem in all structuralist theory is that of the connection between antecedence and constructivism, which raises the following series of questions: "Are those totalities formed by structures composed once and for all, or are they always in the process of construction? How are they constructed? By whom?"[2] These issues have as much a bearing on Piaget's theses in genetic epistemology as they do, I think, on the theme of this chapter. For despite recent genuinely investigative tendencies in criticism (in, for example, the work of Roland Barthes), certain conventions, persisting as unexamined vestiges of the whole history of ideas, have a strong hold upon the critical imagination as it tries to grasp what a text exactly is. Such a determination is of quite basic importance. Thus certain questions—such as the nature of the author's (beginning and continued) *authority* over his text, the beginnings and development of an author's work, the location in time and society of a text, and the possibility of the sequential construction of a literary totality viewed as an ensemble of made relationships—remain relevant.

Here is how Piaget phrases his own position on structure, which we can consider for the moment to be also his definition of what a text is:

191

The genesis [of a structure, for example] is never more than a transition from one structure to another, *but also a formative transition [passage formateur] that leads [qui conduit] from a weaker to a stronger [de plus faible au plus fort] structure*; structure is never more than a system of transformations, whose roots remain operative (*dont les racines sont opératoires*) and are therefore held to a preexisting formation of adequate instruments.... From this we derive the following conclusion: that the nature of a subject is to constitute a functional center and not an *a priori* seat for a complete edifice. If we were to replace the notion of "subject" with a social unity, or a species, or life, or even the universe, the case would be the same.[3] [Italics mine]

Of the two important observations here, I shall consider the second one first. Piaget makes a distinction between two possible conceptions of the subject ("la nature du sujet")—that is, the effective, centering motive principle in a structure. One is a conception of subject as preexisting given, as a necessary *a priori* condition for the fully formed structure. The perspective adopted by this conception is wholly that of the completed structure—not as developing, but rather as already developed. Opposed to this conception (which clearly fails to please Piaget) is a view of the subject as a germinal or beginning principle whose force extends throughout, and therefore empowers, a developing, constituting structure. In simple terms, then, Piaget is contrasting a Platonic essence of priority, more formal and logically necessary than efficient, with a plastic, quasi-organic principle of growth proceeding from the simple to the more complex. At any rate, the latter conception is central, whereas the former is practically marginal. I think it ought to be added that Piaget himself would be likely to consider this contrast as by no means exhausting our notions of "subject," nor certainly of center, nor of genesis. The polarity he establishes is not only extreme but convenient, and this for reasons that have mostly to do with the type of experiments in psychological development he has been conducting for many years.*

The clause I emphasized in quoting from Piaget above is crucial: *passage formateur* implies simultaneous graduation, conservation, and formation; the idea of a movement leading toward something (*qui conduit*) suggests intention and direction; and *de*

---

*For an example of the polemical uses to which the polarity might be put (but wouldn't be, I think, by Piaget himself), see Lucien Goldmann's two essays on Piaget in *Recherches dialectiques*. Then, too, there is the relevance of Jacques Derrida's important variations on center, decentering, and difference—themes whose relevance to the fundamentals of classification and opposition is particularly valuable—in *L'Écriture et la différence* and *De la grammatologie*.

plus faible au plus fort requires, I believe, not only greater efficiency and strength in the structure thereby in the process of creation, but also an intensified concentration upon the achievement of completeness. In becoming "stronger," the structure realizes more of its latent powers of incorporation and drops some of the freight that had been hindering its encompassing movement. I am mixing metaphors a little, but I wish to avoid talking of developing force and form in organicist language. What I have in mind is a somewhat abstract scheme that allows one to describe a structure gathering force according to its own special beginnings and laws, not according to those derived generally from nature. Coleridge, for whom the analogy of intellectual growth with natural growth was more or less habitual, brilliantly bypasses the recourse to organicism in the essay on "Method" (number IV of *The Friend*): what Piaget terms "strength" Coleridge calls "generality." Structure develops from mere specificity to impressive, overmastering scope and generality. Thus another meaning for *strength* is wider incorporation and firmness of grasp. As Coleridge sums it up in the fifth essay in the same series: "All method supposes a principle of unity with progression."[5] And since Piaget rightly speaks of structuralism as a method of thought, the link between him and Coleridge is worth making. The two of them, however, remain open to C. S. Peirce's critique of synechism in "The Law of Mind":

> There is but one law of mind, namely, that ideas tend to spread continuously and to affect certain others which stand to them in a peculiar relation of affectability. In this spreading they lose intensity, and especially the power of affecting others, but gain generality and become welded with other ideas.[6]

Loss of intensity is the damaging point here, but one can admit that and still allow that a loss of one kind of intensity is replaced by gaining another kind: direct immediacy is replaced by a greater immediacy of continuity itself ("in this spreading they . . . become welded with other ideas").

All these dangerous abstractions will have been justified if a connection between them and, for the use of a critic of literature, the characterization of a text can be demonstrated. What is first of all necessary is that we situate our discussion as radically as possible; from that vantage point we do not view the text simply, neither as the printed book, an object, nor as a completed edifice of some sort.[7] The given assumptions (usually unexamined) of most literary criticism today can be plainly described as permitting

193

the confrontation of an inquiring critic with a resisting text—that is, between a flexible subject and a completed object. All the activity derives from the critic, to whose swoops and thrusts the text offers a resisting but ultimately compliant surface. Whether the critic seeks out depths (psychological, social, or otherwise) concealed in or by the texts so taken, whether he demonstrates formal relationships (between figures, parts, or otherwise) across the text, or whether he combines both approaches, his *pied-à-terre* is the text-as-completed-book. In the end, as Jorge Luis Borges made the point cleverly in "Pierre Menard, Author of *The Quixote*," although the text is enriched, it is still the same text with which the critic began. If ever the problem of identity were taken up—namely, the question of how an uninterpreted text differs from an interpreted text—we would find all these assumptions supporting a view that the interpreted text was *more like* the uninterpreted one than not. This is because the critic assumes, even imputes, problems to an uninterpreted text (i.e., what does it mean?), and after solving them offers us an object *no longer in need of interpretation*, partially purged (for his purposes) of its problematics. The text is returned to a canon, or a tradition, *more itself* than it had been before.

My earlier discussion of Piaget was designed to force upon us a different approach, the aim of which is to consider the text as a structure in the process of being composed from a certain beginning intention, in the process of realizing a structure. Yet the history of a text—as one contemporary example will prove—reveals the large number of quite different ideas, even if at first glance that seems not to be the case. In the criticism of the Geneva school, preeminently in the monumental studies of Georges Poulet, we have an approach somewhat resembling the one I have just mentioned. Poulet tries first to locate a germinal point out of which the author's project develops, then he shows the project developing, and finally arriving at a point resembling the first.[8] By that time the project is far more deeply and strongly understood. The writer's real text is his "work" taken as a vast and intricate web of connections between various parts. This method is not unlike Spitzer's, which is based on what he called the "circle of understanding," except that Poulet claims to parallel in his own writing, and therefore duplicates, the author's consciousness of totality. The difficulty with Poulet and others working in his school, however, is that no realistic allowance is made for either the brute temporal sequence of an author's production or the author's shaping of the works into independent formal texts.[9] For the Genevans, text is an underlying plenitude of consciousness which, according to Poulet, is only existentially (but not ontologically) compromised by the individual work of art. Poulet's commentary is not metalanguage but a sort of primal language, which can also be characterized as purporting to be the language of unmediated consciousness. What supports it is, of course, Poulet's marvelously penetrating, sympathetic critical imagination. Whether examining Pascal, Amiel, or Proust, Poulet's writing aspires to a privileged level of awareness that runs beneath or above or within (it does not matter which) the finished text-as-product.

The varied range of relationships possible between critic and text is more properly treated as a topic within the sociology of knowledge generally, and the historical and conceptual changes induced in even so apparently unchanging an "object" as the text. Moreover, each historical moment produces its own characteristic forms of the critical act, its own arena in which critic and text challenge one another, and thereby its own depictions of what constitutes a literary text. Consequently, it is wrong to pretend that there is a single notion of text, constant for all literary criticism, just waiting to be discovered. There is definite value, however, in recognizing the philosophical prejudices that have operated, from antiquity to the present, when editors are "establishing a text." For there is an entire history and philosophy surrounding the notion of a reliable text, a history and a philosophy as varied as often as they are concealed, and the editor who takes the naively positivistic attitude that a text can be finally secured on the page does so in unjustified bad faith.*

In this chapter I shall be arguing that the experience of certain major writers who aspire toward a highly specialized ideal of textual achievement as the *beginning* condition of their work must necessarily govern the critic's depiction of a text. What is constant for the critic is that there is always an "authorial" process which, in individual cases, can be grasped once its most notable patterns

*Once one begins to examine the way in which critics today define their relationship to a secure text, a number of curious facts emerge. The most common metaphors used for such definition are spatial, physical, or military: the critic is "close" or "far" from the text; one reads in "slow motion" in order to "get" the sense better; there are "defenses of reading"; and prepositions like "within" and "inside" proliferate. One rarely finds, however, an English-language critic asking where a text takes place, or how it takes place, or what it is, just as it is uncommon for him to consider writing—in its French sense of *écriture*—as anything more than the author's having to take a necessary step along the way to publishing a book or a poem.

are identified. Yet we cannot be truly privy to an author's innermost struggles—except, of course, through his own retrospective, and perhaps inaccurate, accounts. Thus our alternative is to take the author's career as wholly oriented toward and synonymous with the production of a text, especially if the author himself seems obsessively concerned with just that concern over technique or craftsmanship. A further implication is that the author's career is a course whose record is his work and whose goal is the integral text that adequately represents the efforts expended on its behalf. Therefore, the text is a multidimensional structure extending from the beginning to the end of the writer's career. A text is the source and the aim of a man's desire to be an author, it is the form of his attempts, it contains the elements of his coherence, and in a whole range of complex and differing ways it incarnates the pressures upon the writer of his psychology, his time, his society. The unity between career and text, then, is a unity between an intelligible pattern of events and for the most part their increasingly conscious transformation into writing.

If this formulation were left to stand unqualified, it would be open to major criticism. For underlying this view of the text as growing consciousness, regardless of how diverse the expression of this growth, is an accepted teleological progress and development. All of which is true. But of greater moment is the way in which the author's thought succeeds itself in time, and is therefore conscious of passing formatively (Piaget's phrase) from one stage to the next. The sheer weight of completed work, for instance, influences the writer's thought by providing him with examples he need not repeat and experiments he need not try again—or, if he does, at least he knows that he is doing just that. In the sense that he is aware of what he has done, he is more generally conscious of what he can do even if, to take a common enough case, he unconsciously parodies himself some of the time. I shall argue that although the text resembles a never-to-be-fulfilled ideal, a finality never attained even if desired from the very beginning, the author's asymptotic movement toward his goal gives him an increasingly acute sense of what he is doing all the time. Another more convenient way of settling in with a myth of progress here is to say that I shall be concerned with some modern authors whose common trait is that they require from the critic a central thematic of development, one organized around prominent levels of growth from the beginning to the completion of a text.

Yet before entering upon that discussion, I think that a general consideration of some ideas and methods characterizing a text is necessary. In the preceding chapter I examined Freud's *The Interpretation of Dreams* as a work whose subject matter and attitudes are close enough to those of the novel to merit study as a text along with or near the novel. Here I shall propose a different, narrower focus. By restricting myself now to writers from whom a text is in and of itself an actuality of technical, critical, and theoretical moment, I hope to be able later to illuminate generally the modern writer's special problems with his text and its quite particular beginning significance for him. Such a pair of steps will thus permit a relatively disciplined way of understanding a text—neither as a "creative" masterpiece nor as a fact of nature, but as something whose *beginning* condition, irreducibly, is that *it must always be produced, constantly.*

II

Most of the time, the concept of a text carries with it an idea if not of unequivocal achievement, then of distinction, or of prestige based on simple language in use. There are occasions, of course, when *text* is a fairly neutral or even secondary work—for example, when one says of a letter from a friend that its text has such and such a tone or quality. The usual sort of prestige suggested by *text* is preservation: on the assumption that only what has distinction is preserved, the text lifts out or perhaps rescues language from the bustle of time and keeps it in writing. The reason for the preservation, the method of it, the mode, the success, the failure, the persistence of it—all these are aspects of a text that can be subordinated to the idea of preservation itself. The other main distinction of a text is that as a presence it occupies a place actively. Another way of putting this is to say that in being present a text displaces one or a thousand other things; were it not for a text, something else might have been in its place. If that something else is not another text, it could be speech, silence, chaos, etc.; but the presence of a text, usually associated with a *document*, is not simply reducible to what it has displaced nor to an inert object. That is perhaps sometimes the case, but in order to understand what a text is, most theorists have considered it to be something quite positively its own, however much it may stand for, symbolize, produce, or connote meanings in addition to itself.

197

Some illustrations of what I have been saying best demonstrate these distinctions of a text. The place occupied in classical antiquity by the Homeric poems, as well as the perennially renewed Homeric problem in classical scholarship, are central to the problem of the text and the preservation of Homer's work. For Plato, for Zenodotus of Ephesus, for Friedrich August Wolf, as for Nietzsche, the relationships between a set of received images in verse and how they are to be understood as passing from speech into ethical or textual existence are crucial matters that only the text of Homer's poems can resolve. Entire periods of history are thus basically apprehended as functions of a text—that is, either made sensible by a text or given identity by a text. Instances of the former are the Rosetta stone and the Qumran scrolls, and of the latter, Renaissance humanism based on classical scholarship in general and Petrarch's discovery of Cicero's letters in Verona in 1345 in particular. The text acts in two directions: toward the past, which gains actuality, and toward the present, which gains in knowledge. In these instances the material existence of a text, quite apart from its use or its interpretation, has a unique intellectual and historical value. Always this value derives from a text out of a past whose contemporary privileged relevance is derived from the enhanced or restored fact of its preservation in textual form. The four editions by Erasmus (1515-1527) of a Greek New Testament are a celebrated confirmation of such a value.

In the West the classics and the Bible are the best-preserved, the most worked over, the most transmitted, and hence the most original texts of all. Many institutions, including both the Church and the university, are devoted to preserving the texts—prolonging them, as it were—even as a part of their own preservation. Standing very near the center of intellectual life in the West is the tradition of classical scholarship, whose record in Sir John Sandys's three-volume *History of Classical Scholarship* is a humbling one for the contemporary critic.[10] To this tradition it is possible to relate not only Dante's use of Virgil, Joyce's of Homer, the work of Curtius and Auerbach, and innumerable poets and philosophers, but also such important peculiarities and such impressive sports as the battle of the Ancients and the Moderns, Nietzsche's *Birth of Tragedy,* Bentley's edition of Milton, Vico's *New Science*, and Chapman's Homer. A probable reason for the fertility of the great classical texts is that access to them, their preservation, and their transmission is irrevocably connected to their original appearance in three different "foreign" languages. Hebrew, Greek, Latin and then the numerous vernaculars have accounted for the continuing need of translations, editors, and interpreters whose cultural and institutional focus is the text. As Vico put it in *The New Science*, a virtue of Europe is "the Christian religion, which teaches truths so sublime that it receives into service the most learned philosophies of the gentiles and cultivates three languages as its own [*ch'insegna verità cotanto sublimi che vi si sono ricevute a servirla le piu dotte filosofie de' gentili, e coltiva tre lingue come sue*] : Hebrew, the most ancient in the world; Greek, the most delicate; and Latin, the grandest."[11]

Outside the Judeo-Christian textual tradition—in the Arab-Islamic, for instance—rather different conditions prevail. One of them is *cidjaz*, a concept which describes the uniqueness of the Koran as rendering all other texts impotent by comparison. Thus since the central text is in Arabic, and since, unlike the Gospels or even the Torah, it is given as unitary and complete, textual traditions are essentially supportive, not restorative. All texts are secondary to the Koran, which is inimitable. (Note the absence of the problems of the formal imperfections of Scripture, of mixed styles, of incomplete or partially transmitted texts, and so on—all of which obtain in the Christian Europe that Vico described.) There is nevertheless a hierarchy of disciplines and of books in relation to the Koran. Thus two sciences above all other, jurisprudence (*fiqh*) and tradition (*hadith*), sets of systematic textual customs, control the editor's work, and in the case of the *hadith* they are very elaborate and systematic customs indeed. Every tradition is judged according to a canon of valid sources. One ranking judges that the best tradition is heard, then following that perhaps traditions recited, licensed, handed over, obtained by correspondence or by bequest, or found. When not dealing with texts associated with the Koran, Islamic editors made use of the system of *idjaza* (license to transmit), which although originally the third method of transmitting Koranic traditions in print, came to be used for all other manuscripts.[12] Thus every Arabic text during the "manuscript age"—the period from the seventh up to around the end of the fifteenth century—generally opens with a list of *isnads* (*asaneed*) or witnesses, linking the text to a univocal source through a series of oral transmitters.

In Islam, the dialectic between oral and written language is traditionally very near the surface of any text. Preeminence is given to what is spoken, inasmuch as the Koran was dictated or spoken to the Prophet; knowledge, on the other hand, is characteristically described by the great writer al-Jahiz as that which can be put down black on white. Paradoxically, then, texts are simultaneously important and yet not so important. Franz Rosenthal speculates that the comparative lack of system in Islamic textual practice during and after the manuscript age was due to the continued presence of the Koran and an unbroken tradition, whereas

the survival of no more than scattered fragments of ancient civilization made it imperative for the Occident to husband its meager cultural resources by administering them in the most economic—i.e., systematic—manner. . . . Western intellectual poverty, which knew little except scholastic philosophy facilitated the formation of a systematic approach to research. Since only a limited number of ideas was at the disposal of Western scholars, these scholars were forced to dissect and put together those selfsame ideas over and over again. This procedure resulted in the creation of refined forms of literary presentation.[13]

By contrast, in the Islamic tradition there was no distinction made between actual collation of texts and a sort of free emendation of a text according to the precepts of one's teacher.[14] Nevertheless, there is an amusing converse of this practice: a writer might destroy his own text as a way of dramatizing the eminence of another's. "Twice I composed *maqamat*, but my work did not please me, and I destroyed it. I wonder whether God might not have created me for the sole purpose of emphasizing Ibn al-Hariri's superiority."[15]

Despite the differences between the Islamic and Judeo-Christian textual traditions, before the age of printing there was extraordinary difficulty in both traditions when references from one text to another were attempted. An author could never be sure that a manuscript he referred to existed in more than one handwritten copy, so references were exceedingly cumbersome, and usually involved digressive summaries. In the West, if such references were often prohibitive, then the fragments that received the most textual attention and reproduction—usually Scriptural ones—bred an internal system of organization that, I think, far exceeds anything to be found in the Islamic tradition. The recent study of biblical codices has revealed a wide range of textual devices, all concentrated upon preserving texts and making them more useful. On the one hand there are formal systems that include colophons, scholia, onomastica, catenae, commentaries, superscription, subscription, and so forth; on the other, as Bruce

Metzger has amusingly pointed out, there is a fair variety of informal social devices that brought the text from a distant and revered past into the present:

> [There are] conversational jottings which occasionally stand at the close of a manuscript or in the margins of folios throughout a document. Though scribes were forbidden to talk to one another in the scriptorium, the more irrepressible found devious ways to communicate with each other. One such means was to jot remarks on the margin of the page being transcribed and to show it to one's neighbour. The margins of a ninth-century Latin manuscript of Cassiodorus' commentary on the Psalms contains a variety of commonplace remarks written in Irish. For example: "It is cold today." "That is natural; it is winter." "The lamp gives a bad light." "It is time for us to begin to do some work." "Well, this vellum is certainly heavy!" "Well, I call this vellum thin!" "I feel quite dull today; I don't know what's wrong with me."[16]

If a preserved text is thought of as displacing something by its presence, there is, I think, one especially interesting consequence: not only does a text enjoy an existence quite special to it, but in addition it becomes less and less possible, the longer it survives, to consider it as analogous with, parallel to, or symbolic of the human lifetime. The authority of *The Aeneid* is transhuman. Virgil himself is thought of less as a biographical subject than as a topos worthy of many lifetimes' study. The tendency in philological work since the eighteenth century has been toward the sort of attitude, capable of including high specialization and that of *Altertumswissenschaft,* that considers a text as the representation of complex, collective phenomena in an irreducibly particular mode. The quasi-logical extension of such a tendency leads to the sort of images found in Borges's short story "The Library of Babel," in which human life is simply one of the less ingenious and less interesting items among a world of texts. The interpretive traditions upon which most modern conceptions of the humanities are based employ texts to give a suprahuman continuity to the tradition, just as the history of the humanities is dotted with individual quests—like those of the protagonist in James's *The Aspern Papers*—after a text that becomes a *raison d'être* of a lifetime. In effect, this is not so contradictory, since in the humanities a central text is regarded as a kind of ideal as well as practical goal for the individual humanist; the literal meaning of *philology* makes this clear enough.

In everything I have so far said, reading is paradoxically not always so important a process to the life of a text as one might assume. Granted, an unread text is often equivalent to no text at all; but what I mean is that regarding a text fundamentally as *that which is read* (the object that one reads) is to miss the enormously variegated activity of writing and rewriting that a text breeds. No text ought to be viewed as a sort of mathematical balance between writing and reading, nor as the material result of reading, nor as an effect of reading. The trouble with such formulas is that they place the act of reading prior to that of writing, whereas in fact the production of a text is an event, physically and spiritually, which has its own genealogy that cannot begin with its reading. The point here is that the filiations of a text have much more to do with writing than with reading—at least for the type of analysis I have been attempting here and elsewhere. A text is in part a continuing desire to write one: as Roland Barthes has said in making the textual distinction between *lisible* and *scriptible*, "Le texte scriptible est un présent perpetuel, sur lequel ne peut se poser aucune parole *conséquente* (qui le transformerait, fatalement, en passé); le texte scriptible, c'est *nous en train* d'écrire."[17] To begin to write is to begin to produce a text, although writing can go though a very large number of refinements before it *is* a text, at least to its author. In this way, too, a text is disjunctive with the human lifetime: the writing career follows a pattern by no means connected necessarily with that of a dateable cycle, a subject to which I shall return later on.

A helpful insight is gained by comparing Thomas Kuhn's description, in *The Structure of Scientific Revolutions*, of the role played by the science textbook with the nonscientific text in general. In a chapter entitled "The Invisibility of Revolutions," Kuhn advances the thesis that science textbooks are sources of authority whose role is to describe the outcome of a scientific revolution as something linear or cumulative.[18] Such a misconstruction, Kuhn observes, is unexceptionable pedagogy, but in effect science "textbooks thus begin by truncating the scientist's sense of his discipline's history and then proceed to supply a substitute for what they have eliminated." Kuhn's interest in science textbooks is that, because they are sources of information about scientific research, the pedagogic image of science they present determines the common view of science—as discovery and invention—held by most scientists. Such textbooks therefore conceal the real history of research and discovery by displacing them. They also preserve the results of research in such a way as to obscure the complex process of paradigm production, testing, and rejection that, Kuhn contends, forms the basis of all scientific revolution. In any case, Kuhn's characterization of the scientific text(book) directly connects the linear authority of a printed text with its displacing, misconstructing, and pedagogic functions. The printed texts begin the act of defining a discipline by truncating history, by making it seem as if history begins from a discrete, determinable point and proceeds thereafter in a straight line. Such a presentation thus invents an image of history to which, in its neatly etched peripheries, the text corresponds.

In a sense, therefore, Kuhn argues that the science textbook is a sort of obstruction within the ongoing activity of scientific research. A text presents this activity as something hard and already achieved instead of as the multidimensional and plastic effort which it really is. Two views that almost exactly correspond with Kuhn's are those of Nietzsche and Vico, both of whom argue that every text, whether the tables of Roman law or the revered texts of Athenian tragedy, stands between the scholar and the historical past—or rather, the text, in its didactic simplicity, is often interpreted (because of its seeming clarity) as the reality of a past that its linear textual form misconstrues. The text is therefore Apollonian, at least in its ability to hold back a far more fluid poetry than words can convey with what Nietzsche calls an Olympian structure. Vico states that "men are naturally impelled to preserve the memories of the laws and institutions that bind them in their societies."[19] They do so in texts (poems, codes, histories, myths) that preserve the past in uniformity, but which the "conceit of the scholars" overrates as if "what they know must have been eminently understood from the beginning of the world." Vico concludes that "for purposes of this inquiry [in *The New Science*] we must reckon as if there were no books in the world."[20] In *The Use and Abuse of History* Nietzsche says that "there is a hygiene of life near the volumes of science," and that the essence of this hygiene is the unhistorical and the super-historical, both of which counteract the "malady of history."[21] Within these "volumes of science" one can find the study of history and modern philosophy, which "is political and official, bound down to be a mere phantasmagoria of learning by our modern governments, churches, universities, moralities, and cowardices."[22]

The images of imprisonment and obstruction with which a text has often been identified are not unexpected ones, even if the identification is not so polemical as Nietzsche's. For example, the opening poem of Blake's *Songs of Innocence* represents the poet as using a reed—"a rural pen"—to write his happy songs for the joy of every child. His paper is the water which is stained as he "writes": but one's inclination is to associate innocence in the poem with the impossibility of a permanent inscription in the water. The one line of the poem that suggests a troubling of innocence is "And I stain'd the water clear." Nevertheless, the ambiguously placed adjective "clear" offsets the threat in "stain'd," so that one can read the line to mean either "I stained the water until it became clear" or "my pen stained the clear water": in both cases the conclusion is that because he writes on water, which even if momentarily stained would not retain the imprint, the poet composes happy (and clear) songs. This conventional imagery is systematically strengthened by the context of "innocence" and by contrast with the forging, imprisoning imagery so frequent in *Songs of Experience*.

The converse is to be found in Swift's "Verses wrote on a Lady's Ivory Table-Book." The speaker is the book itself, whose hardness is evident as well in the writing inscribed on it:

> Peruse my Leaves thro' ev'ry Part,
> And think thou seest my owners Heart,
> Scrawl'd o'er with Trifles thus; and quite
> As hard, as sensless, and as light.

This is an admittedly special book, "expos'd to every Coxcomb's Eyes," but all that Swift does in the poem is to meditate on the oddness of the book's textual hardness as it unites heartless inscriptions with vulnerable openness. Since the text is a surface that preserves what is inscribed there, it invites attention indiscriminately, at the same time being hostile to and repelling "deep" understanding.

Both Swift and Blake differ from Keats, for whom a text on two notable occasions has less unfavorable meanings—but for the reason that, in Keats's case, the physical characteristic of a text, the fact that it is written down, is either transmuted into another element or given a very special signficance. Chapman's Homer is not a document-text but a voice-text: Keats says that he never breathed "the pure serene" of Homer's world "Till I heard Chapman speak out loud and bold." And in the sonnet "When I have fears that I may cease to be," the poet's intensified sense of his mortality is connected with his inability to fill books with writing, to glean his brain with his pen, to trace the romance in the shadows of "the night's starr'd face." Writing is the means of gaining Fame, just as looking upon a beloved face gains one the relish "of unreflecting love." The writer's text, therefore, immediately averts nothingness; Keats's perspective is that of a man fearing extinction, of a man for whom the very act of inscription (as opposed to any particular text he produces) assures him that so long as he writes he is alive.

Keats's way of avoiding the text's almost physically bound existence is related, I believe, to all those techniques of rewriting the text during the act of interpretations. When writing is considered to be not the solitary act of an individual, nor the imprisonment of sense in graphological inscription, but rather an act that constitutes participation in various cultural processes, then the text as obstruction becomes text as pathway to new texts. This transformation is at the center of Dilthey's system of interpretation, although the system is encompassed by the long history of hermeneutics with its antecedents in such interpreters as Porphyry. The tradition views a text as something to be converted slowly and by much study into further texts, which in turn permit others to appear. In Karl Barth's theological hermeneutics, for example, his "methodology, as he describes it in . . . the *Römerbrief*, is to live with the text until it disappears and one is confronted with the divine word itself."[23] For nontheological hermeneutics each text is polytextual, just as in the epistolary novel one letter is the occasion of another letter. The text's preserving and obstructing and displacing functions are taken as resisting rewriting (which is what hermeneutical interpretation is at bottom), but the beginning premise of this rewriting is that the text's resistance is principally a formal matter. Ultimately, that is, each text as an obstruction can be circumvented or dissolved. What puts Vico and Nietzsche to one side of this attitude is that for them a text is *fundamentally* a fact of power and displacement, whereas in Dilthey's work the text presents itself to the historical consciousness as an aspect of "mental life," and as such the text's form is a fact of *distribution* in that life, not of threatening obstruction.[24] Perhaps because the text is writing—which, in the hermeneutic philosophy expounded by Hans-Georg Gadamer, is "a self-estrangement from speech" (*Selbstentfremdung der Sprache*)[25] —it can be considered as *essentially vulnerable* to interpretation and rewriting.

There is another way in which the text is vulnerable, and the practice of textual criticism is an attempt to deal with it. Once again the physical act of writing a text involves "self-estrangement," but not from speaking. Rather, as A. E. Housman puts it in "The Application of Thought to Textual Criticism," a modern *locus classicus* of textual criticism, the text can be estranged from an original version (in this sense a "pure" version) by transcribing scribes: "Scribes," he says, "will alter a less familiar form to a more familiar, if they see nothing to prevent them."[26] Since textual criticism "is the science of discovering error in texts and the art of removing it," there is no excuse for considering its practice as having anything to do with mystery or mathematics. An original text is a given existing outside the field of the textual critic's practice: he attempts to restore that which by definition is not within the scope of his knowledge and experience. "Thought" enables him to establish a correct text based upon transmitted (transcribed) versions. Thus for each restored text, a family of copies is assumed to exist, although the critic must build a family tree for his text before it can be considered "present." Housman is careful to show how textual criticism deals with "things which [do not] present themselves clearly and sharply to the mind."[27] For each section in a text, dozens of prejudices, historical errors, and varieties of fantasy can intervene; so the critic must act *as if* the words he uses have sensuous qualities. In this way he can more readily tell whether he has been foolish or not: his actions can be seen to have practical consequences. But "our conclusions regarding the truth or falsehood of a MS. reading can never be confirmed or corrected by an equally decisive test [as in a chemical experiment]; for the only equally decisive test would be the production of the author's autograph."[28]

Housman consistently refers to textual criticism as a sort of internal space inhabited largely by "deplorably intellectual" objects. His view of the text is, I think, quite similar. Since there can be no absolutely correct and "original" text firmly anchoring subsequent transcriptions in reality, all texts exist in a constantly moving tangle of imagination and error. The job of the textual critic is, by fixing one text securely on the page, to arrange all other versions of that text in some sort of linear sequence with it. Housman's preface to his edition of Manilius describes exactly that. Nevertheless, discursive prose about a text only makes explicit the implicit filiation which the cumulative emendations and restorations of the edited text have established. The inner space occupied by texts of the same family is restricted, and partly caused by, the absence of an "original" father-text. A recension is a copy whose "parents" are other texts, themselves copies, which the editor can only trace back as far as an "archetype."

Paul Maas's *Textual Criticism,* whose theoretical predecessors are Johann Jakob Griesbach and Karl Lachmann, uses these terms to describe the text so as to minimize those confusions inherent in textuality. Maas's contribution is to employ stemmatics—a method and vocabulary borrowed from genealogy—to exhibit "the inter-relationship of the witnesses" or copies. If a copy can be traced back to one witness or tradition (*codex unicus*), recension "is a matter of describing and deciphering as accurately as possible the single witness."[29] Where there have been "splits," the editor's job is considerably more difficult. Since each tradition is related to an "archetype"—which is not the original text but only the first copy of it—a given text's filiation is very complex. Each text (*textus receptus*) undergoes critical examination in such a way that transmitted errors (*errores significativi*) are used to validate editorial changes in the text's corrected version (*constitutio textus*). The editor's rationale is that in providing his text with the best possible, most reliable pedigree (*code optimus*), he is elucidating the connections between his recension and the archetype. The picture of a family of texts is drawn by Maas as follows:

> A river comes from an inaccessible source under the peak of a high mountain. It divides underground, its branches divide further, and some of these branches then come to the surface on the mountain side as springs; the water of these springs at once drains away and may come to the surface at several places farther down the mountain side and finally flows onward in visible form overground. The water from its source onwards is of ever-changing but fine and pure colors. In its subterranean course it flows past several places at which coloring matters from time to time dissolve into the water; the same thing happens every time the stream divides and every time it comes to the surface in a spring. Every influx changes the colour of a certain part of the stream, and this part keeps the colour permanently; only very slight colour changes are eliminated by natural processes .... The object of the investigation is to test the genuineness of the colour or colours on the evidence of the springs.[30]

Note that according to the logic of Maas's imagery, the origin of the family, its paternal source, is defined as inaccessible, which amounts to saying that so far as a text is concerned there is no original but only copies. Thus the beginning of a textual tradition is the first appearance (archetype) of a presumably faithful copy of the inaccessible original. Again logically, any text that falls within the course of the main current is related to all the others as members of the same family. Mistakes in transcription are "natural" concomitants of filiation, so there can be no appeal to an outside authority, to what Housman calls a "decisive test." Even outright forgeries, completely fanciful copies, and thought-less recensions can be treated as tributaries of the main stream. In other words, each version of a text is a modification of the original's positivity, even though, as we said, the original is inaccessible, at best a fertile power. Every user of the text is caught within the net of relationships (which includes editors, scribes, traditions, and schools) that involves any instance of the text as a variant of every instance. The distinguishing mark of the textual critic is that he, more than the scribe, is aware of the *family* relationships between texts, whereas all other "consumers" are satisfied with a vague knowledge of kinship among versions of the same text.

Whether the textual critic uses Maas's genealogical method, Joseph Bédier's "best-text" method, or any of the statistical techniques now available, the claims made for a purified text encroach upon the author's ground. When James Thorpe says that if "there is no editing, texts perish,"[31] he is arguing that textual criticism *prolongs* the author's impulse. The subject matter of textual criticism is a work of art, and its ideal as a discipline is "to present what the author intended."[32] Yet according to Morse Peckham, such views "urge us to pursue an unattainable idea: this is true hagiolatry."[33] For not only is the notion of a "text" a construct, but "the term 'author' (the intensive is 'poet') ascribes to a human organism conceived of primarily as producer of language the gift of God's grace or charisma."[34] Yet Peckham's summation of his argument, for all its radicality and frankness, does not completely shake off the meliorist and serial biases of textual criticism:

> The task of the textual editor is to produce a new version from a series of a postulated text by a postulated author by making up for the policing, validating, and changing deficiencies in the long, complex and interlocking series of behaviors the consequence of which was the production of that series. There is no "definitive" version at which he must or can arrive. There is no one set of instructions which can mediate his behavior to the exclusion of all other sets. His activities are multi-purposeful; his problem is empirical; it cannot be solved a priori. His situation is open.[35]

From an ethical point of view—that is, if one regards the copy as having opened up the postulated integrity of the original—each new copy of the text can be said in some way to *exceed* its predecessors. Not only is the risk of error increased, but the distance between original, archetype, and copies, if not increased, is then varied. Each copy spends more of the original capital than its predecessors, and in so doing it transgresses, if it does not actually contaminate, the previous version. There are, however, limits to these excesses. One is a principle of similarity that keeps texts "strong" by virtue of their exact resemblance to the archetype: this paradox is the insight around which Borges's story of Pierre Menard is built. A second limit is that textual traditions, very broadly considered, coalesce to form larger matrices: two examples are the notions of *Weltliteratur* and of *Romania.*[36] Even though these wide groupings do not antedate the authority of any "original" text, they nevertheless act as a sort of conceptual armor for groups of texts descended from those originals. In addition to the support of other texts in the same family, each single text thus implies—and draws from the power of—other families connected through the matrix of a universal language like Latin, or of a universal idea like that of *Weltliteratur.*

None of these conservative dynamics of textual survival can work, however, were it not for the fact that a text is a very particular sort of graphological memory. Once again we must talk of the text's preserving and displacing functions. For in an unmistakable way the presence of a text-as-copy displaces (and by virtue of similarity preserves a memory of displacing) some original—an idea, or an implicit priority, or an intransitive power, or an uncopied autograph. At certain moments in textual history the displacement appears more strikingly than at others. During the eleventh century the subordination of all rhetoric to the art of writing copies of dictating classical models, the so-called *ars dictaminis,* is one such example. Each text pushes aside ordinary discourse in order to place before the world a textual composition whose authority derives from two sources: the ancient originals whose style is being copied and the present text's appearance in the form of a preserved duration. To put pen to a text is to begin the movement away from the original; it is to enter the world of the text-as-beginning as copy and as parricide.

The Oedipal motif lurking beneath many discussions of the text (Housman and Maas, for instance, are no exceptions) makes more sense if we regard the text-copy as totem and the making of such a text as the beginning parricidal deed (performed on a paternal original) that Freud spoke of in *Totem and Taboo.* If the reference to Freud seems farfetched here, it is because the enormous increase in the dissemination of books, the effect of radical modernism, the absence of a central pedagogical tradition based on the classics, and the textual upheavals of the Higher Criticism during the nineteenth century have diminished the quasi-totemic status of texts. But when we read, as we shall presently, *Totem and Taboo* as a gloss upon popular works of textual criticism—such as Renan's *Vie de Jésus*—its relevance is considerably enhanced. As an instance, there is Freud's account of the "binding force attributed to eating and drinking"[37] among members of a community. Such ritual in primitive societies signifies kinship, participation in "a common substance,"[38] which binds the society together in commemoration of a "beginning" deed. The obligation laid upon all users of a text like the *Odyssey,* whether translators, editors, or modern novelists, is to acknowledge that their kinship is defined by their common point of reference—the text itself. Even when they use the text as outrageously as Samuel Butler does in proving that Nausicaa wrote the poem, they declare their sense of community with the whole textual tradition, which is one of common guilt: "I may comfort myself," says Butler in chapter 1 of *The Authoress of the Odyssey,* "by reflecting that however much I may deserve stoning there is no one who can stone me with a clear conscience."[39] Butler is referring to the change in opinion by which it is now commonly assumed that the *Iliad* and *Odyssey* had different authors. The passage of time increases the number of copies of the text, changes ideas about the text, and more intensely than before provides the textual community with opportunities to violate the text's putative original state. For what could more invade the poem's privacy than to treat its actual composition, forever left behind once a text appeared to replace an original bardic rhapsody, as a subject of irreverent controversy?

Publication of a text, or at least the appearance of the text as an object to be diffused, is a ceremonious repetition of the parricidal deed by virtue of which copies proceed to supplant what Maas calls an inaccessible source. I am speaking of publication in a very general way, but it should be noted that in the Christian West the central text, the New Testament, has formally existed as Gospels whose physical existence commemorates a communal guilt and redemption. If Jesus is the father of the Christian community, every instance of writing signifies his death, or at least the transfer of his spoken words to a written document and the community's ambivalent relation to it. In either case, his presence is transmuted into or sacrificed for words, just as, conversely, he was the Word made flesh; the idea of Christian sacrifice therefore "offers satisfaction to the father for the outrage inflicted on him in the same act in which that deed is commemorated."[40] Christ's death makes possible the presence of an apostolic community forever stained with guilt; and that community is perpetuated whenever loyalty to crucial Gospels is instituted as the sign of kinship. Through adherence to the Gospels, all men are made as brothers, especially since such kinship requires the loyal observance of rules inspired by the text. Of these rules, *imitatio*, as Erich Auerbach has shown, seems to have survived most energetically so far as the making of a *Christian* text is concerned—*imitatio* as mixture of styles, as *figura*, as mimetic representation, as allegory, and as form. "Do this in remembrance of me and like me" is thus the Christian injunction for the making of texts subordinate and analogous to a central and antecedent one. Auerbach's *Mimesis* demonstrates powerfully the extraordinary effect of the Christian texts upon the classical notions of *imitatio*, an effect that permitted Dante and Cervantes, for instance, to exploit as well as submit to fraternal kinship *after* the archetypal inscription.

Even on a stylistic level, as a result of Christ's sacrifice the central Christian text influenced such dynamics as those set in motion by the *sermo humilis*, a mode that combined "low" locutions with sublime subject matter, in the manner of the Scriptures. And yet

most educated pagans regarded the early Christian writings as ludicrous, confused, and abhorrent, and this applied to the Latin even more than the Greek versions. The content struck them as childish and absurd superstition, and the form as an affront to good taste . . . . How could the profoundest of problems, the enlightenment and redemption of mankind, be treated in such barbarous works? In order to eliminate this stumbling block educated Christians might well have decided at an early date (here we are speaking of the Latin texts) to correct the first translations of Scripture which had been done by men without education or experience and adapt them to good literary usage. But this was not done. The first Latin translations, with their very peculiar style, were never replaced by a Bible text in the classical taste. The texts in the *Vetus latina* had quickly acquired such authority among the congregations, they were so appropriate to the social and intellectual level of the first Latin-speaking Christians, that they soon became a firmly established normative tradition. A more cultivated literary version would never have found acceptance.[41]

One of the strengths of the *sermo humilis* "is its power to express human brotherhood, an immediate bond between men."[42] That is, the *sermo humilis* provided Christians with what Freud called "a common substance"; the form and content of the textual substance had a binding force similar to that of a ritual meal. It is not surprising, therefore, that the greatest of medieval Christian poets, Dante, on the one hand had an

extreme subjectivity, or at least a subjectivity hitherto unequalled in its vast range and sharpness of expression, [which on the other hand] had sprung from a devoted Imitation of Christ and an endeavor to record faithfully what is enacted (not only decided, but actually carried out) in the kingdom of God .... Dante [thus] created a public not for himself alone but for his successors as well. He molded, as potential readers of his poem, a community which was scarcely in existence at the time when he wrote and which was gradually built up by his poem and by the poets who came after him.[43]

In no small way, then, the idea of a Christian text imposed upon writer and audience a voluntary discipline, a confraternity of liberties and restrictions, that could be said to have arisen from Christ's sacrifice of his living speech to the alternate mode of written language. I think that Auerbach's assessment of Dante as the inaugurator of modern European literature gains still more validity if one sees *The Divine Comedy* as an implantation of the Biblical text in the here and now.[44] In seeing—and portraying—the contemporary world as if with the eyes of the Gospels and the words of the vernacular, Dante commemorated the Passion not only as a text to be repeated, as if spoken by Christ, but also as an event to be prolonged into the present.

On this point, the difference between Dante and Milton is very instructive. Blake's ideas about Milton's intransigence emphasize, among other things, the overreaching quality of *Paradise Lost* as a text setting itself up to rewrite the Gospels. Milton's

> advent'rous Song,
> That with no middle flight intends to soar
> Above th' Aonian Mount, while it pursues
> Things unattempted yet in Prose or Rhime
> (1.13-16)

is everywhere characterized by the intention to exceed all previous texts, perhaps not excluding even the Gospels. His "answerable style" inscribes the sort of text capable, like Raphael, of sailing "between worlds and worlds" (5.268). Curiously, too, Milton's imagery for his accomplishments as writer in the poem always includes reminders that he flies higher than anyone else:

> Mee of these
> Nor skilled nor studious, higher Argument

Remaines, sufficient of itself to raise
That name, unless an age too late, or cold
Climat, or Years damp my intended wing
Deprest. . . .

(9.41-45)

To Dante the original texts require confirmation and incarnation
in what Auerbach calls the earthly world, whereas Milton sees his
text aspiring to the place of inauguration, as if to protest the
usurpation of the beginning place by an antecedent text, a *codex
unicus.*

Challenges to the text as paternal authority by new texts
comprise a major theme in literature and thought since Milton.
The battle of the books, the investigations of the
eighteenth-century encyclopedists, the romantic revolt—all these
repeat the filial quarrel with a dominating father-text. Earlier in
this book I have argued that the novelistic impulse was to take for
the writer a paternal role, to give the novel itself an internal and
autonomous filiation which depended upon the writer's beginning
inventiveness. An example of what I mean is the role of Cide
Hamete Benengeli's "found" manuscript in *Don Quixote:* that
invention stands inside Cervantes's text in order to prove that the
novel's antecedent was a text named, and created, by the novel
itself, and not a text simply there for the novelist to submit to. As
for the enormous problem of influences between writers (as
explored most recently by W. J. Bate and Harold Bloom), that,
too, can be understood as an aspect of the relationships between
texts in the terms we have been using here. If I focus here so
single-mindedly upon the text, and not upon authors or person-
alities, it is in order to insist upon the actual positivity of a text as
the beginning problem faced by every writer. For one can easily
see that the modern writer as text maker—e.g., Mallarmé, Hopkins,
Proust, Joyce, Eliot, and many others—is no less single-minded
about the type of difficulty encountered than I have been.

In order more exactly to understand modern writing generally
as the author's particular problems with a text there is much to be
learned, I think, from the nineteenth-century exploration of
biblical texts, hitherto a neglected type of writing so far as literary
criticism is concerned. The major signposts are well enough
known: Bishop Colenso's work on the Pentateuch; *Essays and
Reviews*; Strauss's *Leben Jesu*; the Higher Criticism generally,
including Schleiermacher, Baur, and Kiem; Renan's *Vie de Jésus*;
and so on.[45] Similarly, the type of effect, or outcry, they caused

213

is also well known. Yet what bears closer scrutiny is the drama of their textual revisionism, the struggle endured—explicitly in some cases and implicitly in others—over their treatment of "original" texts as *beginning* ones. We may consider the struggle as one for the right to a text of one's own contemporary establishment, despite the awesome residue of sheer sacred priority accorded the biblical text. Vico, for example, simply avoided the Bible when he studied "primitive" texts like the *Iliad.* When he speaks of "the first men," Vico, unlike Milton in his audacity speaking of Adam as "our Author," designates the gentiles, by no means the people of the Bible. Not so the Higher Critics, whom one of their enemies, W. H. Green, charged with committing a dangerous "perversion" in thought and seriousness. Green asserted that investigations attempting to show that the biblical texts are neither as primitive, nor as unified, nor as reliable as previously claimed are to be fought. Even so, in his preface to *The Higher Criticism of the Pentateuch,* Green said confidently:

> The books of the Bible have nothing to fear from such investigations, however searching and thorough, and however fearlessly pursued. They can only result in establishing more firmly the truth of the claims, which the Bible makes for itself, in every particular. The Bible stands upon a rock from which it can never be dislodged.[46]

Higher Criticism attempted generally to redispose the unitary text of the Bible, or parts thereof, into a set of disparate documents with miscellaneous histories. That is, the text of the Bible as treated in the text of the contemporary critic would become merely the focus of philological and circumstantial textual evidence, not the *fons et origo* of all subsequent history and writing. Green, on the other hand, contends that

> the Old Testament is a product of the Spirit of God, wrought out through the instrumentality of many human agents who were all inspired by him, directed by him, and adapted by him to the accomplishment of his own fixed ends . . . . Everything in the Old Testament tends to Christ and is to be estimated from him. Everything in the New Testament unfolds from Christ and is likewise to be estimated from him.[47]

Green understands that the thrust of Higher Criticism, which he sees as already having being practiced in the eighteenth century, is to refute supernaturalism entirely. Each biblical text is treated, not as being delivered by God to man, but as transcribed from documents. Green's anger with this perspective is worth citing: he characterizes the "Fragment Hypothesis" of the Pentateuch (maintained by Johann Vater and Anton Hartmann) as "the

214

Document Hypothesis run mad."[48] He reminds his readers that "it is no mere literary question . . . which this style of criticism raises . . . . The truth and evidence of the entire Mosaic history are at stake."[49] If such criticism succeeds in its aim, then "it nullifies at once the Mosaic authorship of the Pentateuch, and substitutes anonymous documents of late age in an imperfect state of preservation, which have been woven together, and to some extent modified, by anonymous redactors."[50] To anyone who does not suppose that such a nullification is a textual issue of the highest consequence, Green spells it out in detail:

> If we abandon the Mosaic authorship, which is so explicitly and repeatedly certified by the earliest tradition that we are able to summon, we are out upon the open sea with nothing to direct our course . . . . We go blindly groping along the centuries in quest of authors. All is unwarranted conjecture; there is no firm lodgement anywhere . . . . The Scripture is no longer reliable in its present form. The inspiration of its writers has been surrendered. We have lost our infallible guide . . . . In yielding the principle everything has been conceded that is involved in it and follows from it. The avalanche cannot be arrested midway in its descent.[51]

While it would be perhaps melodramatic to associate an avalanche with the efforts of so scholarly and reputable an investigator as Ernest Renan, there is no question that his *Vie de Jésus* represents a considerably threatening and, to the student of modern literature, interesting textual innovation. The text of *his* book is sober enough, but what it does to the textual forms of the Gospels, their matter and their existence, is highly adventurous, particularly if we take account of the extraordinarily imaginative connection made by Renan between a subject like Jesus, textual records of his life and teaching, and retrospective critical analysis. There is a remarkable psychoanalytic dimension to Renan's project; consequently, *Totem and Taboo* (as I discussed it with regard to textual practice and theory) will be implicit in my analysis of the *Vie de Jésus*. My contention is that if we understand correctly what Renan explicitly is doing, we are far better able to understand not only what subsequent modern authors have accomplished in their texts but what they have made of them. Such radical attention to the text for a critic therefore makes more precise the idea of a concrete beginning point, what Freud calls the "beginning event," since the text is the primary point of convergence for every variety of writer.

Throughout his book Renan's attitude to Jesus the historical personality is consistent. For Renan, the Galilean, while the author of an astonishing spiritual, moral, and historical revolution, is nevertheless neither supernatural nor capable of supernatural feats. What Renan admires more than anything else is Jesus' *originality*—the word turns up constantly—in having cut through every legal and institutional religious obstacle in order to institute what Renan calls a religion of the Son. "Même il est probable," Renan says on one of many similar occasions, "que, dès ses premiers pas, il s'envisage avec Dieu dans la relation d'un fils avec son père. Là est son grand acte d'originalité; en cela il n'est nullement de sa race."*[52] From this act many consequences flow. Jesus took for himself the title of "Son," whether of God or of Man, and the power that this entailed:

> Cette puissance n'a pas de limites. Son Père lui a donné tout pouvoir. Il a le droit de changer même le sabbat. Nul ne connait le Père que par lui. Le Père lui a transmis le droit de juger. La nature lui obéit; mais elle obéit aussi a quiquonque croit et prie; la foi peut tout. . . . La position qu'il s'attribuait était celle d'un être surhumain, et il voulait qu'on le regardât comme ayant avec Dieu un rapport plus élevé que celui des autres hommes.†[53]

An intrinsic aspect of this higher relationship to God seems to have been Jesus' opposition to the notion of codifying and writing about his faith or about his morality.[54] Therefore, the texts that have survived throughout history, and which comprise the New Testament, are original in that they record Jesus' discourses. Of a lesser originality is "the collection of anecdotes and bits of information that Mark wrote according to Peter's recollections."[55] The first two extant Gospels dispose between them a common document, which appears intermittently in the texts according to Matthew and Mark; yet these two gospels themselves are "arrangements in which an effort has been made to fill the lacunae in one text by pieces of another."[56]

Renan's introduction to his *Life of Jesus* attempts to show how the original records of Jesus' life and discourses "were not therefore texts that had been stopped and fixed dogmatically."[57] For about two centuries there was no hesitation, for example, in

---

*"It is even probable that ever since his first steps, he envisaged himself with God in the relationship of a son to his father. That was his great, original act; in that he did not belong to his race."

†"This power has no limits. His father had given him every power. He has the right even to change the sabbath. No one could know the Father except through him. The Father had transmitted to him the right to judge. Nature obeys him; but she also obeyed whoever believed and prayed; faith can do anything. . . . The position he attributed to himself was that of a superhuman being, and he wanted people to regard him as having an understanding with God that was higher than that allowed to other men."

interpreting additions to the texts of eyewitness reports. Speaking of oral tradition and a general disregard of texts as such so far as Jesus' life and teachings are concerned Renan says: "It is when the tradition weakened in the second half of the century that texts bearing either apostles' names or the names of apostolic men accrue decisive authority and begin to have the force of law."[58] He goes on to describe three stages through which the texts have passed: (1) "The original documentary stage [of Matthew and Mark] first versions no longer extant"; (2) "the stage of simple mixture, in which original documents have been incorporated without any effort at composition . . . (The present Gospels of Matthew and Mark)"; and (3) "the stage of combination, of intended and reflective editing, in which one perceives the effort made to reconcile the different versions (Gospel of Luke, Gospels of Marcion, of Tatien, etc.). The Gospel of John . . . forms a whole of another sort entirely, and altogether of another order.[59] Renan's purpose in the book, therefore, is to treat his subject "as a living organism" despite the factual knowledge that reveals texts to be *at times* hardly more than fanciful embroidery. The result, he hopes, is not a caricature of life but rather something analogous to the reproduction of a Greek statue, "the general spirit of the work, one of the ways in which it might have existed."[60]

Let us try now to articulate in another way what Renan says he is doing. The true origin of his biography is a living, speaking man who, except as the author of a continuing spiritual revolution, has disappeared forever. Then there emerges a series of texts consequent upon this life *and* this disappearance. Renan imagines the texts as first continuing, then replacing, then displacing a textless original (i.e., one spoken and lived) that is inaccessible through ordinary, natural means. That is, in the early stages of Christian history, Jesus' life was the common spiritual property of friends and apostles; no one document contained his life complete. Each version in its own way continued his life, gently and silently replacing a previous version with a "fuller" one, which everyone presumably welcomed. Authority appears, or begins, when this process of silent replacement stops. *The authority of a text, according to Renan, is tied to the realization that a text has outlived whomever participated in its original making.* This rift between textual authority and the historical individual lifetime further means that a document becomes a text with authority when emendations, excisions, additions, editions, and revisions of it become intentional textual acts displacing earlier textual acts instead of, as before, matters of communal tacit agreement. For the communal document there can be no question of textuality, since anyone who intervenes in it does so out of love and common memory: such a document increases in value each time something (an anecdote) is added to it and fills it out. For the text, however, each change is viewed as making its "textuality" more secure, safer from willy-nilly rifling (or displacement) of its contents. Instead of the common experience of the votary who tells yet another part of the whole story, the text's discipline yokes to it an editor who guards the text, screens it from defilement, exorcises its errors, ultimately gives it higher authority.

The text leaves behind its origin (which in the case of the New Testament is Jesus), for the text is the beginning of a series of substitutions which altogether comprise the formal object we call a text.[61] This is neither as tautological nor as metaphysical as it seems. Every text is something first composed, then transmitted, then received, then edited and interpreted, then reconsidered. Yet the moment that composition—the setting of pen to paper—takes place, each of these processes is somehow involved: since there is really no such thing as an absolutely primal text, each act of composition involves other texts, and so each writing transmits itself, receives other writing, is an interpretation of other writing, reconstitutes (by displacement) other writing. What is common to each of these analytical differentiations of a text is an image of *affirmation,* in which a text in some form can be seen persisting as positive textuality for some duration, by virtue of *excluding* other possibilities. Thus Renan must (and does) recognize that the Gospels have persisted in the Vulgate, for instance, because, no matter how much original validity they may have lost, they began their textual existence as affirmative substitutions for informal common documents; when Renan says of a Gospel that it is "according to Mark," he understands the name "Mark" as being a substitute for, and a check upon, unlimited emendation.

An even more complex matter remains. Renan's feeling for Jesus is everywhere evident in the book. Jesus was a man of extraordinary gifts, no one of which could be appropriately contained in a text. Everything about Jesus as Renan describes him resists textuality, beginning with the "originality" of his unmediated filial relationship with the Divine: "Du reste, [il n'y a] nulle trace, dans l'enseignement de Jésus, d'une morale appliquée ni d'un droit canonique tant soit peu défini. . . . Nulle théologie

218

non plus, nul symbole."*[62] Just as Jesus in his life and faith put himself directly next to God, so in his *Life of Jesus* Renan describes Jesus *as he could have existed* were it not for the intervening and authoritatively Christian text of the Gospels. The filial relation seems for Renan to be extratextual, not to say imaginative. Opposed to the unmediated Son-Father relationship envisaged by Renan is the Father-Son genealogy with all the institutions of religion and textuality maintaining the hierarchy. [63] It is precisely because he claimed a direct association with the Father that Jesus was a revolutionary dedicated to a popular (in the literal sense) idea that collapsed hierarchical relationships:

> Sorti de l'affirmation hardie d'un homme du peuple, éclos devant le peuple, aimé et admiré d'abord du peuple, le Christianisme fut empreint d'un caractère originel qui ne s'effacera pas jamais. Il fut le premier triomphe de la revolution, la victoire du sentiment populaire, l'avénement des simples de coeur, l'inauguration du beau comme le peuple l'entend. Jésus ouvrit ainsi dans les societés aristocratiques de l'antiquité la brèche par laquelle tout passera.†[64]

The class structure of institutions such as Christianity does in fact threaten to efface the "popular" inauguration of Jesus. And this effacement derives from the inability of Jesus' apostles—of whom the evangelists (Matthew, Mark, Luke) are far superior to Paul, John, and the other authors—to duplicate Jesus' achievement. Thus "ne disons pas que la gloire de la fondation du Christianisme doit revenir à la foule des premiers chrétiens, et non à celui que la legende à a déifié .... Bien loin que Jesus ait été crée par ses disciples, Jésus se montre en tout superieur à ses disciples."‡[65] Each writer who attempts intentionally to bequeath us Jesus' image in writing constantly disfigures him.[66] Thus Renan describes the makers of an official text: "On entrevoit à chaque ligne un original d'un beauté divine trahi par des redacteurs qui ne le comprennent pas, et qui substituent leurs propres idées à celles

---

*"For the rest, [there is] no trace in Jesus' teaching of applied morality nor even of an implied canonic law .... No trace either of a theology, and no symbol."

† "Sprung from the dauntless affirmation of a man of the people, come to light before the people, first loved and admired by the people, Christianity was stamped with an originality which will never be effaced. Christianity was the revolution's first triumph, the victory of popular sentiment, the advent of the simple in heart, the inauguration of the beautiful that the people understands. Jesus thus opened the breach in ancient aristocratic society through which everything would flow."

‡ "let us not say that the glory of having founded Christianity should be credited to the mob of early Christians, nor to the credit of the man deified by legend .... Far from having been created by his disciples Jesus in everything showed himself superior to his disciples."

qu'ils ne saisissent qu'à demi."*[67] Within, or behind, or apart from each line of text there is another communication or expression that was never intended for a text. For as Jesus was able to speak directly to God, so too he spoke directly to the people, thereby causing breaches in the polity of his time. The essential violence of Jesus' message is repaired by the text: the intimacy between Son and Father gives way to the genealogical subordination of son to father, of interpretation, sect, authorities, and priesthood to a text, of contemporary presence to prior absence. In having inaugurated a religion of the Son, Jesus was really taking unto himself, and standing in the place of, the Father. The only priority recognized by Jesus is that of what Renan calls "an original purity," to which the old Father of the Law and tradition has no title whatever.

Renan's biography, then, is the account of a dialectic in which the text is a genre representing succession, the establishment of hierarchical paternal authority, and interpretable sense, all in conflict with Jesus, "drapeau de nos contradictions, . . . le signe autour duquel se livrera la plus ardente bataille, . . . la pierre angulaire de l'humanité, qu'arracher ton nom de ce monde serait l'ébranler jusqu'aux fondements."†[68] The narrative of Jesus' life is Renan's way of reaching the pure sign of his name; that is, the narrative told apart from the biblical texts enables Renan to address Jesus directly, just as Jesus transgressed the authoritative texts of his time in favor of his direct filiality with God the Father. In both cases the intimacy achieved contradicts the principle of temporal succession ordinarily submitting, or second-ing, a son to his father. Just how personally Renan himself judged this contradiction is manifest in his shift from the third to the second person on two occasions: once during the peroration I have just quoted, and once in his dedication of the book "à l'âme pure de ma soeur Henriette." On both occasions he bursts through the textual conventions of historical writing to address dead people whose living presence truly exists only in the pure sign of their names. Thus the purity and sufficiency of the title Jesus took for himself—"the Son"—transcends the genealogies of laws, texts, and nature. It stands for a sort of stubborn transgression against

---

*"In each line we catch a glimpse of a divine original betrayed by editors who did not understand it, and who substituted their own ideas for those they could only half grasp."

†"banner of our contradictions, . . . the sign around which the fiercest battle will be waged, . . . the cornerstone of humanity, the banishment of whose name from the world would be to shake earth to its foundations."

the hierarchies normally established once a name passes from being a pure sign to one sign among many in the social system of a text. And yet such a pure sign can exist only despite the text; this is another way of saying that were it not for the antagonistic text, the pure sign would have no place—even if, paradoxically, that place must be forced away from the text.

Jesus the Son is also Jesus the father of Christianity. In the Gospels this contradiction is embodied in the fact that he is the subject but not the author of texts whose intention is to subordinate the old to the new, the Father to the Son. Another instance of this contradiction is how Jesus at the same time represents the originality of Christianity, its textually inaccessible purity, and Christianity's beginning, its ordained point of departure in history. There is a balance in Renan's own text between these notions, as if he wanted to make each side of the contradiction neutralize the other. His mode is not so much the biographical as the rebiographical—that is, the sort of structure whose necessary reliance upon other texts is really a method for going past the texts to a human career or project which all of them cannot fully express. In other words, the very complexity of Renan's awareness of Jesus and of the textual traditions that have conveyed his life and teaching contradictorily into the present indicates an essential *excessiveness* with regard to both the nature of a text and what a text stands for. Thus a text exceeds its subject (Jesus) in codifying what he does not intend to be codified; a text exceeds what it stands for—Christianity, the history of the Church, religious authority—by offering the writer (Renan) an opportunity formally to use biography for an extrabiographical purpose: achieving intimacy and fraternity with an archetypal filial rebel. Moreover, this chosen intimacy signifies the inevitable inadequacy of biography as a mode for expressing the archetypal son (whom, we may recall, is for Renan the main agent for displacing the father).

Renan's *Vie de Jésus* is an instance, therefore, of how far the text is from being a passive object, of how far it also is from being (adequately described as) an image, or a symbol, or a metaphor for something else. A text is an actuality which engages a particular problematic or style of thought in the writer. There is perhaps something ingenuous in calling a text a beginning for the writer, since it is perfectly obvious that a produced text, even more than the act of writing, claims priority so far as the active writer is concerned. My rationale for dwelling here on the texts of the classics and of the Bible, however, is based on the remarkable extent to which even such indubitably beginning texts as these have themselves provoked a rich and complex sort of thought and written action, as it were, concerning the connections between beginnings and texts: the priority and eminence of both the classics and the Bible does not spare them from reflections of the sort undertaken by Renan, Nietzsche, or Milton.

Nietzsche, as Jaspers so persuasively characterizes him, typifies the modern writer for whom the text-as-beginning can become text-as-existence. This potential transfiguration is another, more extravagant aspect of what I have called the text's excessiveness, which includes the text's capacity to blur the distinction between beginning and beginning-again, or writing and rewriting, or positive text and interpretation. Here is Jaspers:

> The text, precisely because of its multiplicity of meanings, is almost non-existent, and thus there is a tendency to lose sight of it as the standard of truth of the interpretation. But, in another connection, Nietzsche insists all the more that the genuine text must be preserved from contamination by mistaken exegesis. . . .
>
> Here, where any unambiguous exposition would fail, Nietzsche's contradictions show what he is driving at. Existence both provides and is a product of exegesis. It is regarded as a circle that renews itself constantly while seeming to annul itself. It is now objectivity and now subjectivity; it appears first as substance and then as constantly annulled substance; though unquestionably there, it is constantly questioning and questionable; it is both being and non-being, the real and the apparent.[69]

The text calls into question the fundamental differences between writing as existential career and the stability of what is written; in Renan's case, this goes back to the dialectic between biographical texts and the pure sign, the first contaminating the second, the second dependent upon the first, which it scorns.

The pervasiveness of such practical and theoretical prejudices that one discovers lurking on the peripheries of modern writing (i.e., among textual critics, the Higher Critics and their opponents, individualists like Milton, the philologists Vico and Nietzsche, Freud in his theory of totem and sacrifice) become suddenly dramatic, even momentous, when encountered in such a work as Jean-Paul Sartre's La Nausée. Sartre's text is itself a "found" text that records the making of a text, its abandonment, and the action to which it gives rise. Roquentin's scholarly endeavors are set off against the library of Bouville, haunted by that poor creature of texts and their alphabetic tyranny, "L'Autodidacte." The scholar's failing impulse to produce a text coincides, throughout the novel, with the Autodidacte's quiet progress (and subsequent unhappiness) through texts. It is no fortuitous recurrence that when Roquentin confronts his text while writing, he sees the present in all its perplexing sufficiency and resistance: "Cette phrase, je l'avais pensée, elle avait d'abord été un peu de moi-même. A présent elle s'etait gravée dans le papier, elle faisait bloc contre moi . . . . Je jetai un regard anxieux autour de moi: du présent, rien d'autre que du présent."*[70] The text seems to actualize existence, to enable the sort of consciousness so misleadingly far from, for example, that of textual critics like Maas or even Renan.

As definite presence, as positivity, the text occupies a place from which everything else, especially the past, has been crowded out. Yet for the writer the text is also that made thing by virtue of which his career signifies its beginning, its course, and its goal. According to this formulation, then, the text is a pure sign of the writer's career, a sign—Roquentin muses—whose sheer force might residually inform even the writer's life: "Mais il viendrait bien un moment où le livre serait écrit, serait derriere moi et je pense qu'un peu de clarté tomberait sur mon passé."†[70a] But with a text, as with all beginnings, such clarity belongs either to constructions of fiction or to an unrecoverable past:

> Peut-être qu'un jour, en pensant precisement a cette heure-ci, à cette heure moine ou j'attends, le dos rond, qu'il soit temps de rentrer dans le train, peut-être que je sentirais mon coeur battre plus vite et que je me dirais: "C'est ce jour-là, à cette heure-là que toute a commencé." Et j'arriverais—au passé, rien qu'au passé—à m'accepter.‡[71]

These are the sort of pathetic distances and temporal ironies of which only the text is capable—or at least so the modern writer, from Mallarmé, Hopkins, and Conrad to Proust, Eliot, and Kafka, has discovered.

---

*"This sentence, I had thought, had once been a part of myself. Now it etched itself into the paper, it seemed to stand against me. . . . I looked anxiously around me: the present, nothing but the present."

† "But a time will come when the book will have been written, will be behind me, and I think then that a little light will be shed on my past."

‡ "Maybe one day, thinking precisely of this present moment, of this monkish hour as I wait, round-shouldered, that it may be time to climb back into the train, perhaps I shall feel my heart beating faster and I shall say to myself: 'That is the day, at that very hour, from which everything began.' And I will come to accept myself—in the past, only in the past."

III

At certain moments in the history of literature and, to make the point more general, in the work of certain writers at other moments in that history, producing a text—as an ideal goal for the writer—is extremely problematical. This is specially true of the modern writer. Why this is so is something I shall be speculating about a little later. The difficulty for such writers, as for such times, is in being able to distinguish adequately between the author as a human being (whatever his self-characterization), the author as a producing writer, and his production. Those moments and those writers ought to become a more prevalent theme of literary study, for their exemplary uncertainty, which to them appears abnormal, brings into question otherwise reified, "normal" notions held about texts.[72] Just as the digressions in *Tristram Shandy* or *A Tale of a Tub* shed important light upon accepted notions of plot and narrative continuity, just as eccentric writers like Milton and Swift challenge and even modify prevailing norms, so too the times and writers alluded to require rethinking what it means to produce and complete a text. If, as Piaget says, structuralism is in one of its negative aspects a method "dirigée contre quelques tendances dominantes à l'époque,"[73] then we can say that at certain times a writer's sense of the text he wishes to produce runs counter to the way in which the culture at large views a text.

The attitudes Ludwig Wittgenstein expresses toward the text he produced in *Philosophical Investigations* are interesting for the inner conflict they reflect. His unit of composition, the *Bemerkung* (note), he says in his preface, has turned the book into an "album" instead of "a good book." The reason for this is his inability to forge the *Bemerkungen* into a unity. And yet, according to G. E. M. Anscombe, Wittgenstein very carefully organized the book: "It is the assemblage of many *Bemerkungen*, together constituting a multifarious and ramified attack on the problems of philosophy that produces the effect that is intended .... So we have a very large number of worked and polished building blocks put together to make a whole."[74] This is the case despite the admitted fact that the transitions in the *Investigations,* together with a zigzag method of proceeding through the "wide field of thought," give an impression of a sort of failed text. Anscombe remarks earlier that Wittgenstein's method in the "Blue Book" was discontinuous dictation to students: "He would discuss for a while and then say, 'Now there's something you can take down' and dictate, then break off the discussion for further discussion and so on."[75] So Wittgenstein evidently felt that a text was what could be taken down, and yet he also felt that the completeness of treatment and perfection of statement that merits writing out can sometimes be abandoned for catholicity of scope. The *Investigations* seemed to have sacrificed one for the other, with the result, according to Anscombe, that Wittgenstein feared his book was "only remarks."

This immediately raises the question of what it is that a text contains if not "only remarks," and, related to it, the question of whether everything that is written is therefore a text. A text is not simply the record of an immediate desire to write; there is no analogy between writing and, let us say, eating as the consequence of hunger. Rather, a text distributes various textual intentions, regularly and on several axes; what unifies these intentions or impulses is something very difficult to generalize about. Foucault's analyses, while on the whole abstract, at least have the great merit of showing that a text is less a unit bound together by an individual author, a period, or the idea of a "work" or of an "idea" than it is a *discursive formation* made up of *statements.*[76] To those who persist in making of contingent printing devices (manuscript, book, document, newspaper, etc.) ontological units of irreducible value, it is possible to say that a text is a fundamental *epistemological judgment.* And like all judgments, it is largely circumstantial.

It is worth following Foucault a bit further here, since his argument contends that contrary to vulgar opinion, texts, properly speaking, are difficult to produce. The statements made by a text (contained in a text) are *conditions met* at a particular cultural time and place in a particular way: they are rarer than mere speaking and writing. A statement is not necessarily a sentence (just as for Wittgenstein a *Bemerkung* was not one necessarily either), nor is it simply a unit that can be described using grammar and logic. Moreover, since it is in and of discourse, a statement cannot be something latent that is realized by discourse: a statement is not the surface of which discourse is the depth. Yet the more Foucault rejects such descriptions of a statement, the more evident it is that a statement is rare and that it is a unit of effectiveness:

> The statement is not just another unity—above or below—sentences and

225

propositions; it is always invested in unities of this kind, or even in sequences of signs that do not obey their laws (and which may be lists, chance series, tables); it characterizes not what is given in them, but the very fact that they are given, and the way in which they are given [their effectiveness]. It has the quasi-invisibility of the "there is," which is effected in the very thing of which one can say: "there is this or that thing."[77]

Perhaps a prefiguration of what Foucault means by a statement is to be found in the smile of the Cheshire cat—or, as he himself says in the opening pages of *Les Mots et les choses,* in the list of animals given in a Chinese encyclopedia referred to in "The Analytical Language of John Wilkins" by Borges: "Although the statement cannot be hidden it is not visible either . . . . It is like the over-familiar that constantly eludes one." Another important aspect of the statement is that it is correlative with a *lack:* "There may in fact be—and always are—in the conditions of emergence of statements, exclusions, limits, or gaps that divide up their referential, validate only one series of modalities, enclose groups of coexistence, and prevent certain forms of use."[78] Thus a statement emerging prevents another utterance from emerging; conversely, with regard to a whole series of possibilities, a statement *emerges to be something else*—namely, a statement, but not an idea, or a sentence, or a passing remark.

At all events, one thing at least must be emphasized here: that the analysis of discourse [and of statements in and by discourse] thus understood, does not reveal the universality of a meaning, but brings to light the action of imposed rarity, with a fundamental power of affirmation. Rarity and affirmation: rarity, in the last resort of affirmation [Swyer's translation here is impossibly garbled: Foucault says, "the rarity of affirmation"]—certainly not any continuous outpouring of meaning, and certainly not any monarchy of the signifier.[79]

My notion is thus that certain writers for whom producing a text is an achievement fraught with problems represent and are constantly troubled by this curious mixture of affirmation and rarity. For them the text is the statement of a career fully commanded by neither public pressure (even though that plays a part) nor the ordinary conventions that prescribe a literary vocation. On the contrary, the career is aboriginal; hence its problems. To write for Grub Street is abhorrent, as is also the idea of writing a mere collection of works. The desired goal is a true whole, in which individual segments are subordinated to the totality of collective integration and collective affirmation. Further, the career in its rarity is even thought of as aberrant, not to say criminal. Thus whatever work is in fact produced suffers from radical uncertainty at the beginning; it is highly unconventional; it possesses its own inner dynamic; it is a constantly experienced but strangely impalpable whole partially revealing itself in individual works; it is haunted by antecedence, difference, sameness, and the future; and it never finally accomplishes its ideal aims, at least in its author's opinion. The writer's life, his career, and his text form a system of relationships whose configuration *in real human time* becomes progressively stronger (i.e., more distinct, more individualized and exacerbated). In fact, these relationships gradually become the writer's all-encompassing subject. On a pragmatic level, then, his text is his statement of the temporal course of his career, inscribed in language, and shot through and through with precisely these matters.

"Career" is the key notion in what I have been saying so far about the writer. For any author, his writing life is what sets him off from the normal quotidian element. During the earlier European tradition great poets like Dante and Virgil were considered inspired by the poetic afflatus, which also shaped their poetic vocation and guaranteed special allowances for them as vatic seers: a well-known example of this attitude, cited by Curtius in his chapter on the Muses, is found in Virgil's *Georgics* (2.475 ff.): "Me vero primum dulces ante omnia Musae solidus,/Quarum sacra fero ingenti percussus amore," etc.[80] In the modern period (my primary consideration here), the author's career is not something impelled into a specific course by "outside" agencies, whether they are called inspiration, Muses, or vision. I sacrifice considerable detail by skipping over whole periods of literary history until about the last quarter of the nineteenth century in Europe generally and in Britain and France especially in order to remark that the idea of a poetic or authorial vocation as a common cultural myth underwent severe change. Blake once described the change prophetically as the "Fair Nine, forsaking Poetry." So thorough had been the subjectivization of approach, so detached from traditional practices had the writing enterprise become—our discussion of Renan makes this point repeatedly—and so individualistic a tone had the literary voice produced—at least among writers whose aspiration was to uncommon status—that the poetic *vocation,* in the classical sense, had come to be replaced by a poetic *career.* Whereas the former required taking certain memorial steps and imitating a ritual progress, in the latter the writer had to create not only his art but also the very course of his writings. In ethical terms, therefore, a statement was for such writers without precedent. This had been a problem for the romantics certainly, as they vacillated between following classical models and stubbornly hewing out their own ways.[81] But by the mid-1870s in England, the self—or, as Meredith called the self-centered person in his novel, the egoist—had become one of the central themes in literature and indeed one of the author's main personal concerns.

To highlight the change between one generation and the next, we need to contrast a great popular institution like Dickens, whose career virtually included the public, with someone like Henry James. James is not only less accessible as a writer than Dickens: his novels and critical writings portray the lone figure surveying other writers or individuals who are under pressure to make difficult choices regarding virtually unprecedented problems. This is especially true of the characters in James's novels. Thus whereas Pip's ambitions in *Great Expectations* are modeled after conventional patterns—to rise in the world, become a gentleman, gain social position, and so forth—Isabel Archer's in *A Portrait of a Lady* are vaguer: indeed, her career is, she thinks egoistically, entirely of her own making.

Now, very little of what I have just been saying is more than common literary history—that the modern writer, his form, his characters, his subjects, and his style have become more private, less predictable. Still, certain consequences must be taken into account in characterizing literary texts appearing under these conditions. For example, the critic must acknowledge that the poet's text has become less ascertainable as the text's meaning has become more obscure: in and of themselves, words on a page become more and more essentially just that, words on a page, less easily interchangeable with unilateral sense fixed for the reader in and by the words. The words of a modern author gain meaning when juxtaposed with the words from another of his works, and the whole "figure in the carpet" slowly emerges as the entire corpus is viewed in this comparative manner. In the end, we see that there is an almost annoying resemblance between an author's egoism and the character of his work. Or, to put it differently, there is a real, unavoidable coincidence between an author's egocentricity and the kind of eccentricity found exclusively in his text.

Some light is shed on this coincidence by Foucault in the final pages of *Les Mots et les choses,* where he remarks how, after such writers as de Sade, Mallarmé, and Nietzsche, mimetic representation could convey neither an author's desires nor his eccentric psychological discoveries. Concurrently, the logic of syntax as well as the linear sequence of printed language in the work of the authors just cited is assaulted (and found wanting) by a wish to express nonsyntactic, nonsequential, and radically eccentric thought. Together with these writers, Marx, Saussure and Freud (as we saw in our analysis of *The Interpretation of Dreams*) invented systems of thought which no image in words could adequately represent. Renan's *Vie de Jésus* obviously falls into more or less the same category, for in all these cases we are dealing with writers for whom the notion of *logos* is taken in the most literal and *beginning* sense. Thus writing could no longer exhibit a predictive form like that of the classical realistic novel or the simple biographical continuum, form based either upon biological growth or a representative governing image. Instead, writing sought to constitute its own realm, inhabited from the beginning entirely by words and the spaces between them. In turn, the relationships between this realm and empirical reality were established according to particular strategies and enunciative functions.

Thus an author's role is now more the result of a performance (as Richard Poirier has recently shown[82]) than of a personality. It is possible, of course, to maintain that this predominance of function over entelechy has always been the case: all writers are in part performers. At the point in the modern period under discussion, however, the balance shifted so much that the writer seemed to be left with a role only when writing. Blanchot puts it this way: "The poet only exists poetically, as the possibility of a poem and, in this way, after the poem, although the poet exists opposite the poem."[83] A writer occupies no particular role once he ceases writing directly, as Dickens did, for a consuming public. Pushed back in on himself, the writer experiences his vitality in the process of composition, which, since it both nourishes and depletes the writer's identity, he sees as a system with ill-defined terminals and boundaries that is always encroaching upon his intimacy. The writer becomes what Conrad called "the worker" in language, and his activity "simply the conversion of nervous force into phrases." In writing there is no longer any proper starting or stopping, only activity resumed or interrupted—and this because for the self there is no stopping or starting, only a selfhood resumed or interrupted at some risk to the individual's security.

Nevertheless, the confusion between selfhood and the act of

writing makes the coincidence between an author's egocentricity and textual eccentricity seem to defy a rational comprehension of what a text is. This need not be the case, however, despite as in Conrad's case, an often querulous inability, as reflected in letters on extratextual dicta, to grasp his text rationally. A text is a statement made with signs, and those signs constitute a judgment already made that as signs they *shall be.* This judgment-statement excludes other signs, just as it includes the ones it intends.

Such a way of describing a text is *ethical,* in the widest sense of that term; furthermore, it is a method that refrains from discussing the origins of statement or its source in some absolute way. Rather, such a definition considers statement as an ethic of language, with a beginning made up or organized as well as sanctioned exclusions and inclusions, a setting amid other permitted statements, a continuity and ascertainable transformations that connect it with other statements in the order of discourse. Foucault's method is precisely to employ these descriptions, and because he deals with social instances of statement (in *Folie et déraison*) his discoveries are fairly dramatic. When leprosy was no longer the scourge of society at the end of the Middle Ages, society isolated "folly" and transformed it variously—despite its exclusion from society—into madness, irrationality, immorality, depravity, and so on. These exclusions entail designations and statements saying that such and such behavior is "folly" or "madness." Moreover, these designations become institutionalized—in hospitals, houses of correction, asylums, penal colonies, and the like. The relevance of all of Foucault's analyses (as we shall see in chapter 5) is that they enable one to understand, unmistakably, that statement has social and, preeminently, ethical force—of an admittedly particular technical (and discursive) kind.

Discourse is therefore the organized social ethic of language as statement making or as text making: "I am supposing that in every society the production of discourse is at once controlled, selected, organized and redistributed according to a certain number of procedures, whose role is to avert its powers and its dangers, to cope with chance events, to evade its ponderous, awesome materiality."[84] In 1916 Walter Benjamin put a similar ethical insight into language at the center of an essay on language in general and human language in particular. Before man's expulsion from Eden, Benjamin says, the only knowledge without a name was the knowledge of good and evil. All things have a name, all knowledge is nouns. The serpent tempts man with new knowledge, of good and evil, which thereafter

abandons the name. . . . [This new knowledge] is exterior knowledge, the uncreative imitation of [God's] creative verb. The name steps away from itself in this knowledge: the Fall is the moment of birth of man's language [*des menschlichen Wortes*], that in which the name no longer remains intact, that which has left behind a language that names and the language—one can say—that knew its own imminent magic, all this in order for language now to make itself deliberately magical from the outside. The word must communicate *something* now, outside itself. [*Das Wort soll "etwas" ausser sich selbst.*] This is really the original sin of the spirit of language. As it communicates outside of itself the word is something of a parody, by an explicitly mediate word, of the explicitly immediate word, of God's creative word [*das schaffende Gotteswort*]; it is the Fall of a fortunate essence of language [*der Verfall des seligen Sprachgeistes*] in Adam, who stands in the middle. There is indeed a basic sameness between the word which, according to the serpent's promise, perceives good and evil and the word which on the surface conveys information. The knowledge of things is based on the name, but knowledge of good and evil is, in the profound sense in which Kierkegaard conceives this word, idle chatter [*Geschwätz*] and chatter capable only of the purification and elevation to which the babbling man, i.e. the sinner, also had to submit, namely Judgement.[85]

Discourse, says Foucault, is things that are said (*les chose dites*)—what seems to be mere idle talk—whose rarity in a text (the occasion of their purification and elevation) is the form of judgment (on what is being excluded and on whomever does the exclusion), exteriority, and knowledge. The rarity of a text, in other words, has an overt public side to it which we have connected with the author's career and his "performance." There are no innocent texts.

How can we now discuss these matters specifically with reference to literary texts as they are produced in a given culture during a given period? At the outset there is the problem of evidence. At one pole we have unmanageably large bodies of information to deal with, and, at the other extreme, units so small as to take us into infinite regression. For example, how can we begin to speak of *a* culture? Conversely, at what precise moment in a writer's life, at what stage in his psychological development, can we locate his seminal insights? I propose a set of very gross, but I think useful, oppositions that structure an author's career. As I conceive of them, these oppositions are not abstractions that support a scheme, but rather practical exigencies in the form of choices between polar alternatives that an author faces during his career. They might even be called the technicoethical conditions of a writing career, conditions that make a career and a text possible once the framework of a poetic vocation (in the earlier sense) is no longer available. Perhaps Yeats was referring to something like these oppositions when he intimated in his *Autobiography* that no mind can engender till divided into two. [86] These conditions are respected by both the writer and his critic, the job of the latter being to redistinguish the outlines of the author's career in his (the critic's) writing. These oppositions therefore correspond to different phases of a career; yet even though one follows the other, the influence of each persists throughout the career. For example, Conrad's feeling that his career had no starting point—a reflection obviously connected with his fragile sense of beginnings—was something to which his mind and temperament consistently reverted even after years of sustained production. Consider, for example, the following written to Edward Garnett in 1896, after Conrad had already completed at least six important works:

> Other writers have some starting point. Something to catch hold of. They start from an anecdote—from a newspaper paragraph (a book may be suggested by a casual sentence in an old almanack). They lean on dialect—or on tradition—or on history—or on the prejudice or the fad of the hour; they trade upon some tie or some conviction of their time—or upon the absence of these things—which they can abuse or praise. But at any rate they know something to begin with—while I don't. I have had some impressions, some sensations of common things. And it's all faded—my very being seems faded and thin like the ghost of a blonde and sentimental woman, haunting romantic ruins pervaded by rats. I am exceedingly miserable. My task appears to me as sensible as lifting the world without that fulcrum which even that conceited ass, Archimedes, admitted to be necessary.[87]

This sort of preliminary concern, part of the very earliest sort of quandary faced by a writer, testifies to Piaget's observation that "les racines sont opératoires." Even in his mature fiction Conrad's mind was attracted to reflections upon, scenes of, and feelings at the *beginning*—as for example in this haunting, famous passage from *Heart of Darkness:*

> Going up the river was like traveling back to the earliest beginnings of the world, when vegetation rioted on the earth and the big trees were kings. An empty stream, a great silence, an impenetrable forest .... We were wanderers on prehistoric earth, on an earth that wore the aspect of an unknown planet. We could have fancied ourselves the first of men taking possession of an accursed inheritance to be subdued at the cost of profound anguish and of excessive toil .... The streamer toiled along slowly on the edge of a black and incomprehensible frenzy. The prehistoric man was cursing us, praying to us, welcoming us—who could tell? We were cut off from the

comprehension of our surroundings; we glided past like phantoms, wondering and secretly appalled, as sane men would be before an enthusiastic outbreak in a madhouse. We could not understand because we were too far and could not remember, because we were traveling in the night of first ages, of those ages that are gone, leaving hardly a sign—and no memories.[88]

Although the opposition (which I shall presently enumerate) follow each other, then, they are all potentially present in every career and in every phase of a career; *time and the sense of a course being traversed are responsible for revealing one or the other of them more decisively.* What is most important about these oppositions is that together they compose the author's career into a development that, from the point of view of his production, is the process that actively creates and finally fulfills his text. Another necessary qualification is that whereas I am primarily discussing a period of about fifty years in European (particularly British and French) literary history—years that give rise to a radical rethinking of what it means to create a text—there are examples from other periods for which some of the modern examples are relevant. All writers have faced the problems of the conflict between coherent development, let us say, and the mere dispersion of energy. All writers, certainly from the Renaissance on, have meditated in language upon the peculiarities of language. So while we can and do cite examples from many periods in history, these fifty years provide us with a sustained examination of the issues at other times. Such writers as Wilde, Hopkins, Proust, James, Conrad, and T. E. Lawrence in their works and lives completely transform the text from an object to be gained into an unceasing struggle to be a writer, into what Lawrence called "the everlasting effort to write."

In these writers, then, we find attitudes toward writing that, judged by most standards, are monstrously exaggerated. When Wilde adopted Axel's dictum that living is for servants, he might have also been implying that living in the ordinary sense isn't for writers. As a project, being a writer takes up most of one's energy. Here again is Conrad complaining to Garnett:

I seem to have lost all *sense* of style and yet I am haunted, mercilessly haunted by the *necessity* of style. And that story I can't write weaves itself into all I see, into all I speak, into all I think, into the lines of every book I try to read. I haven't read for days. You know how bad it is when one feels one's liver, or lungs. Well I feel my brain. I am distinctly conscious of the contents of my head. My story is there in a fluid—in an evading shape. I can't get hold of it. It is all there—to bursting, yet I can't get hold of it no more than you can grasp a handful of water.[89]

233

The pressure of such experiences prompted the following outburst (already quoted in chapter 3) from Conrad to A. H. Davray: "La solitude me gagne; elle m'absorbe. Je ne vois rien, je ne lis rien. C'est comme une éspèce de tombe, qui serait en même temps un enfer, où il faut écrire, écrire, écrire." Conrad saw everything in the tormenting framework of the writing life, whose imperatives seemed limitless. The result of undergoing such tyrannical domination was that even the writer's personal life—for the critic as well as for the writer himself—became matter for the writing project.

This is, I think, a significant critical point, since it has far-reaching importance for the kind of literary study such writers have inspired. After two generations, beginning about 1875, of writers like Joyce, Hopkins, Eliot, Conrad, Kafka, Mallarmé, and so on—writers whose every ounce of energy was sapped by their continual efforts to experience and to will their production into written life—there is considerable pressure on the present-day critic to consider everything committed to paper by the writer (letters, notes, revisions, drafts, autobiography) as influencing the writer's career. Therefore, the practical notion of "text" is obliged to include a very wide network of relationships: between notes (for instance) and a "final" version, between letters and a tale, between revisions and early drafts, and so on. By the time most of these relationships have been reconstructed by the critic, the simple sequence of events in the writer's life will have undergone considerable modification. A recent case in point is the posthumous publication of the original version of *The Wasteland*: our knowledge of Eliot and of the poem is thereby considerably refined, perhaps even significantly changed; new possibilities for knowledge about Eliot's poetry as a whole now appear; and Eliot's reader can recognize elements omitted from the standard text of the poem insinuating themselves in later poems.[90]

But this type of modification in knowledge happens regularly, for both critic and reader. The very process of composition obviously causes the integral text to seem constantly in the act of changing; new units appear to assemble sections of work into other significant wholes. What every writer—this is no less true of the critic—militates against is mere dispersion, the fear that his writing is only a bunch of scattered occasions. He has an interest in preventing the work from degenerating into a miscellany of writings, governed successfully by neither personality nor time. For the writer, as for the critic, the notion of career as statement becomes privileged, if only because such shorthand terms as

"Milton says . . ." or "In Eliot . . ." signify the existence of a text absolutely coextensive and even identical with a career intending the text. The career permits one to see a sequence of intelligible development, not simply of accumulation. In marshaling his energies to shape his artistic life, the writer accepts the passage of time on his own terms: time is transvalued into a sequence of personal achievements connected by a dynamic of their own. The displacement of empirical time by artistic time is one of the happier results of the displacements of the normal human life by the writing career.

One of two qualifications remains to be made before proceeding to describe the seminal oppositions alluded to above. In an examination of this relatively modest length, it is obviously impossible to write anything resembling a full literary history. The alternative, then, is to choose a number of figures who make of the period a structural unity by virtue of two important qualities: their own systematic struggle with the difficulties of coherence, and the strength of their work, which compels the literary history of their period into their forms and idioms. This is especially paradoxical with the writers in question, for no writers could be more idiosyncratic: how can they, then, be considered exemplary of a period? Because the polar extremities to which their thought took them establish an axis from which all less extreme thought is measured. Thus although there was much other literary production contemporary with them, they abide as the major authors for whom production was always problematic. To them the text was above all the metaphor for an ideal resolution, for the exteriority that affirms the will to write over and above mere being. More than the average user of language, such writers exaggerate and make plain in their eccentricity and solitude the text's exteriority, that is, the true alienation of all writing as it stands out from the natural order. What is heroic about this exaggeration is the willingness to accept the terrifying freedom of individuality. To make, as they did, "I write" into a solitary sovereignty is to be free of a great number of social and psychological limitations, except those of the literary career. A text in such a view of it does not depend for its validity upon communication, a social act, neither upon mimetic representation, nor upon a single point of origin. Rather, the text is constantly produced, constantly justified during and by its author's career. Thus a text can never be simply completed as a voyage is completed, in stages, but is conceived in terms of something beyond even the massive effort that characterizes the continuing enterprise of the career. Such writers as I shall be describing rarely viewed their text face to face as a man looks at an object. As T. E. Lawrence put it in *The Mint:* "When we write we are not happy: we only recollect it: and a recollection of the exceeding subtlety of happiness has something of the infect, unlawful: it being an overdraft on life."[91] The text, from the beginning, is *excess.*

IV

The first opposition (or pair of opposed, alternative choices for the writer) is the one that concerns us most directly when we discuss any writer: the conflict, constant in some cases, between an author's career as a productive writer and either the beginning or the end of that career—i.e., those times when he has not yet begun to write or when he has stopped writing entirely. Sometimes the career is threatened with extinction during its progress. What matters to the writer then is preeminently what matters to us as well: whether or not that which he is in the process of writing will finally appear on the page, in print, or in a book, as a text preserved. Can he keep appearing? He may, as we shall see, endlessly bewail his inability to appear, and even do his complaining in writing. Writing about his writing can then be not writing at all, from his point of view, just as appearing—in Hopkins's case, for example—is entirely sterile, without issue, almost as bad as not appearing at all.

The first opposition, between career and noncareer, is capable of many modulations and gradations, all of which are fully evident to the writer himself. When it comes to seeing the differences between writing and not writing, again very little is lost on him. Thus he sees his life before he started his career as wholly distinct from his writing life. He worries whether he can continue to produce. He wonders what will make him stop. He examines the amount of time it takes him to write and notes the moment when his immediate project is completed. In all cases, the polarity between career and noncareer is a matter for radical perception, and its evidence is a text in the course (or not) of being constituted. From the beginning, then, according to Merleau-Ponty,

the experience of perception is our presence at the moment when things, truths, values are constituted for us; that perception is a nascent *logos;* that it teaches us, outside all dogmatism, the true conditions of objectivity itself; that it summons us to the tasks of knowledge and action. It is not a question of reducing human knowledge to sensation, but of assisting at the birth of this knowledge, to make it as sensible as possible, to recover the consciousness of rationality. This experience of rationality is lost when we take it for granted as self-evident, but is on the contrary, re-discovered when it is made to appear against the background of non-human nature.[92]

For the writer, "perception" of his text is literally the act of constituting—that is, of writing—his nascent *logos.* Without such a material fact there can be no rationality and, of course, no career. Each incremental addition to the text is a rediscovery of what is for the writer privileged evidence of his *raison d'être.*

Yet the rationality of the text and of the career conflicts, I think, with the natural and the human: Merleau-Ponty's comments ought to end with "the background of *human* nature." Modern literature converts a dependence on writing into a method for isolating writing and the writer from what is natural and human. The writer's peculiarity is that he is a writer or, as Baudelaire once put it, that he is "un faux accord dans la divine symphonie"[93] (a discord in the divine symphony). Writing is an acquired mannerism, a performance, a characteristic gesture of inscription that separates the spaces of the page from the spaces of "life." To Mallarmé there is a miracle in the disappearance of a fact of nature as a result of the play of language ("selon le jeu de la parole").[94] To Wilde, "Nature's lack of design, her curious crudities, her extraordinary monotony, her absolutely unfinished condition" makes art "a spirited protest, our gallant attempt to teach Nature her proper place."[95] From the beginning of a writer's career, art is an activity that leaves behind Pater's "mere machinery of nature"; "la composition," Baudelaire said marginally, "implique la complication."[96]

T. E. Lawrence, Conrad, Hopkins, and Wilde are of paramount importance in exemplifying the kind of harrowing complication which this antagonism between more or less "naturally" living and writing can represent to a writer. All were men to whom the writing life was literally secondary; that is, it followed and in most ways conflicted with another life. Conrad was a sailor, Hopkins a priest, Lawrence a man of action, Wilde a public personality. To none of them did writing come easily, and as a result each developed mannerisms of style and thought that make them seem endowed with what Hopkins calls "a vice of queerness." Most of these mannerisms reflect the attempts by each to find suitable means for expressing, in writing, experiences taken from his "other" life. In each case, the interplay of forces between the writing career and the antecedent or (for Wilde and Hopkins) concurrent form of life produced an intense specialization of literary technique—so specialized as to make the writing truly begin something new in the most active and literal sense. Wilde's epigrammatic flair, to take one example, gained in intensity and in the ability to show how brilliant it was possible to be in life as he became increasingly better known as a writer whose plays reflected the ethos of his outrageous nonliterary life. By the time of *The Importance of Being Earnest* (1895), his manner had become so willful that at the end of the play his characters, through a remarkably brilliant series of moves, are able to originate themselves in the mock baptismal rituals of the last act. Algernon and Jack are brothers because a book says so, and it is only when their fancy soars impossibly high to match the book that their brotherhood becomes a fact of birth. Just as Wilde created himself—at what was later revealed to be an exorbitant expense—so too do his fictional creations seem to be what Yeats called "self-born mockers" of ordinary middle-class life.

The public demands on Wilde made him pursue his vertiginous course to a conclusion that finally destroyed him as writer and as citizen. Yet in what Wilde considered a penitent work, *De Profundis,* he is far busier shaping his career than being penitent. If (he says to "Bosie" Douglas) I was formerly like the Marquis de Sade or Gilles de Retz, now, in prison, I am paying the price, but my new model is Christ. Wilde cannot help turning the brutal experiences of his life into a statement whose form elegantly detains his writing and public lives on the page so that they may be balanced: the plays, epigrams, stories, and fables of his demonic career are redeemed, set off, neutralized by his horrible punishment and subsequent conversion. Thus in *De Profundis* Wilde substitutes a fully shaped, fully written-out or stated career composed of nice balances (sin, punishment, redemption: wit, jail, Christianity: writer-dandy, fall from favor, penitence) in place of any attempt psychologically, morally, or socially to understand what he was all about. There is to be no comment about this career, except that it is as special as, say, an epigram like "Only the shallow know themselves." The most Wilde can say is that he has stated the pattern of his life—which really means that, like one of his plots, his career has triumphed, at least in his writing about himself. And Proust perfectly understood Wilde's aesthetic attitude. Commenting on Wilde's "sadness" over Lucien de Rubempré's death (in Balzac's *Splendeurs et misères de courtisanes*), Proust adds in vindication that Wilde

etait un lecteur particulièrement bien choisi et élu pour adopter ce point de vue plus complètement que la plupart des lecteurs. Mais on ne peut s'empêcher de penser que, quelque années plus tard, il devait être Lucien de Rubempré lui-même. Et la fin de Lucien . . . à la Conciergerie, voyant toute sa brillante existence mondaine écroulée sur la preuve qui est faite qu'il vivait dans l'intimité d'un forçat, n'etait que l'anticipation—inconnue encore de Wilde, il est vraie—de ce qui devait précisément arriver à Wilde.*[97]

The extent to which the formality of the writing career can from the very beginning oppose the threats of real life is more startlingly shown in *The Seven Pillars of Wisdom*. Of this book and its author, the *emptiness* that Malraux remarked properly refers to Lawrence's role in the Arab revolt. At first enthusiastically himself, then leader-initiator of the revolt, then double-dealing British agent, then finally a man shocked at his hypocrisy, Lawrence turns himself into an author quite late in the book. Here is an important passage from chapter 99:

It was a hard task for me to straddle feeling and action. I had had one craving all my life—for the power of self-expression in some imaginative form—but had been too diffuse ever to acquire a technique. At last accident, with perverted humour, in casting me as a man of action had given me a place in the Arab Revolt, a theme ready and epic to a direct eye and hand, thus offering me an outlet in literature, the technique-less art. Whereupon I became excited only over mechanism.[98]

By then the revolt had gone its own way. Damascus was soon to be liberated, and all Lawrence could do was formally reconstruct his role and his dubious achievement. There seemed to him no way to do that, and somehow also save himself in the bargain, except by creating himself when he began to write as historian-*manqué*, as author of epic mechanisms without conclusive meaning and leading to no point except an aesthetic one. Even when subsequently he did untold damage to his personality by trying to commit "mind-suicide" in the ranks of the RAF, he still sought for literary exoneration in *The Mint,* a precise and frank account of his conversion into common coin, which he rendered, paradoxically, in the most "worked" prose he could manage.

*"was a particularly well-chosen, predestined reader to adopt this point of view more completely than the majority of readers. But one cannot help thinking that several years later he was himself to be Lucien de Rubempré. And Lucien's end . . . at the Conciergerie, watching his brilliant worldly existence collapsing because he now lived a life whose intimacy was that of a convict, all this had been an anticipation—hitherto unknown to Wilde—of what precisely was to be Wilde's own fate."

BEGINNINGS

The relationship between a writing career and a life of taking physical risks was accompanied in Lawrence's case, not accidentally, by an extraordinary solicitude for the actual manuscripts he produced, which (strangely enough) he was constantly losing. One of the most curious themes running through the literature and literary mythology of the period we are discussing is how very hard it was for the writer to make his works last, literally and materially in written form. This threat of impermanence was a perpetual reminder of how slender was the evidence that the career had begun and was proceeding. The first manuscript of *The Seven Pillars of Wisdom* was destroyed unaccountably, and Lawrence believed that a mysterious plot lay behind the loss. Hopkins burnt his poems periodically. Wilde averred (comically, it is true) that it took him half a day to put in a comma, then half a day to take it out. Mallarmé agonized over destroying the paper's blankness. Conrad's efforts physically to write were dogged with every known variety of psychosomatic illness, including gout, arthritis, and cramps. Proust's years of writing were a near-lethal existence. Perhaps the most pitiless account of the writer's physical trouble in trying to make the text a printed object is Gissing's *New Grub Street,* a novelistic diagnosis of the period under discussion. Every writer in the novel dies or loses his manuscript, so fearful are the dangers of print, so humanly destructive the conditions of its production. In all this we find the writer afflicted with terror for having dared transgress an apprehensible, but generally unknowable, force which his career has in some way offended. Such is part of the price of being, according to Rimbaud, "le grand malade, le grand criminel, le grand maudit."

Mysterious threats, therefore, sometimes necessitate the initial formulation of the authorial project on another level, where its ability to persist is rather devious. The writer's project, nurtured within the special environment of a career besieged on all sides and accomplished (if ever) in the solitary transcendance of a text always becoming, can be described in unique languages of effort and invisibility, and of originality and repetition. Effort and invisibility comprise a language grounded in negatives whose preponderance manages to stir the author's yearnings into expressions of almost unimaginable goals. One finds some of this described in the twenty-third of Rilke's *Sonnets to Orpheus,* Part 1, where the Being attained at the end of the poem is associated with a hyperbolic, non-specific and uncircumstantial place.

240

O erst *dann,* wenn der Flug
nicht mehr um seinetwillen
wird in die Himmelsstillen
steigen, sich selber genug,

um in lichten Profilen,
als das Gerät, das gelang,
Liebling der Winde zu spielen,
sicher schwenkend und schlank,—

erst wenn ein reines Wohin
wachsender Apparate
Knabenstolz Überwiegt,

wir, überstürzt von Gewinn,
jener den Fernen Genahte
sein, was er einsam erfliegt.*[99]

And also in Merleau-Ponty's fascinated regard for Cézanne, who saw his work as "only an essay, an approach to painting," whose aim was to mix "up all our categories in laying out its oneiric universe of carnal essences, of affective likenesses, of mute meanings." The artist located his work in a hesitating place "at the beginning of the world." His work thus located, the artist becomes "oriented toward the idea of the project of an infinite Logos,"[100] or, as Proust says, "l'idée de mon oeuvre etait dans ma tête . . . en perpetual devenir."†[101]

These images of the artist's work at its beginning as a kind of hyperbole are related to another sort of language used to characterize the text as the beginning of a literary career. In both cases, however, the text intended is a pure sign, free of

*"O not till the time when flight
no longer will mount for its own sake
into the sky stillnesses,
sufficient unto itself,

that in luminous profiling
as the tool that succeeded,
it may play the winds' favorite,
surely curving and slim,—

not till a pure whither
outweighs boyish pride
of growing machines,

will, headlong with winning,
one who has neared the distances
be his lone flight's attaining."

†"the idea of my work was lodged within my head . . . in a state of perpetual becoming."

interpretation, of the (generally) difficult circumstances of its production, of interventions in its own internal play. It stands in no complex system of relationships with history and society, but only in one-to-one correspondence with the artist's career, of which it is, from beginning to infinity, the only statement. To say this the writer employs a vocabulary expressing extreme originality and extreme repetition. All the genres of contemporary writing except literature, according to Mallarmé, are reportage. On the other hand, in poetry

le vers qui de plusieurs vocables refait un mot total, neuf, étranger à la langue et comme incantatoire, achève cet isolement de la parole: niant, d'un trait souverain, le hasard demeuré aux termes malgré l'artifice de leur retrempe alternée en le sens et la sonorité, et vous cause cette surprise de n'avoir ouï jamais tel fragment ordinaire d'élocution, en même temps que la reminiscence de l'objet nommé baigne dans une neuve atmosphère.*[102]

The motifs of isolation, extreme originality, sovereignty, and novelty alternate in this description with those of the ordinary, the repeated, the habitual. Similarly in Mallarmé's most celebrated critical phrase, a complex idea unites the extreme subjectivity (and originality) of the poet with the most common of all literary objects, the book: "Une proposition qui émane de moi . . . sommaire veut, que tout, au monde, existe pour aboutir à un livre."[103]   Writing is therefore rewriting, which has all the force of original—i.e., first-time—writing.

This internal contradiction in Mallarmé's comments on the literary text heightens the hyperbole deliberately. A text is no longer *a* book, but *The Book;* just as, by extension, writing is everything and all, not merely something. The consequence is to use this fortified hyperbole to make the text, and the writing career, different from all other human productions. This is an essential part of what Renato Poggioli has called *the transhumanizing tendency* of avant-garde poetics;[104]   in Mallarmé the goal is to make of the text "l'oeuvre pur" or, as he says elsewhere, the unsigned "hymne, harmonie et joie, comme pur ensemble groupé dans quelque circonstance fulgurante, des relations entre tout."†[105]   But such a metamorphosis of writing into a trans-

*"the verse which out of several vocables, remakes a total word, a new word, a stranger to the language, as if incantatory, achieves an isolation of speech: cancelling, by virtue of a sovereign trait (*niant, d'un trait souverain*) the risk lodged in terms despite the artifice of their being steeped alternately in sense and sonority, causes you that surprise of never having heard (*de n'avoir ouï jamais*) that ordinarily familiar sounding fragment, at the same time that recollection of the named object bathes in a new atmosphere."

†"hymn, harmony and joy as a pure ensemble grouped together in some floating circumstance, of relationships between all."

human work entails also a metamorphosis of time, and here Proust provides the most scrupulous account.

In *Le Temps retrouvé,* there is an extraordinary, finely detailed description of a man beginning to think as a writer about to begin his work. Placed at the (unfinished) conclusion of an enormously rich novel, the initial process of Marcel's meditation upon a literary project, and his special loyalty to it, vastly magnifies our sense of sharing the intimacy of his choice to be a writer. Throughout those final pages a contrast is sustained between his empirical self, exposed to interior and exterior dangers, and his artistic self, whose creation he intends as an ultimate replacement for the loss of memory, will, and existence in his empirical self. What is common to both selves is the idea of death, which he says "me tenait une compagnie aussi incessante que l'idée du moi."[106] In this condition, half-dead already, he begins to plan his writing. He will write so that there will be no discontinuity in the world of past time he has inhabited and now carries within him in order to transcribe it. His point of departure is the evening when his mother gave in to him, and when he remembers hearing a bell announcing Swann's departure and his mother's return:

> Il fallait qu'il n'y eût pas eu discontinuité, que je n'eusse pas un instant cessé d'exister, de penser, d'avoir conscience de moi, puisque cet instant ancien tenait encore à moi, que je pouvais encore retourner jusqu'à lui, rien qu'en descendant plus profondément en moi.*[107]

But such ambitions, as well as those to make his work like a cathedral, a refuge from oblivion, are refinements of a will to write set in motion in the course of a morning at the Guermantes house. And that material experience is the culmination of many other experiences of increased awareness, of which this final one is a climax as much as the end.

The whole of *A la recherche du temps perdu* is a preparation for the writing career which, it has not escaped some critics, Marcel by the end of the novel is unlikely ever really to begin. [108] Nevertheless, Proust's analyses of the tension between the man *tout court* and the incipient writer are more relevant to our point, the initial opposition between career and no career, especially as they take place within the literary text itself. Even if the actual

---

*"It was necessary to have had no discontinuity, that I would not have ceased to exist for an instant, nor to have not thought, nor to have had no self-consciousness, in order for this instant from out of the past to have held me enough for me to return to it just by going within myself more deeply."

beginning of Marcel's work is forever postponed, Proust's own highly managed text appears literally to be a sort of pre-text for Marcel's. The peculiarity of this illusion making is that, like Joyce in *Ulysses,* Proust uses his text to assimilate all phases of the writer's life including those that precede the writer's life, whereas Marcel and Dedalus exist exclusively as writers-to-be: the work of each of the latter is a project of a never-to-be attained future, incorporated as a beginning into another work. Yet Joyce and Proust encourage the reader to assume that were Dedalus and Marcel actually to produce texts, these would resemble *Ulysses* and *A la recherche.* The effect is reminiscent of Pericles' "Thou that beget'st him that did beget"; the text is polymorphous to the extent that it includes not only the career of the writer who (might have) produced it, but also his life before he was a producer and a description of its putative genesis. Leo Bersani perceptively notes that "the world [Marcel] sets out to describe is first of all in his own mind, and its existence outside his mind cannot extend beyond his decisions as a writer. Reality is now bearable because, by re-creating it from the perspective of memory, he has made of it, as Gaetan Picon writes, 'an *anteriority* from which aggressions and surprises can no longer come.' " [109] Reality *before* the writing life is seen as part of beginning to write.

Proust's aesthetic, of course, is built on the differences between the writing life and all other forms: the heavy polemic in *Contre Sainte-Beuve* repeats the difference in many ways. "He [Sainte-Beuve] made no distinction between the literary life . . . and conversation."[110] The writer is "the self which had awaited its turn while one's social self had been in the company of others."[111] Although the attack on Sainte-Beuve is imagined as, interestingly enough, a conversation with Proust's mother, there seems to be no doubt in Proust's mind that writing is a principle of intentional, radical individuality rationally divorced from ordinary life. Here is how he sums up the process of begetting a text using a *rarefied* language of procreation and enjoyment (note how the author's filial sentiments somehow get included):

Ne pas oublier: le talent est le critérium de l'originalité, l'originalité est le critérium de la sincérité, le plaisir (pour celui qui écrit) est peut-être le critérium de la vérité du talent.

Ne pas oublier qu'il est presque aussi stupide de dire pour parler d'un livre: "C'est très intelligent," que "Il aimait bien sa mère." Mais le premier n'est pas encore mis en lumière.

Ne pas oublier: les livres sont l'oeuvre de la solitude et les *enfants du silence.* Les enfants du silence ne doivent rien avoir de commun avec les enfants de la parole. . . .

Ne pas oublier: la matière de nos livres, la substance de nos phrases doit être immatérielle, non prise telle quelle dans la réalité, mais nos phrases elles-mêmes et les épisodes aussi doivent être faits de la substance transparente de nos minutes les meilleures, où nous sommes hors de la réalité et du présent.*[112]

A book's intelligence is no more an issue than a man's love for his mother; both are natural enough without being more than occasional, or circumstantial, and initially necessary. It is the use to which they are put that counts, just as in conceiving of an author's life before he begins to write Proust transforms it into a *beginning for* that life. Or, to add another parallel, it is like Proust's ability to imagine a novel and a work of criticism (*A la recherche* and *Contre Sainte-Beuve*) as mutually interchangeable only so long as both are *written* texts and not mere children of speech.

The whole of *A la recherche* dramatically demonstrates these ideas. Bergotte, for example, scarcely seems to believe that he is both the author of his own book and also the officious snob he evidently is;[113] for Marcel, a writer's work is so novel as to make the connections between things appear totally different;[114] the matter of art must be "distincte, nouvelle, d'une transparence, d'une sonorité speciales, compacte, fraichissante et rose." †[115] In short, the beginning premise of all writing is loss ("les vrais paradis sont les paradis qu'on a perdus" ‡[116]): to begin to write, as Marcel sees in *Le Temps retrouvé*, is to view all the temporal losses one has endured as leading inevitably to a career (the word Marcel uses is a *vocation*—"une vocation" [117]). Far from being a succession of described objects, the text *begins* to take form, and "ne commencera qu'au moment où l'ecrivain prendra deux objets différents, posera leur rapport . . . et les enfermera dans les

---

*"Do not forget: talent is the criterion of originality, originality is the criterion of sincerity, pleasure (for he who writes) is perhaps the criterion of the reality of talent.

Do not forget that it is almost as stupid to say of a book that 'it is very intelligent' as to say 'he really likes his mother.' But the first statement hasn't yet been shown up for what it is.

Do not forget: books are the work of solitude and are the *children of silence.* Children of silence ought to have nothing in common with children of speech, with ideas born out of a desire for something, out of a sense of blame, out of an opinion, that is, out of an obscure idea.

Do not forget: the material of our books, the substance of our sentences have to be immaterial, not taken directly from reality, but our sentences themselves as well as the episodes must be made out of the transparent substance of our best moments, in which we are outside of reality and of the present."

† "distinct, new, of a special transparency and sonority, compact, cool."

‡ "real paradises are lost paradises"

anneaux nécessaires d'un beau style." *[118]   In giving up the immediacy of objects, the writer enters the realm of the relationships among them, their real essences, which he must perforce imagine (or recollect) retrospectively.

Here we reach the central paradox of the text as representing and including the beginning and the career in opposition to empirical time and human time. What Marcel thinks about in the Guermantes library is what he projects for the future: his career, what a text ought to be, the *oeuvre* to come. Thus all his past—as memory, and not simply as occurrence—is preparation for the text to come. And yet *A la recherche* itself is memory: materially, that is, as a textual entity, it contains all the elements of the future text. Since Marcel's intention to write is formed within the novel, then we can say of *A la recherche* that it is the event which begins the career and the text. In a fairly literal double sense the novel before us is beginning itself: it begins, and it is the beginning. It is all of that anteriority which leads to the present (memory); it is the beginning that intends the future. Blanchot catches this peculiarly interesting situation when he says: "Ce que [l'oeuvre] dit ce n'est pas seulement ce qu'elle est au moment de naître, quand elle commence, mais elle dit toujours sous une lumière ou sous une autre: commencement. C'est en cela que l'histoire lui appartient et que cependant elle lui échappe." †[119]

Because the text of Proust's novel is where memory and future exist, there are further coincidences present as well. One is Proust's interest in sexual inversion, which, he says at the end of the excursus on homosexuality in *Sodom et Gomorrhe*, dates back "à cet hermaphroditisme initial dont quelques rudiments d'organes male dans l'anatomie de la femme et d'organes femelles dans l'anatomie de l'homme semblent conserver la trace." ‡[120]   So, too, the text preserves the traces of fertile memory and of a potent future, traces always poised at the beginning of some great work completely prepared for and still to be done: "Les choses, en effet, sont pour le moins doubles." §[121]   Albertine and Saint-Loup

---

*"will only begin at the moment the writer chooses two different objects, postulates their relationship to each other . . . and then encloses them in the necessary rings of a fine style."

†"what [the work] says is not only what it is at the moment of birth, but, in one way or another, it always says: beginning. It is in this way that history belongs to it and, however, it escapes history."

‡"to that initial hermaphroditism of which some rudimentary male organs in the woman's anatomy and female organs in the man's anatomy seem to conserve the trace."

§"In effect things are at least double."

are later revealed to have "un secret parallele et que je n'avais pas soupçonné." *[122] It is this discovery which immediately precedes, and reflects, Marcel's morning at the Guermantes when he recognizes the doubleness of his own life—as man and as incipient writer. The unity of antitheses he perceives between all the diametric oppositions in the characters themselves beautifully suggests his consciousness in the library of his career and his past, opposed and yet bound together:

> Et c'était eux qui étaient morts, eux dont je pouvais, separées par un intervelle en somme si bref, mettre en regard l'image ultime, devant la tranchée, dans la rivière, de l'image première qui, même pour Albertine, ne valait plus pour moi que par son association avec celle du soleil couchant sur la mer.†[123]

The juxtaposition of images for Marcel the writer-to-be, however, takes a specifically material form (again during his sojourn in the library) of the text as a produced work. His unpremeditated choice of Sand's *François le Champi* from the shelves stimulates his memory involuntarily; it is the climactic experience in a series of four such memories that morning, each one triggered by a physical sensation, each returning Marcel to some particular episode in the near or distant past, each one resurrecting the past so vividly as to give Marcel the impression of an essence outside time. But in each case the experience derives from a place or an object, from a place and a sensation, never from an abstract essence or theoretical situation: "Toujours, dans ces resurrections-là, le lieu lointain engendré autour de la sensation commune s'était accouplé un instant, comme un lutteur, au lieu actual." ‡[124] Thus the actual book of *François le Champi* returns Marcel to his childhood in Combray ("pendant la nuit peut-être la plus douce et la plus triste de ma vie"§[125]). And immediately after experiencing this return he starts to reflect on his future career as a writer, all of this now imagined prospectively through the book he holds in his hands "retrouvé aujourd'hui dans la bibliothèque des Guermantes précisément, par le jour plus beau et dont s'éclairaient soudain non seulement les tâtonnements anciens

---

* "a secret parallelism that I had never suspected."

†"They had died; yet for them I had been able, separated by an interval which was finally so brief, to link together the final image ... with the first image which, also for Albertine, was valuable for me only by its association with the sun setting on the sea."

‡"Always, in those resurrections, the distant locale, which was given rise to by the common sensation, coupled with, like a wrestler, the present locale."

§ "during what was perhaps the saddest and sweetest night of my life"

de ma pensée, mais même le but de ma vie et peut-être de l'art."* [126]

Proust's strategy in making a book in Marcel's hands the last of that series of memories triggered by the *madeleine* is profoundly just. At once the most original of objects (as the writer's first text, the reader's first experience of reading, the first instance of numerous copies) and one of the most common (as one copy among the virtually infinite number of books written, read, printed, and preserved), a book releases for Marcel a special stream of reflections:

> La première edition d'un ouvrage m'eut été plus precieuse que les autres, mais j'aurais entendu par elle l'édition où je le lu pour la première fois. Je rechercherais les éditions originales, je veux dire celles où j'eus de ce livre une impression originale. Car les impressions suivantes ne le sont plus. Je collectionnerais pour les romans les reliures d'autrefois, celles du temps où je lus mes premiers romans et qui entendaient tant de fois papa me dire: "Tiens-toi droit." Comme la robe où nous vîmes pour la première fois une femme, elles m'aideraient à retrouver l'amour que j'avais alors, la beauté sur laquelle j'ai superposé tant d'images de moins en moins aimées, pour pouvoir retrouver la première, moi qui ne suis pas le moi qui l'aie vue et qui dois céder la place au moi que j'étais alors, s'il appelle la chose qu'il connut et que mon moi d'aujourd'hui ne connait point.† [127]

The fundamental passivity of these thoughts is exactly what Marcel vows to replace with his own "original" text once he becomes a writer. From being a haphazard collector of pleasures, Marcel will actively seek out objects to connect with one another, to establish that "rapport unique que l'écrivain doit retrouver pour en enchainer à jamais dans sa phrase." ‡ [128] The act of writing, the physical growth of the text, the gradually more impersonal and distant character taken on by a text—all these *ground* the intimate relationships between a man and his work in the writing, which is

---

* "re-found today here in the Guermantes library, during the very finest day, a book by which not only my mind's early gropings but also the whole purposes of my life and perhaps art were suddenly illuminated."

† "The first edition of a book had been more precious to me than other editions, but I would have always meant by that the actual copy I read for the first time. I would always look for original editions, I mean those of the book from which I had received the original impression. For the impressions that followed were no longer of that sort. I would collect old bindings for novels, bindings of the period when I read my first novels and heard papa say to me so many times: "sit up straight." Like the dress in which we saw a woman for the first time, they helped me to find again the love I once had, the beauty on which I had superimposed too many images I loved less and less, all of which made it hard to find the first one, I who was no longer the "I" who had seen it, and who had to cede his place to the "I" that had once been."

‡ "unique relationship that the writer must find again in order to enchain it forever in his sentence."

an incarnation for Marcel of memory and repetition, of originality and loss. The beginning of a career is the moment when the writer is an incarnation for Marcel of memory and repetition, of originality and loss. The beginning of a career is the moment when the writer looks to his text as any man looks to the future, so all-inclusive are the exigencies of his work: "A ce premier point de vue l'oeuvre doit être considérée seulement comme un amour malheureux qui en présage fatalement d'autres et qui fera que la vie ressemblera à l'oeuvre, que le poète n'aura presque plus besoin d'écrire, tant il pourra trouver dans ce qu'il a écrit la figure anticipée de ce qui arrivera." *[129]

Marcel's meditations on his future text indicate, as I said above, the exaggerated value attached by the writer to his career. They certainly reflect Proust's own case, if not in every detail then in the fact of detail, as well as in the temporal hyperbole by which thoughts of or about a text yet to be produced seem to engulf even the practical, everyday acts of writing without which no text can be produced. Benjamin rightly says that "since the Spiritual Exercises of Loyola there has hardly been a more radical attempt at self-absorption." [130] Therefore, Proust and Joyce map the limits to which, in the modern period we are discussing, the text as a writer's initial choice or intention can be forced. The intention seems a drawn-out one, and thereafter writers speak of their work as an obstacle course. The initial decision to make a text is renewed at each successive step of the way. As he writes, the author repeats his inaugural devotion to the career he has chosen and to the text—that pure sign of his career—he has intended. This is an instance of what Poggioli calls "agonism, . . . the pathos of a Laocoön struggling in his ultimate spasm to make his own suffering immortal and fecund." [131] We shall see later how the agonism of a writer's first step toward his text imposes upon him a polysexual role to which Proust's interest in "les hommes-femmes" is finely related.

Thus the first opposition is a total and an inaugural one for the writer; it is the radical question he must ask himself, the radical decision he must make at the outset of his career and also at every moment throughout the career. Coeval with his ordeal by initiation is the second opposition, which mobilizes the writer's

---

*"from this point of view the work must be considered only as an unhappy love affair that fatally presages others, and that causes life to resemble the work, so much so that the poet might not have any need to write, since such a great deal of what he had written already prefigures what will take place."

sense of being on a course, launched upon a career, yet increasingly concerned with knowing, trying to ascertain, whether that course is the right one. Ought he, for instance, to be producing one kind of sequence of works, or another? Does a given subject attract him for the right reasons, or for the wrong ones? What are the best solutions to questions raised by, and in, the continuity of his text? A classic account of this set of issues, all of which derive from and illustrate the opposition I mentioned, is Henry James's story "The Next Time." Ralph Limbert is a writer who vows, the next time, to write a book suited to the public. He never does, for "he had floated away into a grand indifference, into a reckless consciousness of art":[132] but James places his moment shortly before Limbert's death. The career has run its course out of life entirely, although the right progress had been Limbert's most lively concern.

Although James does not say so explicitly, Limbert's predicament is that he views writing his text as a wholly different matter from having his work read by his audience, or pleasing his audience, or being approved by it. This realization applies to most of the artist-characters James created during the 1880s and '90s. In his usual flamboyant manner, Wilde averred that "the artist works with his eye on the object. Nothing else interests him. What people are likely to say does not even occur to him. He is fascinated by what he has in hand."[133] Wilde of course exaggerates by stating that for a writer there are problematical issues of a technical sort whose importance antedates, if it does not completely efface, the writer's sense of his audience—antedates, and is privileged by virtue of that antecedence, which is immediacy and directness for the writer writing. In his *Logical Investigations,* Husserl makes a useful distinction between meaning-conferring acts (or meaning intention) and meaning-fulfilling acts:[134] for the writer, conferring meaning is essential "to the expression as such," whereas fulfilling the meaning, "confirming, realizing it more or less adequately, and so actualizing its relation to its object," is something he only hopes to achieve. For a writer to fulfill the meaning is to realize his text—to produce a text in the honorific sense of the word—but for the reader, or audience, this consideration is comparatively arcane. The reader wants to read and consume and understand. The aesthetic of production is secondary for the reader.

Now, if for a writer like Marcel Proust (either as narrator or as author) the text is a work of the future, if its fulfillment or actualization as a text is distant, then as a producing writer his focus is necessarily upon meaning conferral, upon writing as something one always does *before the text* or *toward the text*. Writing is a species of investigation, of preparation leading up to the text. Words in writing therefore become truer (than in ordinary use) for the purposes of a text. Once he is embarked upon a career, the writer's production vacillates questioningly between sketch and final draft, which may or may not be adequate, finally, for inclusion in the text. It is commonplace in literary history for writers, while preparing a collected edition of their works, to delete, edit, interpolate, and generally meddle with previously published material. This sort of intervention is part of the process of meaning fulfillment, and no writer after he has begun his career can avoid the ethical-technical questions involved therein. So what I am speaking about now is the whole set of questions he deals with as he writes, of which the questions having to do with a collected, integral edition are a much later and more public example.

One of the critical distinctions of modern literature is the importance given by the writer to his own paratexts—writings that explore his working problems in making a text. James's *Notebooks* come immediately to mind, as also do Gide's *Journals*, Rilke's *Letters*, Valéry's *Cahiers*, and Hopkins's letters to Bridges. Often, as Georges Bataille has often shown, paratexts may exist solely for the writer to burn off some of his writing in a deliberate gesture of waste, in reaction to the pressure of having always to think of the text as representing supreme moral virtue. In no writer's career, however, does this second phase, with its characteristic set of alternatives and questions, seem so engrossing and complex as in Kafka's. And there exists to my knowledge no more careful study of Kafka's example than Blanchot's in *L'Espace littéraire*. [135] Blanchot remarks that in his 1914 journal Kafka seemed preoccupied with three related personal concerns: that only literature satisfied him; that he doubted his own powers, which always "thwarted his plans"; and that this doubt was connected to whatever was extreme, or eccentric, in his work, "'l'exigence centrale, mortelle, que 'n'est malheureusement pas la mort,' qui est la mort mais tenue à distance, 'les eternels tourments du Mourir.' "*[136] The more Kafka wrote, the more he realized that of all activities only writing provides no security whatever. As a

---

*"that central mortal exigency which 'unfortunately is not death,' but death held at a distance, 'the eternal torments of Dying.' "

writer, Kafka's rigorous exertions were neither a compensation for unhappiness, nor a form of reverie, nor a construction, nor a means of describing truth. Art, for Kafka, according to Blanchot, is "lié, précisément comme l'est Kafka, à ce qui est 'hors' du monde et il exprime la profondeur de ce dehors sans intimité et sans repos." *[137]

With powerful insight Blanchot intimates that for Kafka the figure of the surveyor K. is a sort of extension from his journals into his text: K. is the character whose profession, with its concern for direction, distance, measurement, and decision, signifies the writer's troubled course once he has begun to write. Kafka's alienation made the course into a trial by error, not a trial toward truth. What Kafka punishes in himself and in K. is impatience, that desire to force a work to its conclusion, the wish to transform partial achievement into the total certainty of full conclusion. K.'s fault, in other words, is that he engenders an *image*—or an idol—representing a premature goal; once figured, this image gives K. a temporary sense of achievement and of unity, even as it makes real achievement and unity inaccessible. [138] Kafka's work begins and continues for a while, but he can never reach the end of any story he begins, so troubled is he always by the distances symbolized by images of promise (such as those associated with the castle) stretching before him. His self-imposed regimen of slowness and detail of composition developed not from any corresponding need in reality, but rather solely from the text's exigencies, what Blanchot calls its condemnation.

Kafka's feelings about his work are extreme, but they at least illustrate the type of enterprise a writer engages in. The text's condemnation is based on the fact that so far as the writer is concerned *all* questions—about his life, his work, his mind—are referable to it, are surveyed from its viewpoint. Everything he writes, whether letters, notes, sketches, or riddles, bears upon it the mark of responsibility to the text. If it is rare to find a writer since Dr. Johnson and Savage for whom writing is unalloyed pleasure (this does not contradict what Proust felt—that writing is necessary for the author's health), then since the late nineteenth century it is even rarer to find writers for whom writing is not a combination of suffering and loneliness, and almost always because the imperatives of a text seemed limitless. Merleau-Ponty comments on the paradox of "l'auteur et de l'homme, ce que

---

* "is connected, exactly as in Kafka, to that which is 'outside' the world; Kafka expresses the profundity of this 'outside' without intimacy and without rest."

l'homme a vécu faisant évidement la substance de son oeuvre, mais ayant besoin, pour *devenir vrai,* d'une préparation qui précisément retranche l'écrivain du nombre des vivants."*[139] With every advancing moment of the career, the life seems impoverished as the text gains in reality on the basis of what Wilde called "her own lines." The price of those "lines" is characterized by Joyce in writing *Ulysses* as follows:

> The word *scorching* has a peculiar significance for my superstititious mind not so much because of any quality or merit in the writing itself as for the fact that the progress of the book is in fact like the progress of some sandblast. As soon as I mention or include any person in it I hear of his or her death or departure or misfortune: and each successive episode, dealing with some province of artistic culture (rhetoric or music or dialectic), leaves behind it a burnt up field.[140]

The dynamic of impoverishment and problematical enrichment (since there is no guarantee that sacrifices made for the text will be of service) brings with it what one might call abandonment of the image. By *abandonment* I mean the sort of scorching out of every image from the past or the present that might represent the text's fulfillment in the future. The absence of what R. P. Blackmur calls predictive form in modern literature is, I think, attributable to this scorching out of an image.[141] No discrete analogies for the "growth" of a text and its completion seem apposite—neither organic ones, nor visual ones, nor schematic ones. To hope to complete the production of a text, the writer cannot project a course in time which is made intelligible, for example, by the image of a man *becoming mature.* The disparity I spoke of above between lifetime and text-time increases rather than diminishes. Thus, as Mallarmé recognizes, whereas in "life" chance remains in force, in the text chance is gradually eliminated. James's "figure in the carpet"—its unsayability, its elusiveness, its resistance to formulation, its unheeding and perfect inviolability—controls chance in the text, even as for author, reader, and curious spectator "life" has no great respect.

Yet there remains a conflict for the writer at this stage, and so long as he writes, between the *status* of his text and its *volume.* The status of Limbert's work, for example, has to do with its reception, its reputation, its earning power, and so on; he seems to have discounted all these in favor of giving a greater volume to his

---

*"the author and the man, that which the man lived making up the substance of his work, yet needing, in order to *become true,* a preparation causing the writer to withdraw from the ranks of the living."

text. James's parable—for it is just that—greatly simplifies the complexities of an author's dilemma. During the modern period, volume, in the cases of Mallarmé, Hopkins, Eliot, Joyce, Valéry, Kafka, and Wilde has to do with density, rarity, and irregularity. Status has to do with the text's inaccessibility to the "ordinary" public and, concomitantly, with its extraordinary capacity for being with, or being a part of, other literature; that is, the explicit terms of reference of the text are far less relevant to an audience than to other literature. Thus, as Blanchot says of Kafka, writing is an "unstable equilibrium" between "an increasingly rigorous spiritual monism" and "a certain artistic idolatry." [142] Mallarmé's and Wilde's numerous references to art, Eliot's to tradition, Valéry's to poetry—all these are instances in which the author's text is oriented toward a kind of commanding metatext or supertext, whereas his writing is evidence of penalties imposed, of obstacles cleared, for having undertaken the task of producing a text.

A necessary part of the status and volume of a text is style, which for the author producing his text is the language of his career. Syntactically, style is the extended signature of a writer, his characteristic way of connecting signs to one another; semantically, style is the writer's device for connecting his signs to a text they intended to complete. Style is *not* the *origin* of a text, but that which the *beginning* of a text *intends*. Style is writing which blots out origin, and substitutes for it the beginning, which is the writer writing his text. (In this discussion I am limiting style dogmatically not to an object or phenomenon of analysis—as in stylistics [143] —but to that activity of writing that begins with the writer composing his text.) Moreover, style displaces speech, just as the text—by virtue of its volume and status—displaces every origin. Thus a beginning, which intends the textuality of a text, can *transform* language generally into a specific text by a particular writer.

In the gradual development of a writer's career there occurs a time when be becomes aware of certain idiomatic patterns in the work, or even of his work's idiolect. Being aware does not necessarily mean that he is obsessively vigilant—although that is possible (there are the cases of Mallarmé and James)—but that he can quote himself, refer to himself, be himself in ways that have become habitual for him *because of* the work he has already done. What starts to concern him now is the conflict between fidelity to his manner, to his already matured idiom, and the desire to discover new formulations for himself. This, then, is the third opposition within the career. Swift, for example, is an interesting earlier figure insofar as this conflict is present almost continually in his writing. So adept is he at impersonation that in each new piece, whether *The Bickerstaff Papers, The Conduct of the Allies, The Drapier's Letters,* or *Gulliver's Travels,* a new voice emerges. And yet there is nowhere any mistaking the Swiftian manner, nor, more importantly, is there any mistaking Swift's devastating mimicry of his enemies. Originality and habit in this case coexist in a truly productive tension. With Milton and Pope we feel that the gain in elegance has almost overwhelmed the innovations, although in both writers the later style (of *Paradise Lost* or the *Dunciad* respectively) draws out a variety of new sounds and builds on a solid store of reserves. At a ripe moment in the career, a writer like Yeats can even schematize his earlier achievements in *A Vision* in order either to vary his present and later poems or to make it possible and convenient to use them synoptically. If and when such a moment occurs, it is an entirely fortunate phase in the career.

Hopkins was particularly concerned with the tension between innovation and repetition in his work. In a set of notes made in 1873-74 entitled "Poetry and Verse," he claimed for poetry the task of presenting the "inscape" (special distinguishing particularity, inner structure) of speech, "over and above its interest of meaning":

> Poetry is in fact speech only employed to carry the inscape of speech for the inscape's sake—and therefore the inscape must be dwelt on. Now if this can be done without repeating it *once* of the inscape will be enough for art and beauty and poetry but then at least the inscape must be understood as so standing by itself that it could be copied and repeated. If not/repetition, *oftening, over-and-overing, aftering* of the inscape must take place in order to detach it to the mind and in this light poetry is speech which afters and oftens its inscape, speech couched in a repeating figure and verse is spoken sound having a repeating figure .... Now there is speech which wholly or partially repeats the same figure of grammar and this may be framed to be heard for its own sake and interest over and above its interest of meaning. Poetry then may be couched in this, and therefore all poetry is not verse but all poetry is either verse or falls under this or some still further development of what verse is, speech wholly or partially repeating some kind of figure which is over and above meaning, at least the grammatical, historical and logical meaning. [144]

"Oftening, over-and-overing, aftering" are effects that cannot be reduced to our habitual view of things. For they achieve the detachment of sense from the logic of sequential reason, and the delivery of sense into figures or patterns whose chief feature is an individuality remarkable for its own (verbal) sake. Because they are marked and repeatable, such figures enhance the language from which they have been fashioned: by exaggeration, they help us to perceive what is there but not readily perceptible, or at least not perceptible in a single encounter. Such figures arise from going over and over sounds, stressing them out of the ordinary into prominence. The dynamic of repetition (as Kierkegaard also saw) keeps one within reality even as a sort of new reality is being created. Hopkins used the technique in his own verse, thereby creating a new idiom—based on "sprung rhythm," with its heavy alliteration, and an entire vocabulary of powerful neologisms. He believed that his verse was closely imitative of the fertile processes of nature, which while producing the essential rhythms of repeated events (spring, dawn, harvest) made them new each time. In this Hopkins prefigures such poetics as those of Pound and of the Russian formalists (especially in the notion of what Mukarovsky called "the foregrounding of the utterance").

And yet Hopkins's comments on poetry and speech suggest other, still more interesting ways of describing this third phase. During this third period in the career, innovation and repetition not only constitute the writer's judgments of what he is doing, they also parallel judgments of him made by his audience, by now accustomed to his idiom and to the particular place he occupies, through his text, in its mind. But whether or not author and audience agree in their judgment, it is nevertheless true that during this phase the writer judges his work much as a reader would. The career has its particular identity, as does the text: because of the writer's past accomplishments, his text will be read in a particular way; and because its idiom is more or less established, it will produce sense in a particular way. In short, at this stage the text will *speak* to the reader in a manner that the work of a new writer cannot emulate. Hopkins describes *speaking to*, in the literary mode, as a function of "oftening"—that is, of those repeated verbal idiomatic performances whose purpose is identifying, inscaping, heightening that characteristic verbal performance we have called producing a text. Each time an author writes during this phase he is also idiomatically speaking to his audience which, quite apart from the meaning of what he says, recognizes his language as characteristically his. And this act of recognition now enables the next act of recognition (of innovation or repetition),

256

and so on until he stops writing. Thus the text is the sign that stands for the prolongation, or continuity, of a career.

A rather delicate system of relationships sustains a text at this stage. One is the relationship between the writer and his text, which he views as exerting pressure on him insofar as its volume and idiom dictate certain utterances; his text is thus a limitation on the innovation he aims to achieve. Another relationship is the one between text and reader. A third is that between text and the institutions of its dissemination, preservation, and judgment—that is, publishing, criticism, and so forth. Thus by having remained in production until the stage we are now discussing, the text engages each of these relationships with the others. Altogether these relationships make it virtually impossible for the text either to repeat itself without limit or to renew itself without limit. In other words, repetition and innovation for the writer take place within a certain historical regularity that is the text's way of speaking, or its manner of *speaking to* both the writer and the world.

But how does writing speak? Is there not a gross contradiction that makes it foolish to describe a written language functioning as a spoken one? In general, studies of style, and stylistics as a discipline, attempt to characterize those aspects of written language whose "over-and-overing" seems to address the reader as if orally from the page. *Speaking* is thus a term for denoting stresses in the writing (style) whose function is not to convey information, but only the relatively pure sign of, the relatively pure activity of, a writer's presence at a specified moment in literary history. Hopkins has this in mind when he says that "poetry is speech which afters and oftens its inscape." No writer, however, can do this, or make his text do this, at will: analysts of style sometimes obscure this fact by assuming that *any writing* has attained this particular phase in the production of a text, whereas style is really a comparatively privileged *moment* in the life of a text. The speech of a text emerges at a midpoint in the writer's career, after a certain amount of his writing has appeared as writing only—that is, as nonspeech. A text can speak once the writer's subjectivity has fully appropriated to itself an entire textual language in which the "I" of the writer/speaker designates an ego functioning in a reality created by that language. Benveniste calls this reality *discourse*, [145] and when Foucault studies discourse he has in mind just what Benveniste describes. My thesis is that at a crucial midpoint in the career, the writer's text *has itself become a discourse,* a praxis by which statements can be made, statements whose purpose—since we are discussing literary texts here—is not to convey information but *to speak* to the reader. Thus the time of the text is not primarily 1895 or in the past, present, or future, but, as Benveniste says, " 'the time at which one *is speaking*.' This is the eternally 'present' moment, although it never relates to the same events of an 'objective' chronology because it is determined for each speaker by each of the instances of discourse related to it." [146]

For the writer the eternally present moment arrives when his text can speak as a discursive formation "bringing out ... subjectivity" in language—*his* subjectivity, Hopkins said, "as a point of reference *and* a belonging field." [147] As Benveniste goes on to say, discourse not only "takes over the expression of temporality, but it creates the category of person" [148] —in this case, that of the writer whose authority is to write a text as if speaking to the reader. And this can only occur if the text has already acquired the volume to authorize statements, or utterances, or further writing, that confirm the text as text. To use Foucault's terminology, the text's volume is a sort of historical a priori fact permitting the formulation of new statements. It is a rule-bound order that does not, however, deny the writer the power to innovate. The writer's role, paradoxically, is to use the subtle constraints of his discourse (the text's volume) to expand their reach, to make his discourse capable of repeating its present and its rules in new ways: thus the dialectic of repetition and innovation seems to announce the writer's presence to the reader, to the text, to the institutions (professional, economic, social, political) that sustain it. Nevertheless—and this cannot be overemphasized—the writer is not at liberty to make statements, or merely to add to the text at will: statements are rare, and they are difficult, so strong is the text's anterior constraint upon him. [149]

As an almost programmatic instance of what I have been discussing, Eliot's "Ash Wednesday" is very explicit, especially in the first of the six poems. [150] The "I" in the poem gains much of its prior authority not from the sincerity of its statements, nor from its quasi-liturgical rhythm and repetition, but from its echoes of earlier uses of "I" in the discourse created by Eliot's previous poems. This ego rejects, one by one, in perfect symmetry, a series of possibilities: knowing, turning, drinking, thinking. Each of these verbs refers to objects denoted by the demonstratives, indicators of *deixis,* "this," "that," "the," "the one," "such," "these." For over twenty lines the ego summons a series of relationships from the past only to abrogate them "because" they no longer serve to foster hope as they once did. The "I" of Eliot's earlier verse is typically in motion, seeking rest and nourishment among those objects, persons, and ideas that drive it to activity but not to fulfillment. In "Ash Wednesday" these are renounced without much description as somehow extrinsic; the ego consequently rejoices, "having to construct something upon which to rejoice." What is renounced is from the past, but what is here and now is that which, according to Benveniste, is linguistic time, and self-referential. "What is actual," says ego, "is actual only for one time." It is as if Eliot were saying that the "I" of his poetry is concerned now with its ability to speak exclusively at the level of the text ("the air which is now thoroughly small and dry"), not through fragments of life and literature as before, nor to that sort of audience which searches for intelligibility as if it existed in a maze of quotations.

The shift in the poem from ego alone to "I" and "us" together is accompanied by the use of liturgical forms ("pray for us sinners now") commonly used both privately and publicly. In speaking both to and with his readers, the speaker protects his utterance from the privacy ("these matters that with myself I too much discuss") of purely inward meditation: instead, the text takes on the disciplined accents of the prayer service, which verbally reconstructs the moment and the manner that make statements possible. The range of these statements is made evident in the following five poems, with the bewildering complexity of their content. Yet in those latter five poems the ego's manner is restricted to delocutive statements, statements based on locutions, which are in turn based on religious formulas. The ego *speaks* now—he does not *write*, "Lord, I am not worthy . . . I turned and saw below . . . Sovegna vos . . . O my people, what have I done unto thee," and so on. The text goes forward as if a voice were superimposed on it making statements that identify the poet as Eliot, in this state, "between dying and birth," unturning, speaking, creating. The text has become an event for the poet's voice to exploit.

When such an event becomes an unhappy one, it is because the opposition between repetition and innovation has changed for the worse. Whereas formerly habitual patterns and originality intersect in the writer's consciousness, now mere repetition is viewed as one alternative of a pair, where the opposite is the career's disruption by a failing impulse. Here, too, Hopkins tells a great deal. In his later poems, the "terrible" sonnets, one theme recurs with frightening insistence: unproductive repetition is the poet's lot. Tied to this is the certainty that what is being repeated is himself, sterile, uncreating, "widow of an insight." In Hopkins's later verse, the alliteration, which earlier signified diversity and exuberance, is merely dull and repetitious:

> birds build—but not I build; no but strain,
> Time's eunuch, and not breed one work that wakes.[151]

In another poem he says:

> I am gall, I am heartburn. God's most deep decree
> Bitter would have me taste: my taste was me.[152]

Hopkins's highly developed sense of self included a sizable amount of self-loathing, as if in reaction to having entirely surrounded nature and motion with his ego. This is not true of Wilde, who in writing *De Profundis* essentially repeated himself in the figure of Christ without realizing how familiar were his locutions and his poses.

The fourth and final opposition, or dilemma of concerns, becomes influential when the writer begins to view himself as nearing the end of his career, tempted with the idea of going on, yet often able to recognize that his writing has reached its conclusion. Works of recapitulation are common: Yeats's "The Circus Animals' Desertion" and a much earlier analogue, Swift's "Verses on the Death of Dr. Swift," are two perfect examples. In the latter poem the poet not only projects his own death, but goes on to project the life he will lead in posterity. Swift's vision is to double the career by perpetuating it after his death.[153] The main distinction of this phase is the writer's fear that his career has spent itself as a result of its own logic of continuity, but not necessarily because he has completed his text. The opposition is more accurately described as that between the subject of ending (in a work like *The Tempest*), on the one hand, and, on the other hand, writing at or near the ending. A failing impulse produces suitably matching work with frequent references to an antipoetic old age and to the need for what Yeats called "frenzy":

> Here at life's end
> Neither loose imagination,
> Nor the mill of the mind
> Consuming its rag and bone,
> Can make the truth known.

> Grant me an old man's frenzy,
> Myself I must remake
> Till I am Timon and Lear
> Or that William Blake
> Who beat upon the wall
> Till Truth obeyed his call. [154]

For Yeats the writer's old age provokes a sort of anatomizing spirit: in its sources and its achievements the career is reduced to a foul rag-and-bone shop. This Swiftian motif is found everywhere in Samuel Beckett's career, of course, but many of the writers we are discussing (including Yeats) come up with temporizing antidotes to the actual end of a career. Frequently, however, these antidotes are but symptoms of inevitable decay. One such antidote is transfiguration, as when Yeats desires to be remade into Blake and his frenzy. Another antidote is recourse to a recapitulatory, essential image, such as Conrad's Peyrol in *The Rover* of Gide's *Thesée;* this image is really a vehicle for the author's superannuated "voice," with all the fruits of senescence added to it, sometimes embarrassingly. Another antidote is, as in Eliot's *Four Quartets,* the invasion of the text by "explanation," as if because it is ending, the text is suitably vulnerable to the encroachments of mere prose. In all instances employing these tactics, the ending curiously is not equivalent to a finished text; but then—as we have seen—writing is the production of meaning, never its achievement. [155] Except for Borges's Aleph (which is an image of beginning and of engulfment) no modern image for the end of writing a text can be anything but ironic (such as Yeats's circus master), or apologetic and pontifical (Gide's Theseus), or evasive (Eliot). A text is not the result of a career: rather, it is the career which, when the text reaches an "end," stops when the writing stops. The rare perfected text, however, is like Mallarmé's *Livre* or Joyce's *Finnegans Wake*—a form of perpetual writing, always at the beginning.

V

What organizes the literary career and knits together the four sets of oppositions I have described is the constantly tantalizing dilemma of whether the writing life conflicts with, runs parallel to, uniquely imitates, or finally stunts human empirical existence, the life that Wordsworth called "the still, sad music of humanity."

Literary theorists from Plato to the romantics to I. A. Richards have often maintained that the writer is different from other men only in degree, not kind, of experience; yet the more common sentiment is to be found in statements such as this one by Giacomo Leopardi:

> To a sensitive and imaginative man, who lives as I have lived for a long time, constantly feeling and imagining, the world and its objects are, in a way, double. He sees with his eyes a tower, a landscape; he hears with his ears the sound of a bell; and at the same time his imagination sees *another* tower, *another* bell, and hears *another* sound. [156] [Italics mine]

To *another* we can add *alternative* in apposition. Conrad called himself *homo duplex,* since no one was more sensitive than he to the eccentricities of two lives existing in permanent correlation, and hence conflict, with one another. What is notable, however, is how the modern writer has used his career to reconstruct his intimate private life into a poetic—that is, alternative—career. Even apart from the world of literature, psychologists such as Freud, philosophers such as Nietzsche and Kierkegaard, and anthropologists such as Lévi-Strauss all define the characteristically human in terms of what one might call the possibility of an alternative, or a second time. In all these cases, language is excellent testimony to the Vichian manner in which a naive initial *corso* becomes transformed into a cultural or verbal second *ricorso.* And yet it is the problematical and alienating (or gentile) quality of the *ricorso* that the modern poetic career exemplifies.

Vico, however, had said that the repetitions (*ricorsi*) of history are exact: Each cycle duplicates the three phases through which primitive man passes on the path from bestiality to civilization. Vico believed that history is the history of families, so that in the *corsi* and again during the *ricorsi* families are formed, they flourished, then they perished; this pattern informs the rise and fall of civilizations. But during the period I have been discussing the *ricorso* represented by a poetic career is far from being an exact repetition of the natural human *corso.* A poetic or literary career does not reflect the man's life, it absorbs it, overwhelms it, gets on top of it, in Norman O. Brown's phrase.[157] The correlation between career and "life" begins as discontinuous adjacency—as when, for instance, Marcel forms his decision to write *aside from* the otherwise banal experience of a morning in the Guermantes house. Later the writer's career distorts "life," and, as we have seen, its prerogatives enclose the writer in a logic of development without any "natural" equivalent or any predictive form. In Chapter 3 my theme was how classical narrative fiction is linked intimately with an attempt, at the beginning, to reproduce in language the mysteries of human procreation: in a sense, such an attempt constitutes the fiction of fiction. Similarly, the effort of making a literary text or work of art generally resemble, and even be, a biological product constitutes one peculiar feature of the text's textuality.

When a literary career *intends* the literary text there is a need to determine the degree of correspondence, and character of the relationship, between literary career and the writer's life outside the career. As an alternative, a literary career begins—as we saw above—by being different from all other sorts of life. Yet such difference is haunted by a certain sameness, so powerful is the image of physical engenderment, and so common both to writing and procreation the notion that what one makes is one's child, one's progeny, one's temporal legacy. In his drama Ibsen foregoes naturalism—a more exact sort of realism—in order to explore the persuasive powers of art, powers of the sort that can endow the artist with the ability, through his text, to lead a life strikingly similar to biological life, yet without its limitation. Ibsen's late plays (such as *Hedda Gabler, The Master Builder,* and *When We Dead Awaken*) frequently depict an artist whose work is "his child," even though Ibsen can himself see tragedy awaiting the quasiprogenitors (Hedda and Lorborg, Kaya and Solness, Irene and Rubek). What these characters do not seem to recognize is the illicit nature of their alternative artistic projects, the peculiar transgression one commits by devoting to verbal or artistic material not only the technical care necessary for producing an art work but also the sexual care usually reserved for a human being.

The central symbol for the modern producing writer depicts the physical transfer of an image from man's sexual-procreative life to his artistic one. A writer's writing, in other words, is the result of daring to apply sexual energy or attention to the act of writing. The image of the writer, whether of ascetic priest renouncing all for art (Flaubert, Joyce, Mallarmé), prodigal expender of creative energy (Yeats), enslaved devotee (Conrad, Lawrence), or hedonistic aesthete (Wilde, Proust), is—because, first of all, it is an image, and also because it is transferred illicitly (or at least inappropriately) and audaciously from one activity to another—an intensified confusion of production with product, of career with text, of textuality with sexuality, of image with career. The more a text is produced, the stronger (obviously) the temptation to regard sacrifices made for it, the arid and imageless technical logic of the career suffered for it, as gaining for the writer an overt libidinal gratification and in the long run offspring. The text's volume, its substantial textuality, collects not just the writer's writing, but also those energies, diverted from his sexual life, or procreative engenderment. As a result, then, the text, besides explicitly accumulating words, just as explicitly attracts special sexual attention. Both the words and the sexual energy are signs of the writer's activity: they are his product, his text and child.

It is almost a commonplace to remark that Freud, a contemporary of the writers I have been discussing, generally regarded art as a compensatory activity rooted in the artist's neurosis. But here Freud, too, I think, confused the production of art with the finished product: in making this deliberate confusion, and even in his judgment of it, he belongs with these writers. Like them, his *image* for the artist (or the writer) is transferred from one sphere to another, just as like theirs his *textual practice* (in *The Interpretation of Dreams*) has a logic and a form and a textual identity different in intention from any other form, logic, identity of life. As I said in chapter 3, the text of the *Interpretation* is an invention quite beyond the mimetic realism of, say, the classical realistic novel. Freud's text is a redistribution of language according to a dynamic of dissociation and association. In less abstract terms, this means that Freud takes the images of a dream and dissolves them by putting them into words, then allows these words to make associations with other words and ideas, and so on until a new form of understanding is achieved—an understanding that takes shape existentially in producing a text and that is existentially coterminous with the text. If "tangles" like the Oedipus complex are psychological matters, it is the Freudian text that embodies them; similarly, the polysexual nature of these tangles is realized verbally by the text. Thus the text *presents* the tangles (as images to be unraveled) and then *produces* them as interpreted language (as psychoanalyzed). The author's personal life and his writing life are coupled, just as his literary career and his text are coupled. It is these conjunctions, with both their logic and their sexual punning, that the text is *stating*, outrageously, excessively, uniquely.

Freud's view of art is that the art work formally exceeds the artist's empirical life by materially realizing his neuroses. A writer's decision to write is, we have said, a decision to begin *another* project; the text materially states that beginning, as well as the transferral from empirical life to language of a sexual-procreative ambition, as the intention to author a new creation. Thus the text is a polysexual "tangle" of the writer's various interests; not only is the pen-ink-paper sexual symbolism in operation, but also the text-child complex and the writing-devoted consecration-marriage process. Besides Freud, it is Hopkins whose work is characterized by an intensified confusion of all these things together; it is his writing that performs the working out of a text, the courses of a life and a career, and the omnisexuality of those things taken together, simultaneously and representatively.

Hopkins's poetry begins as a confirmation and a repetition of a divine metaphysic of creation, which involves both beginning and creating. Later his poetry self-consciously considers itself to be a rival to the divinity, so strong has the authority of the poetic self become. Finally, the poet and his project discover themselves imprisoned on a sterile plot totally isolated from God. By this time, however, the poetic career has already been divorced (Hopkins's word is "widowed") from the divine thrust: the poet is now a spiritual eunuch, his text a linguistic mutant that has issued forth from an emasculated pen.

This general account of Hopkins's text cannot help but obscure the constant detail of its production, which is its very life. The inaugural and radical insight of Hopkins's whole career is that in every particular, no matter how small, the world is charged with God's power. At the outset, then, God impregnates undifferentiated matter, so that, as Hopkins says, the creation "is word, expression, news of God": a thing is at once a material object, God's creation, and a sign, or word, of God's male, procreative power. Hopkins always makes these identifications. In poetry, as in nature, there is life, there is power, there is evidence of male thrust. "Sprung Rhythm is the most natural of things" he wrote in his preface to the poems;[158] "stress is the life of it," he told Robert Bridges of a poem in 1878.[159] Stress occupies the center of his compositional theory, which starts by dividing words into marked (stressed) and unmarked (unstressed) sounds. Since all words are live, stress is a relative quality, and therefore each object has its own instress which it is the poet's task to organize along with others in a pattern of sounds, some more stressed than others. The poet must exaggerate the difference between stressed and relatively unstressed phenomena, since perceiving that difference is necessary to finding reality itself intelligible. The poet and his art, then, are the verbal equivalents of that difference, and out of their rhythmic play springs (the word has a truly seminal value for Hopkins) not only "the stress felt," but indeed the drama of procreation that makes the world comprehensible.

In *The Wreck of the Deutschland,* his first major poem, Hopkins repeats the articles of his submission to a divine "fire of stress," which, he says, "hast bound bones and veins in me, fastened me flesh." Married to the principle that made him (God's male authority), as a poet he then becomes the re-creator of a sacrificial scene in which a courageous nun receives God in a moment of extreme crisis. At that moment Hopkins the poet joins the nun through his poetry, and together they celebrate Christ's coming into her:

> But how shall I . . . make me room there:
> Reach me a . . . Fancy, come faster—
> Strike you the sight of it? look at it loom there,
> Thing that she . . . there then! the Master,
> *Ipse,* the only one, Christ, King, Head:
> He was to cure the extremity where he had cast her;
> Do, deal, lord it with living and dead;
> Let him ride, her pride, in his triumph, despatch and
>   have done with his doom there.[160]

Thus the poet writes a scene in which the union between man (or woman) and God has been effected by an art miming the rhythm of incarnation through impregnation. "Let him easter in us, be a dayspring to the dimness of us."[161] And indeed, in all of Hopkins's early poetry (after *The Wreck*) the setting is of a man transcribing nature immediately. As God "fathers-forth" material reality, the poet "utters in notes the very make and species" of things. In a sense the poet's writing refines and alienates in greater detail the life of things, which issues from God and reposes in the "deep down freshness" of Earth:

> And what is Earth's eye, tongue, or heart else, where
> Else, but in dear and dogged man?

Or, as he wrote in his "Comments on the Spiritual Exercises of St. Ignatius Loyola": "Nothing else in nature comes near this unspeakable stress of pitch, distractiveness, and selving, this selfbeing of my own."[162]

As God is to man, so the poet to his poetry. Hopkins gives birth to being by impregnations of fecund originality whose source is his male selfhood. Hence Hopkins's thoroughly distinctive art, which is at once feminine—faithfully mimetic of God's stress or impress upon him—and masculine—creative in relation to a reproduced verbal utterance. In the following lines, the abruptness of the language closely follows the abruptness of the bursts of reality, for in writing the lines the poet himself follows God's fathering-forth:

> All things counter, original, spare, strange;
> Whatever is fickle, freckled (who knows how?)
> With swift, slow; sweet, sour; adazzle, dim;
> He fathers-forth whose beauty is past change:
> Praise him. [163]

As receptive woman, as creative man; as impregnated Christian impregnating the page; as stressed creature himself stressing language into weak and strong thrusts: all these finely balanced roles that Hopkins plays help explain why words like *heaves, springs, darts, charges, rears, bursts,* and *rises* appear so prominently in his writing. He gives as he receives. Yet as creative poet and man-woman he begins to perceive that what he does is not only analogous to what God does, but something more.

In a letter to Canon Dixon, Hopkins wrote the following:

Now this is the artist's most essential quality, masterly execution: it is a kind of male gift and especially marks off men from women, the begetting one's thought on paper, on verse, on whatever the matter is . . . . Moreover on better consideration it strikes me that the mastery I speak of is not so much in the mind as a puberty in the life of that quality. The male quality is the creative gift, which he markedly has . . . . All should, as artists, have come, at all events should in time come, to the puberty, the manhood of those gifts: that should be common to all, above it the gifts may differ. [164]

The artist's work is what he begets on the page—but only, Hopkins says in a later poem, after the artist's mind has been enlivened by "the fine delight that fathers thought." Hopkins's way of relating the production of poetry to sexual capability is very finely articulated; he says that begetting poetry occurs when the creative male gift has reached puberty. That sort of maturity enables the poet to produce *forged* language, not the easy flowing lines to which a less mature poet is prone. Puberty for Hopkins implies abruptness, violence even, a kind of making (as after sexual union) that will produce live children and not just words. Thus the artist begets more than just a replica of himself, and he does more than passively imitate nature: he creates new life.

The difference between biology and writing fades still further as one examines Hopkins's compositional technique. His manneristic style is based upon abruptness and contraction—"forging"—

which replaces the expansive order of narrative sequence with sometimes violent association and conjunction: "it is the rehearsal/Of own, of abrupt self there so thrusts on, so throngs the ear." [165] In banishing connectives and "normal" word order, the poet begets instead a novel, even queer, sort of verbal life on the page. Hopkins's thoughts on creation generally support such a particularly literary activity with a highly suggestive (to the average secular reader, at least) theology of creation: "The first outstress of God's power" (which Hopkins calls "the first intention then of God outside himself") was Christ, who was also God's intention. Hopkins argues that the temporality of this intention is of a different order from, for example, that of the six days of Creation; the latter is mere sequence, the former is "forepitch of execution" in which perfection, or things in their perfect state, are created first. In a sense, Hopkins adds, when, in the time of intention, elect things are created, they correspond with grace, thereby seconding God's designs; and for them it "is like a taking part in their own creation, the creation of their best selves." [166] But why did God allow his Son intentionally to go forth from him? It is worth quoting Hopkins's answer at length:

Why did the Son of God go thus forth from the Father . . .? To give God glory and that by sacrifice, sacrifice offered in the barren wilderness outside of God, as the children of Israel were led into the wilderness to offer sacrifice. This sacrifice and this outward procession is a consequence and shadow of the procession of the Trinity, from which mystery sacrifice takes its rise, but of this I do not mean to write here. It is as if the blissful agony or stress of selving in God had forced out drops of sweat or blood, which drops were the world . . . . The sacrifice would be the Eucharist, and that the victim might be truly victim-like, like motionless, helpless, or lifeless, it must be in matter. Then the Blessed Virgin was intended or predestined to minister that matter. And here then was that mystery of the woman clothed with the sun which appeared in heaven. She followed Christ the nearest, following the sacrificial lamb "whithersoever he went."

In going forth to do sacrifice Christ went not alone but created angels to be his company, lambs to follow him the Lamb . . . . They were to take part in the sacrifice and he was to redeem them all, that is to say / for the sake of the Lamb of God who was God himself God would accept the whole flock . . . . For redeem may be said not only of the recovering from sin to grace or perdition to salvation but also of the raising from worthlessness before God (and all creation is unworthy of God) to worthiness of him, the meriting of God himself, or, so to say, godworthiness. In this sense the Blessed Virgin was beyond all others redeemed, because it was her more than all other creatures that Christ meant to win from nothingness and it was her that he meant to raise the highest.

Christ then like a good shepherd led the way; but when Satan saw the mystery and the humiliation proposed he turned back and rebelled. . . .

Here I have thought of a parable of a marriage cavalcade, in which some as soon as they see the bride's lowly dwelling refuse to go further, are themselves disowned by the bridegroom and driven off, but keep attacking the procession on its road. [167]

Hopkins's extraordinary muddling of roles (in his parable Christ is Mary's bridegroom) is extended further in the pages that follow the above quotation. Satan, the "archsnake" or dragon, fights to win the woman for himself. Hopkins refers throughout to "the pregnant woman" and "the manchild to whom the woman gives birth to . . . like a pleasing sacrifice": the sexual context is clear enough. Christ and Satan struggle to possess Mary, and Christ wins. "At any rate I suppose the vision of the pregnant woman to have been no mere vision but the real fetching, presentment, or 'adduction' of the persons, Christ and Mary, themselves." [168] "Fetching" and "presentment" suggest how in a material way a meaning can be fetched out from obscurity or abstraction and presented, or figured, to the senses for comprehension. Mary made pregnant by Christ is the godworthiness of creation, a celebration for God's glory. But Hopkins elaborates further:

But first I suppose that Christ in his first stead of angelic being, led off the angel choir, . . . calling on all creatures to worship God as by a kind of *Venite adoremus.* They obeyed the call, which indeed was a call into being . . . . This song of Lucifer's [Hopkins refers to Lucifer's song here for the first time: he imagines Christ as leading the angels in singing adoration of God, and Lucifer singing a countersong to seduce them away from Christ] was a dwelling on his own beauty, an instressing of his own being; it was a sounding, as they say, of his own trumpet and a hymn in his own praise. Moreover it became an incantation: others were drawn in; it became a concert of voices, a concerting of selfpraise, an enchantment, a magic, by which they were dizzied, dazzled, and bewitched. They would not listen to the note which summoned each to his own place . . . and distributed them here and there in the liturgy of the sacrifice; they gathered closer and closer home under Lucifer's lead and drowned it, raising a countermusic and counter-temple and altar, a counterpart of dissonance and not of harmony. I suppose they introduced a pathos as of the nobler selves that God was only trying them; that to disobey and substitute themselves, Lucifer above all, as the angelic victim of the world sacrifice was secretly pleasing to him, that selfdevotion of it, the suicide, the semblance of sin was a loveliness of heroism which could only arise in the angelic mind; that it was divine and a meriting and at last a grasp of godhead.

Meanwhile as they drew back from their appointed lots the score of their disobedience rose as in a mirror in the vision of the woman with child: she felt it as birthpangs and cries aloud. For this they despised her the more and hated the presumption of so weak a creature, not knowing the weakness was their own sin. And Lucifer who had drawn so many of the angels into his train prepared to consume, absorb, the woman's offspring too. But this hope and all their hopes of acceptance must have been dashed to the ground by the assumption and acceptance of the newborn child. Was it at that point that they broke out into open rebellion? . . . It was St. Michael and his angels who attacked them, not they St. Michael; it was a sort of crusade undertaken in defense of the woman in whom the sacrificial victim had lain and from whom he had risen, a sort of Holy Sepulchre and a heavenly Jerusalem.[169]

He then goes on to describe the war in heaven, in which

Michael and his angels instressed and distressed them with the thought of their unlikeness to the Most High; they from their selfpraised pinnacle and power of eminence flung themselves, like the sally of a garrison, with the thought of/We are alike the Most High, thinking in their madness their heroism, which was the divine in them, would declare itself as the godhead and would bear them up and its splendour dismay and overwhelm their enemies; but it was a blow struck wide, a leap over a precipice, and the weight of that other word bore them headlong down.

Further I suppose that the procession or liturgy of the angelic host was to have its score upon the world of matter and the angels thus to unfold and by cooperating create the species and the order of the lower world; which in consequence is marked everywhere with the confusion, clashing and wrecking which took place in the higher one and was there repaired at once but here not all at once. If this is so and the beginnings at least of every form were in the first *move* the heavenly hierarchy made one can see how it was possible for Satan to attack man even before his fall, that is before it was complete.[170]

This rather astonishing piece of writing represents Hopkins's struggle to understand—not by any means to reconcile—the physical effort to create artistically and the physical enjoyment gained (nobly and heroically) in the act of artistic creation. In both experiences sexual enjoyment is plainly present, as is the excessive egoism involved in countercreation. Although he condemns the pride of Lucifer's gestures, Hopkins sees the heroism of it, which, since the highest form of behavior (Christ's) is self-sacrifice, he interprets as quasi self-sacrifice, suicide. When he speaks of sacrifice, which runs through the whole passage like a ground bass, Hopkins means self-stressing, self-presentation out of the presence of God—that is, the action by which an individual assumes his quiddity, his independent selfhood, away from the protection of God. The woman's offspring is very ambiguous, and Hopkins does nothing to explain himself on this point. The child is Christ's, and probably as part of "the sacrifice" the mother's birth pangs are the producing of, the begetting of, a "god-worthy" creature. This creature belongs to the world of matter, which, because of Lucifer's rebellion, bears the stress of confusion. Nevertheless, since the child is assumed by God, it is as if what a creature produces away from God (including poetry) makes him undergo the pain of childbirth: the result is that the "child" is made godworthy by "cooperation" with the higher world, even though the time taken is relatively long and the process marked with the confusion caused by Lucifer's pride.

Thus regarding the poet there are several uncomfortable observations to be made. First, there is the peculiar sexual tangle: Christ, Mary, and their child. Second is the analogy between poetic performance and Lucifer's "instressing of his own inscape," as well as the similarity between Lucifer and the Most High. Third, there is the implied connection between the begotten child of Mary and Christ, the poetic work, Lucifer's attack, and the almost masochistic idea of self-sacrifice. It is, I think, no exaggeration to say that Hopkins's gnarled, tangled, abrupt, forged idiom is an accurate verbal reflection of all these conjunctions taken together. No writer with urgent theological beliefs so imaginatively and articulately formulated can avoid in some way incorporating them into his poetic writing. And it is the working out of the logic and of the stresses contained here that Hopkins's unfolding text exposes.

Consider now these lines which, after *The Wreck of the Deutschland,* self-consciously formulate the poetic project:

> I say more: the just man justices;
> Keeps grace: that keeps all his going graces;
> Acts in God's eye what in God's eye he is—
> Christ—for Christ plays in ten thousand places,
> Lovely in limbs, and lovely in eyes not his
> To the Father through the features of men's faces. [171]

This is the sestet of a sonnet, hence "I say more" means primarily that the poet is adding to what he has already said in the octet. But the phrase also draws attention to the poet's power to say more ("I say more"), over and above what is immediately perceptible evidence to the ordinary observer of nature. The poet begins to launch his world. His medium is language, as God's is natural reality, so that in the phrase that follows, the poet makes language produce *more* before our eyes and ears: he creates a new verb by pulling it forth out of an adjective: *just*—*justices.* The poet's power lies not only in issuing forth, but also in conserving through repetition, the opposite of playing out. The last four lines turn around the relationship between the verbs *is* and *plays,* which together unite issuing forth ("plays") and conserving ("is"). There is here an entire series of startling identifications forged by Hopkins: between man and Christ, between Christ the one and Christ the many (he "plays in ten thousand places"), between Christ who is readily identifiable and Christ who takes on other forms ("lovely in eyes not his"). All these identifications together comprise a sort of seductive dance to entrance God (and we are to remember the "sacrifice" by which reality glorifies God): they play *to* the Father who is their progenitor and, since the poet has himself pointed them out, even created them in language, God is literally their prospective mate, also. We are thus left at the end with a unity resembling a polymorphous marriage. Limbs and eyes are given to the Father.

A great deal depends on the poet's generative power and, of course, on his memory of his and God's past accomplishments. When, during Hopkins's fully progressing career, he realizes this, he recognizes that he possesses the power to take life away as well as endow it. Hence the late sonnet "Carrion comfort." God begins to withdraw, so strong is the poet's selfhood and presence, attested to in the body of work, the text, he has hitherto produced. Whereas formerly there had been a balance between the poetic enterprise and the divine, now Hopkins incorporates both roles within himself. In the following poem of imprisonment, the pronouns *we* and *you* all refer to the poet, now unnaturally forcing himself to perform more than one part:

> I wake and feel the fell of dark, not day.
> What hours, O what black hours we have spent
> This night! what sights you, heart, saw; ways you went!
> And more must, in yet longer light's delay.
>
> With witness I speak this. But where I say
> Hours I mean years, mean life. And my lament
> Is cries countless, cries like dead letters sent
> To dearest him that lives alas! away.
>
> I am gall, I am heartburn. God's most deep decree
> Bitter would have me taste: my taste was me;
> Bones built in me, flesh filled, blood brimmed the curse.
>
> Selfyeast of spirit a dull dough sours. I see
> The lost are like this, and their scourge to be
> As I am mine, their sweating selves; but worse. [172]

Soon this omnicompetent, transgressing self will become "Time's eunuch," unable to fecundate itself, even as its language veers alarmingly toward drab repetition. To be creative is not only to create for a reason, but also to bear a parental relation to what one has created. Yet as his letters to Bridges in 1885 show, Hopkins was deeply perplexed by his artistic desires. Should he write with hoped-for recognition and fame in mind, as all artists do, and then dedicate that fame to God? (He once wrote enthusiastically to Dixon that "the only just literary critic is Christ.") Or should he eschew any kind of public recognition—which, apart from diffidently sending his work to Bridges, Dixon, and Coventry Patmore, he did—and resolve to be silent? On all sides the question must have been trying. For to have decided to serve God in silence would not have guaranteed any abatement in the tension between the male creative potential and his priestly vows of chastity. It must have been nearly intolerable. Nonetheless, Hopkins seems to have rationalized some of his hesitations about poetry into a mode of controlled, though uneasy, silence.

He was not curbed for long. The artist's own problem of creativity again took hold of him: Why was he unable to write? He was depressed and uncreative—why? Much of this was apparently resolved by January 12, 1888, when he wrote sadly and resignedly to Bridges:

> All impulse fails me: I can give myself no sufficient reason for going on. Nothing comes: I am a eunuch—but it is for the kingdom of heaven's sake.[173]

We come now to the change from being God's eunuch, from being in a state of dedicated chastity, to becoming "time's eunuch." It is best understood, I think, if one hears with it this verse from Matthew 19:

> For there are some eunuchs which were born so from their mother's womb: and there are some eunuchs, which were made eunuchs of men: and there be eunuchs which have made themselves eunuchs for the kingdom of heaven's sake. He that is able to receive it, let him receive it.

As a foil for Hopkins's thoughts the verse produces the decisive agony that now erupts: he recognizes that a humbling spiritual exercise may have failed of itself and may have become an extended abuse. The abruptness of the heavily vexed rhythm (made even more clublike with its repeated *b*'s) brings this terrible reflection to high intensity in "Thou art indeed just, Lord":

> birds build—but not I build; no, but strain,
> Time's eunuch, and not breed one work that wakes.[174]

Moreover, in these two lines Hopkins has lifted the poem to its climax. When, finally, he writes: "Mine, O thou Lord of life, send my roots rain," it is as if the long monosyllable *mine* is exhaling great pain. The line's last four words mash together nature, submission, pleading and the bruised self.

The most remarkable of Hopkins's last poems, "To R. B.," mourns the tragedy of a poet whose career is completed yet whose sterility knows no relief. The dominating idea is that of the poet's mind bereft of its male thrust. *Wears, bears, cares*—the simple rhymes convey the stale sameness of a poet missing rapture, although able to live on with "hand at work." Instead of "the roll, the rise, the carol, the creation" (radical features of poetic activity), there is only an explanation:

> The fine delight that fathers thought; the strong
> Spur, live and lancing like the blow pipe flame,
> Breathes once and, quenchéd faster than it came,
> Leaves yet the mind a mother of immortal song.
>
> Nine months she then, nay years, nine years she long
> Within her wears, bears, cares and combs the same:
> The widow of an insight lost she lives, with aim
> Now known and hand at work now never wrong.
>
>   Sweet fire the sire of muse, my soul needs this;
> I want the one rapture of an inspiration.
> O then if in my lagging lines you miss
>
> The roll, the rise, the carol, the creation,
> My winter world, that scarcely breathes that bliss
> Now, yields you, with some sighs, our explanation.[175]

The last yielding, which is cruelly opposed to fathering-forth, delivers an explanation—the poorest substitute for a poetic text. In his text Hopkins can upbraid the text for not being what it once was; missing from its "lagging lines" is evidence of its seminal beginnings, "the roll, the rise, the carol, the creation." The words of the poem, therefore, do not inhabit a "creative" text, but are rather the lifeless verbal remnants of a course that has turned, through the logic of self-stressing poetic performance and sacrifice (in Hopkins's special sense), back to its start in the poet's celibate authority. The intense confusion of verbal creation with sexual procreation finally leaves the writer "widowed"—which is to say, alone with his voice and little else. What he speaks now is an explanation outside the text. His language seems to have lost its connection with his creative male gift and retains only its capacity to address the reader directly, sadly, commemoratively.

In a very poignant way, Hopkins recognizes that his "creative" text is now behind him; he has passed it by because he can no longer add to it. In common with most modern writers, Hopkins regards the text and his career as entities that stand apart from the rest of his life; what the text preserves is a potent authority that seems to taunt its beginning source in the author himself. Considering such later encyclopedic works as *Finnegans Wake, Point Counterpoint, Ficciones, 1984,* and *Doktor Faustus,* we can see how as texts they depress individual authority—despite the author's virtuosity—to the level of an "element" in verbal performance. Such a situation in the course of modern textual practice, noted for its eccentricity and individuality, *begins,* I think, in the long debate over language and knowledge and their beginnings. I should like now to discuss that debate, in the following chapters, in its most interesting contemporary setting and in its most compelling early modern analyst, Vico.

———————

Abecedarium Culturae: Absence, Writing, Statement, Discourse, Archeology, Structuralism

I

No reader of *Paradise Lost* is ever likely to have experiences of the kind undergone by Adam; which is why Dr. Johnson insisted on the poem's "inconvenience, that it comprises neither human actions nor human manners."[1] Preeminently an imaginative vision, rather than a true record of actual events, *Paradise Lost* is conceded by Dr. Johnson to be the great poem of a man who "saw Nature, as Dryden expresses it, *through the spectacles of books*."[2] Every inconvenience we normally feel when we find language wanting in its ability to convey experience directly is, in such a poem as Milton's, especially acute. In book 7, for example, Raphael is sent to inform Adam of the events in heaven, events that include the indescribable and "Immediate . . . acts of God, more swift/Than time or motion." From the beginning, therefore, the language of description is not adequate for its intention. Raphael continues to hedge his recital:

> . . . to recount almighty works
> What words or tongue of seraph can suffice,
> Or heart of man suffice to comprehend?
> (112-14)

He goes on, the difficulties notwithstanding, because

> Such commission from above
> I have received, to answer thy desire
> Of knowledge within bounds; beyond abstain
> To ask, not let thine inventions hope
> Things not revealed, which the invisible king,
> Only omniscient, hath suppressed in night,
> To none communicable in earth or heaven:
> Enough is left besides to search and know.
> (118-25)

The Truth is at about five removes from the reader. First suppressed in night, suppressed once again by Raphael (who as an angel knows more than Adam), suppressed still further because Adam after all is the original man from whose priority we have all fallen, suppressed another time by Milton's use of English to convey the conversation in Eden, and finally suppressed by a poetic discourse to which we can relate only after a mediated act (of reading a seventeenth-century epic)—the Truth is actually absent. Words stand for words which stand for other words, and so on. Whatever sense we make of Milton is provided by our use of accepted conventions, or codes, of meaning that allow us to sort out the words into coherent significance. We may take comfort in Raphael's assertion that there had been a Word, a primal unity of Truth, to which such puzzles as "meaning" and "reference" are impertinent.[3] Yet, on the other hand, we have only his *word* for it; not a thing, certainly, and not more than an assertion that depends on other words and an accepted sense-giving code for support.

Milton's theme is loss, or absence, and his whole poem represents and commemorates the loss at the most literal level. Thus Milton's anthropology is based on the very writing of his poem, for only because man has lost does he write about it, must he write about it, can he only write about it—"it" here being what he cannot really name except with the radical qualification that "it" is *only* a name, a word. To read *Paradise Lost* is to be convinced, in Ruskin's phrase, of the idea of power: by its sheer duration and presence, and by its capacity for making sense despite the absence at its center, Milton's verse seems to have overpowered the void within his epic. Only when one questions the writing literally does the obvious disjunction between words and reality become troublesome. Words are endless analogies for one another, although the analogies themselves are for the most part orderly ones. Outside the monotonous sequence of analogies, we presume, is a primeval Origin, but that, like Paradise, is lost forever. Language is one of the actions that succeeds the lost Origin: language *begins* after the Fall. Human discourse, like *Paradise Lost,* lives with the memory of origins long since violently cut off from it: having begun, discourse can never recover its origins in the unity and unspoken Word of God's Being. This, we know, is the human paradigm incarnated in *Paradise Lost.*

Dr. Johnson's reservations about the poem do not prevent him from reading it; the practical difficulties he experiences (the poem's length, its lack of human interest) seem to him merely adjuncts to, or examples of, the intransigence that troubles Milton's poetic achievement. When, however, we read Milton's great poem with the disquieting sense that we are witnessing an "ontology of nothingness"[4]—an infinite regress of truths permanently hidden behind words—then we have entered a phase of knowledge which has been made the domain of contemporary French criticism. For while it may be inappropriate to impose an ideological unity upon the French structuralists in particular and upon an important style of modern French thought in general, we may view each in the same way they very often view other styles of thought—as inhabiting and constituting a certain level of consciousness with its own sense of difference from others, its own idioms, patterns, ambitions, and discoveries.

The importance of this postwar generation of thinkers to a study of beginnings is of a complex nature; the length of this chapter, if not perhaps all of its findings, attests to the difficulties of dealing with the individualized, technical, and diverse events that taken together I have called contemporary French thought. The designation of such a group consciousness works to identify what I consider to be an exemplary rational and contemporary recognition in explicit critical terms of the need to make a beginning. Moreover, this need is connected radically to the *fact* of written language. No contemporary mode of thought, in other words, can lay greater claim to typifying a reasoned confrontation with the predicaments I sketched in the remarks on Milton above. My contention is not that no other modern thinkers have made as acute perceptions into the nature of beginnings as these. Rather, I am saying that these critics have made the problem of beginnings the beginning—and in a sense the center—of their thought. Moreover, such a determination has been tied to the connection between beginnings and language.

A fairly detailed consideration of this group necessarily scants the brilliance of particular contributions, except as these contributions build relatively visible "machines" for thought. For all the provincialism of French writing, I have found that this writing has nevertheless addressed—sometimes only implicitly—and come to terms with the principal currents in the contemporary imagination. Nietzsche, Marx, and Freud are a common patrimony; but then so too are positivism, linguistic analysis, and Durkheim, and phenomenology, revisionist Marxism, Freudianism, Nietzscheanism, and Kafka, Mallarmé, and Rilke. A catalog, however, does not say much. The reception of the names into knowledge, their modification, responses to them, and, above all, their transformation into a working critical and rational instrumentality—all this matters far more. In short, I shall consider these French critics as making a sort of thought by which the contemporary awareness of beginnings is most deeply and typically acted upon, in method and in practice.

The general outlines of this awareness are as follows: knowledge is conceived of, first of all, as radical discontinuity—not that the relationships between finite instances of knowledge are necessarily nondialectical, but rather that the unit of knowledge is an articulation, or an instance, of difference from another unit. Therefore, dialectical knowledge presupposes diacritic knowledge: a dialectic must be *begun,* and the imperative has a method and intention of a special sort which takes into account the given distance between every unit of knowledge. Secondly, the method is postnarrative. As my extended discussion of Foucault will show amply enough, the novelistic model of successive continuity is rejected as somehow inappropriate to the reality of contemporary knowledge and experience. If, as we saw in chapter 3, the form of novelistic narration *begins* from certain historical needs and epistemological conditions, then, I shall argue in this chapter, that novelistic form was displaced by a later form in which discontinuity, dispersion, and rarefaction are the essentials. I mean that we can better perceive the continuities taken for granted by the narrative impulse in the West once we note the consequence of their rejection by the discontinuous method of order and knowledge. Such a rejection is very much at stake in the problematical modern text. The contemporary need for a beginning, as reflected in the concerns of the French thinkers I shall be discussing presently, testifies to an active search (related in some ways to Freud's search) for a nonnarrative way of dealing with nonnarratable units of knowledge. Thirdly, the very acts of apprehending knowledge, whether as that which is written or as that which is read, are filled with a combination of uncertainty and invention. Both are frankly constitutive acts, and yet neither is simply arbitrary. For if the method of reading does not always cover the method of the writing, the latter is nevertheless assumed to be neither a stable object nor a regular succession of lines. Instead, writing is considered a controlled play of forces dispersed in a textual space that is created by the writing and that does not exist before it. Therefore, reading can be said to *repeat* the controlled, arbitrary nature of the text's creation, but not, however, to *duplicate* it. Fourthly, underlying all this discontinuity is a supposition that rational knowledge is possible, regardless of how very complex—and even unattractive—the conditions of its production and acquisition. These four general features are, I believe, to be found in the work of the thinkers with which I am concerned here. These features provide us with the elements by which during the mid-twentieth century *beginnings* have become a central problem: hence the importance to my study of a certain generation of French writers.

Of them all, it is Michel Foucault who has become, in Roland Barthes's words, the very thing his works describe: a consciousness completely awakened to and possessed with the troubled conditions of modern knowledge.[5] Foucault is, to use one of R. P. Blackmur's phrases, a technique of trouble. As history is gradually unveiled in Foucault's explicitly historical investigations, we witness, not an easy chronicle of events, but a succession of functional conditions that give rise to the existence not only of knowledge, but of man himself:[6] hence the subtitle *An Archeology of Human Sciences* to *The Order of Things* (the English translation of *Les Mots et les choses*). Permanently hampered by language, which is the first, and in a sense the last, instrument at his disposal, Foucault's job of getting to the bottom yields only the constantly repeated and varied assertion that man is a temporary interruption, a figure of thought, of what is already begun (*le déjà commencé*). Any human investigation since the nineteenth century (and the relevance of Wittgenstein's later work is crucial to this *aperçu*) is actually bound up in the nature of language. The interpretation of evidence, for example, is exegesis. But when we ask "exegesis of what?" we commit ourselves totally to a perpetual series of the preposition *of*: the modern form of criticism, according to Foucault, is philology as an analysis *of* what is being said in the depths of the discourse.[7] Just as there is no easily ascertainable beginning to the process of exegesis, there is also no end:

> In the sixteenth century, interpretation proceeded from the world (things and texts together) towards the divine Word that could be deciphered in it; our interpretation, or at all events that which was formed in the nineteenth century, proceeds from men, from God, from knowledge or fantasies, towards the words that make them possible; and what it reveals is not the sovereignty of a primal discourse, but the fact that we are already, before the very least of our words, governed and paralysed by language.[8]

The drama of Foucault's work is that he is always coming to terms with language as both the constricting horizon and the energizing atmosphere within and by which all human activity must be understood. Two of Foucault's three major historical works, *Folie et Déraison: Histoire de la folie à l'age classique* and *Les Mots et les choses,* describe respectively how language has permitted the social discriminations of "otherness," and the cognitive connections between the orders of "sameness." In the former work it is madness, isolated in a silence outside rational language, that is made by society to carry the weight of an alienated "otherness"; in the latter work it is through the powers of language that words are made into a universal collection of signs for everything. As with most of the structuralists, Foucault must presume a conceptual unity—variously called historical a priori, an epistemological field, an epistemological unity, or *épistémè*—that anchors and informs linguistic usage at any given time in history; no structuralist to my knowledge has gone to such lengths as Foucault to ascertain and to articulate this "unconscious positivity."[9] In *Les Mots et les choses* he writes that "in a culture, and at a given moment there is never more than one *épistémè* that defines the conditions of possibility of all knowledge."[10] One of the various chores this univocal assertion is made to perform is, as Steven Marcus has remarked,[11] that it gives license to Foucault's literal faith in an era before the modern dissociation of sensibility. For according to Foucault, language in the Renaissance was intimately connected with things; words were believed to be inherent in the script of an ontological discourse (God's Word) that only required reading for the guarantee of their meaning and truth. Words existed inside Being: they reduplicated it; they were its signature; and man's decipherment of language was a direct, whole perception of Being.

Foucault's brilliant analyses of *Don Quixote* and Velasquez's *Las Meñinas* show how the intricate system of resemblances by which things were ultimately linked to a divine Origin began to break down: Don Quixote in his madness is unable to find the creatures of his reading in the world, Velasquez's magistral painting focuses outward and away from the canvas to a point its composition requires but does not contain. The representative space of language has become, by the eighteenth century, an ordered film, a transparency through which the continuity of Being can shine. Thus "the essential problem of classical [or eighteenth-century] thought lay in the relations between *name* and *order:* how to discover a *nomenclature* that would be a *taxonomy,* or again, how to establish a system of signs that would be transparent to the continuity of Being."[12] When words lose the power to represent their interconnections—that is, the power to refer not only to objects but also to the system connecting objects to one another in a universal taxonomy of existence—then we enter the modern period. Not only can the center not hold, but also the network around it begins to lose its cohesive power.

When, in his two major historical books and in his archeology of clinical observation,[13] Foucault embarks on a discussion of the nineteenth and twentieth centuries, it becomes apparent how much his vision of history preceding the modern age is projected back from his apprehension of the contemporary. For like many of the structuralists, Foucault is obsessed with the inescapable fact of ontological discontinuity. In language, for example, "the thing being represented falls outside of the representation itself"[14] ; thus the signifying power of language far exceeds, indeed overwhelms, what is being signified. Another example: the emergence of the *idea* of man (an idea whose advent Foucault associates exclusively with the nineteenth century) coincides with the breakdown in the representative power of language. Man, therefore, is what essentially resists language; he links together what Foucault calls an "empirico-transcendent doublet,"[15] two parallel zones of raw human experience on the one hand and human transcendence on the other, that together are alien to discourse. And discourse is the "analytic of finitude" that comprises modern knowledge and which is made possible by man's alienation from it; for according to Foucault, the discourse of modern knowledge always hungers for what it cannot fully grasp or totally represent. Thus knowledge is perpetually in search of its elusive subject. Here again the fact of discontinuity—or difference, as it is also called—is paramount.

Finally, the densely and portentously argued theme of *Les Mots et les choses* (a book whose literary and philosophical implications are overwhelming) is occupied with the vacant space between things, words, ideas. In the eighteenth century the possibility of representing things in space—as in a painting—derived from the acceptance of temporal succession, which thereby allowed the constitution of spatial simultaneity: the idea that objects could coexist in the privileged space of a painting depended upon an unquestioned belief in the continuing forward movement of time. Spatial togetherness was thus conceived to emanate from temporal succession. Yet in the modern era the

285

profound sense of spatial distance between things, the sense that separates even like things from one another, permits the modern mind to contemplate time as only an illusion of succession, as a promise of unity or of a return to the Origin.[16] Above all, time is the most tenuous of the spatial configurations that attempt to bridge the gap between things. Thus the human sciences and time together occupy the distance that separates (without uniting) biology, economics, and philology, the three fields of knowledge that Foucault regards as essential because they treat, respectively, natural life, value, and representation.[17] As a humanized account of life, psychology stands next to biology; and, by the same argument, sociology stands next to economics, and literature and mythology next to language: in the tension and the discontinuity between each and its adjacent partner we have, according to Foucault, the constituting models of the human sciences. Man is a problem defined in terms of an alternation between impersonal biological functions and psychological norms, between standard-ized economic rules and sociological conflict, and between language as system and the significations of myth and literature. [18] Modern man is the enigmatic structure that with difficulty knits them together.

The effect of Foucault's argument, as much probably as the effect of any general account of it one gives, is that man as we know him is dissolved. Just as in his book on madness Foucault shows how madness consistently and effectively resists language and the postures of reason until the late nineteenth century, in *Les Mots et les choses* he demonstrates how thereafter man himself becomes an irrationality in a special sense, a structure that dramatizes the normally unthinkable relationship between the diversities of knowledge. No longer a coherent *cognito,* man now inhabits the interstices, "the vacant interstellar spaces," not as an object, still less as a subject; rather, man is the *structure,* the generality of relationships among those words and ideas that we call the humanistic, as opposed to the pure, or natural, sciences. [19] The structure is irrational because it is the limit at which thought becomes intelligible, and therefore it cannot be *thought about.* One can just think it—and that only after disciplined "archeologi-cal" research. (The novelty of such a formula in English, as well as the distinction between *thinking* and *thinking about,* is much more acceptable in French: *penser la structure* is a valid construction in the way that "to think structurally" is also valid, although not lucid. In French, however, it is easier to argue—as

Foucault and the structuralists do—that *thinking about* is reflexive, and hence rational, whereas *thinking* itself is mere activity, and hence irrational.) Knowledge, therefore, is a closed system of knowledge *for* or *of* man *by* man. And finally, since knowledge can only be formulated in language, linguistics becomes more a perception than an explanation of man:[20] man is the positive domain, the field, of science and knowledge, but he is not the object of science.[21]

One can therefore say that there is a "human science" not simply wherever man is concerned, but rather wherever one analyzes, in the appropriate dimension of the non-conscious, those norms, rules, and significant ensembles that reveal to consciousness the conditions and the forms of its contents.[22]

The eccentricity of so bleak and antisentimental a view of man is reflected directly in Foucault's prose. Despite the frequently astonishing lucidity of his dissections of intellectual ventures from Cervantes through Linnaeus and Adam Smith to Nietzsche and Freud, one confronts a prose style whose grasp of an author or idea is exceedingly particular but whose revolutionary direction and epistemological radicalism are strikingly general: like Holofernes in *Love's Labour's Lost,* Foucault is usually to be found overglancing the superscript. For if tradition and education train us to take man as the concrete universal, the pivot and the center of awareness, then Foucault's prose, and concurrently his argument, makes us lose our grip on man. If we are inclined to think of man as an entity resisting the flux of experience, then because of Foucault and what he says of linguistics, ethnology, and psychoanalysis, man is dissolved in the overarching waves, in the quanta, the striations of language itself, turning finally into little more than a constituted subject, a speaking pronoun, fixed indecisively in the eternal, ongoing rush of discourse.

Foucault's man is well described in Roland Barthes's clever phrase "a metaphor without brakes" (*métaphore sans frein*).[23] There is an uncanny resemblance between this view of man and that other remarkable dissolution of man in discourse which is Conrad's *Heart of Darkness*. After having described Kurtz as "just a word for me," Marlow continues:

I made the strange discovery that I had never imagined him as doing, you know, but as discoursing. I didn't say to myself, "Now I will never see him," or "Now I will never shake him by the hand," but, "now I will never hear him." The man presented himself as a voice. Not of course that I did not connect him with some sort of action .... That was not the point. The point

287

was in his being a gifted creature, and that of all his gifts the one that stood out preëminently, that carried with it a sense of real presence, was his ability to talk, his word—the gift of expression, the bewildering, the illuminating, the most exalted, and the most contemptible, the pulsating stream of light, or the deceitful flow from the heart of an impenetrable darkness.[24]

In achieving a position of mastery over man, language has reduced him to a discursive function. The world of activity and of human experience stands silently aside while language constitutes order and legislates discovery. When Lévi-Strauss says that "language, an unreflecting totalization, is human reason which has its reason and of which man knows nothing,"[25] he is stating the condition with which serious intellectual work must reckon. Nearly every one of the structuralists acknowledges a tyrannical feedback system in which man is the speaking subject whose actions are always being converted into signs that signify him, which signs he uses in turn to signify other signs, and so on to infinity. Foucault, on the other hand, has been trying to overcome this tyranny by laying bare its workings. Most recently he has ascribed that tyranny to its secrecy; just by naming, describing, classifying where language and discourse pretend to "unknowable" exigencies, the role of society and its class structure, for example, become evident.[26]

II

There are dangers in too quickly defining Foucault's work as philosophical—or even as historical, for that matter. One danger lies in failing to acknowledge that his writing can be of overriding interest to literary critics, novelists, psychologists, medical men, biologists, and linguists (and in general to any professional interested in the past and contemporary states of his discipline). Another, more interesting danger lies in losing sight of the fact that Foucault writes neither philosophy nor history as they are commonly experienced. His is a remarkable angle of vision, a highly disciplined and coherent viewpoint that informs his work to such a degree as to make it *sui generis,* original—a claim Foucault himself would not make for it. The universality of his theories and the intense particularization of their meaning, however, present the reader with a body of writing whose potential effect upon any one discipline has already been neutralized—which is to say that

288

Foucault's theories are not intended to be used as a kind of passkey for unlocking texts. This is an idea to which I shall turn from time to time. Foucault's combination of conceptual power with a kind of ascetic nonchalance is forged in a style of high seriousness and eloquence, and I think that it makes a verbal phenomenon of a unique sort. His name for what he does is "archeology," a term he uses to designate both a basic level of research and the study of collective mental archives as well, that is, epistemological resources that make possible *what* is said at any given period and *where*—in what particular discursive space—it is said. [27]

To the English-speaking reader Foucault's writing may appear abstract, a quality that for some reason is considered to be annoying, especially in work that is vaguely supposed to pertain to human experience. A word that frequently turns up in one after another of his works is *raréfaction*, by which he means the refinement of words into thoroughly special, uncommon, literally abstracted meanings. Now, if Foucault recognizes anything like an absolute law it is that words now, whether "abstract" or "concrete," are delivered already rarefied in statement (*énoncé*). Thus Foucault's language is rarefied, too, and highly saturated with nouns made of verbs of process (*formation, appropriation, transmission,* etc.), but he will maintain that the categories and the classes he formulates for statement and discourse are themselves by definition rarefied in advance; in that way his work meets statement on its own ground and with instruments adequate for describing its states. This at once doubles his point about the polymorphic character of rarefaction, which further intensifies the need for an attitude on the part of an alert scholar that considers *special meaning* to be the signifying activity of discourse. Foucault's position is that language in use is not natural; discourse does violence to nature, just as the use of words like *ohm, coulomb,* and *volt* to describe electrical qualities does violence to an otherwise undifferentiated physical force. On the other hand, it is "natural" for discourse to treat nature as an accident, as *aléa,* in much the way that Yeats's dolls impugn the dollmaker for having accidentally "made" a child.

Quite apart from its real historical discoveries, Foucault's archeological research has a profoundly imaginative side to it, and it is the broad lines of this that I wish to discuss now. The course of his major work has been a gradual exposition of an increasingly more essential and ineluctable poetics of thought. Much the same progress can be found, for example, in the course from *The Birth of Tragedy* to *The Will to Power*. Now, Nietzsche is one of the thinkers for whom Foucault has shown a strong affinity, and the analogy between the former's philology and the latter's archeology is very marked, not least in their common approach to philosophy via recondite historical research. In both cases, since philology and archeology are primarily historical disciplines, it is the special attitude to history that separates these two thinkers from other scholars. Indeed, Nietzsche's perception in the second of his *Untimely Meditations* that the historical sense is a disease of history fairly characterizes the constitutive ambivalence toward history—the medical as well as the critical attitude—in Foucault's work also. Furthermore, Foucault's analytical work, like Nietzsche's manner, is essentially a way of seeing man and his past being disintegrated by the historical sense: "The historical sense . . . must only be the acuity of a view that distinguishes, distributes, disperses, allows free play to deviations and limits—a kind of view that dissociates, is capable of dissociating itself, and is capable of erasing the unity of that human being who is supposed to carry the view in a sovereign manner towards his past."[28] If a scholar's attachment to his discipline is pictured as primarily dynastic—he carries on the work of his predecessors inside the field, whether the field is history or philology—then Foucault's is antidynastic, not the continuation of a line from privileged origin to present consciousness. Thus the relationships that Foucault's work are most concerned with are those of *adjacency, complementarity,* and *correlation,* which are not the same as the linear relationships of succession and interiority;[29] these latter ones are broken up by Foucault and redistributed into the former ones.

It is probably not a coincidence that the novel force of Nietzsche's work at its best comes from his having relegated "pure" philosophy to a secondary role in favor of his passions, venerations, friendships—Wagner, Christ, Socrates, Schopenhauer, Dionysus, the ancient Greeks. In the main, none of these perhaps was a subject that a philosopher need have treated in very great detail, at least so far as the main tradition was concerned. Yet Nietzsche flamboyantly considered his passions as events occurring simultaneously in the history of his spirit and in the history of thought generally. Philosophy's official patrimony obviously includes philosophers and philosophies, and to these as doctrinal entities Nietzsche, like Foucault, pays only tangential attention. Foucault's work feeds its ideas with poetry, the history of science, narrative fiction, linguistics, psychoanalysis—as all these illuminate a given concept with a sense of its situational ambience. Aside from Nietzsche, Marx, and Freud, Foucault's range of interests includes Borges, Hölderlin, Sade, Mallarmé, Beckett, Bataille, Jacques Lacan, Blanchot, and of course all those other authors he discusses at length in *Folie et déraison, Les Mots et les choses, Naissance de la clinique,* and the book on Raymond Roussel. He has a high regard for Georges Canguihelm, Jean Hyppolite, and Gilles Deleuze, a contemporary historian of science and two philosophers, respectively, whose relations with their field he holds to be exemplary for him.

This latter observation is an important one for Foucault, since apart from the idiosyncrasies of his insights, it is as the founder of a new field of research (or of a new way of conceiving and doing research) that he will continue to be known and regarded. The virtual re-presentation and reperception of documentary and historical evidence by Foucault has been done in so unusual and imaginative a way as to have *created* for his evidence a new mental domain—not history, nor philosophy, but "archeology" and "discourse"—and a new habit of thought, a set of rules for knowledge to dominate truth, to make truth as an issue secondary to the successful ordering and wielding of huge masses of actual present knowledge. Most writers tend to place their thought—to locate it as physically as thought can be located—either next to, or under, or apart from other thought. Foucault's central effort is to consider thoughts taking place *primarily as events,* to consider them precisely, consciously, painstakingly as being mastered in his writing in their aleatory and necessary character as occurrences. He has had to reorient and distort the meaning of words and phrases whose use as a means for thought has been so habit-ridden and so literally debasing as to have become completely unthinkable—such words, concepts, and schemata as *change, continuity, relationship, history, interiority, exteriority.* Thus Foucault's work is in effect an attempt at re-thinking and thinking-through the notion of beginning.

In a number of places, most notably in *L'Ordre du discours* (now translated into English as *The Discourse on Language*) and in his essay on Deleuze, Foucault has used the image of theatre to describe the interplay of philosophy and history with which his research is concerned. The image has a good many uses for him. First of all, it serves to fix study in one place and to make study as self-conscious as possible from the very beginning, instead of allowing whatever it is that one studies to be everywhere and no place at the same time, and one's mind a set of vague, superficial notes: hence Foucault's dominant concern with space as the element in which language and thought occur. Second, to an attending spectator, the theatre offers a spectacular event, an event divisible into lesser events, each playing a part on the stage, each moving with reference to every other event on a number of different axes; in short, the theatre's stage is where there occurs a play of events, embodied either in gestures, characters, groups of actions, or even in a changing scene. All this precisely fits Foucault's attitude toward what he calls the existence of discursive events in a culture, their status as events, and also their density as things—that is, their duration and, paradoxically, their monumentality, their character as monuments.

> What I shall call an *archive* is neither the totality of texts which a civilization has preserved, nor the ensemble of traces which have been saved . . . after its disasters, but the play of rules which in a culture determine the appearance and the disappearance of utterances, their paradoxical existence as *events* and as things. To analyze facts of discourse in the general element of the archive is not to consider them as documents (which have a hidden meaning, or . . . a rule of construction), but as *monuments;* and this without reference to any geological metaphor, without assigning them any origin, without the least gesture towards a beginning, an *arché*—not these things, but to do instead what, according to the playful prerogatives of etymology, would be something like an archeology.[30]

The stance implied in this statement is that Foucault examines *said things (les choses dites)* as they happen before him. His attitude toward the past is that of a spectator watching an exhibition of many events, and what Foucault's reader watches is an exciting intellectual exhibition—and I do not by any means intend this to be a pejorative description. In order to be a spectator, which in this case wrongly implies passivity, there must first be a reordering of documents so that they shed their inertness and become a sort of measurable activity: this reordering, or reorienting, of texts from the past takes a maximum of intellectual and scholarly energy.

No idea more crucially connects this reorienting task of Foucault's work with the thought of a surprising majority of contemporary thinkers than the complex one of anonymity—or, in the terms Barthes, Lévi-Strauss, and Lacan have used, the idea of the loss of the subject. This has frequently (and comically) been mistaken simply as an inability to talk about anything—as in "I have no subject for my essay or novel"—although the consequent periphrasis ("without a subject I simply write or talk around a void") is part of the correct meaning of the lost subject. Subject (*sujet*) in its more exact context means the thinking subject or the speaking subject, the *subjectivity* that defines human identity, the *cognito* that enables the Cartesian world of objects. The influence of the thinking subject in Western thought has, of course, been profound. Not only has the subject guaranteed ideas of priority and originality, but also ideas, methods, and schemes of continuity and achievement, endowing them libidinally with a primal urgency underlying all patterns of succession, history, and progress. History in the main has acquired its intelligibility through a kind of anthropomorphism projected onto and into events and collectivities of various sorts; these are then thought of as functions of a subject, and not vice versa. Of course, the influence of the process of human generation has been paramount, forcing us to think of literature, for example, as merely an imitation of the human family.

The two principal forces that have eroded the authority of the human subject in contemporary reflection are, on the one hand, the host of problems that arise in defining the subject's authenticity and, on the other, the development of disciplines like linguistics and ethnology that dramatize the subject's anomalous and unprivileged, even untenable, position in thought.[31] The first force can be viewed as a disturbance taking place at the *interior* of thought, the second as having to do with the subject's *exteriority* to thought. Together they accomplish one end. For of what comfort is a kind of geological descent into identity from level to lower level of identity, if no one point can be said confidently to *be* irreducible, beginning identity? And of what philosophical use is it to be an individual if one's mind and language, the structure of one's primary classifications of reality, are functions of a transpersonal mind so organized as to make individual subjectivity just one function among others?

Foucault's response has been not to dispute these perspectives, but to absorb and understand them fully and then to give them an important basic role to play in his work. I think that it is the positiveness of Foucault's attitude from the beginning toward the loss of the subject as much as his explicit methodological philosophy that determines the invigoration he communicates. Not for him is the noisy appeal to a cult of doctrine, or of apocalypse, or of dogma; he is persistently· interested in the responsibilities and the offices of his method, as well as in the

293

untidiness and the swarming profuseness of detail. Like a medieval Islamic critic of poetry, he formulates rules that cover every instance of authorial flair, thus reducing the originality of any writer he reads to a deliberate accident occurring within the latent, ordered possibilities of all language. The impersonal modesty of Foucault's writing coexists (paradoxically) with an unmistakable tone of voice that can deliver both insight and learning; he gives the impression nonetheless of having experienced first-hand every one of the books he has read. This may seem like something to be expected in the work of any learned scholar, but in Foucault's case the epistemological status of a book, or of a collection of tracts and books, is in his methodology a complex theoretical issue brought to the level of performance in the actual practice of Foucault's writing.

A good way of verifying this is by remarking the extent to which Foucault makes one aware that writing, books, and authors are concepts that do not always entail one another in exactly the same way. Nor is it possible for them to be considered as genetically produced or producing. Moreover, they mean considerably different things at different times. A book like the Koran, for example, is a theme and a myth, as much as it also is an object or the work of an individual author. In several essays scattered throughout his career Foucault has ingeniously explored these variations in stress and meaning, particularly as he finds them taking place among variations in the value of rhetoric, of language, of fiction, of the library. In each case, Foucault distinguishes between the thing itself (in a Kantian or Platonic sense) and thoughts about it or uses made of it. This preliminary demarcation of things—verbal things, that is—into ideal or essential object and specific signifying quality emanating from the word for the object onto a field of verbal praxis is a fundamental one for Foucault, but fundamental in that he treats it as a distinction without a real difference. Essences are words at most, and they do not have the capacity really to divide being into essence and predicates. He permits "essences" no more than as designating powers, and certainly not as powers that divide reality into higher and lower plateaus of being. Words about essences are, of course, words, too; according to Foucault, the job is, then, to place all these words in relation to each other—words as essences (*idea, author, things, book, language*) and words *making contingent use of essences* (*the good, de Sade, Hölderlin's poetry, French,* and so on). Or, to use a notion that Foucault employs continually, the task for the archeologist is to understand words *inter*discursively and *intra*discursively—all words, but especially those with the power to dominate fairly large masses of other words (words like the *author Sade,* whose words fill several large volumes)—and to understand them as *events,* without necessary recourse to a biographical fallacy.

There are some habits of thought that prevent that kind of understanding, and it is to the credit of philosophers like Nietzsche and Deleuze, both of whose philosophies Foucault subjects to appreciative analyses, to have made their philosophy an attack on these habits. Much depends on the role of the subject in maintaining thought away from events and in what Foucault, following Deleuze, calls a Platonization that needs overturning.[32] On a primary epistemological plane, therefore, Foucault sets out to redispose and redeploy thought in a primordial mental space, much as an artist takes the representational space of his work in an active manner, rather than passively as an inert surface. The filled, activated space of a given epoch Foucault calls an *épistémè;* the filling is *discourse,* a body that has temporal duration and is comprised of *énoncés* (statements). (One curious thing about the *épistémè* is that, like structure for the structuralists, it is available neither to introspection nor to the epoch to which it belongs. As Canguihelm puts it: "In order for the *épistémè* of the classical age to have appeared as object it was necessary to situate oneself at the point where, participating in the nineteenth-century *épistémè,* one was far enough away from the classical *épistémè*'s birth to *see* the rupture with the eighteenth century, and near enough to imagine that one was going to *live* another rupture, one after which Man, as Order before him, would appear as an object."[33])

In order to *think* a discursive event in all its immediacy and complexity, Foucault needs coordinately to describe: the field or *épistémè,* in which such an event can be said to take place; the nature of a statement-event; relationships among events; the kind of conceptual changes that events deliver; and, above all, a method adequate to all these tasks. (Incidentally, he is not concerned with the effect of conceptual changes upon man—only with changes in concepts.) Neopositivism, phenomenology, and the philosophy of history, he contends, evade rather than accept the task. The complexity and difficulty of the project is evident. What is not quickly evident perhaps is how much the reader must be involved in a process simultaneously entailing disordering, decreation, and reordering.[34] Moreover, the feats Foucault accomplishes finally come to be seen as comprising a sort of cinematic work of the thoughts and words about thoughts and words. Duplicity—an imaginative and philosophical doubleness—is Foucault's deepest enterprise. It is the game of domination played between thought claiming truth and thought claiming knowledge, a seriously urgent set of moves between truth and the will to truth: "It involves risking the destruction of the subject of knowledge in the infinitely deployed will to knowledge."[35]

Foucault's mind has a predilection for thinking in threes and fours, so it is somewhat useful to juxtapose his themes laterally and in parallel. I shall be concerned to show that Foucault's method is to connect one major tripartite constellation with a major quadrilateral set and thereafter to impose them on one another. The imperatives of archeological research for the present and the future announced by Foucault are as follows:

> The philosophy of the event must move in what *at first glance* appears to be a paradoxical direction: toward a materialism of the incorporeal.

> It is necessary to elaborate—quite outside philosophies of a subject or of time—a theory of discontinuous systematizations.

> One must accept the introduction of chance as a category in the production of events, for in that production one still feels the absence of a theory permitting us to *think* the relationships between chance and thought.[36]

This set of imperatives involves the radical introduction into thought of "*le hasard, le discontinue, et la matérialité.*"[37] In short, Foucault intends the reinclusion into thought of elements that had been banished as disruptive ever since Plato. He argues furthermore that Hegel's dialectic so compelled thought into continuities that any radical philosopher since Hegel has to think against Hegel.

Foucault further asserts that one instrumentality for having kept disruption at bay has been the elision of reality and discourse—that is, the process by which discursive functions, which comprise the focal point of Foucault's analyses and which, more than anything, he is now studying, have been considered an *immediate* making of thought, rather than the series of verbal events (characterized by change, discontinuity, and materiality acting in conjunction with one another and with thought) with a life of their own. Thus the roles of the founding subject (*le sujet fondateur*), of originating experience (*l'expérience originateur*), and of universal mediation (*l'universelle médiation*) have been to embrace and legitimate a philosophical ideology in which discourse is a servile instrument of thought and/or truth, but never an ongoing reality with a behavior (*discursivity*) of its own.[38]

III

In seeking to install chance, discontinuity, and materiality, to locate them as forces operating in discourse, Foucault lists four *exigences de méthode* which he proposes to follow. These exigencies are as much principles controlling study as they are rules maintaining discursivity. This dual role is crucial, for it legitimizes Foucault's method as it describes its object. Foucault's formulation of these rules is in part polemical and in part explanatory. My first reference for each of the four in what follows is to *L'Ordre du discours*,[39] although—as I gloss each one in some detail—much of what Foucault says in this late work draws substantially on what he did in *Folie et déraison, Les Mots et les choses, Naissance de la clinique, L'Archéologie du savoir*, and several of his interpretive essays.

1. The first principle Foucault lists is *reversibility:*

> Wherever according to tradition one believes the source of discourses are to be found, the principle of their increase and of their continuity, in those figures that appear to play a positive role, such as those of the author, of a discipline, or of a will—instead of all that one ought instead to see the active negativity of something cut off, rarefied, into and by discourse.[40]

Those traditional conceptions of primacy such as source or origin, the principles of continuity and development, and those metaphors for originating authority such as *author, discipline,* and *the will to truth* are all more or less canceled by Foucault. For him they are secondary to the discourse: they are functions of it rather than prime movers of it. Much in this reversal depends on what Foucault means by discourse (*discours*), a notion that has a rich history in contemporary French writing.[41] From a linguistic point of view, discourse gains its status as a mode of verbal expression in opposition to historical narration. Emile Benveniste's heuristic definition is based upon correlations between verb tenses and modes of speech, correlations which constitute two quite different systems:

> The *historical* utterance [or *statement* in Foucault's terminology], today reserved to the written language, characterizes the narration of past events. These three terms, "narration," "event," and "past," are of equal

importance. Events that took place at a certain moment of time are presented without any intervention of the speaker in the narration. In order for them to be recorded as having occurred, these events must belong to the past . . . . We shall define historical narration as the mode of utterance that excludes every "autobiographical" linguistic form. The historian will never say *je* or *tu* or *maintenant,* because he will never make use of the formal apparatus of discourse, which resides primarily in the relationship of the persons *je:tu* . . . . The field of temporal expression will be similarly defined. The historical utterance admits of three tenses: the aorist, . . . the imperfect, . . . and the pluperfect.[42]

It must be noted that the events mentioned here are not the events Foucault is interested in. Benveniste is speaking of historical events, not discursive ones. He then notes that, so delimited, historical utterance (statement) necessarily implies a contrasting "plane of *discourse*":

Discourse [*discours*] must be understood in its widest sense: every utterance [statement] assuming a speaker and a hearer, and in the speaker, the intention of influencing the other in some way. It is primarily every variety of oral discourse of every nature and every level, from trivial conversation to the most elaborate oration. But it is also the mass of writing that reproduces oral discourse or that borrows its manner of expression and its purposes: correspondence, memoirs, plays, didactic work, in short, all the genres in which someone addresses himself to someone, proclaims himself as the speaker, and organizes what he says in the category of person. The distinction we are making between historical narration and discourse does not at all coincide with that between the written language and spoken.[43]

Neither of these definitions is anything more than schematic, since historical narration and *discours* shade into one another in practice as often as the speaker changes the intent of his speech from historical narration to discourse and back again. Foucault has used the kind of discrimination made by Benveniste to emphasize discourse as an organized and recognizable manner of intentionally transmitting information or knowledge from one person to another. Thus even a chronicle, while it is primarily a historical narration, belongs to an ensemble of discursive texts transmitting history within an integral institution called historical writing, an institution that has definable relationships to drama, to medical texts, to economic texts, and also to designated readers. Discursivity, then, emerges as largely an intertextual relationship. If the historical narrative as an ideal mode dramatizes the immediacy of passing time, statement as discourse emphasizes the way in which language has taken on the preserved historical form and the materialism of a text—a documentary event subject to specific laws of formation, preservation, and transmission.

A still more complicated notion of discourse of which, I think, Foucault avails himself derives from psychology. Lacan has characterized the patient's speech in the psychoanalytic encounter as the *discours du sujet.* Only here the patient's quasi-objective account of himself as a subjectivity forces him to discover the fundamental alienation that made him, during his life, create himself *as* an *other,* which must always be unmasked *by* an other. ("Car dans ce travail qu'il fait de la construire *pour un autre* il retrouve l'aliénation fondamentale qui la lui a fait construire *comme un autre,* et qui l'a toujours destinée à lui être dérobé *par un autre."* [44]) The essence of this, put simply, is Lacan's contention that self-discourse involves the creation of a paranoiac system for which the model, I think, is Freud's Dr. Schreber. Any attempt made to relay the subject always involves the subject's objectification of himself, which in extreme cases like Schreber's is a fantastic hodgepodge of fantasy and fact; discourse of self, then, is a perpetually distanced speech, emptied of the real, elusive subject in order that the existential self can gain clarity and definition, *for* others, *outside* itself.

Since discourse always implies a speaker and a hearer, Foucault combines linguistic usage with psychological insight in order to assert that speaker and hearer are functions operating in the discourse. They preserve its formality and the assurance that it will be transmitted even as they repress the "true" reality outside, or beneath, the spoken chain. (Needless to say, the "outside" reality loses its solidity, as well as its interest, quite soon in Foucault's writing—not that he is uninterested in anything except words, but the pertinence of his analysis lies in what actually is there in words.) It becomes futile—because radically inaccurate—to view a speaker as really beginning a discourse, still less as being its master. Rather, the speaker is *for* a discourse. His identity gives it a provisional start or finish (this is *découpage* or *raréfaction*), but for its total sense it depends upon circumstances that have to do with the speaker's identity in a very controlled way. In other words, the relationship between discourse and speaker is governed by rules that antedate the speaker's appearance and postdate his disappearance. *Découpage* as negativity and *raréfaction* is Foucault's way of describing the detachment of a single discursive unit—a text by an author, for example—from the main positivity; this lends the text a "rarefied" appearance of individual existence apart from the great number of conditions that override and determine its belonging to the main body.

Earlier in *L'Ordre du discours* Foucault discusses the manner in which an author can be studied as having himself entered the realm of discourse and having distinguished his particular subjectivity from others in the same body. Foucault's notion again is that this is a matter of discernible rules: rituals are performed (initiation ceremonies, the need to belong to societies), certain doctrines are subscribed to, a particular form of education is prescribed, and so forth.[45] A medical doctor who wishes to produce a clinical test and enjoy the status of its authorship must have been to a medical school, belong to a medical society (usually government-accredited), and so on. To speak clinically is to speak of medical subjects in a very special way.[46] Moreover, the "author" in this case produces his own discourse as part of an alternation between repeating the formal rules, on the one hand, and, on the other, varying them to admit his own instances. A given text, therefore, is an event that has appreciable and prepared relationships with other texts or events, and strictly speaking is not a creation in the romantic sense.

2. A principle of *discontinuity*:

> That there are systems of rarefaction does not also mean that beneath or beyond them a great unlimited discourse has reigned, silently and continuously, which is withheld and repressed by these systems, and which it is our task to bring to light, thereby restoring speech to and in it. One must not imagine an unsaid speech or unthought thought that travels through the world and is entwined with all the world's forms and events, and which it is our task finally to articulate or think. Discourses have to be treated as discontinuous practicalities that cross one another, are sometimes juxtaposed with one another, but just as often exclude and ignore one another.[47]

Systems of rarefaction are discursive groups (literature, history, psychology) part of whose self-definition includes the definition or implication of their differences (symbolic, signifying, intentional, formal) from other groups. This idea of differences can be theoretically extended to include differences among societies, or among different orders within a society. Up through and including *Les Mots et les choses* Foucault had been studying the history of the relationships between systems as much to determine their internal cohesion with one another as their differences from one another. *Folie et déraison*, which has been grossly misinterpreted as historical description of madness, was in fact a study of the relationship between sameness and difference expressed in the most basic of social terms; that is, Foucault argued in this early work that a society's identity (its self-rarefaction) rested in some measure upon its detachment from what was not itself. Insofar as members of a society spoke a mutually intelligible language, they were members of a discursive group with countless subdivisions, from which the insane, since the disappearance of leprosy at the end of the Middle Ages, have been excluded. Foucault therefore studied the changing significance of madness—actually, "madness" itself is a dated notion limited to a single era, and is not a universal concept—in the discourse of the nonmad. He shows how a realm that is itself silent with reference to the world of rational discourse is apprehended in the language of reason: as madness, insanity, alienation, irrationality, animality, depravity—in short, as a term of otherness domesticated to the discourse, made to serve its needs and exigencies. As these exigencies are modified socially and institutionally, as well as rationally, the discourse of silence is given differing interpretations, *incorporated, covered,* and *articulated* in the discourse of reason.

Because of his work after *Folie et déraison* and *Les Mots et les choses,* it is not altogether wrong, I think, to surmise that Foucault cares more for histories than he does for History. Since Nietzsche, portmanteau categories like exteriority and interiority, causality, continuity, totality, and genealogy no longer have the power to deal adequately with evidence of the sort Foucault deploys. Yet these categories have traditionally been subordinated to a grand enveloping notion of History, within which they have all functioned. In Foucault's view, history is but one discourse among many,[48] and since the quantity of differing discourses makes the problem of specifying their interrelationship more immediate than the problem of whether one discourse has an absolutely greater or lesser power to command the others, there is a need for developing a kind of affirmative thought "sans contradiction, sans dialectique, sans négation."[49] Evidence is no longer thought of as secondary to a Platonic Idea; multiplicity is made up of a variety of divergencies and disjunctions between equally valid, relatively weightless "bits," and being is ultimately univocal, without levels, hierarchies, or gradations of reality. These features make it difficult to expect Foucault's work to be a narrative chronicle of consecutive events, even though he frequently confines his reflections to a specific historical epoch.

Today, Foucault says, language—whether studied or written— occupies a space which is not defined by rhetoric but by the library.[50] Language no longer can be thought of as anything other than incarnating itself as monotonously as Narcissus viewed himself in the water. The substitution of the library for rhetoric as a conception for thinking of language and human *verbality* is a stunning idea, and it is one among many affinities that Foucault has with Borges. A library is a total, infinitely absorptive system, infinitely self-referential (think of the catalog, of the unlimited possibility of cross-references there and in the books), numerically vast in its elements, and impersonal. So organized and complete a world is at once perfectly repetitive and perfectly actual. The sheer actuality of repeat units (and whether books, words, ideas, or discourses, they are simply modes of language) is sufficient to dismiss any outside or inside extraverbality. Foucault does not insist on this point merely to declare that everything is words, but rather to accentuate the reality of the scholar's enterprise, and in so doing to attack delaying tactics like appeals to the Idea of History which every document is supposed to represent.

Indeed, Foucault's profound distrust of mimetic representation and theological givens goes even further. Correlation, adjacency, and complementarity are, as I said above, the relationships that interest him, but what lies behind them and permits such relationships is no scheme of imitation conceived as representation. A discourse does not represent an idea, nor does it embody a figure: it simply repeats, in a different mode, another discourse.[51] The extraordinary variety of discourse today is a result of the decline in representation. This is a central theme of *Les Mots et les choses.* When language is no longer thought of as a kind of secondary transparency through which shines Being, then the past, for example, becomes only the cumulative repetition of designated words. Such a past lasts only so long as its elements— which make the past possible, and not the other way around—are of value. Thus each epoch defines its forms and its limits of expression, of conservation, of memory, of the reactivation of preceding cultures or foreign ones, of appropriation.[52] And since the very notion of an epoch is itself a function of these limits and forms, it is even more accurate to say that each discursive formulation articulates the limits and forms of its own existence, inseparable from others. Therefore, the library holds together, in ways Foucault tries to specify, a staggeringly vast array of discursive formulations, an array whose essence is that no source, origin, or provenance, no goal, teleology, or purpose can be thought through for it.

Merely affirming this complex notion seems hardly a satisfactory ploy. Foucault had been honestly impressed by the threshold he reached:

> Is that not what Nietzsche was paving the way for when, in the interior space of his language, he killed man and God both at the same time, and thereby promised with the Return the multiple and re-illumined light of the gods? Or must we quite simply admit that such a plethora of questions on the subject of language is no more than a continuance, or at most a culmination, of the event that, as archaeology has shown, came into existence and began to take effect at the end of the eighteenth century? The fragmentation of language, occurring at the same time as its transition to philological objectivity, would in that case be no more than the most recently visible (because the most secret and most fundamental) consequence of the breaking up of Classical order; by making the effort to master this schism and to make language visible in its entirety, we would bring to completion what had occurred before us, and without us, towards the end of the eighteenth century. But what, in that case, would that culmination be? In attempting to reconstitute the lost unity of language, is one carrying to its conclusion a thought which is that of the nineteenth century, or is one pursuing forms that are already incompatible with it? The dispersion of language is linked, in fact, in a fundamental way, with the archaelogical event we may designate as the disappearance of Discourse. To discover the vast play of language contained once more within a single space might be just as decisive a leap towards a wholly new form of thought as to draw to a close a mode of knowing constituted during the previous century.
>
> It is true that I do not know what to reply to such questions, or, given these alternatives, what term I should choose. I cannot even guess whether I shall ever be able to answer them, or whether the day will come when I shall have reasons enough to make any such choice.[53]

Later, with *L'Archéologie du savoir, L'Ordre du discours,* and the two essays on Nietzsche, Foucault began to formulate his decisions and his reasons for reaching them: first, through an attention to dispersion and fragmentation—not to Discourse, but to discourses and discursivity; and second, through an attention to seriality as an internal order within dispersion. That is, Foucault devoted his time to understanding how discourse multiplied itself serially, as a result of its constitution and dynamics, rather than as a secondary repetition in words of natural organic forms. *Archeology* and *order,* the two terms he used in his titles, indicate respectively "an ensemble of rules" that defines the archive of any given period, and the regulative principles within discourse.[54] This leaves him free to treat discourse as discontinuity bound together, if at all, by exigent rules for particular and material, but never transcendent, purposes. He has found Nietzsche's word *Entstehung* useful to describe the "pure distance" separating discoveries from one another and permitting their identities to emerge with reference to one another; this field of distance is, he says, an open space of interdiscursive confrontation.[55]

In all this, language quite obviously plays a central role. Foucault has published numerous essays in which the nature of language has been the underlying subject; but what is curious in all these shorter pieces is the ability he possesses (in common with many of the structuralists) to speak of language as a precisely definable entity. It is something with its own special history, geography, and spirituality, as well as a corporeality; I suppose it is also correct to say that language has its own language, its own mythology and imagination. Foucault's common motif here is that language has been transformed into a human phenomenon. On a number of occasions Foucault imaginatively interprets the *Odyssey* as marking some themes that adumbrate the formerly human nature of language. Like *The Thousand and One Nights,* the *Odyssey* is a text rooted in the postponement of death and disaster. "It is quite possible that the gods sent disasters to beset men so that man might then be able to tell of them: in this possibility speech finds its infinite resourcefulness."[56] Hence Odysseus' brilliant verbal wit. Yet he is also a man who is returning home, and when in Phaeacia he hears his own story told by Demodokos in the past tense, as if it were the tale of a dead hero, he cries, forcing himself to sing the song of his identity. Thus revealed, his identity further distances him from a death seemingly decreed for him by language. This complex of interconnected stories that tell stories with death hovering ever nearby fascinates Foucault. It suggests to him both the play of mirrors that establishes the resourcefulness of language, as well as the presence of death its neighbor. Moreover:

> In western culture to write has meant at the outset to place oneself in the virtual space of self-representation and doubleness; since writing signifies speech and not a thing, the linguistic work has done no more than to move forward more deeply into that impalpable thickness of a mirror, to stir up that double of a double which is writing, to discover an infinite possibility and impossibility, to follow after speech indefinitely, and maintain it beyond the death that condemns it, and to liberate the streaming of a murmur. This presence of speech repeated in writing doubtless gives an ontological status to what we call a work, a status unknown to those cultures in which when one writes it is the thing itself that gets designated—bodily and visibly, and obstinately inaccessible to time.[57]

Elsewhere he asserts that the theme of Odysseus' return, with the influence of its anchoring in a human situation and in a specific place and time, has exercised a fundamental restraint (*une courbe fondamentale*) upon language which, during this century, has been utterly released.[58] Language now has become a thing of space; as a medium, language is *l'espace universel d'inscription,* and it speaks to us by means of "deviation, distance, intermediation, dispersion, fragmentation, difference."[59] These are not literary themes, but givens of today's language. The importance of such writers as Bataille, Sade, and Freud is that because of them even sexuality has been denaturalized, rendered submissive to, and thrown into the empty space of language. Indeed, for Foucault this sort of feat is associated with a new heroism, that of the artist, which has displaced the heroism of the epic hero. In a great essay on Hölderlin, Foucault remarks that the epic quality of the modern artist arose during the Renaissance when representational painters created a new world, which revealed itself to be another version of the same world in which men live: "The attribute of heroism passed from the hero to the one who portrayed him at the very moment that Western culture itself became a world of representations."[60] In the work of an artist like Hölderlin, Foucault finds commemorated simultaneously the death of God and the new sovereign status of language, the connected problematics of absence and presence, and beneath those, the complex interplay of signifiers detached from a stable signified that results (in Hölderlin's extreme case) from the "no" filling the (dead) father's place: all this is made possible when the world is no longer conceived of as representation, but instead, Foucault says in "Nietzsche, Marx, Freud," as *interpretation.*[61]

In the sixteenth century the world was viewed as a system of resemblances (*conventia, sympatheia, emulatio, signatura, analogia*) which together yield a consensus leading directly to God. Opposed to this was an order of *simulacra,* false resemblance, leading directly to the Devil.[62] As we saw earlier, in the nineteenth century the archsignified God-father was perceived as absence. Hence the sign could not be taken as it once was, inhabiting a homogenous and undifferentiated space of reciprocal relationships among man, nature, and God; rather, signs belonged in a far more differentiated, multitiered space which is totally exterior and irreducibly disjunctive. Foucault then describes this verbal space as containing no primary or secondary signs, but rather already-interpreted signs in need of further reinterpretation. It is precisely at this point that Foucault locates his own work, as furthering the work begun by Nietzsche, Marx, and Freud, for each of whom language was an ongoing hermeneutics of itself and not a primary given. Discontinuity, then, is the inaugural principle, the beginning, according to which one could begin to assemble an encyclopedia—"une sorte de Corpus générale"—of interpretations:[63] the discontinuity is based on differences between discourses (themselves interpretive bodies regulated by internal rules, and by their relationships, whether antithetical or sympathetic, with adjacent discourse), whose integral thematic is "la revolution répétitive de l'être autour de la différence."[64] In this convergence of difference and repetition Foucault confirms the triumph of seriality over unity, the latter with its arsenal of a priori categories that elide differences and its nostalgia for organic forms.

3. A principle of *specificity:*

[This is the principle demanding us] not to resolve discourse into a set of preordained significations; not to imagine to oneself that the world turns to us a readable face that we need only decipher simply; the world is not an accessory to our knowledges; there is no prediscursive providence that disposes things our way. One must conceive discourse as a violence we do to things, or in any case, a practicality we impose on them; and it is in that practicality that the events of a discourse find the principle of their regularity.[65]

A major branch of Foucault's historical inquiry has been the definition of how discourse confirms and maintains its individuality. Here, too, Sade plays an epitomizing role, for his work makes monstrously explicit what Foucault calls "the universal Characteristic of Desire." The classical age—roughly the late sixteenth through the eighteenth centuries—had conceived reality in terms of representation: "Language is simply the representation of words; nature is simply the representation of beings; need is simply the representation of needs."[66] Every statement could thereby be referred back to an original source and understood as representing it; in a complete system of taxonomies, therefore, any instance has reference dynastically back to an *Urphänomen*. Underpinning this consensus of representation, however, is a disequilibrium between representation itself and "the empirical domains": in thought, the latter is held in by the former. Then

the end of classical thought—and the *épistémè* that made general grammar, natural history, and the science of wealth possible [these are the modes of knowledge by which language, nature, and value respectively are made accessible to thought in the classical period]—will coincide with the emancipation of language, of the living being, and of need, with regard to representation. The obscure but stubborn spirit of a people who talk, the violence and the endless effort of life, the hidden energy of needs, were all to escape from the mode of being of representation. And representation itself was to be paralleled, limited, circumscribed, mocked perhaps, but in any case regulated from the outside, by the enormous thrust of a freedom, a desire, or a will posited as the metaphysical converse of consciousness. Something like a will or a force was to arise in the modern experience—constituting it perhaps, but in any case indicating that the Classical age was now over, and with it the reign of representative discourse, the dynasty of a representation signifying itself and giving voice in the sequence of its words to the order that lay dormant within things.[67]

The force, will, or desire derives from empirical experience—in Sade's case, a pure libertine desire to name every sexual possibility. And these new possibilities batter down the limits imposed on sexuality by representation. Every one of Sade's scenes is a pure instance of sexuality without precedent, original in itself; hence it stands as a surface without depth, an articulation without an informing rationality.

Between them, Nietzsche and Mallarmé further yield up the essence of discourse and release it from the hold of a social-speaker and representative function. After Sade, a statement is not decipherable simply by tracing it to a source (a speaking subject), whose identity is supposed to be represented by the discourse. Nietzsche dramatizes the difficulty of attribution by inquiring into the identity of each statement's origin as follows: who was the holder of discourse, who was the possessor of the word? The diversity and the totality of discourse, which corresponds in its seriality to the succession of scenes in Sade's fiction, makes it impossible to answer these questions by supplying a name from *outside* the discourse.

Mallarmé's project—that of enclosing all possible discourse within the fragile density of the word, within that slim, material black line traced by ink upon paper—is fundamentally a reply to the question imposed upon philosophy by Nietzsche. For Nietzsche, it was not a matter of knowing what good and evil were in themselves, but of who was being designated, or rather *who was speaking* . . . . To the Nietzschean question: "Who is speaking?" Mallarmé replies—and constantly reverts to that reply—by saying that what is speaking is, in its solitude, in its fragile vibration, in its nothingness, the word itself—not the meaning of the word, but its enigmatic and precarious being. Whereas Nietzsche maintained his questioning as to who is speaking right up to the end, . . . Mallarmé was constantly effacing himself from his own language to the point of not wishing to figure in it except as an executant in a pure ceremony of the Book in which the discourse would compose itself.[68]

The break between speaker and discourse makes it incumbent upon discourse to gain its specificity, its nominal subject, elsewhere, and not with reference back to a manipulative *sujet fondateur.* As an example of the specifically contemporary predicament, Foucault is fond of quoting this line by Beckett: "Qu'importe qui parle, quelqu'un a dit, qu'importe qui parle?"[69] Therefore, the analysis of discourse cannot begin by specifying an author for a given discourse unless authorship is defined precisely with regard to the practical field of the discourse in question. Thus to say that X is the author of Y could mean, for example, that X designates a collection of an unknown writer (Homer, or Dionysus the Areopagite); or that X is the legal author (Sade, whose authority over his novels and tracts involves a criminal liability); or that X is the author of that type of discourse (Freudian or Marxist writing); or that X is believed to be the author of Y because Y resembles Z (the notion of consistency between different works leading to the attribution of a single author); and so forth.[70] The stability of a discourse depends upon something less provisional than an author, both in the short and in the long run.

Discourse is frequently given minimal coherence by the persistence of its subject matter; this is true of both psycho-analytic and clinical writing, for instance. For these examples and others like them, Foucault enumerates three criteria that, oper-ating together, establish the systematic character (that is, the regularity) of the discourse. In *L'Ordre du discours* he adds to this group what he calls procedures of exclusion: procedures that establish, but ceaselessly modify, the limits of its discourse, its frontiers, beyond which everything is nondiscursive and foreign to it. Thus concepts of what is forbidden, what is mad, and what is wrong police the limits of a given discourse, keep out what threatens the permissibility, rationality, and truth enclosed within that discourse.[71] *Inside*—and now we come to the first of the three criteria—there have to be principles of *formation* working to govern the way in which concept, object, theory, and operation—no matter how diverse—partake of the same discursivity; these principles of formation, and not a formal structure, nor a coherent conceptual architecture, nor the unity of a persistent object, are what make it possible to call discourse X "economics" or discourse Y "general grammar." Foucault is attempting to describe an extremely intimate level of activity of the sort that makes it possible for an economist, for example, to use language and thought professionally. This is not a matter only of learning the jargon, but of being able to address others—economists and noneconomists—as an economist speaking economics.

When one's perspective is shifted to account for the role of history in the individualizing of discourse, a second set of principles emerges: principles of threshold or of *transformation*. Here we must recognize that a confluence of different circumstances must take place in order for a discourse to be formed. Not only that, but since discourse is itself a specific process of change, there is good reason for articulating an anterior set of transformations out of which the given discourse appears, as well as a set of presumably future conditions which in its movement in time the discourse will fulfill. Thirdly, there are criteria of *correlation*. Despite its individuality, no discourse is an isolated phenomenon. Consider that one discourse has specific relationships with others—say, clinical discourse with biology, with philosophy, with history—and that in addition to those relationships there are precise nondiscursive relationships (i.e., institutional, political, and economic ones) that maintain the identity of the discourse. Again, clinical discourse is a good example, for it cannot properly be thought of apart from its existence as a discipline, an institution, a system of organization, an outlook, and so forth. The merest clinical statement made by a doctor in his professional capacity is thus supported by a complex, but highly articulated, web of events that have necessarily taken place—they are not vague, or just there—in order for him to speak (or act) clinically. All the criteria Foucault lists are ways of measuring and characterizing the distance between events: discourse, in other words, is the particular occupied space, insofar as it is acted within and upon, that enables *positive* (although not necessarily conscious) knowledge to bear on any coherent activity.[72] How do an economist, a psychiatrist, or a literary critic make their way in their work? What traditions must they assume, what institutions, distinctions, codes, symbolism?—and these without necessary reference to an individual, but always to something called economics, psychiatry, literary criticism: these are some of the questions for which answers are provided by discourse.[73]

The originality of Foucault's criteria is the effect of their use *together*. After all, for *formation* above we can substitute *orthodoxy* (what every economist must know), for *transformation* we can substitute *history*, and for *correlation*, *society*. Putting them together, however, robs any one of them of a privilege over the others: thus the potentially exclusive inwardness of "formation" is corrected by an exterior "correlation." Second, together Foucault's criteria exert a considerably more general power over different sorts of particulars. A frequent problem with the sociology of knowledge has been its reliance upon a narrowly circumscribed Western, industrialized social paradigm; anything beyond that setting seems to resist the method. Foucault's criteria have a tighter internal discipline and a wider general sweep than that. Third, in emphasizing the detailed complications of these criteria, Foucault shows them to be—from the standpoint of a historian—demonstrably effective in separating words from things, in making it clear once and for all that words operate according to laws of their own. What is unexceptionably regular in a discourse is, from a "natural" point of view, completely perverse, even unnatural. Discursivity is a mutual refusal—of nature by language, and of language by nature. Language admits things as things-of-language. A will to truth is above all a will to place things in language, which in the ongoing discipline of a discourse is a phenomenon we might justifiably call "knowledge." Once *of* the discourse, an object occupies a space prepared for it—as Freud's unconscious climaxes a history of psychological probing—but in so doing it must necessarily displace, or at least dislocate, other objects. Hence there is a double violence: of language to things, and of one language to another, and all this takes place as regularly as the discourse proceeds. Every statement is an event that asymmetrically covers up other statements. Insofar as the covering up goes on habitually and repetitively, it is also re-covery, in a dual way: *once again obscuring* other events by its presence, and *bringing up* the discourse to a new level of activity.

No event can long remain an event. Foucault's analysis aims to describe the curve of motion that goes from a statement occurring as a singular irruption to a statement as variation within discourse. The same curve would describe the relationships between one discourse and others, between one *épistémè* and other *épistémès,* each singularity assimilated to a larger order with more or less violence; this is how the intransigent aleatory character of an event is reduced, although never destroyed completely. The verb tense most capable of conveying the movement from irregularity to regularity is the present infinitive,[74] for in it the process leading from *event* to *eventuality* via *reality* can be rendered faithfully. The repetitiveness of the process does away with originality entirely, just as seriality does away with unity, and each event, in its violent displacement of a prior event, does away with creation. And since there is no foreordained, a priori route for the discourse to travel, a route legislated from outside itself, the order of statement, discourse, and *épistémè* bears no resemblance to the traditionally concentric of self, world, and God, which are held together dynastically by three types of time (human, natural, divine) and by three types of continuity, all paternally guaranteed by God the Father.[75] The order of discourse is maintained by *legislated accident,* by chance: "The present is a throw of the dice . . . . The present as return of difference, as repetition styling itself as difference, affirms once for all the totality of chance."[76]

Most theories are so constituted as to be able to compel a large number of different individual details into a smaller set of general principles; this is true, for example, of the theory of generative grammar. The odd, distinctive quality of Foucault's theory, as I have just described it, is that his general principles are designed to illuminate a large number of repetitive phenomena that are continuously appearing with such disconcerting randomness as to seem chaotic. In the mindlessness of their reptition, and the unmotivated gratuitousness of their patterns, they cannot—and perhaps should not—correspond to or fulfill preestablished laws, needs, or desires. Except, one supposes, those of repetition and chance, although I doubt that my vocabulary can go beyond Foucault's in explaining these rather terminal conceptions. I suspect that Foucault is simultaneously addressing the Nietzschean idea of Eternal Recurrence and the disconcerting, surprising effect of Freud's *will to repeat,* in its irrationality: he takes from the former the idea of exact repetition and from the latter the traumatic precision of one exactly defined event that is repeated down to its last detail. According to Deleuze, therefore, Foucault's achievement "is to have discovered and surveyed that unknown realm where a literary form, an everyday sentence, an item of schizophrenic non-sense, etc., are *equally* statements, without however having anything in common with one another, nor anything to which they are all reducible, nor any discursive equivalence with one another. And it is this point to which neither logicians, nor formalists, nor interpreters have ever reached."[77]

4. A principle of *exteriority*:

[This is] not a movement from the discourse to its internal and hidden nucleus, to the heart of thoughts or meaning that are made manifest in the discourse; but with reference to the discourse, in its actual appearance and its regularity, a movement instead toward the discourse's external conditions of possibility, toward that which enables the aleatory series of discursive events, and which determines limits.[78]

Nietzsche, Mallarmé, Artaud, Bataille, Blanchot, and Pierre

Klossowski are cited by Foucault as having deciphered a new form of experience—*la pensée de dehors*—already implanted proleptically in modern culture by Hölderlin and Sade.[79] It is the experience of a kind of transcendental homelessness (Lukacs's phrase is apt here, too). This state is the result of discovering an absolute incompatibility between the realm of totality and the realm of personal interiority, of subjectivity. Hölderlin and Sade personify an extremism so complete in its heedless articulation of impossible desires as to exclude the possibility of accommodating one man's inner self to it. Their works deliver naked desire, totally unconditioned by subjectivity and without contingency: it is a pure serialism unraveling itself, for its own sake. This is paradoxical, for how, then, can men think like Hölderlin and Sade and still retain some semblance of their subjectivity? Foucault argues that the price both writers paid for their daring was virtually to have alienated themselves into unreason: the sign of their exteriority to social discourse was their madness, their act of having turned themselves inside out onto the public domain of their work. A later generation of writers, for whom only language (and not society) was the space of their activity, no longer treated exteriority as an inverted interiority, but as the realm of all knowledge. This freedom of knowledge from subjectivity is posited at the moment that knowledge is understood as a function, not of truth, but of a statement: the "I think" is worked against by the "I speak." The former leads to interiority, the traditional place of truth, the latter to exteriority. Language as being-for-itself stands forth only when subjectivity is engulfed.[80]

Exteriority also means an estrangement from sense—and Foucault is no more justified than here in the use of his theatrical metaphor. Estrangement is dislocation, an effect interestingly attained by Brecht's plays in putting into relief the disparity between audience and message. Similarly, society puts madness outside itself; exteriority, socially speaking, is the displacement of sense outward—paranoia.[81] Ordinarily we discover meaning by claiming sense from the outside world and pressing it into service inward. The opposite process exhausts the self by constituting *another place, another history, another thought* beyond the self, gradually becoming, because stable and overt, more powerful than the self.[82] Discourse is precisely this exteriority given form, just as madness in Western society has been the exteriorization and confinement in asylums of a hidden silent self. The exteriority of discourse makes possible its existence, and it makes possible knowledge, but it does not guarantee its own truth. Exteriority, finally, is the dispersion, the systematic dissociation, of the unified truth of interiority amid the ordered discursive nature of all knowledge.

IV

"One can say that as a field of historicity on which the sciences appear, knowledge is free of any constitutive activity, liberated from any references backwards to an origin or forwards to an historical or transcendental teleology, and detached from any support or ground in subjectivity."[83] Apart from its assertiveness, the most notable thing about this definition of *knowledge* is that it is a series of denials. Knowledge is not constitutive of anything, can be referred neither to an origin nor to a *telos*, is detached from any particular subjectivity. In a certain sense, then, knowledge is epistemologically neutral—not value-*free*, but saturated with *all* values; perhaps it would be better to say not that knowledge *is* anything, but is rather the *possibility* of everything we know. Foucault's enormously complex system of definitions—his rules, criteria, functions, axes, and so forth—continually force the mind from habitual processes to unusual ones whose direction and whose motivation are only minimally apparent.[84] Consider, for example, Foucault's refusal to think in terms of "author" and "work," ready-made continuities he will do everything in his power to avoid. Thus a writer's name is a complex event, and his work is a segment of the archive bound together by "discursivity" whose rules evolve a collection of semantic elements, as well as a collection of operative strategies for getting things said.

All of Foucault's work is an attempt to make the history and indeed the experience of knowledge something as specifically ordered as "nature" has become for modern physics or chemistry. The setting of this order is the library. Nevertheless, I think it is essential to say that far from being (as they appear to be) inhuman models,[85] the "library" and the "archive" in Foucault's project serve a particularly humanizing purpose. Certainly a library is manmade, even if as a collection of discrete entities it cannot be contained in any one man's mind or experience. Still, the library's use for a finite purpose can be subordinated to a human motive—just as an act of speech is humanly motivated, whereas language considered as a system is not. Have the proliferations of knowledge finally left the human subject so completely behind, or is there some method that can bring subjectivity up to the challenge of all knowledge?

Along with the mythological analyses of Barthes and Lévi-Strauss, Foucault's archeologies have had the effect of laying bare a logic inherent in knowledge but no longer dependent upon the manipulation of a constantly intervening subject. In all three cases, this is a logic inhabiting the spaces between the object of thought; but only Foucault among the three has attempted to characterize thought as radically mixed up with chance, discontinuity, and materiality, albeit with regard to language in use. I have already quoted Deleuze's summary of what this means (on page 311), but what I did not then underscore was his use of the phrase "*une terre inconnue.*" Such a description raises the question of whether Foucault has invented a new realm of speculation or rediscovered a long-existing one. Is locating this place a matter of returning, or of reactualization, or of invention?[86] In terms of Foucault's own methodological attitude, each of the three designations is applicable, depending on one's epistemological perspective. Thus his archeology of knowledge is a return to Nietzschean critique and genealogy, a reactualization of a proper way of doing the history of science, consciousness, concepts, and ideas, and then also a polemical invention for harassing establishment historians or philosophers.

Yet in this connection Borges's crucial significance to Foucault cannot be overlooked. I suppose that were he to be asked about why Borges matters to him, Foucault would point to the frequent appearance together in *Ficciones* of terrifically precise detail, inescapably precise repetition, sly duplicity, interestingly monotonous revelation, and the total lack of a scheme of continuity linking details together. All these do not result in a conversion for the reader, just as it is unlikely that the world-view of any of Foucault's readers will suddenly be altered—even if quite literally, his mind is changed. Foucault's imaginative effect,[87] however, is noticeable, and it overrules any desire for getting hold of a method in his writing that one can "apply." In overruling the wish for an applicable method (this is the neutralization I mentioned at the outset), an intellectual event takes place, with a directness we normally associate not with words *meaning* something, but with words *saying* something. In reading Foucault, this event is the result in his writing of having induced thought to happen, without

314

the determining offices of books, authors, or physical perception, except as accidents of thought, secondary attributes of it. Therefore, the prototype of such activity would be Raymond Roussel's language, which always means "something else."[88] But to go on and detail this "something else" would be to make the subversion of our customary mental furniture into an exact science, a stylized theatricality of dissociation which is technically as well as rationally plotted from moment to moment. Housing all this in prose is rather like taking a library very seriously, as an incredible peculiarity and a very powerful adjunct to the history of human effort. The paradox of Foucault is how he maintains such severity, learning, and system—quite without dishonesty or trickiness—with such wisdom and style: there are hardly any scholarly enemies he attacks and no obstacles he avoids. The bookish fragments that Joyce, Eliot, and Mallarmé wove into their respective works return in Foucault, but as postmodern denizens of a wide space that is very generously impersonal, intellectually comprehended for all its discontinuities, and far from being an unheroic field of verbal action. But Foucault has not only faced this field as the beginning place: he has also begun to chart it with instruments of his own making.[89]

V

And yet Foucault and the structuralists share a gloomy theme in the idea of loss and, associated with it, man's unhappy historical insertion into a language game that he can barely understand. This has led to a dominantly linguistic apprehension of reality. But why, we should now ask, must the centrifugal analogies in Holofernes's speeches and the tautologies of Lucky's monologue in *En attendant Godot* stand as emblems for the structuralist vision of man?

The problem as seen by all the structuralists—Lévi-Strauss, Barthes, Louis Althusser, and Emile Benveniste among them—is that the authority of a privileged Origin that commands, guarantees, and perpetuates meaning has been removed. Why this has happened does not seem as important as the fact of its having happened; and this fact is already accepted in *Paradise Lost* and in the work of Vico, the philologists of the early nineteenth century, the great romantic poets and rebels, and the Higher Critics.[90] In other words, man now lives in a circle without a center, in a maze without a way out. If we try to think of action's beginning, for example, we must articulate the beginning in language. And since language for us is a system of written signs, the "first" sign is a momentary exigency of the discourse, never an absolute terminal.[91] So there is no such thing as an absolute beginning for language; or, if there is one, it is an unthinkable event, since, as Emile Benveniste puts it in one of his trenchant essays, we cannot think without language, and language makes only a token concession to a beginning.[92] The categories of thought and language are identical. To complicate matters further, we generally locate origins before beginnings, since the Origin is a latent state from which the beginnings of action move forward: retrospectively considered, then, the Origin is a condition or state that permits beginning. Foucault's way of showing the loss of both a beginning and the Origin behind it is to study the way in which eighteenth-century thought about language underwent radical change during the nineteenth century. Whereas during the classical age the derivation, designation, and articulation of words were thought to be functions of the consistent transparency with which words reflected Being, in the nineteenth century derivation gave its place up to a theory of linguistic families (in the work of the German philologist Franz Bopp), designation ceded its role to a theory of verbal radicals, and articulation was replaced by a theory of internal variations within language.[93] Being, in short, was swallowed up in the internal analysis of language. The structuralist vision of things takes this rationale almost for granted.

As a result of these momentous changes, words now simply double back on themselves: this is why the verb *dédoubler* turns up incessantly in all structuralist writing. It is no longer possible either to designate a beginning or to think of an origin except (in both cases) as concessions to the empty fact or priority. Strictly speaking, I think, a beginning to a modern mind occupies the temporal place in thought that a speaking subject would in a passage of prose. At best, however, a beginning provides an inaugural direction, a provisional orientation in method and intention. Yet because we must always use language to point to a beginning, and because for the structuralist language is always a presence and never a prior state, the origin and the beginning are both hopelessly alien to, and absent from, the stream of discourse. (This is a structuralist position which, in the course of this book, I have implicitly been criticizing and modifying; here, however, I am presenting the position as they have argued it.) Removed by language, which is the very activity it once presumably made possible, the beginning stands outside words, yet is assumed by them; the beginning is like the man at the door of the Law in Kafka's parable, neither able to enter nor permitted to be forgotten. Man the beginning, man as the subject of human thought and activity in what is now seen as the utopia of Renaissance humanism, is admitted to language only as an incipient, and inarticulate, ensemble of relationships among his activities. According to Barthes, *logos* and *praxis* are *praxis* are cut off from one another.[94] Structure remains shyly to fill the void.

Each of the structuralists in his own way alludes to origins that antedate and provide for a beginning event. It is this allusion and this exigency that I wish to play up. The characteristic feature of this event in structuralist writing is the absence of written language; literally, the event is a pre-scriptive beginning. In *Tristes tropiques,* characterized by Maurice Blanchot as full of a fascination with beginnings and original possibilities, Lévi-Strauss encounters the Nambikwara, tribesmen who have not yet discovered writing.[95] There, among them, Lévi-Strauss, speculating on the origins of writing, concludes that writing is the advent of enslavement. Before writing, man lived at a "zero point," described elsewhere by Lévi-Strauss as an original state preceding the neolithic age.[96] Life at the zero point was ruled over by a central "floating signifier," a kind of spiritual etymon, whose ubiquity and perfect consistency endowed it with the power to act as a pure semantic value. This, in Lévi-Strauss's judgment, corresponds to Marcel Mauss's notion of mana, an almost magical value that permits preliterate societies to make a whole range of universal distinctions between force and action, between abstract and concrete, and between quality and state. (The parallels between preliterate cultures and Eden before the Fall are fascinating, indeed.) One beautifully functional key, man, therefore unlocks every signifier because it is the Origin of all signifiers.

The point here, however, is that Lévi-Strauss is attempting, somewhat like Foucault in his analysis of madness, to describe a society and a state to which civilized man can have no real access; this partially explains the enigmatic use of words like *magic* and *zero*, as well as the quasi-fantastic air running throughout his descriptions. Because the observing ethnologist is a product of literate society, and because anthropology itself is subject to the enslaving laws of literacy, the zero state is a forbidden paradise which literacy penetrates only at the same critical moment that the paradise is being obliterated. In the confrontation between preliteracy and literacy, the latter always wins: the illiterate natives learn how to write. In so teaching preliterates (a process recorded with moving philosophical precision in *Tristes tropiques*), civilization disturbs the equanimity and calm of a univocal society in which spoken words and concrete objects had been intertwined in a complex but profoundly logical unity. For a while, nevertheless, the ethnologist can observe a society making its traumatic entry at the *beginning* of literacy, leaving the zero-point Origin behind it forever. (The tragedy is, as Lévi-Strauss observed in one essay, that anthropology inevitably brings and forcibly introduces writing to "primitive" society—in a kind of rape—thereby destroying once and for all a peace never again to be enjoyed in nonliterate solitude.[97]) To sum up, then, the process described by Lévi-Strauss is as follows: zero state, followed by the beginning of writing (literacy), followed by enslavement, which is our present situation. Writing means submission to the logic of language, and the loss of a central and univocal resource of meaning.

There are *two* primitive states. One is the zero-point stability of preliterate society, the other the moment at which writing begins to be learned—in fine, the Origin and the beginning. Yet only one can be actually described (in writing, of course) by the field anthropologist who is recording its loss, or metaphorically evoked by the linguist who notes its absence: and this, then, is the structuralist beginning, which in anthropological or linguistic discourse is converted into a *sign* that initiates the system, a *sign for* or *of* the signifying system. The Origin is a silent zero point, locked within itself. It is the realm of untroubled semantic security, closed to literate man; whereas the beginning is the event that founds the realm of order and writing—syntax, whose weblike wealth continues to impoverish, render obsolete, and cover up the memory of the original germ of pure meaning. Primitive thought, insofar as it can be described by civilized thought, is order at its most essential level, yet the modern mind must conceive it entirely as a system of endless parallels and reflections. There is no center available to the modern thinker, no absolute subject, since the Origin has been curtained off. The modern anthropologist's field trips among primitive people provide us with the most lively means of seeing our loss: as he was for the eighteenth-century writer of philosophical voyages, the primitive is a model for our imaginings of lost plenitude. Literate man is constantly signifying, yet *what* he signifies can only be interpreted as a function of *how* he signifies. Language, which is man's principal means of signification, is, as Barthes says, at once a problem and a model of order.[98]

The structualists' predicament is an accurate symptom of man's condition, mired as he is in his systems of signification. Their work can be construed as an attempt to manipulate their way out of our enslavement by language into an awareness and subsequent mastery of our linguistic situation. If their continuing enterprise is functional (like that of Robinson Crusoe, marooned yet surviving and organizing the possibilities of his island around his needs), then their vision of the past is fondly utopian and their anticipated future dimly apocalyptic. The past contained a meaning they cherish somewhat uselessly because they cannot hold it, although the future may restore it to them. They are structuralists—as, in a way, we all are—because they accept their existential fate inside language, whose mode of being is pitilessly relational: words derive meaning not from any intrinsic value, but from a double system of metaphor and metonymy that links words to one another and that grants words fleeting intelligibility as opposed to detached permanence. Certainly the structuralists are formalists, *content* being for them not much more than a chimera of the kind that, Lévi-Strauss notes, one might expect to dig out of a piece of music:[99] it is no easier to say what writing really means, they contend, than to say what a Beethoven symphony really means. Meaning is dispersed, scattered systematically along the length and depth of the spoken and written chain; but it is virtually incomprehensible at any point in the chain, since language is never present in toto and at once. The most one can do, then, is attempt to understand and perhaps predict the workings of the system—much as in reading a musical score—which at least permits one to function momentarily within the system. The question that they ask is, not "What does the system mean?" but "How does it work?" Thus in the structuralist universe the problem of belief is never relevant, since belief entails a hierarchy of meanings. For structuralism there are only significations, and they are either adequate or inadequate for their signifying intentions.

A major criticism of the structuralists is, I think, that the moving force of life and behavior, the *forma informans,* intention, has been, in their work, totally domesticated by system. This, I believe, is a consequence of gravely underestimating the rational potency of the beginning, which to them is an embarrassment for systematic thought. Only the early Barthes of *Mythologies* and *Le Degré zéro de l'écriture* sees the anything-but-token uses to which beginnings can be put. But more often than not when the structuralist tries to allow gingerly for force, he characteristically relegates it to a token beginning, the moment that for him succeeds the Origin–that follows the silent zero point. When Georges Bataille speaks eloquently of having found traces of "inaugural violence" in Lévi-Strauss's work, his image is meant to convey a correlative for an event, now only a speculation, that initiated a signifying system. As we said, Foucault locates such an event at the end of the Middle Ages, when mad people were incarcerated, violently put away by society. Madness is precisely the zero state that resists the encroachments of reason. And for Foucault this conception of resistance to exclusion *begins* the work of "archeology." The violence of the madman's confinement conversely inaugurates, begins, the era of rationalism in whose discursive practice we continue to live. For Lévi-Strauss, on the other hand, the beginning is the initial violence of language itself, which makes its hypothetical first appearance during the neolithic age in catalogs of property, including lists of slaves. Yet Lévi-Strauss has never systematically introduced this hypothesis (mentioned in an interview with Georges Charbonnier[100]) into his investigations: those do not depend upon an incorporated beginning, such as Foucault's, for their coherence.

The efforts of the structuralists are dedicated to studying the residual *form* of the violence, to attempting to clarify and identify it–which is why form, or structure, is always a difficult mixture of need, absence, loss, and uncertain appropriation. Structure is the *sign* of these things–as much a yearning for plenitude as a memorial to unceasing loss. The structuralists themselves speak like men who stand at the beginning of a new era and at the twilight (their word is *clôture*) of an old one; they forecast a time in which linguistics and anthropology will guide human endeavor, will enable man to reassemble the disparate pieces of his activity into a new unity. Perhaps then semantics will confidently be reintroduced into the systematic matrix of significations. For the moment, however, they are satisfied with collecting and unraveling systems, like Mr. Casaubon working at his Key to All Mythologies–with a view toward synthesizing them into a grand and all-encompassing universality. Yet there is a comic side to their industry. The intensity of their dedication often reminds one of Molière's characters who are so single-minded about their work that they cannot detect the irony in a job done too rationally; as Chrysale says in *Les Femmes savantes*, "Raisonner est l'emploi de toute ma maison, / Et le raisonnement en bannit la raison" (2.7.597-98).

VI

Writing of Lévi-Strauss for a special section in *Annales* in 1964 devoted to the anthropologist's work, Barthes commented that Lévi-Strauss had effectively created the need for new cadres of research in the human sciences.[101] Barthes himself, perhaps independently of the older man's work, had by that time hewn out a whole program of what he called "semiotic research"—the decoding of sign systems, from those as simple as the ones used in advertising posters to others as complex as those that make of ladies' fashion magazines a highly specialized language with its own typical images, idioms, and rhetoric. In his various essays, pamphlets, and books, Barthes was attempting to discover how man communicates his messages to others, how he signifies his intentions and fabricates his contingent meanings, and how order inheres in what Barthes and the other structuralists called an unconscious yet functional awareness. Barthes admitted at first that this was only precriticism, and not by any means a full-fledged project of judgment and evaluation.[102] A short while later, in 1967, in a highly-barbed polemic against the old academic criticism, he was to firm up his views considerably by arguing that criticism can never be more than periphrasis, and that the critical work has as much right as the work criticized to say "I am literature."[103] The critic's language, according to Barthes, covers the work criticized with an appropriate prose; signs are laid, in an orderly and well-thought-out fashion, upon other signs, the several levels illuminating one another. The father of semiotics was acknowledged to be Ferdinand de Saussure, and its tacitly recognized Prospero was Lévi-Strauss.

The underlying rationale of semiology (this had been Saussure's own term, although C. S. Peirce had used it, and the idea itself, quite on his own) reposed in an extremely practical view of language. It had been apparent to Saussure in his *Cours de linguistique générale* (1910-1911) that language is far too complex and various a thing for immediate analysis. The first problem for linguistics, he asserted, is to delimit and define itself.[104]   Of course, this preliminary step is equally necessary in any field of knowledge; a historian, unless he is foolish, will first decide what history he wishes to investigate, thus setting up a kind of anticipatory model of his subject, and then proceed to investigate it. The paradox of linguistics to which Saussure continually returns in his *Cours* is that linguistics must always define itself tautologically—in the very words that it sets out to understand. Hence, he argued with convincing rationality, in linguistics the viewpoint determines the object.[105]   To ground a linguistic viewpoint is first to note that language exists only within a collectivity; moreover, no single speaker exhausts collectivities like French or Spanish.[106]   Thus a totality must be presum- ed—Saussure called it *langue*—from which each individual speaker draws, as from a vast subliminal reservoir, during the course of his speech (*parole*); the interchange between *langue* and *parole* permits variations in meaning and manner sufficient⁻ for the signifying or message-bearing intention. In this view, then, every word is a sign, made up jointly of a concept (*significatum*) and a sound-image (*significans*): these two halves of the sign were coined as and then put into circulation in linguistic jargon as the signified (*le signifié*) and the signifier (*le signifiant*).[107]

One of Saussure's farthest-reaching observations was that the connection between sound and concept, the signifier and the signified, is almost wholly arbitrary.[108]   Words do not derive their meaning from any sense inherent in their sound; nor does a sound, in and of itself, necessarily connote a meaning. To emit a sound is to do no more than that; to communicate sense, however, a word must be compared with another word, and this kind of differ- entiation is what we practice when we use language. The difference between words gives language its meaning. Thus the crucial guarantee of meaning in any language is that the differences between words be orderly and consistent; in other words, differences must always be systematic—meaning is diacritical. Thus for "table" to make sense it must always be differentiated in the same essential ways from "love" or "chair" or "man." Language, therefore, is a pattern, or code, of differences that converts arbitrarily chosen sounds into systematic sense. As far as a linguist can tell, the rules of the system are like those of a game; the parallels here with Wittgenstein and Huizinga (to give only two examples) are evident. Yet what is especially interesting about Saussure's discovery of the arbitrary connection between sound and sense—at least so far as it carries over into structuralist writing—is that as a result the sheer oppressive mass of historical, biological, or psychic determinism is first lifted, then frittered away, then brought back as weightless gamelike rules or protocols. That is, history need not be viewed as the burden of the past; it need only be considered the manner in which other arbitrary connections between sound and sense were first made and then conventionalized into common use. The interpretation of language, then, is an aesthetic activity, a release, so to speak, from the tyranny of time and history. This is why Edmund Leach, writing of Lévi-Strauss's structural and linguistic interpretations of kinship systems (which rely on Saussure's method of systematic decipherment of arbitrarily connected signifier and signified), has noted that it is possible to undertake them solely for the aesthetic pleasure of the exercise.[109] In some structuralist writings—for example, Barthes's superb essay on the Eiffel Tower—sign analysis is carried out with a sort of neutral mental glee in the task. In most structuralist writing we rarely have any sense of Freud's tragic realization that civilization and language both serve to repress man's instinctual nature, nor do we sense any of the pain of Nietzsche's assaults against an obdurate wall of history and custom, nor any of Heidegger's patient yet agonized doom within language. For the most part, the structuralists are adjusted to language and civilization (they see the two as coterminous); they take culture for what it rationally appears to be instead of rebelling against it.

The importance of Saussure's work for the contemporary structuralists is too complicated to be examined in detail here. The chief rule of procedure all of them seem to have learned from Saussure, however, is that every problem, no matter how small, requires explicit delimitation. Borrowing from André Martinet—and obviously echoing Saussure—Barthes speaks cogently of the necessity of "pertinence," which he calls a principled decision to describe facts from only one point of view, even to the exclusion of all others.[110] Most of the time, Saussure's rule of delimitation is used to reduce, in order to render manageable for scrutiny, a very large body of phenomena. Quite aside from its obvious practical advantages, Saussure's procedural rule has, from the standpoint of the structuralist critic, certain moral and emotional advantages as well. In the first place, when he is confronted with an enormous hodgepodge of data, the critic can cut his way through it by asserting the existence of a problem within the mass. It is remarkable that in the work of every structuralist—Barthes, Lévi-Strauss, Foucault, Lucien Sebag, and Louis Althusser included—the same initial methodological step that unites critical discernment with violence always turns up. This step is most often called *découpage,* but it is also frequently called (after Bachelard) *coupure épistémologique;* in both, the verb *couper* ("to cut") figures prominently. Facing an awesome mountain of detail, the critic's mind becomes a confident David going straight for the vulnerable spot in Goliath's forehead. The critic cuts out a patch in the detail as a way of constraining the vast body of which it is a part, and he then focuses exclusively on that patch. Emotionally he asserts his mind's undoubted sway over what seems to be a totally resisting mass of detail; morally he demonstrates his right to control it because he has a victorious tool, proven in the encounter.

There are a few submerged assumptions that support the structuralist *découpage,* that assertive cutting-down to tractable size of intolerable detail. One is that detail is not merely a matter of quantity, but has become a qualitative feature of every human discipline. Any historian or literary critic can verify this by consulting recent bibliographies on even the most trivial subject. The mind tends to be impressed, not with the sheer number of details in and about a field, but with the fact that all these details present a forbidding obstacle to any meaningful penetration of the field. Devising a means for hurdling the obstacle thus becomes the first order of critical business. Clearly, Auerbach's notion of *Ansatzpunkt* is a way of transacting this first step. Another structuralist assumption is that all details have the status of *information*—for the structuralist has decided, as Lévi-Strauss says, that the world of signs is an orderly place, and that if there is order somewhere, it must be everywhere. Now, since order is characterized by an economy of means that renders every detail functional, and since the structuralist model is language, it becomes quite logical, therefore, to assume that every linguistic particle, every verbal emission, conveys information of some sort. Structuralism in fact does not seem to allow for either waste or incoherence: it states, rather, that every item in a sign system is invested with the dignity of message-bearing capability. Finally, the structuralist *découpage* (it is amusing to compare this term with Swift's phrase "every man his own carver") is borne along by a kind of mathematical ambition to turn details into a coherent *field* governed by a *set* whose function it is to *operate* systematically in linking all the details with one another. The history of this kind of cybernetic hope in the West is a long one; it includes the Greek atomists, Lucretius, Leibnitz, and Descartes, then more recently Frege and Wiener, and finally the structuralists. It also finds its way imaginatively and pedagogically into Browne's *Garden of Cyrus,* into the dictionaries, encyclopedias, anatomies, catalogs, and universal grammars of the seventeenth and eighteenth centuries, into Flaubert's *Dictionnaire des idées reçues,* and into Borges's *Aleph.*

In a restrospective comment on his *Structures élémentaires de la parenté* Lévi-Strauss noted how in that work he had "chosen a field that could, at first glance, have called attention to itself only for its incoherent and contingent nature," yet he had tried to show "that it was possible to reduce all of it to a very small number of significant propositions."[111] Kinship systems present a bewildering variety of customs that resist being subjected to a synthetic overview, yet it is by projecting into them the existence of a set of rules that make the entire corpus a working whole that the mind can then absorb the mass as a significant entity. And this is precisely what Lévi-Strauss did. Barthes's manifesto for structuralism hinges on his statement that applauds the method as an activity first of decomposing works—of literature, for instance—into their simplest functional forms, then of recomposing them into wholes dominated by what he called a "sovereign motor principle."[112] This had been the scheme employed by V. I. Propp in *The Morphology of the Folktale* (1928). Foucault's method of *découpage* is to grasp the vagaries of history as a set of discontinuous units—the statements—ruled by laws of discursive formation. René Girard's *Mensonge romantique et verité romanesque,* a literary study carried out with structuralist instruments, views the history of the novel as a set of variations on a simple but enormously fecund "triangular model" of desire. "A basic contention" of Girard's book "is that the great writers apprehend intuitively and concretely, through the medium of their art, if not formally, the system in which they were first imprisoned together with their contemporaries."[113] Finally, Louis Althusser's Marxism has for its method a way of pulling from a text what Althusser calls its "problematic," which is a special mode the text has of taking hold of its subject: regardless of how complicated the philosophy or political program, it can be grasped by the mind as an attempt "ideologically" to see the world for a particular end; and this end, as well as the program itself, can be formulated as a problematic, or specific generality.[114]

In every one one of these examples, the critic first orders his data by delimiting his field in terms of a specific problem, then deduces a rationale from his initial delimitation, then applies this rationale in detail to all the material in an effort to make the material work, or perform systematically. Beginning thus becomes the principal functional step. All of this reductive activity goes on in the critic's writing, which is not only his instrument and the mode of his activity, but also the common fabric in which all human actions are recorded and given a relative stability and intelligibility.

The linguistic apprehension—or perception—of reality is, of course, the most important cutting-down-to-size. We tend to accept this *découpage* when we read a novelist, for example, but it seems more extreme when it is found to be the operative bias of the historian, the sociologist, or even of the psychoanalyst, particularly when only meager allowances are made for brute reality as a mere symbolic fiction. Lévi-Strauss fatalistically marks the fundamental opposition between the discontinuities of symbolism (in this case, one supposes, the totemic world of objects that symbolize values, our everyday world) and the continuity of knowledge—that is, between the world and the mind.[115] The grand model of knowledge, therefore, is language-as-writing, the most continuous of man's enterprises and the one that covers all man's activity with the sheen of prose. At bottom, structuralism is a set of attitudes held toward and expressed in writing: "grammatology." In writing, the structuralist can enact his work actually and actively; his attention to his work is an act of disciplined relevance. Like science, structuralism is meta-linguistic—language studying language, linguistic consciousness appropriating linguistic competence and performance.

When Lévi-Strauss has spoken of primitive thought (*la pensée sauvage*), he is not only describing the way in which the primitive thinks, but also thought itself, as it is, atrophied in its essential about-to-be-thought-about-something. Lévi-Strauss wishes to describe the order of thought, not its substance. This is a very important point, one that Paul Ricoeur emphasized tellingly in a worthwhile exchange with Lévi-Strauss.[116] Order, according to Lévi-Strauss, is what makes thought intelligible as thought; order holds back thought from the verge of chaos. Thus the structuralist substitutes order, or the structure of thought, for a Being that in classical philosophy had informed and nurtured thought. Order is a limit beyond which it is impossible to go, and without which, moreover, it is impossible to think. Order is the result of the mind choosing syntax over semantics, of opting for the existence of momentary, discursive sense instead of the certainty of rigid and detached meaning. The structuralists, in short, do not believe in the immediacy of anything: they are content to understand and to contemplate the alphabetical order of sense as a mediating function rather than as a direct meaning. Order, they claim, is just on our human side of nothingness; it preserves us from the oblivion of unremarked duration. To perceive this order one cannot have recourse to a direct unfolding (as in the *Entfaltung* of hermeneutical interpretation) of the kernel of meaning within a statement: that alternative, we recall, disappeared with the primordial Origin. We are left only with a way of perceiving how something, a sentence, or a statement—in fine, the entire world of experience conceived of as a gigantic script or musical score—works, how it hangs together. We search for structure as *Zusammenhänge,* the "principle of solidarity" among parts, according to Barthes.[117]

Structure hides behind the actuality of our existence because it is the nature of structure to refuse to reveal its presence directly; only language can solicit structure out of the background in which it hovers. Structure is nonrational: it is not thought thinking about anything, but thought itself as the merest possibility of activity. It can offer no rationale for its presence, once discovered, other than its primitive *thereness.* In a most important way, then, as an ensemble of interacting parts, structure replaces the Origin with the play of orderly relationships. A univocal source has ceded to a proliferating systematic web. The character of structure is best understood, I think, if we remark the nature of its status as beginning, its radicality, which derives from a mating of the spirit of Rousseau with the spirit of Sade, of existential and functional primitivism with moral primitivism. The central fact of primitivism is not just its precedence, but its unobjecting affirmation of its own originality. It has no alternative but "to be"; we can see versions of such radical originality in the perpetual spiritual amateurism of Rousseau or in the continual, almost abstract repetitiveness of Sade—or in the "concrete" existence of Australian and Brazilian aborigines whose ways Lévi-Strauss has chronicled so well.

The rule of structure is its superconscious transgression of all conscious rules and the consequent establishment of a grammar whose persistence constrains all vocabularies and simultaneously repels thought and spiritual dimension. The researcher's way to structure is in the semiotic reading of the play of signs on the pages of a culture: method, activity, and end there become totally identified with one another. The structuralist wishes to lose himself in the writing, to become the writing itself. As we saw, Foucault in one place also echoes this ambition. Barthes correctly describes structuralism as an endless activity of imitation founded, not on the analogy of substances, but on the analogy of functions.[118]   And the final key language of structuralism is shelved in the Library of Babel. The elegance and the terror of such a world-view, completely confined to discourse, is a veritable nightmare-utopia composed of nothing but impeccably organized writing: it is the subject of Borges's work. When Barthes wishes to abolish the distinction between art and criticism, he uses the word *writing* (*écriture*) to level the difference between them (here again Borges's work comes to mind). Thus writing illuminates writing, which in turn illuminates other writing—to infinity. The sum total of all writing is silence, zero. The end of a structuralist's job of work is, according to Barthes, silence—the silence that comes with having reached the eschatological limit, with having said all there is to say.[119]   Lévi-Strauss, too, describes a work of his once written as a dead entity, a world in which he had very ardently lived, but that now excludes him from its intimacy.[120]

In Barthes's case, one is willing to accept Gérard Genette's view (presented in a beautifully balanced essay in *Figures I*) that what governs the semiotic project is a nostalgia for objects and bodies whose solid presence has the undeniable reality of Dr. Johnson's stone.[121]   Genette sees Barthes longing for the silent quiddity of objects undisturbed by the intervening yammerings of language. There is I think no less a case for believing that Barthes and the structuralists, but not Foucault, long also for the zero-point calm of original primitivism and wholeness. Such longing, paradoxically, also shores up the integrity of their faith in the irresistible metamorphical powers of language. For if one text might serve them all as a banner, it is Ovid's *Metamorphoses,* that celebration of reality as ceaseless transformation and unhindered function for its own sake. Yet Barthes, along with Lévi-Strauss and Althusser, in fact has a stoically ironic and almost poetic vision of his own position. In the analysis of the play of signifiers he sees not so much a necessity as a luxury. What he calls "acculturation"—the omnivorous swallowing-whole by a linguistic culture of all work, a concept strikingly reminiscent of one that Lionel Trilling discusses in *Beyond Culture*—goes on apace, while the individual critic's activity remains an involuntary trickle in the great stream.[122]

Two disciplines one might find resisting the tide of structuralist functionalism and a linguistic world-view are psychoanalysis and sociology. The first deals with the terminal poles of human behavior, the second with the all-too-solid terminal of social reality: neither can readily succumb to an invasion by language. In Jacques Lacan's return to Freud, however, one discovers psychiatry serving as the interpretive tool for deciphering psychic metaphors that have no ready and anchoring terminal in the unconscious. That faculty has become, according to Lacan, "neither primordial nor instinctual," but instead a floating repository (if that be the best word) for the "elements of the signifier." The method of operation of this unconscious is rigorously grammatical, its symptoms rhetorical, and it first articulates the ego as the expression of a narcissistic relation to itself.[123] The ingenuity of Lacan's understanding of Freud's "talking cure" lies essentially in his taking Freud's term literally: he construes Freud the same way Quintillian construes poetic language. Metaphor and metonymy deliver, or withhold, a Being as absolutely allusive as, I think probably, Freud's unconscious ultimately was not. Nevertheless, Lacan's work is contingent in its deliberate self-limitation upon discursive strategies which, like those described by Foucault, are instruments of highly selective inclusion and exclusion.[124]

The other great structuralist rereading of a venerable radical is to be found in Althusser's Marx. According to Athusser, Marx's retirement behind his own statements in order to insure their rigor, to guarantee their structure (rather than their Origin),[125] creates the possibility for a Marxism, or theory of Marxism, that Marx himself never had time to write. Marx, therefore, is the *beginning* of a reading of society as a complex of ideological strands seen from a new perspective of philosophical differentiation. This differentiation shows how "human societies secrete ideology as the element and the atmosphere indispensable for their respiration and their historical life."[126] Althusser's ruling metaphor is dramatic: Marxism allows us to *see* how society formulates itself *for* itself. Therefore, we are required to remain detached when we read Althusser and, like spectators at a Brecht play, create a historical consciousness by recognizing ideologies that pretend to truth while remaining the victims of their signifying (ideological, propagandistic) activity. Society is like Mother Courage fixed on a skewed course through lies of her own making. Contradiction means the awareness of discontinuity, of ruptures, between one ideology and another. Yet ideology is not a mere accident, but a necessary condition of society—indeed, its fundamental structure.

The precision and elegance of Althusser's spare exhumation of Marx as a style of thought (and a much longer account than I have given would scarcely do Althusser justice) clashes headlong with the late Lucien Goldman's thematic appropriation of revolutionary thought. Goldmann's important study of Pascal and Racine (*Le Dieu caché*, 1955), and his subsequent forays into general theory (propelled by his tutelage under Lukacs and Piaget), show how literary work and society approach homology; yet during the last years of his life, Goldmann, apparently in response to the structural wave, started to describe himself as a "genetic structuralist." The issue between him and Althusser is very clear: for Goldmann the sociology of knowledge must appeal to a hierarchy of values that stands *outside* bourgeois ideology and reveals the *content* of an ideology for either its adequacy or inadequacy with reference to all of social reality. Goldmann's term for "all of social reality" is *totality*—an ideal whole. Totality seems for Goldmann very curiously to be what Jakob Burkhardt called "an Archimedean point outside events." The structuralist's job, according to Goldmann, is to seize the coherence of an artist's or a thinker's work at its "real" origin in time and society, and to see it as submitting to processes of growth implicit in its essential coherence. If as a result of this a given thinker is seen to have grasped the totality of his time, and if his work reflects it coherently, then he is a *dialectician*—for Goldmann, not only a descriptive title, but an honorific one as well. Otherwise, the thinker is an *ideologist*—albeit, as in the case of Pascal, a great one. Althusser pointedly rejects totality—and, for that matter, any privileged ideal reality outside the discourse of ideology. (It is important to note that for Althusser ideology is discourse, at least in its political guise.) All articulated thought is ideology: only the *differences* between ideologies (like the diacritical differences between words in Saussure's linguistics) provide us with knowledge as a structure of relationships. Everything else—including

Goldmann's references to "totality"—is mere fiction, a victim of discourse. Marxism, for Althusser, provides the sharpest instrument for dissociating ideologies from one another into a series of statements made *for* ulterior purposes.

Thus the main group of French structuralists sees the world as a closed set of what J. L. Austin called "performative statements."[127] Closed not because its limits can be grasped as a totality, but because its first and beginning functional principles are a finite set of rules. As Barthes says, a single lexical law can mobilize many different lexicons.[128] Structuralism, however, is a kind of positivism, although like all forms of positivism it has a certain view of what man's activity is all about. And that is what Lévi-Strauss calls *bricolage,* man's ability and destiny to make do with, to formulate projects out of, and because of, fragments, the usable debris that clutters human existence.[129] *Bricolage* is, in the words of Swift's manic persona, "an Art to sodder up the Flaws and Imperfections of Nature." Not accidentally, as Genette has noted with characteristic shrewdness, the French have themselves not only defined the techniques of *bricolage,* but have become virtuosi at the whole business.[130] The reasons Genette cites are French insularity coupled with a native French genius for assembling bits and pieces into imposing models of wit and reason. To probe *bricolage* further than this is to acknowledge also a subtle French sense of order based on uncertainty, on the partial, and on the hidden. This is why *structure* is neither a spatial term nor, for that matter, a temporal one: it is essentially an activity, a cultural version of *bricolage,* and less a philosophy or philosophical method than what Genette, quoting Ernst Cassirer, calls a general tendency of thought.[131] A tendency, we might add, that seeks out and is attracted to the elusive in-betweenness of order: it does not see order as what Freud called a repetition compulsion, but rather as a complement to existence. Although, paradoxically, order is a supplier, it wishes it could linger quietly over, Lévi-Strauss says,

The essence of what our species has been and still is, beyond thought and beneath society: an essence that may be vouchsafed to us in a mineral more beautiful than any work of Man; in the scent, more subtly evolved than our books, that lingers in the heart of a lily; or in the wink of an eye, heavy with patience, serenity, and mutual forgiveness, that sometimes, through an involuntary understanding, one can exchange with a cat.[132]

As a formalist doctrine, structuralism differs in an instructive way from earlier modern modes of formalism. Dilthey's

Weltanschauung philosophy affirms the adhesive power of inner vision as an existential property of human mind: among the first adumbrators of this property was Coleridge, whose doctrine of the secondary imagination, along with his description of the coadunatory and esemplastic shaping powers, granted the highest marks to man's ability to shape experience meaningfully. The later German and Marxist theories of *Gestalt* and/or totality (exemplified variously in the works of Lukacs, Karl Mannheim, Bernard Groethuysen, and others) adapt from Dilthey, but add to his conception the notion of a more rigorous historical necessity; for them the individual is an involuntary participant in a class or group together with other like-interested individuals who act according to a common vision of their origin and destiny. It is the property of history, therefore, to be a totality that makes things inhere formally in thought and action. Finally, there is the more elusive formalism of twentieth-century idealists like Croce, in which a certain executive, almost Platonic, coherence controls, gives theoretic shape to, human action.

For the French structuralists, form is borrowed from the actualities of language considered as a set of fragments (phonemes, words, phrases) that orders itself with binding rules into a constantly earned equilibrium of higher structures (sentences, discourses, narratives). Language is the initial conceiving and productive matrix of human activity, but its wholeness can never really be known—and derived only partially from its rule-bound play. The permanent elusiveness and incompleteness of structure is typified in the eternal discrepancy between the linear flowing chain of language in use—that is, our continuous mode of life—and the circular system of signs that surrounds speech at any one moment. Structure is the unity of linguistic performance and linguistic competence, of *nunc movens* and the *nunc stans*.

As the structuralists see him, the individual is a modern equivalent of Pascalian man—only with this difference, that Pascal's *roseau pensant* is replaced with what Merleau-Ponty called *le sujet parlant*. The linguistic reduction of man (which continues the tradition of Pascal's fascination with and dislike of self) is consistently supported by the structuralist's stubborn desire always to use linguistic terminology in referring to man: man is a name, his necessity a pronoun (since, as Benveniste says, all language requires the inclusion of an "I" and a "you"),[133] his situation is discourse, and his thought metalinguistic. All in all, he is what Lévi-Strauss calls a *bricoleur*. Man, therefore, is inserted into Being either *allegorically,* as a linguistic substitute for presence (which language can only allow by the *absence* of *presence*), or, when he continues to insist on his indispensability to the reality of language, as *parody*—the sheer, endless repetition of himself in the distorting mirrors of social, artistic, psychological, anthropological, historical, or philosophical discourses.

VII

Insofar as one can speak of the central body of work maintaining its fortunes, structuralism resembles an open-ended manual of methodological attitudes—and I wish neither to demean the value of this type of work nor to suggest unqualifiedly that it ought to increase. What does need to be remarked, however, is the congruence between criticism formulated as the account of pure structural functionalism (and with this formulation the abandonment of historical, institutional, biographical, narrative, and psychological pieties of critical faith) and criticism produced according to that formula which dictates patient accounts of *how* a work *might* be done rather than the record *that* it is done.

The problems of communication in an age of mass culture, and of mass confusions, are the problems that structuralism seems destined very ably to reflect. Structuralism after all lives in the world of McLuhanism, although it tidies up that North American sprawl across culture with a good deal of grace and *élan*. One of the chief points of difference between structuralism and the Geneva school of critics (which together make up the central body of French New Criticism) is that the latter group considers the literary work as dissolved in the author's consciousness, whose impulse is articulation for its own sake, whereas the former group takes language, and hence literature, exclusively as a system of interhuman communication. What Josiah Royce called the intersubjective world—namely, the community of interpretation—is for the Genevans actually enacted in the identification of the critic with the author he considers, but for the structuralists there is only the involuntary community of systems of information that are transparent to one another. Yet the division between structuralism and Genevan consciousness-for-itself-and-for-the-critic derives from the dual inner nature of literary language itself as it is realized, for example, in the vocations of individual writers. Some, like Coleridge, Swift, Hopkins, and Joyce, are what Gérard Genette calls technicians of communication;[134] others, like Wordsworth, Yeats, Shelley, and the later Eliot, are poets of interior meditation for whom language, in Heidegger's phrase, is the house of Being.

It is characteristic of the structuralists—here again Lévi-Strauss is the noteworthy exception—that they seem unconcerned with either their counterparts or their intellectual progenitors in other countries. The work of George Herbert Mead, the Chicago Aristotelians, Kenneth Burke, and Northrop Frye, to speak only of North Americans, represents fairly obvious parallels with structuralism and consequently, if the structuralists cared, gains to be made on the basis of those parallels; the similarities, however, are never perceived and, to be blunt about it, seem to be unknown. Aside from respectful bows toward C. S. Peirce, the structuralists express no interest in Anglo-American linguistic critics and philosophers: none in Ogden and Richards, in Empson, in Quine, or in any of the action philosophers. The work of the great German philologues Auerbach, Curtius, and Spitzer seems not to have made much of an impression either, although one would think that the universality and the scope of German romance philology (with its origins in Goethe's idea of *Weltliteratur*) might have suggested at least one other model of linguistic research integrally organized. The same is true of the discipline of comparative literature, whose relevance is nevertheless recognizeable in structuralism's enterprise when the latter is viewed as the science of comparative communication. Still, the contrast between structuralism as an essentializing and universalizing activity and as an insular one remains an odd phenomenon.

Wherever else it is placed, structuralism belongs, with Gallic preciosity, to what Harry Levin has called the Alexandrianism of our time.[135] The organization of a structualist work is always ingenious, sometimes even more interesting than the matter it discusses. The positive response to Barthes's call for new cadres of research is immediately felt in the effort expended in putting together one or another structuralist book. Lévi-Strauss's books present a surface of dazzling arrangement, whether one reads a page or the table of contents. The choice of subject matter in Foucault's work, as much as in Barthes's, Genette's, Althusser's, or Lacan's, is always novel and unexpected; the unkindest cut of all would be to call such novelty, with Raymond Piccard, "dogmatic impressionism." The styles are almost always difficult, whether because they are technical or because they reveal writing turning back on itself to consider, questioningly, its beginning validity and principles. The salutary effect of structuralism goes beyond providing criticism with a few handy catch phrases and florid tricks. Structuralism has demonstrated the value of determinedly rational examination, has displaced the prior mystique of mere appreciation passing itself off as scholarship, and has even stimulated novelists (like Alain Robbe-Grillet and Michel Butor) to a just ascertainment of their own work. As Barthes has noted, structuralism sits securely beside such developments in modern art as the music of Pierre Boulez and the designs of Piet Mondrian,[136] it draws from the peculiar psychological traditions of France as exemplified in the books of Gaston Bachelard, and it has fecundated the brilliant work of an Arabist like Jacques Berque and the parascientific explorations of Gilles Gaston Grainger. Versions of structuralism also contribute to the interest of the more urgently historical (and earlier) work of Georges Dumézil, and to that of his gifted contemporary disciple Jean-Pierre Vernant; to the linguistic work of André Martinet, Edmund Ortigues, and André Leroi-Gourhan; and even to the more purely scientific and mathematical experiments of Abraham Moles and Jean Desanti. With the characteristic unkindness of new movements, structuralism either ignores or attacks the monuments of preceding generations; this is especially poignant in the cases of Malraux and Sartre, less so in the case of Gustave Lanson.

The gravest problem that structuralism has yet to deal with wholeheartedly is how seriously to account for change and force, how to assimilate the powerful and sometimes wasteful behavioral activity of man—what Blackmur calls the Moha—to the numinous order of structure. In Lévi-Strauss's work we find the recognition of force in terms of disruption. In examining the constant passage in both directions within society between ideas and images, he acknowledges a certain measure of contingency and arbitrariness; the systematic organization of society, he concedes regretfully, is endangered by wars, epidemics, and famines.[137] The relationship between order and disorder, therefore, is one of opposition; yet this opposition is expressed not *by* the society itself—or at least, not *necessarily* by the society—but *for* the society by the observer who stands outside it. As Lévi-Strauss says in another place, structure will only appear as the result of observation practiced from the outside;[138] hence *order,* or *structure,* is available for analysis from the outside, while society's *process,* or *force,* can never be grasped because (Lévi-Strauss himself makes the point) it is entirely within the perspective of the social individual engaged in his own historical becoming. In *Totemism* Lévi-Strauss speaks of the internalization ("trying on [oneself]modes of thought taken from elsewhere or simply imagined")[139] that permitted Bergson and Rousseau to apprehend what goes on in the mind of man. This internalization, of course, allows the modern anthropologist to understand what goes on in an observed primitive society.

The situation can now be stated as follows: Within a society a certain energy is acting to make it a society. Outside the society stands an observer who notes constants (included in the kind of essential structure Lévi-Strauss himself had observed in *Les Structures élémentaires de la parenté,* for example), which in turn are internalized and tested by the observer for their logic and coherence. The force or energy or entropy of a society, that which maintains its ongoing historical actuality, is a transparency through which observations on the structure beyond it can be made. Two kinds of force can be distinguished: one, society's force which for the observer is easily gotten by, the other, the observer's force of observation, which though essentially, and curiously, contemplative, has the power to penetrate through the seeming opacity of a foreign culture to a lucidity beyond. All of this, as I said above, seems to take into consideration a conflict between system and contingency which, within a society, always oppose one another. Yet at the beginning of the anthropological observation, discontinuity has already been assembled into a transparent force that had yielded very easily to the observation just practiced. Although the structuralist avers the power of disruption and discontinuity, he replaces it later with a transparent coherence that is very little more than the power of an object, or a society, to be observed. In linguistic terms, force and energy are converted exclusively into the power of signification, which exists to be *read,* to be semiotically deciphered.

This is linguacentricity pushed very far, indeed: the quality of things that makes them significant is almost an ideal third term between language, on the one hand, and men and the world, on the other (one is reminded of the critique of Socrates' ideas in the *Parmenides*). This term, a quality which I shall call *linguicity,* performs very valuable services. Among other things, it informs the activity of what Lévi-Strauss calls the totemic operator, that rational instrument carried within the primitive mind that enables him to divide the observed world into a logic of finely organized species.[140] Furthermore, linguicity permits language to be what I have elsewhere called a totalitarian system.[141] It also insures the availability to language of unlimited signifying opportunities, despite the impoverishment of what is being signified; it guarantees language unlimited linguistic discovery—that is, a sort of permanent finding power; and it provides the links between dimensions of investigation (say, from particular to general, or from discontinuity to discontinuity). In short, linguicity is a privilege taken for granted by structuralist activity; its perpetuation, however, is structuralism's project and purpose. Linguicity is a consequence of the radical discontinuity also presupposed by structuralism. Without linguicity, the structuralist—whether Barthes, Lacan, or Lévi-Strauss—cannot demonstrate analogy and metaphor as intrinsic to the signifying process. For linguicity allows mirror-exchanges between words, between levels of consciousness, between myths. The power to reflect, as in a series of mirrors, assumes the prior existence of clarity of exchange. Structuralism replaces the darkening glass of traditional religion and literature—which forces us to appraisals of our fragile but dear individuality—with a ready antiphony of equal sights and sounds. We might say that linguicity converts the inequities of translation into the equivalence of transcription, and the use of writing (*écriture*) to structuralism thereby becomes even more crucial. Linguicity discounts memory, and history, in the interests of total recall, for structure, which is the child of language and linguicity, has no way of containing its past, but only of delivering its present by "laying all its cards on the table."[142]

What linguicity cannot do, however, is show us why structure structures: structure is always revealed in the condition of having structured, but never, as Jean Starobinski has observed, in the condition of structuring, or of *being structured,* or of failing to structure.[143] This fact, as we saw, separates Foucault from the structuralists. The main structuralist weakness, which is not Foucault's, is that linguicity must remain outside the constitutive structure, even to the point of being rejected by structure, yet it is presumed by structuralism as a precondition for order. Another facet of this weakness lies in the difficulties structuralism has with the problem of a text. In the nonstructural criticism of Georges Poulet, for instance, the individual work is dissolved so that it may be relocated in the irreducible consciousness of the author. For this sort of criticism, mind is the matrix of thought, and the text is a particular instance of consciousness thinking itself (Jean

337

Rousset, another of the Genevans, is relevant here). In Lévi-Strauss, however, myth, or society for that matter, speaks itself; this corresponds to Barthes's formulation of writing as an intransitive activity.[144]   In structuralism no real distance exists between language and any of its individual articulations, since none of the latter is under any more than token obligation to a thinking subject. There can be no tone, in Richards's sense of the word, in any statement, no sense of an individual voice that is its own final authority, since for the structuralists the whole world is contained within a gigantic set of quotation marks. *Everything,* therefore, is a text—or, using the same argument, *nothing* is a text. The inherence of a structure expresses neither an intention nor any more than the barest of constitutive necessities. Communication is absorbed by the structure, since communication can never exhaust a structure or a language. The enduring power of language to signify thus almost completely collapses the beginning into the result, and the tautology completely eliminates both subject and object, and to a certain extent direct communication, too.

The willingness of structuralism to discuss differences between objects—a feat that moves values from the objects to a privileged space between them—is consistent with the structuralist's hesitation, even fear, whenever singularity is an issue. The solitary, crystalline perdurability we feel and know in a poem, the condition of its exile from the communal sea of linguicity, cannot be named by structuralism. Not that anyone else can very readily isolate this quality, since a poem is also a momentary statement. But the effort of naming is at least possibe outside structuralism, if only because one can acknowledge an unknown and keep it alive in thought. Here, I think, the powerful insight of Foucault's notion of the modern deviant artist is sorely lacking. Structuralism's holding power over its subject matter is tenuous: this is at once a strength, when it reminds us of the provisional nature of our efforts, and a weakness, when it commits us to an irretrievable past and the dimensionless obsolescence of the future.

As the ground of structuralism, linguicity requires the notion of play, within rules, to sustain a minimum of discourse (which Barthes calls prose[145]). Linguicity seems to generate and then specify rues of intelligibility by which things appear as telling language, rather than as random bursts of being. As use in structuralism's arguments, these rules comprise a nexus binding statements into progressively clearer units the further one works out their possibilities. Thus by lifting aside one set of signifiers (as we did earlier in lines from *Paradise Lost*) when two or more occur in, for example, works of literature, the threatening jumble of direct presence is channeled off into examples of recognized convention. The structuralist procedure of decoding or reducing the object to a set of statements collected into general rhetorical order somewhat resembles the process of resolving literature into archetypes, a kind of criticism practiced commonly in the United States. The structuralists, and the archetypalists, always wish to avoid direct encounters with language. Instead, they weaken the full-throated spoken chain into a series of signifiers, all of which exist in the chain's linguicity, like the plural meanings of words in a pun. Linguicity forces us, perhaps against our will, to read language and reality together as if they were cleverly hidden in something like Swift's little languages, or in the puns of *Finnegans Wake*.

The trouble with this fairly esoteric view of language is, first of all, that rules insure the safety and the captivity of signification: in a sense, therefore, structuralism is conservatively safeguarding the assured certainty of its own activity. For every contingency, a rule can be discovered lurking in linguicity. Secondly, the number of rules is, also conservatively, kept to a workable minimum. To be willing to admit that (1) there are no rules for some situations and (2) there is no limit to the number of rules would mean the necessity of believing in (*a*) an infinite vocabulary and (*b*) a finally useless catalog of infinite rules. And these latter two eventualities are ones the structuralist will not admit. Borges's Irenes Funes does admit this, however, and he is locked in "the stammering grandeur" of his vertiginous world of numberless particulars. Linguicity, then, is the alternative to avoiding the peculiar traps of infinite particularity—and of nonsensical dispersion. The difference between structuralist linguicity and Foucault's notion of discursivity is that, whereas the latter deals expressly with what one may call the delinquencies of reason that persist in and behind language, the former does not.

The peculiar problems of the French structuralist outlook are purposefully and deservedly exposed in Jacques Derrida's writing.[146] A philosopher in his own right, Derrida deserves mention in any consideration of structuralism because one side of his work (admittedly, a special side) is a critique, by grotesque explicitation, of the structuralists. Thus like Nietzsche's outpouring of philosophy that is already in the throes of self-destruction, Derrida's writing converts the principles of structuralism into surreal, large objects whose overaccurate relationship to the original versions mocks them, overwhelms them, plays havoc with them. The sense of structuralism is, in Derrida, writ large—too large. The inflation is evident on many levels. First, in the organization of his books, which make normal structural preciosity look primly demure. *De la grammatologie,* for instance, is a study of writing "pure" and "simple"; its first half is titled "Writing Before the Letter," but before the section begins (and Derrida is obsessed with continually prior states) there is a short digression titled "Exergue," and immediately following that, chapter 1: "The End of the Book and the Beginning of Writing." A later chapter is headed enigmatically "The Outside Is the Inside." Second, Derrida's prose style, which is sometimes very self-indulgent, has a quiet yet nearly maniacal complexity to it that defies translation and perhaps even description. Its central features are, first, a habit of italicizing grammatological terms that causes them to become ontological terms (*trace, letter, inscription, archwriting*) and the italicization of ontological terms so that those will act as grammatological ones (*beginning, end, violence, transgression, reduction*). Second, Derrida specializes terms into near-parodies of their commonsense meaning: he performs this operation on words like *difference* (see also his invention of words like *différence*[147]), *works, economy, alteration, iteration, writing, presence, supplement, auto-affection,* and, finally, *structure.* At one point he describes his manner of exposition as "hesitancy" since, he admits, his subject is the movement of deconstruction— that is, the opposite of structuring.[148]   Precisely because Derrida believes that structuralism is logocentric—it is a philosophy, that is, of written texts, which are understood as supplementary to speech—he argues that structuralist notions of evidence and necessity are forms of desire. In tracing this idea back to Rousseau, Derrida wishes to show that textuality in the modern West has been conceived as the abyss in which the presence of reality is represented as absence. The *exorbitance* of a text is an excessive desire in it to *be* presence; linguicity, then, in the supplementary verbal richness of a text, is the articulation of this desire.

The last essay in *L'Ecriture et la différence* collects these and other of Derrida's metaphysical and cultural reflections very admirably. What he undertakes to fix in our mind's eye is the paradox of structural knowledge that takes order as the unified play of elements (pure signifiers) that do not have a center, or Origin, or dominant *significatum:*

> This then is the moment when language invades the universal and problematic field [of human existence], it is the moment where, in the absence of center or origin, everything becomes discourse—on the condition that this word is understood—that is, a system in which the central signified, whether it derives from an origin or whether it is transcendental, is never absolutely present outside a system of differences. The absence of a transcendental signified [*significatum*] stretches the field and the play of significations to infinity.[149]

Derrida goes on to speak of the difficulty of locating an event in time at which decentering took place. To attribute the event to the work of either Freud or Nietzsche, say, is in fact to submit once again to the circle without a center, not at all to get beyond it. For the vicious circle of signifiers, globally considered, is itself the relationship between the history of metaphysics and the destruction of that history by radicals like Freud and Nietzsche; outside language we do not possess any way of describing destruction in a manner that does not also rely on the same structure whose order is being challenged. To speak of Freud and Nietzsche means first to accept the structure of philosophy, then to try, without much hope of success, to show the structure breaking down; yet a breakdown can only be described in terms, or signs, provided by the prior order. The damning difficulty of the whole matter, according to Derrida, is that opposition, or difference-between, remains the inescapable basis of a signifier. This, we recall, has always been one of the cardinal points in the structuralist creed: the meaning of a word, of a sign, is diacritical; the meaning of a word is not intrinsic to the word, but is rather the quality of its *difference from* another word. A structuralist like Lévi-Strauss, Derrida argues, is in the position of a man who wishes to conserve the value of an instrument (language as a sign system) whose truth value he is criticizing.[150] This is no less true of Nietzsche and Freud, the one attacking philosophy philosophically, the other attacking psychology psychologically. Derrida's grasp of the bewildering dilemma of modern critical knowledge resembles, in its awareness of the debilitating paradoxes that hobble knowledge, the works of Dostoevski.

Thus language—and the sciences that it commands, ethnography in particular—emerges as a new, provisional center destined to replace the phiosophic and/or epistemological center, or Origin, that it has criticized and exorcised. One myth cedes to another.[151] The play (*jeu*) of signifiers, which Derrida calls a series of infinite substitutions, takes place on a field, or space, of language that is limited and marked by the lack of a center. Infinity is the result of a specific and finite absence. Play, which is another way of characterizing the totality of structures in language as they reflect one another, is supplementary to absence. Here we are to recall Barthes's uneasy awareness of the luxury of signifiers by comparison with the poverty of "signifieds." Therefore, play is the eternal disruption of the presence of a center (or Origin)—in short, of presence itself, since the center identifies presence, while its lack signifies absence. Derrida then goes on to distinguish two attitudes toward absence: one is Rousseau's—negative, guilty, nostalgic; the other Nietzsche's—affirmative, joyous, forward-looking. The first, which includes Lévi-Strauss's work, looks sentimentally in the present, *into* its current efforts, for a new inspiration that will hopefully rejoin, regain, refind the lost Origin.[152]

Yet Derrida concludes—I think incorrectly—by saying that the choice between the two attitdes is not a real current possibility. It is only partly true that we live in a world in which the forms of the first attitude predominate: as Derrida's writing demonstrates, they infect our representation of our condition, they provide our mental activity with kinds of organization, and they fix aspects of our direction. This is why we continue to be logocentric, and our minds remain rooted in a doctrine of signs, fastened upon the paradox of absence, committed to difference rather than value. All we can do now is to catch a glimpse of the coming change in our outlook; we can do so in the spirit of Yeat's trembling question: "And what rough beast, its hour come round at last,/Slouches towards Bethlehem to be born?" Yet the development of Foucault's attitude, as I have tried to show, differs from all this in its affirmativeness, its progressivism, and its energetic discoveries.

An important aspect of the structuralist position, unlike Foucault's, has been its choice of an often-nostalgic myth over practice as the subject of analysis. To this aspect the rest of Derrida's work until 1968 was devoted. In it he pulled apart and terrorized the conceptual glue of structuralism. *De la grammatologie* and *La Voix et le phénomène* analyze language respectively as the autoerotic myth of ethnocentric man (Derrida's texts are Rousseau, Saussure, and Lévi-Strauss) and as the outer, phenomenological expression of an inner voice that remains "wanting-to-speak." Derrida's gaze remains fixed upon writing that has been dislodged from its status as secondary production and given instead the responsibility of coping with the ontological absence of speaking. Acceptance of this responsibility, despite ethnocentric dreams of an Origin (banished when writing replaced speaking) miracuously turning up in writing, makes writing, for Derrida the grammatologist, a game of pure risk; writing participates constantly in the violence of each trace it makes, and thereby it achieves a vigilance coterminous with pure differentiation (*différance*) that somehow exists before the initiation of individual differences and the creation of individual signs.

Derrida's critiques and appreciations of Freud, Artaud, Bataille, and Levinas are practiced with structuralist instruments· and nihilistic radicality. His work, therefore, busily traverses the place in mind between structuralism as the alphabet of cultural order on one side, and, on the other, the bare outlines, the traces of writing that shimmers just a hair beyond utter blankness. Structuralism, we must agree with his implications, is a conservative force with unrealized—because unthinkable by structuralism—possibilities. Yet the classical realistic novel had filled that mysterious and beseeching space between action and potential, just as philosophers like Foucault, novelists and critics like Butor, Garcia Marquez, Borges, and Beckett today research, and chart, the possibilities of a new inventive order. Yet, as we saw in chapter 4, between the presence in Western Europe of the classical novel and the crisis of discontinuity represented by Foucault and the structuralists there intervenes an intentional process, a logic of writing, and of making texts, which *took place.* In its richness this process meant very much more than precedence: it involved rethought forms of continuity, permanence, appropriation, vision, and revision. All of these occur in the complex event I have been calling the beginning. What this event has also meant, aside from the thought I have been discussing in this chapter, is the subject of the next and final chapter.

Conclusion: Vico in His Work and in This

I

One of the "elements" of Vico's *New Science* (1744) is the following axiom: "Doctrines must take their beginning from that of the matters of which they treat" (par. 314).[1] This seems scarcely more than an observation that any historically intelligible account of an institution, for example, ought itself to begin at that institution's beginning. Begin at the beginning. Yet why did Vico consider this a novel axiom and claim it as his exclusive discovery? Unlike Descartes, Vico believed that the human mind had "an indefinite nature" (*l'indiffinita natura della mente umane*).[2] Clear and distinct ideas are the last rather than the first things to be thought, for before he becomes a philosopher, a man, like all men without exception, begins his life as a child who in time sheds his childish beliefs and acquires the less imaginative, less poetic ideas commonly known as clear, distinct, and mature ones. Historically, therefore, the first instances of human thought are obscure images; only at a relatively late stage of historical development do men have the power to think in clear abstractions, just as according to "the universal principle of etymology in all languages, . . . words are carried over from bodies and from the properties of bodies to signify the institutions of the mind and spirit" (par. 237). Similarly, history is the passage from the obscure birth (*nascimento*) of things to their developed, institutional state: only then do they become clear, although their nature is determined by their beginning. A philosopher who tries to understand an institution like law uses a conceptual language far removed from the distant and murky circumstances from which the law originally derived. How, then, can Vico's simple beginning axiom be followed? For according to Vico, in becoming more definite, more accurate, more scientific, the human mind in time became less grounded in the body, more abstract, less able directly to grasp its own essential self, less capable of beginning at the beginning, less capable of defining itself. Or equally paradoxical, rational description is by definition a less accurate, more indefinite means than is imagery for describing certain concrete things. Just as children have indefinite ideas about philosophy, so too do philosophers have indefinite, or at least inappropriate, ideas about the childhood of institutions.

This intransigent fact cost Vico "the persistent research of almost all . . . his literary life" (par. 34). So universal a subject as his—"the common nature of the nations"—rested upon a simple axiom: one should begin such a study by discussing the beginning of nations. Yet all his and his readers' learning could not have been preparation enough for the following bizarre discovery of fabulous beginnings, arrived at after twenty years of research:

> [This Science] must begin where its subject matter began, as we said in the Axioms. We must therefore go back with the philologians and fetch it from the stones of Deucalion and Pyrrha, from the rocks of Amphion, from the men who sprang up from the furrows of Cadmus or the hard oak of Vergil. With the philosophers we must fetch it from the frogs of Epicurus, from the cicadas of Hobbes, from the simpletons of Grotius; from the men cast into this world without care or aid of God, of whom Pufendorf speaks, as clumsy and wild as the giants called "Big Feet," who are said to be found near the Straits of Magellan; which is as much to say from the Cyclopes of Homer, in whom Plato recognizes the first fathers in the state of the families. (This is the science the philologians and the philosophers have given us of the principles of humanity!) Our treatment of it must take its start from the time these creatures began to think humanly. In their monstrous savagery and unbridled bestial freedom there was no means to tame the former or bridle the latter but the frightful thought of some divinity, the fear of whom is the only powerful means of reducing to duty a liberty gone wild. To discover the way in which this first human thinking arose in the gentile world, we encountered exasperating difficulties which have cost us the research of a good twenty years. We had to descend from these human and refined natures of ours to those quite wild and savage natures, which we cannot at all imagine and can comprehend only with great effort. (par. 338)

Man's world begins among stones, rocks, frogs, and cicadas, rather like Yeats's "foul rag-and-bone shop of the heart." This is quite another world from Plato's realm of forms or from Descartes's clear and distinct ideas. All of Vico's great book is an effort to give substance to the otherwise banished beginnings of human reality. Yet every time he describes man's beginning, Vico drastically qualifies his characterization with something like "we cannot at all imagine and can comprehend only with great effort. . . ." Thus not only is it hard for modern man to locate his beginning, but even when he becomes aware of his historical aboriginality he cannot even truly imagine what it is.

Vico's place at the conclusion of a book on beginnings is earned by precisely this truth, as well as by the attitude toward scholarship it entails. So far as I have been able to discover, Vico is the prototypical modern thinker who, as we shall presently see, perceives beginning as an activity requiring the writer to maintain an unstraying obligation to practical reality and sympathetic imagination in equally strong parts; and in order to understand the debt owed Vico by a study on beginnings we must attempt finally to understand his work as having begun a significant process. By *obligation* I mean here the precision with which the concrete circumstances of any undertaking oblige the mind to take them into account—the obligation not just passively to continue, but the obligation to begin by learning, first, that there is no schematic method that makes all things simple, then second, whatever with reference to one's circumstances is necessary in order to begin, given one's field of study. And by referring to *sympathetic imagination* I mean that to begin to write is to "know" what at the outset cannot be known except by inventing it, exactly, intentionally, autodidactically. It is the interrelation between this obligation and the sympathetic imagination, however, that is crucial.

For the searching modern mind, as for our savage first fathers, a principle of "divinity" arrived at through fear and not reason "reduces a liberty gone wild." Only by *imagining* (divining = inventing) a force anterior to our origin, a force for Vico capable of preventing further regress into irremediable savagery, can we begin to intend to be human. The coincidence between bridles upon the primitive and the philosophical man is not gratuitous. Both the savage and the philosopher are alien to God's temporal order, to sacred history; for according to Vico, most history is a human and *gentile* affliction, whereas for the Jews there is a life "founded by the true God." Here Vico is at his most profoundly suggestive, and he uses etymological puns to make his point beautifully. A gentile savage or philosopher is tamed by the frightful thought of some divinity; "by contrast the Hebrew religion was founded by the true God on the prohibition of the divination on which all the gentile nations arose" (*sul divieto della divinazione, sullaquale sursero tutte le nazione gentili*) (par. 167). The crucial distinction is between the gentiles who divine or imagine divinity, on the one hand, and the Hebrews whose true God prohibits divination, on the other. To be a gentile is to be denied access to the true God, to have recourse for thought to divination, to live permanently in history, in an order other than God's, to be able genetically to produce that order of history. Vico's concerns are everywhere with this other order, the word of history made by men.

Vico's idea of beginnings has, I think, very far-reaching importance; for the modern reader to discover the accuracy of so proleptic and poetic an intelligence as Vico's is an exhilarating experience. He is the first philosopher of beginnings, not because he was the first in time to think as he did (actually, Vico usually credits Bacon with that heroic achievement), but because for him a beginning is at once never given and always indefinite or divined and yet always asserted at considerable expense. He is also the first beause, having rethought beginnings, he saw that no one could really be first, neither the savage man nor the reflective philosopher, because each made a beginning and hence was always *being first*. Vico's discovery of a beginning common to primitive and contemporary man was the result of three tributary impulses, which in large measure have borne also upon the present book and which constitute a large part of its method.

First, Vico undertook to demonstrate that in certain provinces of thought or writing, a theory and an actual experience are interchangeable because directly adjacent. The notion of man, as the humanist conceives it, and the experience that man actually undergoes, in all its untidy diversity, are for Vico two sides of the same coin. To ascertain an actual point of historical departure (called today the search for roots) and to speculate on the nature of things in terms of an abstract origin not renderable accurately in language; these are the extreme opposites that Vico, as philologist and student of language, is able to think and maintain. He did this by diminishing the uniqueness of neither. This is why such grand ideas as the "mental dictionary" or the cycles of *corsi* and *recorsi* stand without intermediaries directly next to his descriptions of the primitive fathers copulating with their women in the mountain caves. It is no exaggeration to say that such feats as this were made possibe for Vico by his special understanding of language. In language, Vico seems to have thought, either an abstract or a concrete word signifies (a) an indefinite meaning first, (b) thereafter, as one demands definition, a conditional meaning, and (c) a greater or a lesser distance from a main body of significance and from particular experience. The latter signification (*c*) needs some explanation. Like other eighteenth-century figures (for example Lord Monboddo, Rousseau, Hamann, and Herder), Vico tried to account for the first appearance of language in history. Unlike almost every other such thinker, Vico was a professional etymologist. Words for him were unimaginable as simply emanations from the lips of some primitive being. Every word carries—indeed, is—a system of relationships to other words; *The New Science* much of the time is a virtuoso, if not always accurate, display of etymological and correlative explanations. To explain how a name and a character (the concrete and the abstract) had the same meaning, Vico says:

> In Roman law *nomen* signifies right. Similarly, in Greek *nomos* signifies law, and from *nomos* comes *nomisma*, money, as Aristotle notes; and according to etymologists, *nomos* becomes in Latin *numus*. In French, *loi* means law, and *aloi* means money, and among the second barbarians the term "canon" was applied both to ecclesiastical law and to the annual rent paid by the feudal leaseholder to the lord of the land held in fief. (par. 433)

Such a habit of mind makes genealogical sequence, by which a word is traced back mechanically in a straight line to some root, a weak and unattractive prospect by itself. Vico always feels the presence of adjacent lines: *nomen, numus, loi.* When he wishes to characterize the earliest historical period, he breaks it down into a set of complementary systems of knowledge he calls *poetic*: poetic metaphysics, poetic logic, poetic history, poetic geography, and so forth. No one alone can exist without the others. Soon it appears to Vico that all knowledge during every historical moment is poetic in that the sinews between different branches bind these branches together despite an appearance of dispersion. The term *Poetic* therefore signifies a relationship of adjacency asserted against logical, sequential continuity; a perfect analogy is the set of relationships obtaining between parts of the human body. As men grow more reflective and capable of seeing something other than their body, words reach further than the body and become abstract. The sum total of all words is a reflective idea that rather startlingly prefigures Mallarmé's *Livre* containing all books. Each word in a dictionary is related to every other, again by systematic adjacency, much more rarely in genealogical lines. A poetic understanding of knowledge in a reflective period is what Vico calls philological science.

This, then, is the first tributary impulse in Vico's thought: the direct presence to one another of the abstract and concrete in language is based upon the fundamental poetic adjacency of words to one another, another, an adjacency that Vico also sees in the first men congregating in families. All this entails a method of argument that moves from one constellation or cluster of ideas to another. For example, Vico says that *pa* is the first syllable uttered by man in imitation of a frightening thunderbolt. Doubled it becomes *pape* (father Jove), and Vico shows how all the primitive gods were imagined as fathers and mothers. Then he discusses *patrare*, the verbs *impetrare*, and *impetrire*; finally he asserts that "the first interpretation [*interpretatio*, as if for *interpatratio*]was the interpretation of the divine laws declared by the auspices" (par. 448). Although Vico's subject is the common law of nations, and his ambition is to find a common beginning—a genealogical project—his "topical" method is everywhere to amass evidence by correlation, complementarity, and adjacency. Although his desire is to locate a primeval beginning, a line of direct filiality, the material testimony of language and his learning restrain his desire, engaging it instead with the susceptibility of language to divination and poetry. A distant and irrecoverable origin is not yearned after fruitlessly, because the mind can reexperience its making power by forging novel connections (the parallel etymologies of *pa*, for instance) again and again—thus *adjacency, complementarity, parallelism,* and *correlation as methods employed in the interests of a genealogical goal.* In what Vico called the gentile world, this does away entirely with such common hierarchies as a spirit higher than body, a meaning higher than evidence, a father who because he is older is wiser than his son, a philosopher or a logician who is more "rational" than a poet, an idea that is higher than clusters of words. It also does away with the Beginning that stands over and above all human effort.

The second tributary is Vico's ambition to understand himself and others in terms of a collective fate. In no philosopher before Marx, Freud, or Nietzsche does one find an assimilative capacity as great as Vico's. Because he takes words as his subject, no aspect of human experience can be relegated to the status of mere detail. In no respect is the enormous difference between Vico and his later eighteenth-century contemporry Sade so minimal as in the catholicity of their interest in the detailed movement of bodies, for which words are an extension and symbol. This interest breaks down barriers between nations and dissolves hierarchical taboos; moreover, it is expressed as a gesture against nature (or—even though Vico would never have admitted it—against religion).[3]

Man's collective fate lies in the creation of another world, which Vico called gentile.

As to the role of God or even of divine providence, Vico appears clearly a believer. "The clear and simple observation we have made on the entire human race," he says near the end of *The New Science* ". . . would lead us to say certainly that this is the great city of nations that was founded and is governed by God" (par. 1107). A few sentences later he says that the endurance of man's world "is a counsel of a superhuman wisdom" (par. 1107)—which, he adds in the next sentence, divinely rules and conducts [the city of man]." *Divinely* here is not an unintended word. In recalling the *divination* upon which the gentiles base their polity (that is, the whole process of thought that makes the pun on *divinity/indefinite* a telling one), this phrase also prepares us for the following great summation, in which God or divine providence plays a nonexistent role:

It is true that men have themselves made this world of nations (and we took this as the first incontestable principle of our Science, since we despaired of finding it from the philosophers and philologists) but this world without doubt has issued from a mind often diverse, at times quite contrary, and always superior to the particular ends that men had proposed to themselves; which narrow ends, made means to serve wider ends, it has always employed to preserve the human race upon this earth. Men mean to gratify their bestial lust and abandon their offspring, and they inaugurate the chastity of marriage from which the families arise. The fathers mean to exercise without restraint their paternal power over their clients, and they subject them to the civil powers from which the cities arise. . . . [Here follows a series of parallel sentences, each beginning by saying that men *mean* to do what they did.] The nations mean to dissolve themselves, and their remnants flee for safety to the wilderness, whence, like the phoenix, they rise again. That which did all this was mind, for men did it with intelligence; it was not fate, for they did it by choice; not chance, for the results of their always so acting are perpetually the same. (par. 1108)

In one thing above all else is man's indefinite mind definite: in its intention *to be*, an intention which is the zero point of man's existence. Human intelligence means for Vico the willed perpetration, the constantly experienced order of being. The collective human fate is far from a simple choice over extinction. It entails the historical creation (also constantly experienced) of an order of meaning *different from* (hence gentile—i.e., the world of the *gentes* and *families*) the order of God's sacred history. Man's beginning is a transgression; and so long as man exists, the fact of his existence asserts the beginning-as-transgression.

Yet Vico is too honest to his senses to ignore time and diversity. His primitive savages are conceived as having begun the gentile world, but not with having prescribed all its later developments. When he says that "mind did all this" (meaning human history), he is saying that human history is an order of repetition, not of spontaneous and perpetual originality. Theoretically, repetition implies sameness; but practically, as one looks around, one sees difference: different ideas, men, countries, habits, languages. Repetition is a reasonable idea, and it accounts for Vico's reduction of all history to a recurrent set of three unvarying cycles, the ages of gods, heroes and men. And yet, in fact, difference or diversity is the detail—like the parallel and wildly varying etymologies of the same words in different languages—that is the *unreasonable* chaotic reality implied by reason. The curious coming and going in Vico's *The New Science* between the relatively uninteresting sterility of the three cycles and the really powerful community of intractable human detail which Vico pours out with that unstinting philological zeal of his might very well have been of the kind Samuel Butler imagined for the Erewhonian Colleges of Unreason. "Unreason," the colleges maintain, "is a part of reason; it must therefore be allowed its full share in stating the initial conditions." [4] Mind for Vico determines the choice men make when they make decisions, and also it determines the "perpetually sane" results. Analyzed further, the statement says that choice (not fate) makes as many different decisions as there are occasions. In their staggering variety they appear irrational—but only until their unreasonable chanciness is reduced to a set of categories (the three cycles) that seem after the fact to repeat a finite pattern of sameness ad infinitum. After that they appear rational.

If the second tributary impulse of Vico's thought aids us methodologically to apprehend a collective human fate that embraces reason on the one hand and unreason on the other hand, his third impulse is to find a mode of expression in which to deliver his ideas. For the modern reader *The New Science* is not a tidy book, and its often postponed arrival at any sort of conclusion makes it perhaps a bad example of expository prose. Nevertheless, let us allow Vico to state his views on what he is doing:

There must in the nature of human institutions be a mental language common to all nations, which uniformly grasps the substance of things feasible in human social life and expresses it with as many diverse modifications as these same things may have diverse aspects. A proof of this is afforded by proverbs or maxims of vulgar wisdom, in which substantially the same meanings find as many diverse expressions as there are nations ancient and modern. This common mental language is proper to our Science, by whose light scholars will be enabled to construct a mental vocabulary common to all the various articulate languages living and dead. . . . As far as our small erudition will permit, we shall make use of this vocabulary in all the matters we discuss. (par. 161)

Vico's subject matter is viewed as a language, not as a series of events that actually took place. He posits a kind of concordance between "things feasible in human social life" and a set of conceptual formulations already existing in the mind. Just as what Vico elsewhere calls "the quasi-divine nature of mind" has an irreducible tendency to move itself, to transform its concepts inventively, this *ingegno* in mind virtually creates new social circumstances which express it. Yet his insistence upon the common and the feasible emphasizes Vico's belief that mind is a finite set of possibilities, capable of many many combinations and permutations, all of which are kept from *infinite* multiplicity by internal restraints. In short, he is arguing that although man's mind is capable of so many transformations as to be inventive and creative, it is also restrained finally by its own rules based on the need for human community and social order. Those rules guarantee the endurance of man upon earth.

Consequently, *The New Science* never loses sight of its intention to describe man among men. Vico's "small erudition" extended into several disciplines and languages: he therefore could write *for* and *about* the community of men. He was being consistent with his ambitions as a professor, set out with unusual eloquence as far back as 1708 in his *De nostri temporis studiorum natione*. If the structure of *The New Science* is unusual at all, it is because at the level of the individual sentence and at the level of a section Vico is trying to describe the multitiered, but organized, realms of mind. His account of poetic morals, for example, goes from start to finish by describing the development of "virtues" from the most simple to the most complex; whereas in the next chapter, on poetic economy, Vico repeats the progression from simple to complex using different materials and arriving at a different sort of "poetic" structure. While all these sections can only be comprehended sequentially, by means of the parallels, correspondences, and allusions among them Vico aims to render them as though they occurred simultaneously.

The locus of Vico's attention in his writing is the fable, which is strictly speaking not a historical narrative, nor an entirely fanciful invention, nor an unimportant embellishment of morals (as it was to many of his contemporaries). The fable is figured language, it is communal, it has a kind of repeatable originality, it is autochthonous—that is, it is set in a specific history and language. When Vico recounts Homer's description of Achilles' shield or the fable of Cadmus, he calls them *repilogamenti della storia poetica* (Vico's English translators render *repilogamenti* as *epitomes*, not entirely an accurate choice, as I shall show in a moment). This is very different from the kind of attitude toward Greek myth one finds in Porphyry or Henry Reynolds, for example. Vico maintains that these fables recapitulate, in compressed language, *general* stages of real history. He ridicules none other than Erasmus for actually believing that Cadmus' fable "contains the story of the invention of letters by Cadmus" (par. 679). What the *repilogamenti* are valuable for is that they are recapitulations (not symbols, nor epitomes) by the Greeks themselves of their own history. These fables, therefore: (*a*) use a language that is at once historical and transparently belonging to "the mental language common to all nations"; (*b*) possess a particular narrative logic of their own so far as events in the story are concerned, although they are *generally* true to the main stages through which a period of history passed; (*c*) are original creations, and yet have neither a particular individual author nor any pretense to being more than rewritings of popular legend. Above all, the *repilogamenti* recapitulate history in such a way as to make that history available, through the disseminating power of "a common mental language," to subsequent generations and other races.

One especially Vichian irony must be noted. *Repilogamenti* is a word related in its root to our word *epilogue*. How does one account for the conflation here of Vico's thinking about beginnings and origins with his interest in a genre whose aim is to recapitulate in a final sense? I think Vico considered such peculiar human constructs as fables to possess the kind of primitive freshness that we still associate with folktale and legend, as well as a kind of *intentional* power for generality and truth that we normally associate with the classical historians or with the great national epics. Insofar as they are written—or at any rate, disseminated in time—the *repilogamenti* therefore cry out for decipherment and study. Because of their privileged position at the beginning moments of human actuality, they are also privileged subjects for late study; indeed, they are the final goal of study, even if they are not historically "true." As Vico says in the first sentence of his essay on laughter, to contrast man's inventive faculties with truth is absurd. Man's divining, creative power is his first and—using the word in its double sense of "dominant" and "beginning"—his *principal* gift.[5] All his subsequent efforts as a thinker should be directed at trying ultimately to understand that gift. In the words of Hölderlin:

> Was der Alten Gesang von Kindern Gottes geweissagt,
> Siche! wir sind es, wir; Frucht von Hesperien ists.*[6]

II

Vico's thought, as I have so far described it, is extraordinarily useful at this stage in that it parallels my key arguments throughout the preceding five chapters. Here is a schematic list of seven Vichian signposts that have helped me, from the beginning, to discuss beginnings and to sketch a method:

a. The initial distinction between the gentile or historical and the sacred or original—paralleling my distinction between beginning and an origin.

b. The combination in intellectual work of a special, idiosyncratic problem and a very strong interest in human collectivity—a combination that occurs in this text from the beginning.

c. An acute awareness not only of genealogical succession (except as its biological foundations obviously persist), but also of parallelism, adjacency, and complementarity—that is, all those relationships that emphasize the lateral and the dispersed rather than the linear and the sequential.

d. A central interplay between beginning and repetition, or between beginning and beginning-again.

e. Language as *rewriting*, as history conditioned by repetition, as encipherment and dissemination—the instability, and the richness, of a text as practice and as idea.

f. Topics for critical analysis that do not fall neatly into the categories of commentary, chronicle, or thematic tracings.

g. The beginning in writing as inaugurating and subsequently maintaining *another* order of meaning from previous or already existing writing. Here, once again, the distinction (made in *a,* above) between gentile and sacred becomes relevant.

---

*"What of the children of God was foretold in the songs of the ancients/Look, we are it, ourselves; fruit of Hesperia it is!"

III

Vico's own beginning, he tells us over and over again in his *Autobiography*, is himself. For he was preeminently an autodidact *(autodidascolo)*; this is the honorific title bestowed upon him by his friend Gregorio Caloprese.[7] Everything he learned, he learned for and by himself; he seems to have been convinced of his individuality and strength of mind from his earliest days, and most of the time his *Autobiography* is an account of this self-learning. But, as Croce suggests,[8] it is valuable to read the *Autobiography* in the spirit of *The New Science*, and to do this one can begin by performing an interesting exercise on the term *autodidact* in the manner of *The New Science*.

The first investigative step is always philological, says Vico. In other words, a word has to be examined for its shades of meaning, and so we turn immediately to his philological account in *The New Science*. There he tells us that the second principal aspect of *The New Science* is a philosophy of authority. Now, *authority*, as a word, has for its original meaning "property." The reason for this, Vico goes on to say (par. 386), is that *auctor* certainly comes from *autos*, which equals *proprius* or *suus ipsius*. Keeping in mind the starting point of our discussion here—the term *autodidact*, particularly the prefix *auto*, and its application to Vico the man—we look next to paragraph 388, where Vico tells us that human authority, in the full philosophical sense of the phrase, "is the property of human nature which not even God can take from man without destroying him. . . . This authority is the free use of the will, the intellect, on the other hand, being a passive power subject to truth." Thus in calling himself an autodidact Vico is insisting with philological astuteness on the self teaching itself with the authority—which is its property—of its humanity; and this human property resides completely in an exercise of will, or conation. When one learns something, one first performs an act of will, because only by intending or willing to learn can one learn.

That, however, is only half of teaching, because in becoming conscious of what one learns (for one cannot learn *and* be unconscious of it) one is doing something more. In distinguishing both the object of will and the will itself, the mind achieves consciousness *(conscienza)*; the completion, therefore, of the act of teaching is when the principle that underlies consciousness is understood *as a principle,* when the imminent principle is abstracted by induction from the consciousness to the intellect. Hence *videre et cogitare.* Then we have science (*scienza*), or truth, or philosophy. Thus the full sense of the word *autodidact* includes the whole process just described, which, when it is philologically taken, is *conscienza,* and, when the principle is grasped philosophically, is *scienza.* What Vico is trying to describe is the mind in its double aspect of active conation (or will) and reflective intellect, the mind both acting and observing itself acting. One can best describe this, I think, as a voluntary mental action simultaneously reflected upon.

A great deal more, however, needs to be said of this "free use of the will" which is the active aspect of the mind. Let us return to the middle of the *Autobiography.* Vico had by this time decided that he was neither a materialist nor a Cartesian, at least insofar as either of those philosophies could be construed as denying the mind and its ideas on the one hand, or, on the other, positing the mind as the foundation of empirial science. What Cartesians and materialists would not acknowledge is that the world of nature, the world of natural objects that one presumes to have been made, is the artifact of God—or, if not of God, then certainly not of man. One thinks here of Dr. Johnson disproving Bishop Berkeley "thus"—by kicking that so obviously present stone. Objective nature is impenetrable—not, as Descartes believed, penetrable by the cogitating ego. The arrogant René (who is roughly handled by Vico) is extremely ahistorical, even antihistorical; for armed with the tools of science and mathematics, Descartes was wont to declare: Who needs the humanistic, historical disciplines? There is the mind and its science, the world and God: that is all.

Vico's criticisms were directed at Descartes's concept of the "thinking mind": what it perceives is no doubt certain, says Vico, and what is certain to it is therefore true for it. But this is not nature. For the act of perception involves (as we saw earlier) a beginning act of will, and who is foolish enough to claim that nature depends on human will for its reality? If one were simply to face a table, one could will all one liked and the table would neither move nor change thereby, for effectively it has only presence, and neither beginning nor end; the tragicomedy arising from such ineffectual self-delusion carried to an optimistic extreme is the essence of Voltaire's *Candide.* The table is simply a table, the world is the world. One can presume, however, that for God, so great

359

and effective an act of will is possible. Thus Vico tells us that the world is God's perception; which means that by an authoritative act of divine appropriation in the beginning God made the world.

What emerges from all this is that (a) perception from the beginning involves creation and (b) human perception involves creation of quite another sort than the kind God performs, or has performed, in order to create nature from the beginning. Vico here talks of "investigating the wisdom of the ancients" under Bacon's supremely intelligent aegis, only to discover that among the ancient Egyptians it had been believed that "the instrument with which nature makes everything was the wedge, and this was what they meant their pyramids to signify. Now the Latins called nature *ingenium*, whose principal property is sharpness; thus intimating that nature forms and deforms every form with the chisel of air."[9] Vico then goes on to discuss the etymological relationship between *ingenium* ("nature"), *anima* ("air"), and *mens* ("thought"). This is, to us, a curious alchemical exercise, but it is highly suggestive because, as usual, Vico's etymologies lead us back to the mind. In this "fabulous" Egyptian story Vico begins to detect a historical prejudice, which is based, in the case of the Egyptians, on ignorance, and, when it appears centuries later in Descartes's thought, on arrogance. The prejudice is that men have always wanted to believe that they have understood nature and its creation, and that in some way nature corresponds to them, or that it depends on them. Because each successive generation of men provides a different theory for expressing this prejudice (and one perceives the differences in the philological and historical variations of the words used to formulate the theory), one knows instantly that what appears certain to one group of minds is not true for another which is separated from the first in time and space. So that what for the Latins had been nature (*ingenium*) and air (*anima*) has become for us *ingenuity* and *spirit*. Vico tells us that he had learned to see men as they were, as both the creatures and the creators of their beliefs, from Tacitus. He keeps implicitly insisting that Descartes's arrogance stems from his inability to see the obvious historical lesson to be learned from someone like Tacitus, that René's theories are but a historical episode.

From Plato, however, Vico had learned that metaphysical abstractions exist, if only because all men, at all times, have believed in an eternal idea, if only an eternal idea of their own mind. One can read history as a study in the eternal persistence of the idea of man's mind; and that idea, when it is temporally considered (which has to do with the world of nature only as a sort of parallel to it), becomes narrative history. On occasion, Vico is wont to characterize man's ideas as dealing with the outside of things, with their surface continuities and forms; God, on the other hand, deals with things from within, because he truly made them from within.[10] Since the idea is an idea of man's mind, and since the idea persists in different forms, a true historian can view history—which man makes—from the perspective of eternal, or ever-present, or *inner* persistence. History then becomes the mind considered as synchronous structure (an ideal persistent architecture), as the inner form of man's activity, and as diachronous modality, or temporal modifications, or sequential continuity: above all, it is necessary to understand that history is neither one nor the other exclusively.

At this point in the *Autobiography* Vico relates how he formulated all of this into a proper metaphysics. Two of his commentators, Croce and H. P. Adams, characterize this metaphysics as fantastical.[11] Their reason for so calling it is that, in formulating it, Vico first confused the two Zenos (the Eleatic and the Stoic) and then proceeded to propound what he considered to be the Zenoistic theory of points, which is a peculiar hodgepodge of shrewdness and fantasy. But as Vico himself said, just because a belief is fantastic to us now does not mean that that belief did not serve some valid purpose for the mind that created it and held it: this is the most insistent lesson of his historiography. And while the theory is quasi-mathematical, Vico transposes it into metaphysical doctrine. At its simplest, the theory argues that just as in geometry one can posit a hypothetical beginning point from which lines can be extended (the point remaining a postulate, but one which is valid because all lines are divisible into infinitesimal indivisible points), so too in metaphysical terms one can posit a beginning point which is neither entirely mind (or abstraction) nor matter (or concreteness). The so-called metaphysical point then becomes conation—what in this book I have been calling beginning intention—which in history is human will, understood both temporally and absolutely. Human will, we recall, is the property of humanity, and as such it is radically less effective than divine will; but it is nonetheless an imperfect model of divine will, albeit an imperfect one. It needs to be said that Vico realizes that, when one perceives the obvious fact that the theory of metaphysical points is only a theory—which assures us once again that it has a temporal meaning (for Vico himself) and an eternal or philosophical meaning—then one is redemonstrating the mind's characteristics.

God, conceived of as pure mind, wills intentionally, and then matter or nature comes into existence from that beginning act of will. Man, in his mind, wills intentionally, and then, not nature, but a different version of it comes into existence from *that* beginning or intentional act of will. Thus we see that the doctrine of metaphysical points is in fact fantastic or fictional—if one can use such terms without implying rational superiority to them— because it is human and therefore inadequate, plainly so. (Indeed, Vico had used just that word—*fictional*—in his *Wisdom of the Ancient Italians* of 1710.[12]) Human will, or conation, then, is precisely like an initial, or beginning, or inaugural wedge between man and nature. That is why every metaphysical theory attempts intellectual mastery of impenetrable nature and succeeds only in providing a certain but different version of nature, which the mind then pronounces to be true. Thus human intellectual activity is, to use Coleridge's terms in the thirteenth chapter of the *Biographia Literaria*, "a repetition in the finite mind of the eternal act of creation in the infinite I AM."[13] When God says *cogito ergo sum*, he wills himself into material and spiritual existence. When man says it at the beginning, he wills only himself and *his* world—quite another thing—into existence. From a reflective, historical standpoint, all human things (or institutions) are, from the beginning, created by the mind, *mind* understood as that which can begin intentionally to act in the world of men.

Vico's entire reasoning is therefore comparative (because it compares itself to the wholly true thinking of God) and at the same time is based on acknowledged inadequacy (because God succeeds in influencing nature, whereas man succeeds only in influencing himself). The only time man is more successful than not in his creation is when he reasons geometrically, in the analytic manner of Descartes and Arnauld. There one has mind, conation, and the geometric object which has been willed into existence; but what a far cry from a meadow or a tree is a line or a surface! Geometrical thought is almost ridicuously limited, and man is far too alive and active to be restricted to that sort of accuracy. Because of his humanity, man continues to will, and his whole universe is created by him; but his universe is the world of institutions and of history, whose record is one of unending failure to create a permanent, sequential, or orderly world.

The modes of geometrical reasoning are used nevertheless

throughout *The New Science,* and are especially apparent in the way the book is arranged. The book opens with an exhaustively comprehensive description of a painting that is itself almost incredibly detailed, then proceeds to rehearse many indisputable axioms, and finally runs through a series of proofs that illustrate and support certain major principles. But the book is eminently critical of itself and of human reasoning: notice that the first few axioms pronounce the mind to be weak and inadequate. Within the mind's limitations, *The New Science* aspires to the same elegance and severity in describing human affairs that geometry possesses in describing the figures with which it is concerned. An organic unity thus binds the ambitions of *The New Science* to Vico's career as a professor of eloquence and as skillful and subtle lawyer: there is always present a concern for separating the configurations of a certain truth from falsehood and for describing those configurations as skillfully and as intensely as possible. But because the mind is weak and inadequate, as Vico says so very often, *The New Science* is to be read as an *aspra e continova meditazione* on the limitations of the mind. The great achievement of *The New Science* is that within those very severe limitations a great many modifications are possible and discernible once the beginning will to begin is exercised. This accounts for the book's astonishing subtlety and variety. What needs emphasis, however, is Vico's passionate concern with the fundamentally severe and economical operations of the autodidactic humanistic mind.

This concern, then, condones, even requires, the application of *The New Science* to the *Autobiography* and vice versa. For the *Autobiography* is Vico's history of himself viewed temporally as a series of successive episodes in the life of a thinker, and *The New Science* is a history of the modifications of man's mind viewed in their eternal aspect—as an enduring thought. Yet neither book portrays and employs the mind in only one of these two aspects. It is just that Vico uses the outer structure of etymological philology or sequential reasoning in the *Autobiography,* and the outer structure of geometric or philosophical reasoning in *The New Science.* Croce quite aptly says that the *Autobiography* is written in the spirit of *The New Science;*[14] but the converse is no less true. As Auerbach, Vico's principal and most profound literary student, says, "the simple fact [is] that a man's work stems from his existence and that consequently everything we can find out about his life serves to interpret the work."[15] Thus in the *Autobiography* one notes Vico's search for what he so suggestively calls the *universal principle* of law; and in the monumentality of *The New Science* one notes the temporal succession of events, the three ages of man. The beginning is an intentional reconciliation between temporality and universality.

The common background of the two books can now be stated as follows. Confronted with the objective presence of nature and the very subjective presence of human thought, Vico's problem, like Descartes's, Spinoza's, and Leibnitz's, was to bring those opposites together in a meaningful relationship. The mind, however, can be finally certain only of itself, and then only conditionally: certainty implies knowledge that comes from having observed, and observation implies will. But will is practically appetitive, and it is soon discovered that intellectual will has little real effect on nature. Human will has, to be sure, a real effect on what is intellectual and human; yet the substance of thought is sense perception, which is recorded in the mind as imagery of one kind or another. Men, however, are gifted with language; and language, because it is associated with the mind, expresses the result of sense perception. Thus Vico is able to postulate a primitive man who, like a child, made sounds that resembled his sense impressions as closely as possible. Each linguistic expression represents a beginning act of choice, of will, for in making a sound man is confirming a sense impression, becoming conscious of it.

History's records are primarily verbal: language itself is the foremost historical document. This Vico knew both by training and from common sense. Yet his early training in Naples always left him dissatisfied; he felt, he implies, that the traditional manner of study was far too stylized and superficial. Left to his own resources, Vico, like the primitive men he was to describe in *The New Science,* discovered the basically utilitarian inner function of language, which is to make man's impressions of the world intelligible to him. Understanding means defining and restricting, it means isolating the essential from among a welter of tumbling impressions. In the very act of understanding the world, man is in reality understanding himself. The language that a man speaks, then, makes the man, and not man the language.

The most overwhelming sense impression, the one closest to man, is that of man's body. The human body is the first object of knowledge, but it is not the only one. There are mountains and trees, the sky, water, land, thunder and lightning, and other men. How, then, is one to describe the mind's apprehension of all these competing natural objects? How is one to describe—from the point of view of a fully self-conscious mind, which Vico was—the first shock of knowledge? How—and this is the real problem—is one to show that the mind, for all its supercivilized subtlety and knowledge, has a functional beginning and not a sacred origin? The brilliant economy of Vico's philosophy, which has the greatest value methodologically for the argument of the present work, lies in the fact that Vico proves essential inadequacy, not simply in terms of self-aggrandizing abstractions (which he uses in his fantastic metaphysics), but in terms of dramatic images that convey in their concreteness and their desperation the operations of the human mind as a pathetic and yet grand wedge differentiating at the very outset between the encroachments of the divine and the natural.

These threatening encroachments are described by Vico as the result of a divinely willed flood, which I take to be an image for the inner crisis of self-knowledge that each man must face at the very beginning of any conscious undertaking. The analogy in Vico's *Autobiography* of the universal flood is the prolonged personal crisis of self-alienation from full philosophical knowledge and self-knowledge that Vico faces until the publication of his major work, *The New Science*. The minor successes of his orations, his poems, and his treatises reveal bits of the truth to him, but he is always striving with great effort to come literally into his own. The result of all his learning—the *Autobiography* artfully wishes us to believe—is *The New Science*, a major work that puts all his earlier life and work in proper perspective, as well as providing the beginning for a novel, rational method of further study. The important fact is that Vico the autodidact teaches himself everything, and not until he has a viable universal law formulated in *The New Science* can his autodidacticism be said to have reached its objective. In *The New Science* the first men, those imaginative poetic characters, are in a state of unconscious ferality until the flashes of lightning, glimmers of some far-distant sense of unified truth, begin. They create Jove in their image. But this is not enough: they have been animallike in their huge passions, their ways have been undisciplined and furious. They create a whole world of gods or words or images that correspond to each act of self-discipline, each act of self-conscious choice that carries with it a whole burden of guilt and inadequacy. Theirs is a poetic world where *poetic* is an adjective the Vico intends in three ways: as imagistic and hence inadequate, as creative and hence human and grand, and as descriptive of the beginning.

Central to this picture of the first men arriving at some sort of self-consciousness is their creation of themselves. Here, in a superb passage from the second book of *The New Science,* Vico pauses to describe this "poetic economy." Man, he says, has to make himself into a figure that economically matches the world he has created (note the two Latin words whose meaning he ponders):

> The heroes apprehended with human senses those two truths which make up the whole of economic doctrine, and which were preserved in the two Latin verbs *educere* and *educare.* In the prevailing best usage the first of these applies to the education of the spirit and the second to that of the body. The first, by a learned metaphor, was transferred by the natural philosophers to the bringing forth of forms from matter. For heroic education began to bring forth in a certain way the form of the human soul which had been completely submerged in the huge bodies of the giants, and began likewise to bring forth the form of the human body itself in its just dimensions from the disproportionate giant bodies. (par. 520)

Like these first men, Vico was an autodidact: he has applied to himself the meanings of *educare* and *educere.* By extracting his body out of a gigantic object of awe-inspiring signification, man places his bodily person as an object among objects. And by extracting his soul out of the welter of matter, he has perceived a form that inheres in and yet overrides the world of objects. Man, in short, has become a historic being—in the two senses, temporal and eternal, of that word. He has become a historic object and, in his soul, an eternal or formal one. This, after all, is autodidacticism in the most profound sense. Man, Vico, has become a philological object and a philosophical one at the same time. Similarly, the beginning has become the same sort of object.

IV

Vico's way of pairing philology with philosophy—in *The New Science* the terms are almost always used side by side—suggests the necessary complementarity of the two sciences. Not only are they close because love motivates the adherents of both—or because "conceit" is an affliction their adherents both share—but also because philosophy deals with the true, philology with the certain. These are subjects that Vico intends us to see as practically close: both the true and the certain lay claim to belief, both to urgency, both to conviction—most of all, both to man's mind, which can, and ought, to live with both. When reflected upon, human experience has a *certain* aspect and a *true* one. Many years before *The New Science,* Vico prophetically united philosophy with philology in his survey "The Study Methods of Our Time." Because he was a professor of eloquence, he averred, he could survey all the sciences of his time. But why do so, and what is the connection between professing eloquence and being able to oversee all learning?

> In answer, I will say: As G. B. Vico, I have no concern; but as a professor of eloquence, great concern in this undertaking. Our ancestors, the founders of this University [of Naples] clearly showed, by assigning the professor of eloquence the task of delivering every year a speech exhorting our students to the study of the principles of various sciences and arts, that they felt he should be well versed in all fields of knowledge. Nor was it without reason that the great man, Bacon, when called upon to give advice to James, King of England, concerning the organization of a university, insisted that young scholars should not be admitted to the study of eloquence unless they had previously studied their way through the whole curriculum of learning.
>
> What is eloquence, in effect, but wisdom, ornately and copiously delivered in words appropriate to the common opinion of mankind? Shall the professor of eloquence, to whom no student may have access unless previously trained in all sciences and arts, be ignorant of those subjects which are required by his teaching duties? The man who is deputed to exhort young students to grapple with all kinds of disciplines, and to discourse about their advantages and disadvantages, so that they may attain those and escape these, should he not be competent to expound his opinions on such knowledge?[16]

Eloquence is what makes possible an understanding of the true and the certain: this is what Vico seems to be saying. Eloquence involves not only the best use of words, but also their most *copious* articulation. Thus, since philosophy and philology must employ words, Vico saw his role as professor of eloquence as providing a place, almost literally, for philosophy and philology to enrich one another. And that place was language—or more specifically, Vico's own copious, eloquent discourse. Later in the above oration Vico insists that he speaks as he does without "the desire to diminish the prestige of a colleague or to place myself in the spotlight."[17] In a certain sense, Vico's authority as the maker of copious discourse rises above his personality; I think, too, that Vico's claims for impartiality are strengthened by his lifelong attempts to subordinate the contingencies of time to the universal laws governing human history. His audience, he says in a letter to Bernardo Maria Giacco on October 25, 1725, is among the very largest, most noble, most greathearted, most learned.[18] And yet, in every one of his works, Vico's human authority, his character or person, is very strongly in evidence. That is, there is no doubt in the reader's mind that he is encountering a powerful originality. For not only is the subject matter of Vico's discourse new, but also the tone is novel, the organization eccentric, and the digressions central. One sees at work a stubborn intellect, prodigiously learned and well versed in the academic tradition of his time, but homemade, original, quirky in its undertaking.

The use of the word *method* to describe Vico's procedure has to everyone (Vico himself not excepted) seemed fairly inaccurate. It is not just that as he grew older Vico opposed his "topical" manner to the Cartesian-Port-Royal geometric method. That opposition was methodical and polemical, by which the "invention" of arguments around a subject exposed the thinness of straight deduction;[19] Vico's circular manner as I have described it in the first and third sections of this chapter pitted the wealth of human diversity against the poverty of philosophy mathematically considered. But not just all that. Vico's obsession with details, each of which confirmed, even if it obscured, the human historical presence—this obsession itself also obscured method. When he argued for a new science, or for a considered rational appraisal of contemporary methods of study, Vico's tendency was to turn away from schematic methods that could be lifted out of his text; instead, he advocated wideness of scope, broad comparisons, the love of detail linked to large universal principles—all intended to load down schemata beyond usefulness. The power of Vico's rhetoric always takes one away from method, rationalistially considered, to knowedge as pathos, invention, imagination—with their pitfalls unobscured.

And such a route returns the reader, as it does Vico, to language, which is where Vico teaches us always to begin. After describing his six orations, delivered "at the annual opening of studies in the Royal University," Vico concludes in the *Autobiography:*

> Whence Vico proves that the pain of our corruption must be headed by virtue, knowledge, and eloquence; for through these three things only does one man feel the same as another. This brings Vico to the end of the various studies, and fixes the point of view from which he considers the order of study. He shows that as languages were the most powerful means for setting up human society, so the studies should begin with them, since they depend altogether on memory which in childhood is marvelously strong.[20]

Hence *eloquence* standing at the end of a sequence recapitulating progress from a child's beginning *with* language to a man's achievement *in* language. Copiousness at the end, the marvelous memory and attraction to language of a child at the beginning. Both terminals are contained—Vico wants us to believe—in the gradually developing, exemplary discourse of *his* work. As an instance there is this: "From the time of the first oration of which we have spoken, it is evident both in it and in all that followed . . . that Vico was agitating in his mind a theme both new and grand, to unite in one principle all knowledge human and divine."[21]   The ceaseless activity of mind delivers language and is delivered by and in language, Vico's own, and it is precisely this that characterizes Vico's novelty and originality.

Everywhere in Vico's work there is to be found the sometimes paradoxical play between, on the one hand, learning, tradition, history, method, pedagogy—in short, applied and pure reason in all their dynastic forms—and, on the other hand, originality, personality, the marvelous, detailed, and often heroic style in all its dispersed forms. This interplay, in addition to the hortatory inclination of his every sentence, puts Vico very close to Rousseau, his near-contemporary. Both men write as teachers to the world at large, each appealing in his own style to a valorized personal experience as a support for theoretical arguments. Like Vico, Rousseau is interested in the conjunction of language, at its source in human experience, with passion. And if we compare Rousseau's pedagogical programs in *Emile* with Vico's, the resemblances are more striking still, since in both men there is a subtle interplay of traditional authority with a sort of humanistic quasi freedom. The purpose of education, says Rousseau, is to produce men ("en sortant de mes mains . . . il sera premièrement homme"*[22]); what is crucial is to adapt educational schemes to men, and not vice versa ("appropriez l'education de l'homme à l'homme, et non pas à ce qui n'est point lui"[23]). The principle of all human action, Rousseau continues, is the will of a free man,[24] which is not to say, however, that philosphers know what that means.[25] Rather, we must remember the animistic philosophy of primitive men—here Rousseau's image exactly resembles Vico's *gigante*—and that although man begins to think with difficulty, once he begins he never stops.[26] As for language, it is best that the child be founded in only one, so that copiousness of linguistic knowledge be something he learns as he matures.[27]

All these notions, so similar to Vico's, are rooted in Rousseau's

*"when he leaves my care . . . he will be first of all a man"

experiences and personality as a man in the world of men: "J'éxiste, et j'ai des sens par lesquels je suis affectés. Voilà la première vérité qui me frappe et à laquelle je suis forcé d'acquiescer."*[28]   Yet immediately after making such an affirmation Rousseau, unlike Vico, expresses doubt whether his sense of his own existence is anything more than mere sensation. For this doubt is what it comes to in Rousseau, whereas for Vico, education, or self-education, *brings out* mind from the body, thus assuring mind of a real existence. Not that mind is independent of sensations; rather, mind for Vico, even while it is derived from the immediacy of sense experience, can enjoy a continuity, a coherence, a style of its own. It is precisely this duration of mind in the world, after the beginning in animistic sensation, that underlies Vico's *method* in *The New Science*. On the other hand, Rousseau's discourse deliberately refrains from taking *that* particular step in that certain direction.

Both mid-eighteenth-century writers, however, appeal in an enormously important, urgent manner away from traditional learning and toward personally learned certainties. If Vico is the quasi-medieval scholar in his recondite learning, and Rousseau seems the relentless amateur, what is true of both men is the earned authority of each as a writer whose experience is instructive as well as exemplary for having done things *on his own.* In both men, method is self-taught and, more important, self-teaching. Together they symbolize the great shift in knowledge away from dynastic continuity and toward that of radical discontinuity, toward that mode in which the beginning of intellectual work and writing cannot be detached either from thought about or the actual activity of beginning.[29] Moreover—and this is, I think, especially true of Vico—the "scientific" or methodological innovation of each derives from urging upon his readers something more like a constant experience of self-teaching than a schematic para-Cartesian method. Both men gain in importance for what their discourses silently make possible in later writers. Vico's I believe to be the more instructive case for what it means now to begin a course of reflective study, especially since his appeal as a writer is especially relevant to readers for whom (as for me) the beginning is principally an activity of reconstruction, repetition, restoration, redeployment.

In everything I have so far said, whether about Vico or about

---

* "I exist, and I have sensuous faculties by which I am affected. That is the first truth that strikes me, and to which I must submit."

Vico and Rousseau, a sense of loss is implicit. That is, Vico's *The New Science* smacks of the newness of aftermath rather than the newness of Edenic immediacy. While Vico never says that he is trying by means of scholarship to resupply the world with what it has lost as a result of either of those two great diminishments, the Fall or the Flood, the first, far more obscurely than the second, haunts all his pages. His laborious commentary on the allegorical frontispiece to *The New Science* includes this glossing passage on the funerary urn that stands at picture center:

> The second human institution is burial. (Indeed *humanitas* in Latin comes first and properly from *humando*, burying.) This institution is symbolized by a cinerary urn . . . . The urn indicates also the origin among the gentiles of the division of the fields to which is to be traced the distinction of cities and peoples and finally nations. (par. 12)

The first institution is matrimony, but it ought not to be lost on the reader that it is burial that for Vico gives rise to history, not mere conjugation. The "giants" who begin human history divide the earth into intelligible physical, intellectual, and moral units; their name (giants) is "a Greek word meaning 'sons of the earth,' i.e., descendants of those who have been buried" (par. 13). They bury their ancestors because, unlike beasts, they maintain long residence in a place, which to Vico signifies fear of the divine and a desire to hide. The giants cannot live surrounded by putrefying corpses, so in burying them they undertake, for the first time in human history, an intentional order by which the dead and the living are related to one another.

> Hence they considered themselves noble, justly ascribing their nobility in that first state of human institutions to their having been humanly engendered in the fear of the divinity. From this manner of human engendering and not fom anything else, what is called human generation took its name. (par. 13)

We must remember, too, that by *generation* Vico means "parturition" as well as the act of bringing forth (*educere/educare*) bodies of human, as opposed to gigantic, size. Adam, "the prince of all mankind," was of "proper size" because God made him so; human beings, gentile descendants of the giants, are reduced by *their own effort* to proper size, by the intentional beginning act of will to have a history and a continuity or genealogy. This can only come about when the masses of dead bodies—Vico's metaphor for the undifferentiated, polymorphously perverse desire for that unlimited presence which is ahistoric existence—are buried, and thereby ordered into intelligible sequence. Once they have disappeared, language becomes possible. Because the dead are imagined as having immortal souls extending, as it were, from the past into the present, words then link man with things fantastically (that is, by a sort of fictional process).

> For that first language, spoken by the theological poets, was not a language in accord with the nature of the things it dealt with (as must have been the sacred language invented by Adam, to whom God granted divine onomathesia, the giving of names according to the nature of each), but was a fantastic speech making use of physical substances endowed with life and most of them imagined to be divine. (par. 401)

In time, language losses its fantastic quality, just as, analogously, men shrink from giant to human size. Vico is of course describing shifts in perception by which the senses stop seeing things as divinely original in order to begin seeing them as humanly regular. From being fabulously extraordinary, men and words become ordinary because they become human, continuous, intelligible; yet such a shift is possible only because man effects it, because he *begins* to effect it. In time, fantastic myths give way to bloodless abstractions. Vico hints even that Adam and Noah are apprehensible by man only as two versions of an abstract concept called "the beginning." Yet it is *The New Science* in whose generous discursive and textual space the loss of vivacity and immediacy accompanying the shift from divine originality to human beginning is given acknowledgment. This is an achievement I have kept in mind as I have been writing about beginnings.

V

A major thesis of this book is that beginning is a consciously intentional, productive activity, and that, moreover, it is activity whose circumstances include a sense of loss. Furthermore, as Vico's *New Science* demonstrates, the activity of beginning follows a sort of historical dialectic that changes its character and meaning during the processes of writing and intellectual production. Thus beginning has influences upon what follows from it: in the paradoxical manner, then, according to which beginnings as events are not necessarily confined to the beginning, we realize that a major shift in perspective and knowledge has taken place. The state of mind that is concerned with origins is, I have said, theological. By contrast, and this is the shift, beginnings are eminently secular, or gentile, continuing activities. Another difference must be noted briefly here, since in my discussions of Freud and of modern texts I have already examined one aspect of this difference in detail: a beginning intends meaning, but the continuities and methods developing from it are generally *orders of dispersion,* of *adjacency,* and of *complementarity.* A different way of putting this is to say that whereas an origin *centrally* dominates what derives from it, the beginning (especially the modern beginning), encourages nonlinear development, a logic giving rise to the sort of multileveled coherence of dispersion we find in Freud's text, in the texts of modern writers, or in Foucault's archeological investigations.

To lay this difference at Vico's feet is, if not an exaggeration, then a way of recognizing how *The New Science* prophetically suggests terms for comprehending a very modern polemic. When Vico said that *human* comes from the root *to bury,* he might not have realized that his humanistic philosophy contained in it the elements of its own negation. *To bury,* in Vico's sense, is to engender difference; and to engender difference, as Derrida has argued, is to *defer* presence, to temporize, to introduce absence. As we saw, Vico connects human history with language, the former having been made possible by the latter. What Vico only hints at, however, is that language effectively displaces human presence, just as history is engendered only by the burial (removal, displacement) of immediacy. This act of deferring can be understood as part of Vico's continuing attack upon Descartes, upon the centrality of the *cogito,* and upon geometric method. When Vico speaks of a mental language common to all nations, he is, therefore, asserting the verbal community binding men together at the expense of their immediate existential presence to one another. Such common language—which in modern writing has appeared as Freud's unconscious, as Orwell's newspeak, as Lévi-Strauss's savage mind, as Foucault's *épistémè,* as Fanon's doctrine of imperialism—defers the human center or *cogito* in the (sometimes tyrannical) interest of universal, systematic relationships. Participation in these relationships is scarcely voluntary, only intermittently perceptible as participation in any egaliterian sense, and hardly amenable to human scrutiny.

Humanism thus engenders its own opposite. I cannot here discuss the implications of this, except methodologically, and only in a limited way at that. In the United States and France during the past decade there has been going on a unique, fairly widespread, often intensely militant analysis of the situation in the humanities. The French quarrel between an increasingly inaudible academic establishment, on one side, and the New Criticism—in literature, sociology, anthropology, psychiatry, epistemology, and ontology—on the other, has centered on the human content or subject of these humanistic disciplines. I simplify a very complex debate (to which I have alluded in detail in chapter 5) if I say that the general line of French New Criticism has been entirely to doubt and subsequently nullify the constitutive, authorizing powers of the human subject in the so-called human sciences. Instead of maintaining an unexamined core of "humanism" as an original validating center of the humanities (the "old critical" position, generally speaking), such writers as Barthes, Foucault, Derrida, and Lacan have contested that view with intricate and proliferating rules that account for human reality without recourse to an originating, privileged human subject: this, of course, is one side of Vico's "humanistic" science. These writers have sought to show that literature, psychology, philosophy, and language are too independent of direct and constant human intervention to be reduced to the traditional creeds of humanism for explanation or understanding—that is, that these disciplines have acquired rule-governed lives of their own that include man while never being subordinate to or dominated by him, nor, moreover, accessible to him by retrospection. Man is occasionally *a* measure of things, but by no means is he *the* measure. There are systems, distributions, and structures that by virtue of sheer variety and number supersede the power of a dominating, permanent human center to activate them; a whole new array of disciplines, concepts, and orientations have appeared more adequate than the individual *cogito,* and these have been contained by difficult technical disciplines that proceed internally by discontinuous steps, not humanistic beliefs. Unlike the futurists or the surrealists (despite the latter's asseverations to the contrary), the New Critics in their work have claimed—correctly, I think—to occupy a political position on the left.

In the United States the battle between the old and the new, or the establishment and the countercultures, if it has had a focus at all, has largely been concerned with issues connected to the politics of culture. The famous question of "relevance," as much as Lionel Trilling's celebrated book *Beyond Culture,* or the truly widely (and qualitatively) varied efforts of such radical or revisionist writers as Theodore Roszak, Noam Chomsky, Gabriel

Kolko, Louis Kampf, Herbert Marcuse, Susan Sontag, and many others, or the enterprising and speculative criticism of men like Richard Poirier, Angus Fletcher, Frederick Crews, and Harold Bloom—all these represent difficulties for the traditionally bred humanist who attempts to employ "school" knowledge to account for modern phenomena that either bypass or overwhelm that knowledge. These phenomena are of three sorts: sociopolitical behavior not explainable or understandable behavioristically; artistic activity that conforms to canons other than those of practicable creativity, construction, or profit; and instances of an intellectual potential (conscious or unconscious) whose experience stubbornly resists the habitual categories of explanation based on the stability of history and *cogito*. What was the general culture to do: retrace its steps to traditional ideas, recoil in anger and bewilderment, or meet the challenge with knowledge constructed on new bases?

Of course, in the United States the Vietnam War and the strong opposition to it provided an urgent setting for debate and drew it forth. But a general difference between the American and French polemics, in my opinion, is that, so far as the human sciences are concerned, in France there have been sustained efforts made to theorize and systematize the issues around which debate has centered; whereas in the United States this has been far less true (except, I think, in linguistics, owing largely to Chomsky's extraordinary labors), and for two reasons. The first is the propensity, perhaps a national-cultural one, to avoid theory as a subject pertaining to the study of humanism in general and of literature in particular. Concerning the one influential (and Canadian) exception—Northrop Frye's theory of literature and criticism—I shall have something to say in a moment. Secondly, with a few notable exceptions, parties to the debate in criticism seem to have confined their work mainly to celebration or complaint, and much less to audacious speculation.

The net effect, and to an extent also the cause, of this debate in France and the United States has been to discourage "academic" or "scholarly" study. Each has come to seem a pedantic exercise, and most American scholars probably agree that even the idea evoked by scholarship lacks dignity. Trilling's recent Jefferson Lecture puts the blame for these symptoms globally upon a denigration of mind, an impoverishment that increases uncertainty about intellectual values and diminishes mind's authority.[30] Yet the very fact that since the Second World War in France, for example, there has been going on what in my opinion is an astonishing and fascinating production of thought attests to a continued belief in mind, albeit a radically altered view of scholarship. As Paul de Man once wrote, the American view of modernism has always stressed the dark, confused side of its nihilism[31] —neglecting that aspect of Nietzsche's nihilism, for instance, which was a revitalized sense of rational learning and a radically *constitutive* sense of the human sciences. I am trying here to insist on the *surface espousal* of modernist nihilism in America,[32] and trying also to insist that if the work of Sartre, Lévi-Strauss, Foucault, Robbe-Grillet and others has any value or originality, it is in having harnessed the *methodological* vitality of modernism over and beyond its not especially novel discoveries of an all-enveloping darkness.

A principal aspect of methodology so comprehended is, as I said above, rejection of the human subject as grounding center for human knowledge. Derrida, Foucault, and Deleuze have gone further than the rejection. Epistemologically they have spoken of contemporary knowledge (*savoir*) as decentered; Deleuze's formulation is that knowledge, insofar as it is intelligible, is apprehensible in terms of *nomadic centers,* provisional structures that are never permanent, always straying from one set of information to another.[33] When this position is compared with that of Frye's *Anatomy of Criticism,* the difference between them is seen to be dramatic. *Anatomy of Criticism,* after all, is a major piece of intelligence and systematization; it has played the dominant part, and deservedly so, in giving critical discourse in English today an important share of coherence. Nevertheless, Frye's monumental edifice of historical, ethical, archetypal, and rhetorical criticism, with its corresponding modes, symbols, myths, and genres, is premised upon structural principles for which Frye's analogies are tonal music and Platonic Christianity. The former gives him a well-tempered circle within which to enclose all literary discourse, the latter a *logos* by which to center all literary experience. I do not intend this observation as an index of Frye's limitations, because in my quasi-journalistic account of his theory I have perhaps inadvertently failed sufficiently to analyze the openness of his aim[34] and the prodigious élan with which his work tries to reforge "the broken link between creation and knowledge, art and science, myth and concept."[35] What I wish to indicate is the need in Frye's theory for a center—not always a stated one perhaps, but

376

one nevertheless assumed to be present and to perform a centering and originating function for critical discourse.

It is precisely Frye's view—that "verbal languages" have "a centripetal character"[36]—that the three French philosophers mentioned above firmly dispute. Curiously Lévi-Strauss, whose analyses are of preliterate cultures and who has often been indiscriminately lumped together with those three, takes a view in the "Overture" to his *Mythologies* not wholly unlike Frye's—that myths have (like music) a *center* which is not stated, but which is like the tonal system embodied in disparate expressions.[37] Frye and Lévi-Strauss both argue that meaning is distributed in an orderly way throughout the total system by an original center or *logos;* Deleuze's position is that the system delivers as much nonmeaning (*non-sens*) because meaning is produced, never originated or grounded in something prior to it, and because meaning *begins* at the zero point at which *nonmeaning* can be distinguished from *no meaning* as derived from a fecundating Origin or Center, and because meaning is a "machine" producing local instances of sense. It is worth quoting Deleuze a little on this point:

> It is therefore pleasant that good news resound today: meaning is never principle or origin, it is always something produced. It is not something to be discovered, restored, or re-employed, it is to be produced by new mechanisms. It belongs neither to any heighth nor to any depth; it is an effect of the surface, inseparable from the surface as its proper dimensions. Not that meaning lacks depth, or heighth, but rather that heighth and depth lack surface and lack meaning (or if not that, then they have meaning only as an "effect" presupposing meaning). We no longer ask if the "original meaning" of religion exists in a God betrayed by human norms, nor do we ask if man contains that meaning, lost now because he has alienated himself from God's image.[38]

For each appeal to the absolute, profound, or transcendent Origin, Deleuze—and this is a methodological principle I support— would oppose in answer an instance of surface, which is the place at which meaning begins. Freud and Nietzsche represent this answer of his at its most fierce. Yet interestingly, both Frye and Deleuze view meaning—whether at the level of production (for Deleuze) or at the level of embodiment or analogy (for Frye)—as a form of repetition. Satire, according to Frye, repeats the mythos of winter, romance (in each and every example of it) that of summer. According to Deleuze, who adapts Nietzsche's Eternal Recurrence to his philosophy, repetition signifies the absence of an assignable origin: what is repeated, therefore, is not the One but the many, not the same but the different, not the necessary but the aleatory.[39] Frye's theory of repetition restrains the system, cordons off its possibilities at the limits of resemblance to an archetypal set. Deleuze's theory, he has said recently, multiplies meaning because it is articulated as an account of production, not of a priori validation based on resemblance.

I do not think Foucault and Deleuze are unjustified in seeing their philosophy of decenterment as revolutionary, at least in its reliance upon an intellectual who views his role within his discipline and its institutional supports as an adversary one. "Le rôle de l'intellectuel," says Foucault,

n'est plus de ce placer "un peu en avant ou un peu à côté" pour dire la verité muette de tous; c'est plutôt de lutter contre les formes de pouvoir là où il en est à la fois l'objet et l' instrument: dans l'ordre du "savoir," de la "verité," de la "conscience," du discours."*[40]

The intellectual makes it his task to controvert the dynastic role thrust upon him by history or habit. He does not see himself as subordinate even to concepts such as "truth" or "knowledge" insofar as those *descend* (figuratively or literally) from on high or *ascend* from the Origin to the surface. True theory, says Deleuze, does not totalize, it multiplies.[41] Instead of reducing phenomena to corresponding ideas, theory releases phenomena and experience from the limitations of having happened. Theory does not contain, envelop, or aggrandize experience and knowledge, and neither does it hand them on in the form of processed truth. Theory assumes the evident irregularity and discontinuity of knowledge— and hence its lack of a single central *logos*—but goes on to elucidate or to produce the order of dispersion in which knowledge takes place.

Here Foucault and Deleuze rejoin the adversary epistemological current found in Vico, in Marx and Engels, in Lukacs, in Fanon, and also in the radical political writings of Chomsky, Kolko, Bertrand Russell, William A. Williams, and others. Writing is the act of taking hold of language (*prendre la parole*) in order to do something, not merely in order to repeat an idea verbatim. Foucault again:

Si désigner les foyers, les dénoncer, en parler publiquement, c'est une

---

*"The intellectual's role is no longer to place himself "a little to the side or a little ahead" in order to express everyone's silent truth; it is rather to fight against the forms of power wherever that role is an object and an instrument: in the order of 'knowledge,' of 'truth,' of 'consciousness,' of 'discourse.' "

lutte, ce n'est pas parce que personne n'en avait encore conscience, mais c'est parce que prendre la parole à ce sujet, forcer le réseau de l'information institutionelle, nommer, dire qui a fait, quoi, désigner la cible, c'est un premier retournement du pouvoir, c'est un premier pas pour d'autres luttes contre le pouvoir. . . . Le discours de lutte ne s'oppose pas à l'inconscient: il s'oppose au secret.* [42]

An active, not to say aggressive, sense of writing underpins this passage: for *prendre la parole* usually means "to begin to speak"—to take the floor, to occupy the foreground. To make explicit what is usually allowed to remain implicit; to state that which, because of professional consensus, is ordinarily not stated or questioned; to begin again rather than to take up writing dutifully at a designated point and in a way ordained by tradition; above all, to write in and as an act of discovery rather than out of respectful obedience to established "truth"—these add up to the production of knowledge, they summarize the method of beginning about which this book turns.

From all of the French critics I have mentioned, and from the Americans, too, one receives a vivid picture of the institutions of knowledge against which contemporary scholarship, if it is to be scholarship in the Vichian sense, must take action. Among these institutions—best analyzed by Foucault in *L'Ordre du discours* and by Chomsky in his "Objectivity and Liberal Scholarship"—is specialization, an ideological professionalism, and a hierarchical system of values that places the reinforcement of traditional explanations at the top (by granting rewards and prestige) and keeps beginning speculations that deal heedlessly with the artificial barriers between "original" and "critical" works at the very bottom. These institutions are characterized by Foucault and Chomsky (correctly, I think) as representing power. Thus, according to Chomsky, "one might anticipate that as power becomes more accessible the inequities of the society will recede from vision, the status quo will seem less flawed, and the preservation of order will become a matter of transcendant importance."[43] In the study of literature, not only has a thoroughly pernicious and unexamined distinction been perpetuated between the primacy of "creative" writing and secondary

---

*"if designating the thresholds [of power], denouncing them, speaking of them publicly, is a struggle, it is not because no one has been aware of this, but rather because taking hold of language [*prendre la parole*] about this subject, challenging the network of institutional information, naming, saying who has done what, designating the target—all these make up a first turning back of power, a first step made for other struggles against power . . . The discourse of struggle does not oppose what is unconscious: it opposes what is secret."

writing (so that the novel, for example, is thought of as the grandest form, because the most enormously present and eternal, instead of as the most circumstantial of all genres), but also there has been maintained an almost Platonic view of a text or of an author, a view that militates totally against the realities of producing a text. Moreover, what Conor Cruise O'Brien (quoted by Chomsky) characterizes as counterrevolutionary subordination also applies to that notion of the study of literature which insists upon "art" as standing apart from the conditions of its appearance and as well from tendencies around it of which it is a part.

Beginnings, therefore, are for me opposed to originalities, or to those ideal Presences whose ideal originality Yeats called "self-born mockers of man's enterprise." A beginning is what I think scholarship ought to see itself as, for in that light scholarship or criticism revitalizes itself. Yet it would be rank folly to understand this kind of scholarship as an immediate, direct call to arms, for such impulsiveness as that is often the clearest proof of "the long tradition of naiveté and self righteousness that disfigures our intellectual history."[44] Rather, a beginning methodologically unites a practical need with a theory, an intention with a method. For the scholar or researcher, a beginning develops when the conditions of his reality become equal to the generosity of his, of everyman's, intellectual potential. To call this a *radical* beginning is to risk repeating a hackneyed expression. Yet a root is always one among many, and I believe the beginning radically to be a method or intention among many, never *the* radical method or intention. Thus beginnings for the critic restructure and animate knowledge, not as already-achieved result, but "as something to be done, as a task and as a search." Such radicalism—to continue the quotation from Pierre Thevenaz—"aims at fusing together the moral will and the grasping of evidence."[45]

To have reached such a propaedeutic conclusion in a book about beginnings is perhaps too neat a trick. One (apologetic) way of allowing it to stand is to add that "beginning" is an eminently renewable subject. In the course of studying for and writing this book, I have opened, I think, possibilities for myself (and hopefully for others) of further problematics to be explored. Some of them are: the question of language as an object of speculation, as an object occupying for the writer a privileged first place; the formal and psychological question of the inter-dependence of literary and sociological approaches in dealing with how English, for example, is at once a national and a world language (for some writers a first and for others a second language); the question of comparative literature itself, in terms of fields of dispersion among themes, motifs, and genres, in which beginning is an absolutely crucial step; the question of the cultural domination of one intellectual or national domain over another (one culture is more "developed" than—having begun earlier and "arrived" before—another); and the questions of liberty, or freedom, or originality as they obtain in complex social and intellectual orders of repetition. These are studies to which I hope our moral will shall be equal—if in part *this* beginning has fulfilled its purpose.

NOTES

CHAPTER ONE

1. Leo Spitzer, *Linguistics and Literary History: Essays in Stylistics* (Princeton: Princeton University Press, 1948), pp. 4-5.

2. Ibid., p. 3.

3. Erwin Panofsky, *Meaning in the Visual Arts: Papers in and on Art History* (New York: Doubleday Anchor, 1955), pp. 321-46.

4. W. J. Bate, *The Burden of the Past and the English Poet* (Cambridge: Harvard University Press, 1970) and Harold Bloom, *The Anxiety of Influence: A Theory of Poetry* (New York: Oxford University Press, 1973).

5. Roland Barthes, *Critique et verité* (Paris: Editions du Seuil, 1966), p. 76. The point is made many times by Barthes, notably in his *Essais critiques* (1964), *Critical Essays,* trans. Richard Howard (Evanston, Ill.: Northwestern University Press, 1972). For a good recent analysis of Bachelard's work on the de-forming powers of the imagination, see Edward K. Kaplan, "Gaston Bachelard's Philosophy of Imagination: An Introduction," *Philosophy and Phenomenological Research* 33, no. 2 (September 1972): 1-24.

6. This image is George Steiner's. He uses it to describe an influential aspect of modern literature in his *Extraterritorial: Papers on Literature and the Language Revolution* (New York: Atheneum, 1971).

7. Michel Foucault, *The Archeology of Knowledge and the Discourse on Language,* trans. A. M. Sheridan Smith (New York: Pantheon, 1972), pp. 3-6.

8. The relevant documents of the controversy raised by Nietzsche's work—blasts and counterblasts—are contained in Karlfried Gründer, *Der Streit um Nietzsches "Geburt der Tragödie": Die Schriften von E. Rohde, R. Wagner, und U. v. Wilamovitz-Moellendorf* (Hildesheim: G. Olms, 1969).

9. Stephane Mallarmé, *Oeuvres complètes,* ed. Henri Mondor and G. Jean-Aubry (Paris: Gallimard, 1945), p. 455.

10. Georg Lukacs, *The Theory of the Novel,* trans. Anna Bostock (London: Merlin Press, 1971), pp. 41ff.

11. Giambattista Vico, *The New Science,* trans. Thomas Goddard Bergin and Max Harold Fisch (Ithaca, N.Y.: Cornell University Press, 1948), p. 69. Here as elsewhere in this book, I have constantly used Fausto Nicolini's edition of Vico's work, *Opere* (Milan: Riccardo Ricciardi, 1953). Vico uses the word *gentile* to distinguish human from divine and sacred history. For an anti-Platonic univocal thesis on contemporary *gentile* history, see Gilles Deleuze, *Différence et répétition* (Paris: Presses Universitaires de France, 1968), p. 53 *et passim.*

12. See Edward W. Said, "On Originality," in *Uses of Literature,* ed. Monroe Engel, Harvard English Studies No. 4 (Cambridge: Harvard University Press, 1973), pp. 49-65.

13. Michel Foucault, "Qu'est-ce qu'un auteur?" *Bulletin de la societé francaise de philosophie,* 63rd year, no. 3 (July-September 1969); 75-95.

14. Stuart Hampshire, "Commitment and Imagination," in *The Morality of Scholarship,* ed. Max Black (Ithaca, N.Y.: Cornell University Press, 1962), p. 46.

15. Paul de Man, *Blindness and Insight: Essays in the Rhetoric of Contemporary Criticism* (New York: Oxford University Press, 1971), p. 106.

Notes

16. Paul Valéry, "Letter about Mallarmé," in *Leonardo, Poe, Mallarmé,* trans. Malcolm Cowley and James R. Lawler (Princeton: Princeton University Press, 1972), p. 241.

17. Roland Barthes, "Par où commencer?" in *Le Degré zero de l'écriture suivi de nouveaux essais critiques* (Paris: Editions du Seuil, 1972), p. 146.

18. Thomas S. Kuhn, *The Structure of Scientific Revolutions,* 2nd ed. (Chicago: University of Chicago Press, 1970), p. 10 *et passim.*

19. Maurice Merleau-Ponty, *The Visible and the Invisible,* trans. Alphonso Lingis (Evanston, Ill.: Northwestern University Press, 1968), p. 155.

20. Ibid., p. 153.

21. Rainer Maria Rilke, *Rodin,* trans. Jessie Lamont and Hans Trausil (New York: Fine Editions Press, 1945), p. 11.

22. The complete title of Kenner's book is *Flaubert, Joyce, and Beckett: The Stoic Comedians* (Boston: Beacon Press, 1962).

23. Ernst Robert Curtius, *European Literature and the Latin Middle Ages,* trans. W. R. Trask (New York: Pantheon, 1953).

24. Bloom, *The Anxiety of Influence,* pp. 93-96.

25. Jonathan Swift, *A Tale of a Tub,* in *Prose Works,* ed. Herbert Davis (Oxford: Blackwell Press, 1939-64), 1:26.

26. Samuel Taylor Coleridge, "To William Wordsworth," in *The Complete Poetical Works,* ed. E. H. Coleridge (Oxford: Clarendon Press, 1912), 1:406.

27. Ibid., p. 408.

28. Bate, *The Burden of the Past,* p. 107 *et passim.*

29. Wilhelm Dilthey, "The Rise of Hermeneutics," trans. Frederic Jameson, *New Literary History* 3, no. 2 (Winter 1972): 232.

30. For a brilliant account of how an initiatory act of writing takes place, see Steven Marcus's description of Dickens's invention of Pickwick in "Language into Structure: Pickwick Revisited," *Daedalus,* 101 (Winter 1972); 183-202.

31. "Hopkins's Letters to His Brother," ed. A. Bischoff, *Times Literary Supplement,* December 8, 1972, p. 1511.

32. Jean-Paul Sartre, *Saint Genet: Comédien et martyr* (Paris: Gallimard, 1952), p. 396.

33. Roland Barthes, "Réponses," *Tel Quel* 47 (Autumn 1971): 104.

34. Foucault has systematically dealt with this problem. See his book *The Order of Things* (the English translation of *Les Mots et les choses*) (New York: Pantheon, 1970), pp. 355-87. See also Foucault's early description of the library displacing rhetoric; "Le Langage à l'infini," *Tel Quel* 15 (Autumn 1963): 44-53.

35. Barthes, "Réponses," pp. 105-6.

36. Joseph Conrad, *Lord Jim* (Garden City, N.Y.: Doubleday, Page, 1926), p. 33. See also Edward W. Said, "Conrad: The Presentation of Narrative," *Novel* 7, no. 2 (Winter 1972): 116-32.

CHAPTER TWO

1. Claude Lévi-Strauss, *The Savage Mind* (Chicago: University of Chicago Press, 1966), pp. 58, 252.

2. There is of course a vast literature on utopias. Four contemporary works in particular are relevant to the problem of utopias and beginnings: Ernst Bloch, *Das Prinzip Hoffnung,* 3 vols. (Berlin: Aufbau Verlag, 1953-1959); Robert C. Elliott, *The Shape of Utopia: Studies in a Literary Genre* (Chicago: University of Chicago Press, 1970); Harry Levin, *The Myth of the Golden Age in the Renaissance* (New York: Oxford University Press, 1969); and Frank E. Manuel, ed., *Utopias and Utopian Thought* (Boston: Houghton Mifflin, 1966).

3. Swift, *Gulliver's Travels* in *Prose Works,* 11: 179-80.

4. Swift, "The Conduct of the Allies," in *Prose Works,* 6: 64.

5. Swift, "A Proposal for Correcting the English Language," in *Prose Works,* 4:14, 15.

6. Most of volume 3 of Bloch's *Das Prinzip Hoffnung* is devoted to this theme.

7. One of the more striking, even polemical, characterizations of a beginning as different from passive (and divine) origins is given by Herder in his 1770 essay *Über den Ursprung der Sprache* (Berlin: Akademie Verlag, 1959), p. 60 *et passim.* That the romantics saw an active beginning as having a great deal to do with the rejection of an origin (usually a divine origin) is connected to the linguistic discoveries of the late eighteenth century and the empirical discrediting of the idea of a divine, original language. See Raymond Schwab, *La Renaissance orientale* (Paris: Payot, 1950). Also see Hegal's *Wissenschaft der Logik* (1812), book one especially.

8. *Rosa Luxemburg Speaks,* ed. Mary-Alice Waters (New York: Pathfinder Press, 1970), p. 395.

9. Georges Canguihelm has studied this problem—especially with regard to the "filiation" of concepts, the "birth" of an idea, a first "appearance"—in the history of science. See his *Le Normal et le pathologique* (Paris: Presses Universitaires de France, 1966) and *Etudes d'histoire et de philosophie des sciences* (Paris: J. Vrin, 1970). There is a useful discussion of Canguihelm's ideas on the subject (as well as discussion on Bachelard and Foucault) in Dominique Lecourt, *Pour une critique de l'épistémologie* (Paris: François Maspèro, 1972).

10. Erik H. Erikson, "The First Psychoanalyst," *Yale Review* 46 (Autumn 1956): 47.

11. Ibid., p. 62.

12. Ibid., p. 62.

13. Foucault, "Qu'est-ce qu'un auteur?" pp. 89-94.

14. Descartes, *Philosophical Works,* trans. Elizabeth S. Haldane and G. R. T. Ross (New York: Dover, 1931), 1:10.

15. Erikson, *Young Man Luther: A Study in Psychoanalysis and History* (New York: Norton, 1958), p. 36.

16. Johan Huizinga, "The Idea of History," trans. Rosalie Colie, in *The Varieties of History: From Voltaire to the Present,* ed. Fritz Stern (New York: Vintage Books, 1973), p. 290.

17. Erich Auerbach, (1952) "Philology and *Weltliteratur,*" trans. M. Said and E. W. Said, *Centennial Review* 13, no. 1 (Winter 1969): 8-9.

18. Ferdinand de Saussure, *Course in General Linguistics,* trans. Wade Baskin (New York: McGraw-Hill, 1966), pp. 7-9.

19. Ibid., p. 9.

20. Nietzsche, *Das Philosophenbuch: Theoretische Studien* (Paris: Aubier-Flammarion, 1969), p. 140.

21. Ibid., p. 46.

22. Ibid., pp. 180-182. The translation I have used of this passage is found in *The Portable Nietzsche,* ed. and trans. Walter Kaufmann (New York: Viking, 1954), pp. 46-47.

23. See, for example, *Das Philosophenbuch,* p. 50, paragraph 33.

24. For the most lucid discussion of the pronoun as shifter see Emile Benveniste, "The Nature of Pronouns," in *Problems in General Linguistics,* trans. Mary Elizabeth Meek (Coral Gables, Fla.: University of Miami Press, 1971), pp. 217-22. See also "Subjectivity in Language" in the same volume, pp. 223-30.

25. Bachelard, *L'Engagement rationaliste* (Paris: Presses Universitaires de France, 1972), p. 7.

26. Ibid., pp. 9, 11.

27. Karl Marx, *The Poverty of Philosophy* (New York: International Publishers, 1963), p. 150. See also Lukacs, *History and Class Consciousness: Studies in Marxist Dialectics,* trans. Rodney Livingstone (London: Merlin Press, 1971), pp. 48ff.

Notes

28. Marx, *The Poverty of Philosophy,* pp. 109 ff.

29. A recent study of romanticism, for example, is based on the formulation and expression of this need among the period's major figures; hence the major romantics' work can be read as a reworking of man's fall and redemption. See M. H. Abrams, *Natural Supernaturalism: Tradition and Revolution in Romantic Literature* (New York: Norton, 1971).

30. Nietzsche, *Das Philosophenbuch,* p. 112.

31. Lukacs, *History and Class Consciousness,* p. 178. Lukacs refers here to ascribed or imputed consciousness (*zugerechnet Bewusstsein*), which is uniquely a function of the proletariat as a class. I have borrowed the notion of ascription without limiting it as he does to the proletariat.

32. Nietzsche, *Das Philosophenbuch,* p. 112, paragraph 109.

33. Kenneth Burke, *The Rhetoric of Religion: Studies in Logology* (Boston: Beacon Press, 1961). In this extraordinary and far-too-little-known book, Burke shows working connections between natural and supernatural words, between logology and theology.

34. Nietzsche, *Beyond Good and Evil: Prelude to a Philosophy of the Future,* trans. Walter Kaufmann (New York: Vintage Books, 1966), p. 27.

35. Nietzsche, *Das Philosophenbuch,* p. 116, paragraph 118.

36. Nietzsche, *Beyond Good and Evil,* p. 27. For a recent attempt to sort out temporal functions in language, see Barthes's account of *temps chronique* and *temps de langage* in "To Write: An Intransitive Verb?" in *The Languages of Criticism and the Sciences of Man: The Structuralist Controversy,* ed. Richard Macksey and Eugenio Donato (Baltimore: Johns Hopkins University Press, 1970), pp. 136-37.

37. William Wordsworth, *The Prelude* in *Selected Poems and Prefaces,* ed. Jack Stillinger (Boston: Houghton Mifflin, 1965), p. 193.

38. John Milton, *Paradise Lost,* ed. Merritt Hughes (New York: Odyssey Press, 1962), p. 13.

39. Wordsworth, *The Prelude,* p. 206. See also the powerful insights to be found in Geoffrey Hartman, *Wordsworth's Poetry, 1787-1814* (New Haven: Yale University Press, 1964), pp. 33-55.

40. Wordsworth, *The Prelude,* p. 356.

41. Milton, *Paradise Lost,* p. 191.

42. Ibid., p. 301.

43. Frank Manuel, *The Eighteenth Century Confronts the Gods* (Cambridge: Harvard University Press, 1959); for Bate, see *The Burden of the Past and the English Poet.* Bate's major period of concern is the eighteenth century.

44. The psychological meaning of such an interrelation between words and experience in Rousseau is developed by Jean Starobinski in "Jean-Jacques Rousseau et le péril de la reflexion," *L'Oeil vivant* (Paris: Gallimard, 1961). See also Chapter 6 of the present work.

45. Coleridge, "On Method," in *The Friend,* ed. Barbara E. Rooke (Princeton: Princeton University Press, 1969), p. 1:451.

46. Wordsworth, *The Prelude,* p. 194.

47. Paul Valéry, *Leonardo, Poe, Mallarmé,* p. 13.

48. Ibid., p. 79.

49. Valéry, *Masters and Friends,* trans. Martin Turnell (Princeton: Princeton University Press, 1968), p. 31.

50. Husserl is preoccupied with this throughout his *Cartesian Meditations: An Introduction to Phenomenology,* trans. Dorion Cairns (The Hague: Martinus Nijhoff, 1960), principally pp. 7-26 and 151-57.

51. Husserl, *Phenomenology and the Crisis of Philosophy,* trans. Quentin Lauer (New York: Harper & Row, 1965), p. 146. See also *Cartesian Meditations,* p. 5.

386

52. Pierre Thevenaz, *"What is Phenomenology?" and Other Essays,* trans. James M. Edie (Chicago: Quadrangle Books, 1962), pp. 104, 107, 108.

53. Husserl, *Phenomenology and the Crisis of Philosophy,* p. 140.

54. Most of Valéry's writing on Descartes is a variation of one sort or another of this idea. See *Masters and Friends,* pp. 6-85.

55. Hans Vaihinger, *The Philosophy of As-If: A System of the Theoretical, Practical, and Religious Fictions of Mankind,* trans. C. K. Ogden (London: Routledge, 1968), pp. 38-39.

56. Frank Kermode, *The Sense of an Ending* (New York: Oxford University Press, 1967).

57. Foucault has discussed this state of affairs in *The Order of Things,* pp. 328-35. For a rather different, but highly influential, discussion of the same issues, see Jacques Derrida, *De la grammatologie* (Paris: Editions de Minuit, 1967), pp. 140 ff.

58. See Kuhn, *The Structure of Scientific Revolutions,* p. 10 *et passim.* For a discussion by Foucault of *épistème,* see "Réponse à une question," *Esprit,* no. 5 (May 1968): 850-74.

59. See Foucault's essay "Nietzsche, Marx, Freud," in *Nietzsche* (Paris: Editions de Minuit, 1967), 183-92.

60. Jean Starobinski, *Les Mots sous les mots: Les Anagrammes de Ferdinand de Saussure* (Paris: Gallimard, 1971).

61. Ibid., pp. 29, 70.

62. Ibid., pp. 64-65.

63. A principal source of these traditions with regard to language is Plato's dialogue *Cratylus,* which does not resolve the conflict.

64. Varro, *De Lingua Latina,* bk. 8, 21 ff. I have used the Loeb edition and translation by Roland G. Kent (Cambridge: Harvard University Press, 1938).

65. See John Haywood, *Arabic Lexicography* (Leyden: Brill, 1960).

66. In *The New Science* Vico's polemic is directed against the diffusionist theory of linguistic development. See my discussion of the "mental dictionary" in Chapter 6.

67. Keith Thomas, *Religion and the Decline of Magic: Studies in Popular Belief in Sixteenth and Seventeenth Century England* (London: Weidenfeld and Nicolson, 1971) and Francis A. Yates, *The Art of Memory* (Chicago: University of Chicago Press, 1966).

68. Karl Polanyi, *The Great Transformation* (Boston: Beacon Press, 1964), pp. 258, 249, 238.

69. Lévi-Strauss, *The Raw and the Cooked,* trans. John Weightman and Doreen Weightman (New York: Harper & Row, 1969), p. 10.

70. See Noam Chomsky's *Aspects of the Theory of Syntax* (Cambridge: M.I.T. Press, 1965); *Cartesian Linguistics* (New York: Harper & Row, 1966); *Language and Mind* (New York: Harcourt Brace and World, 1968); and *Problems of Freedom and Knowledge: The Russell Lectures* (New York: Pantheon, 1971).

71. Nietzsche, *The Complete Works,* ed. Oscar Levy (Edinburgh: T. N. Foulis, 1909-13), 3:155.

72. Ibid., pp. 164, 165, 167.

73. Ibid., p. 170.

74. Ibid., p. 169.

75. This is a cardinal point in Wilde's aesthetics; it is made emphatically in *Intentions.* See *The Artist as Critic: Critical Writings of Oscar Wilde,* ed. Richard Ellmann (New York: Random House, 1969).

76. The idea is Lukacs's originally (*zugerechnet Bewusstsein*) but Goldmann makes innovative use of it in *The Hidden God: A Study of Tragic Vision in the "Pensées" of Pascal and the Tragedies of Racine,* trans. Philip Thody (New York: Humanities Press, 1964). For an excellent analysis of Lukacs's notion, see Gareth Steadman Jones, "The Marxism of the Early Lukacs: An Evaluation," *New Left Review,* no. 70 (November-December 1971): 27-64.

Notes

77. See Foucault, "Nietzsche, Marx, Freud."

78. See Said "On Originality," for a discussion of this view; also Chapter 4 of the present work.

79. Freud, *Moses and Monotheism,* in *The Standard Edition of the Complete Psychological Works of Sigmund Freud* trans. and ed. James Strachey (London: Hogarth Press, 1964), 23: 43.

80. The other two are "Note and Digression" (1919) and "Leonardo and the Philosophers" (1929); both in *Leonardo, Poe, Mallarmé.*

81. Valéry, *Leonardo, Poe, Mallarmé,* p. 5.

82. Ibid., p. 7.

83. Ibid., p. 132.

84. Ibid., p. 13.

85. Ibid., p. 72.

86. Ibid., p. 41.

87. Ibid., p. 125.

88. Ibid., p. 41.

89. Ibid., p. 112.

90. Ibid., p. 32.

91. Ibid., pp. 38-39.

92. Ibid., p. 152.

93. Ibid., pp. 92-93.

94. Ibid., p. 95.

95. Ibid., pp. 51-52.

96. Mallarmé, Preface to "Un coup de dés," in *Oeuvres Complètes,* p. 455.

97. Valéry, *Leonardo, Poe, Mallarmé,* p. 106.

98. Freud, *Moses and Monotheism,* pp. 258-59.

99. Ibid., p. 260.

100. Ibid., p. 266.

101. Ibid., pp. 268-69.

102. Mallarmé, "Le démon de l'analogie" in *Oeuvres Complètes,* p. 273.

103. Ibid., p. 273.

104. See note 17 above for citation of the 1969 English translation. The original essay was published in 1952.

105. Auerbach, "Philology and *Weltliteratur,*" p. 16.

106. Spitzer, *Linguistics and Literary History,* p. 32.

107. Husserl, *Cartesian Meditations,* p. 5.

108. Mallarmé, *Les Mots anglais* in *Oeuvres Complètes,* p. 900.

109. Jorge Luis Borges, *Labyrinths: Selected Stories and Other Writings,* trans. Donald A. Yates and James E. Irby (New York: New Directions, 1964), pp. 199-201.

110. Valéry, *Idée Fixe,* trans. David Paul (Princeton: Princeton University Press, 1965), p. 57.

111. Merleau-Ponty, *La Prose du monde,* ed. Claude Lefort (Paris: Gallimard, 1969), p. 11.

112. R. P. Blackmur, "The Language of Silence: A Citation," *The Sewanee Review,* 63, no. 3 (Summer 1955): 382.

113. Valéry, *Idée Fixe,* p. 52.

114. The notion is developed in the first part of Sartre's *Critique de la raison dialectique,* vol. 1 (Paris: Gallimard, 1960), subtitled *Question de méthode.* This section prefigures Sartre's study of Flaubert, *L'Idiot de la famille.*

115. Rilke, *The Notebooks of Malte Laurids Brigge,* trans. M. D. Herder Norton (New York: Capricorn Books, 1958), p. 67.

116. Sartre, *Saint Genet,* p. 396.

117. Quoted in John Lynen, *The Design of the Present: Essays on Time and Form in American Literature* (New Haven: Yale University Press, 1969), p. 367. The remarks are from Lynen's fine study of Eliot in this book, and are taken from Eliot's extended work on F. H. Bradley and from Eliot's *Poetry and Drama.*

118. Harry Levin, *Refractions: Essays in Comparative Literature* (New York: Oxford University Press, 1966).

119. Blackmur, "The Language of Silence," p. 387.

120. Freud, "The Antithetical Meanings of Primal Words." in *The Standard Edition,* 11:158.

121. Benveniste, "Language and Human Experience," *Diogenes,* no. 51 (Fall 1965): 5.

122. Valéry, *Idée Fixe,* p. 29.

123. Malraux, *The Temptation of the West,* trans. Robert Hollander (New York: Vintage, 1961), p. 117.

124. Merleau-Ponty, *The Visible and the Invisible,* p. 125.

CHAPTER THREE

1. See Levin's discussion of this throughout his *Gates of Horn: A Study of Five French Realists* (New York: Oxford University Press, 1963). See also his essay "Literature as an Institution," *Accent* 6, no. 3 (Spring 1946); 159-68.

2. In Alain Robbe-Grillet, *For a New Novel: Essays on Fiction,* trans. Richard Howard (New York: Grove Press, 1966). Originally published as *Pour un nouveau roman* (1963).

3. Eric Partridge, *Origins: A Short Etymological Dictionary of Modern English* (New York: Macmillan, 1966), p. 32.

4. Sören Kierkegaard, *The Point of View for My Work as an Author,* trans. Walter Lowrie (London: Oxford University Press, 1939), p. 17.

5. Ibid., p. 40.

6. Ibid., p. 65.

7. Kierkegaard, *Fear and Trembling: A Dialectical Lyric,* trans. Walter Lowrie (Princeton: Princeton University Press, 1941), p. 6.

8. Wayne Booth, *The Rhetoric of Fiction* (Chicago: University of Chicago Press, 1961).

9. Gilles Deleuze, *Différence et répétition,* p. 14.

10. Kierkegaard, *Repetition: An Essay in Experimental Psychology* (Princeton: Princeton University Press, 1941), p. 6.

11. Kierkegaard, *The Concept of Irony: With Constant Reference to Socrates,* trans. Lee M. Capel (London: William Collins, 1966), p. 270.

12. Ibid., p. 276.

13. Mark Twain, *The Adventures of Huckleberry Finn* (Hartford: American Publishing Company, 1899), p. 15.

14. Marx, *Capital and Other Writings,* ed. Max Eastman (New York: Modern Library, 1932), pp. 183-84.

15. Vico, *The New Science,* p. 121.

16. Ibid., bk. 2, "Poetic Wisdom," pp. 109-297.

17. See Lukacs, *The Theory of the Novel,* pp. 120 ff.; also see Paul de Man, "The Rhetoric of Temporality," in *Interpretation: Theory and Practice,* ed. Charles Singleton (Baltimore: Johns Hopkins University Press, 1969), pp. 173-209.

18. See Lévi-Strauss, *The Savage Mind,* p. 17, for a description of Wemmick as *bricoleur.*

19. Dickens, *Great Expectations* (New York: Charles Scribner's Sons, 1902), p. 562.

20. Ibid., pp. 540-41.

Notes

21. All references to *Nostromo* (1904) are to the Modern Library edition (New York: Random House, 1951), which includes a superb introduction by Robert Penn Warren. Page numbers are indicated parenthetically following quotations.

22. Charles Gould's dedication to the rebirth and progress of the mine is a perverted and, I think, intentional analogy to the history of Christianity. Like Christianity, the mine exerts a power over its devotees that begins with the fabled resurrection of a dead enterprise, proceeds to inspire heretical struggles for control of its emerging force, and culminates with the establishment of an institutionalized faith (in silver). The perversion occurs from the beginning: whereas Christianity promises a free and quickened life, the mine requires the spiritual enslavement of its followers, for only as shackled fetishists can they be kept serviceable to the mine.

23. Douglas Hewitt, *Conrad: A Reassessment* (Cambridge, England: Bowes and Bowes, 1952), p. 50.

24. While it is difficult to date Conrad's note exactly, it is certain that he wrote one for *Nostromo* between 1919 and 1922, most probably toward the end of 1919.

25. Gerard Jean-Aubry, *Joseph Conrad: Life and Letters* (Garden City, N.Y.: Doubleday, 1927), 1:311.

26. Edward Garnett, *Letters from Joseph Conrad, 1895-1924* (Indianapolis: Bobbs-Merrill, 1928), p. 184.

27. Ibid., p. 187.

28. Conrad, *Lettres françaises,* ed. Gerard Jean-Aubry (Paris: Gallimard, 1930), p. 50.

29. Jean-Aubry, *Joseph Conrad,* 1:317.

30. Ibid., p. 321.

31. Conrad, *Lettres françaises,* p. 60.

32. This crisis (which had its origins in 1898) and its implications for Conrad's development are discussed in Edward W. Said, *Joseph Conrad and the Fiction of Autobiography* (Cambridge: Harvard University Press, 1966).

33. See Ibid., pp. 58-63.

34. Jean-Aubry, *Joseph Conrad,* 1:329.

35. *Joseph Conrad: Letters to William Blackwood and David S. Meldrum,* ed. William Blackburn (Durham, N. Car.: Duke University Press, 1958), p. 180.

36. Conrad, letter 5, "Letters to William Rothenstein, 1903-1921," unpublished manuscript letters, Houghton Library, Harvard University, Cambridge, Mass.

37. Conrad, *Lettres françaises,* p. 120.

38. The comparison is made in Jocelyn Baines, *Joseph Conrad: A Critical Biography* (London: Weidenfeld and Nicolson, 1959), p. 297.

39. In *Complete Works* (Garden City, N.Y.: Doubleday, 1925), 16:150.

40. John Galsworthy, *Castles in Spain* (London: Heinemann, 1928), p. 91.

41. Their relationship is discussed provocatively by Bernard Meyer, *Joseph Conrad: A Psychoanalytic Biography* (Princeton: Princeton University Press, 1967).

42. November 22, 1912, *Twenty Letters to Joseph Conrad,* ed. Gerard Jean-Aubry (London: First Edition Club, 1926).

43. July 20, 1894, *Letters of Joseph Conrad to Marguerite Poradowska, 1890-1920,* trans. and ed. John A. Gee and Paul J. Sturm (New Haven: Yale University Press, 1940), p. 72.

44. Garnett, *Letters,* p. 59.

45. July 17, 1895, Jean-Aubry, *Joseph Conrad,* 1:176.

46. March 23, 1896, *Letters,* p. 46.

47. Jean-Aubry, *Joseph Conrad,* 2:83-84; Ibid., p. 51.

48. August 26, 1901, Conrad, *Letters to Blackwood,* p. 133.

49. November 11, 1901, Jean-Aubry, *Joseph Conrad,* 1:301.

50. Ernest Hemingway, *Death in the Afternoon,* (London: Jonathan Cape, 1963), pp. 78-83.

51. Garnett, *Letters,* p. 153.

52. Jean-Aubry, *Joseph Conrad,* 2:14.

53. See Gustav Morf, *The Polish Heritage of Joseph Conrad* (London: Sampson Low, Marston, 1950).

54. *Lettres françaises,* p. 56.

55. See Said, *Conrad,* pp. 58-63.

56. In Conrad, *Heart of Darkness* in *Complete Works,* 16:50-51.

57. Jean-Aubry, *Joseph Conrad,* 1:216.

58. Henry James, *The Art of the Novel,* ed. R. P. Blackmur (New York: Scribner's, 1934), p. 84.

59. Thomas Hardy, *Jude the Obscure* (New York: Harper, 1899), p. 399.

60. For an interesting account of the structure of Hardy's poetry, see Samuel Hynes, *The Pattern of Hardy's Poetry* (Chapel Hill: University of North Carolina Press, 1961).

61. Hardy, *Collected Poems* (New York: Macmillan, 1928), p. 289.

62. See Florence Emily Hardy, *The Later Years of Thomas Hardy, 1892-1928* (New York: Macmillan, 1930), p. 48.

63. For Levin, see note 1 of this chapter; René Girard, *Mensonge romantique et verité romanesque* (Paris: Grasset, 1961) whose English version is *Deceit, Desire, and the Novel: Self and Other in Literary Structure,* trans. Yvonne Freccero (Baltimore: Johns Hopkins Press, 1969); and Lukacs, *The Theory of the Novel.*

64. See the discussion in Chapter 4 of the problem of a text and of a sacred text as antitype.

65. In Erich Auerbach, *Mimesis: The Representation of Reality in Western Literature,* trans. Willard Trask (Princeton: Princeton University Press, 1953) and E. R. Curtius, *European Literature and the Latin Middle Ages.*

66. Lukacs, *The Theory of the Novel,* pp. 112-31.

67. For an interesting analogy between narrative and the family, see Lionel Trilling, *Sincerity and Authenticity* (Cambridge: Harvard University Press, 1973), pp. 101-33.

68. Marx, "The Power of Money," in *Economic and Philosophical Manuscripts of 1844* (Moscow, 1961), p. 140. Also see Zola's essay "L'Argent dans la littérature," in *Le Roman expérimental,* ed. Maurice LeBlond (Paris: Bernouard, 1928).

69. Gustave Flaubert, *Madame Bovary,* ed. and trans. Paul de Man (New York: W. W. Norton, 1965), p. 140.

70. Ibid., p. 140.

71. Lukacs, *The Theory of the Novel,* pp. 125-26.

72. In Flaubert, *Oeuvres,* ed. A. Thibaudet and R. Dumesnil (Paris: Gallimard, 1951), 2: 449-53.

73. Ibid., p. 457.

74. Dostoievsky, *The Possessed,* trans. Constance Garnett (New York: Modern Library, 1936), p. 5.

75. Ibid., p. 719.

76. Ibid., p. 730.

77. James Joyce, *Ulysses* (New York: Modern Library, 1934), p. 8.

78. The two opposed views on repetition are to be found in Marx's *Eighteenth Brumaire of Louis Napoleon* (1852) and Kierkegaard's *Repetition* (1844).

79. Nietzsche, *Will to Power,* trans. Walter Kaufman and R. J. Hollingdale (New York: Vintage, 1968), pp. 298-99.

80. For a perceptive discussion of the relationship between history and fiction in Lawrence, see Albert Cook, *The Meaning of Fiction* (Detroit: Wayne State University Press, 1960), pp. 273-79.

81. In T. E. Lawrence, *Oriental Assembly,* ed. A. W. Lawrence (London: Williams and Norgate, 1939), pp. 142-43.

82. *The Letters of T. E. Lawrence,* ed. David Garnett (New York: Doubleday, Doran, 1938), p. 360.

83. Lawrence, *The Seven Pillars of Wisdom: A Triumph* (Garden City, N.Y.: Doubleday, Doran, 1935), p. 91.

Notes

84. Ibid., p. 78.

85. Ibid., p. 450.

86. Ibid., pp. 192-96.

87. Ibid., p. 551-52.

88. *Letters of T. E. Lawrence,* pp. 417, 300.

89. André Malraux, "Lawrence and the Demon of the Absolute," *Hudson Review* 8, no. 4 (Winter 1956); 527.

90. *Letters to T. E. Lawrence,* ed. A. W. Lawrence (London: Jonathan Cape, 1962), p. 59.

91. Nietzsche, *Beyond Good and Evil,* p. 161.

92. Ibid., pp. 161-62.

93. Ibid., p. 162.

94. In W. B. Yeats, *Collected Poems* (New York: Macmillan, 1951), p. 197.

95. In the discussion of Freud that follows I am indebted generally to Jacques Derrida's essay "Freud et la scène de l'écriture," in his *L'Ecriture et la différence* (Paris: Editions du Seuil, 1967), pp. 293-340.

96. Freud, *The Interpretation of Dreams,* in *The Standard Edition,* Vols. 3 and 4. Page numbers of quotations from this text appear parenthetically following quotations.

97. See Barthes, *Critical Essays,* pp. 171-83; and Kuhn, *The Structure of Scientific Revolutions,* pp. 136-43.

98. The formula is used by Freud again in 1925; see *The Standard Edition,* 20:45.

99. See Jacques Lacan, *Ecrits* (Paris: Editions du Seuil, 1967), and Foucault, *The Order of Things,* p. 374.

100. The whole of Deleuze's *Différence et répétition* is taken up with this problematic. See also Foucault, "Theatrum Philosophicum," *Critique* 282 (November 1970): 885-908.

101. Freud, *Moses and Monotheism,* p. 114.

102. See also *The Interpretation of Dreams,* pp. 349, 353.

103. Freud, "An Autobiographical Study," in *The Standard Edition,* 20:42.

104. Nietzsche, *On the Genealogy of Morals,* trans. Walter Kaufman and R. J. Hollingdale (New York: Vintage, 1969), pp. 77-78.

105. See Freud, *The Origins of Psychoanalysis: Letters to Wilhelm Fliess—Drafts and Notes, 1887-1902,* ed. Marie Bonaparte, Anna Freud, Ernst Kris; trans. Eric Mosbacher and James Strachey (New York: Basic Books, 1954), p. 297.

106. Freud, *Moses and Monotheism,* p. 114.

107. Freud, "Analysis Terminable and Interminable," in *The Standard Edition,* 23:216-53.

108. Foucault, "Qu'est ce-qu'un auteur?" pp. 89-94.

109. Freud, "The History of the Psycho-Analytic Movement," in *The Standard Edition,* 14:15.

110. See also my article on Lévi-Strauss—Edward W. Said, "The Totaliterianism of Mind," *Kenyon Review* 29, no. 2 (March 1967); 257-68—for a discussion on the omnipresence of order.

111. Thomas Mann, *Doctor Faustus: The Life of the German Composer, Adrian Leverkuhn as told by a Friend,* trans. H. T. Lowe-Porter (New York: Random House, Modern Library, 1966), p. 240.

112. Ibid., p. 242.

113. Ibid., pp. 244-45.

114. Ibid., p. 252.

115. Ibid., pp. 253-54.

116. Ibid., p. 181.

117. Ibid., p. 6.

118. Ibid., p. 9.

119. Ibid., p. 509.

CHAPTER FOUR

1. Jean Piaget, *Le Structuralisme* (Paris: Presses Universiatires de France, 1968), pp. 5-16.

2. Ibid., p. 10.

3. Ibid., pp. 121-23.

4. Lucien Goldmann, *Recherches dialectiques* (Paris: Gallimard, 1959), pp. 118-45; Jacques Derrida, *L'Ecriture et la différence* (Paris: Editions du Seuil, 1967), and idem, *De la grammatologie* (Paris: Editions de Minuit, 1967).

5. Samuel Taylor Coleridge, *The Friend,* 1: 476.

6. "The Law of Mind," in *Philosophical Writings of Peirce,* ed. Justus Buchler (New York: Dover, 1955), p. 340.

7. See Chapter 3, note 97, as well as the discussion in that chapter of textual conventions and mannerisms.

8. See Georges Poulet, *Etudes sur le temps humain* (Paris: Plon, 1950) as well as all of Poulet's works that have followed therefrom.

9. This is less true of Jean Rousset; see his *Forme et signification: Essais sur les structures de Corneille à Claudel* (Paris: Corti, 1964).

10. John Sandys, *A History of Classical Scholarship* (London: Oxford University Press,1908), 3 vols. See also Rudolf Pfeiffer, *History of Classical Scholarship From the Beginnings to the End of the Hellenistic Age* (Oxford: Clarendon Press, 1968), and Madeline V.-David, *Le Débat sur les écritures et l'hieroglyphe aux XVIIe et XVIIIe siècles et l'application de la notion de déchiffrement aux écritures mortes* (Paris: SEVPEN, 1965).

11. Giambattista Vico, *The New Science,* p. 414.

12. *The Encyclopedia of Islam,* new ed., s.v. "idjaza" (Leiden: Brill, and London: Luzac, 1971).

13. Franz Rosenthal, *The Technique and Approach of Muslim Scholarship* (Rome: Pontificum Institutum Biblicum, 1947), p. 2.

14. Ibid., p. 22.

15. Ibid., p. 49. The *Maqamat,* or Assemblies, are a series of fifty stories composed in a highly virtuosic rhymed prose by the Basran writer Muhammad al-Qasim al-Hariri (1054-1122). The *Maqamat* are traditionally considered second only to the Koran in epitomizing Arabic literary expression.

16. Bruce Metzger, *The Text of the New Testament,* 2nd ed. (New York: Oxford University Press, 1968), pp. 20-21. For an authoritative account of some Old Testament textual problems, see Umberto Cassuto, *La Questione della Genesi* (Florence: Felice le Monnier, 1934).

17. Barthes, *S/Z* (Paris: Editions du Seuil, 1970), p. 11.

18. Kuhn, *The Structure of Scientific Revolutions,* pp. 136-43.

19. Vico, *The New Science,* p. 73.

20. Ibid., p. 96.

21. Nietzsche, *The Use and Abuse of History,* trans. Adrian Collins (New York: Liberal Arts Press, 1957), pp. 69-70.

22. Ibid., p. 31.

23. Robert W. Funk, *Language, Hermeneutic, and Word of God: The Problem of Language in the New Testament and Contemporary Theology* (New York: Harper & Row, 1966), p. 11.

24. Dilthey, *Gesammelte Schriften* (Gottingen: Vandenhoeck and Ruprecht, 1913), 1:24-26.

25. See Hans-Georg Gadamer, *Warheit und Methode: Grundzuge einer Philosophischen Hermeneutik,* 2nd. ed. (Tubingen: Mohr, 1965), pp. 370-71.

26. A. E. Housman in *Selected Prose,* ed. John Carter (Cambridge: Cambridge University Press, 1962), p. 147.

27. Ibid., p. 136.

28. Ibid., p. 137.

29. Paul Maas, *Textual Criticism,* trans. Barbara Flower (Oxford: Oxford University Press, 1958), p. 2.

30. Ibid., p. 20.

31. James Thorpe, *Principles of Textual Criticism* (San Marino, Calif.: Huntington Library, 1972), p. 54.

32. Ibid., p. 50.

33. Morse Peckham, "Reflections on the Foundations of Modern Textual Editing," in *Proof: The Yearbook of American Bibliographical and Textual Studies,* ed. Joseph Katz (Columbia: University of South Carolina Press, 1971), 1:138. In this work, as in Thorpe's (see note 31), the textual critical theories of Fredson Bowers and W. W. Greg are discussed at some length.

34. Ibid., p. 137.

35. Ibid., p. 155. For an earlier version of some of Peckham's views, see William P. Shepard, "Recent Theories of Textual Criticism," *Modern Philology* 28 (November 1930): 129-41.

36. For a dissenting view on Romania as a privileged idea, see Peter Brooks, "Romania and the Widening Gyre," *PMLA,* 87 (January 1972); 7-11.

37. Freud, *Totem and Taboo, The Standard Edition,* 13:134.

38. Ibid., p. 135.

39. Samuel Butler, *The Authoress of the Odyssey* (London: Fifield, 1897), p. 5.

40. Freud, *Totem and Taboo,* p. 150.

41. Erich Auerbach, *Literary Language and Its Public in Late Latin Antiquity and in the Middle Ages,* trans. Ralph Manheim (New York: Pantheon, 1965), p. 45.

42. Ibid., p. 57.

43. Ibid., pp. 310, 312.

44. See Auerbach's own book on this subject, *Dante: Poet of the Secular World,* trans. Ralph Manheim (Chicago: University of Chicago Press, 1961).

45. A good account of the whole controversy can be found in J. Estlin Carpenter, *The Bible in the Nineteenth Century* (London: Longmans, Green, 1903). I would argue additionally that much of the Higher Criticism is related directly to the rise of the New Philology, one of the results of which was to challenge the divine authority of Hebrew, and hence of biblical texts in Hebrew. Nietzsche's brilliant characterization of Jesus in *The Will to Power,* p. 108, as "a zero in the beginning" deserves mention here.

46. W. H. Green, *The Higher Criticism of the Pentateuch* (New York: Scribner's, 1896), p. vi. See also Emil Reich, *The Failure of the "Higher Criticism" of the Bible* (London: James Nisbet, 1905).

47. Green, *The Higher Criticism,* pp. 2, 11.

48. Ibid., p. 71.

49. Ibid., p. 164.

50. Ibid., p. 167.

51. Ibid., pp. 168, 172.

52. Particularly also if we remember that Renan's *Vie de Jésus* is the first volume—the *beginning* volume, in the strictest sense—of his seven-volume work *Histoire des origines du christianisme.* That a beginning makes possible an origin will be evident as our discussion proceeds.

53. Renan, *Vie de Jésus,* 13th ed. (Paris: Calmann-Lévy, 1867 [originally published 1863]), pp. 80-81. It is this sort of attitude toward Jesus and, consequently, toward texts about him that will in some measure allow for the prodigious labor of Adolph von Harnack; see, for instance, his *Sources of the Apostolic Canons,* trans. Leonard A. Wheatley (London: Adam and Charles Black, 1895), or *Luke the Physician: The Author of the Third Gospel and the Acts of the Apostles,* trans. J. R. Wilkinson (New York: Putnam's, 1907).

54. Renan, *Vie de Jésus,* pp. 255-56.

55. Ibid., p. 311.

56. Ibid., p. liv.

57. Ibid., p. liii.

58. Ibid., p. liv.

59. Ibid., pp. lvi-lvii.

60. Ibid., pp. lxxxvii-lxxxxviii.

61. Ibid., p. lii.

62. Ibid., p. 309.

63. For an interesting, eccentric analogy, see Erik Erikson, *Young Man Luther,* p. 208.

64. Renan, *Vie de Jésus,* p. 456.

65. Ibid., p. 466.

66. Ibid.

67. Ibid., pp. 466-67.

68. Ibid., pp. 440-41.

69. Karl Jaspers, *Nietzsche: An Introduction to an Understanding of His Philosophical Activity,* trans. Charles F. Wallraff and Frederick J. Schmitz (Tucson: University of Arizona Press, 1965), p. 290.

70. Jean-Paul Sartre, *La Nausée* (Paris: Gallimard, 1938), p. 137.

71. Ibid., p. 248.

72. For a parallel idea, that of the *"texte-limite,"* see Barthes, *Critical Essays,* p. 77.

73. Piaget, "Le Structuralisme," *Cahiers Internationaux de Symbolisme* 18-19 (1969): 76.

74. G. E. M. Anscombe, "On the Form of Wittgenstein's Writing," in *La Philosophie contemporaine,* ed. Raymond Klibansky (Florence: Nuova Italia Editrice, 1969), 3:377.

75. Ibid., p. 373.

76. See Foucault's *Archeology of Knowledge,* p. 111.

77. Ibid.

78. Ibid., pp. 110-11.

79. Ibid., p. 234.

80. Discussed in Curtius, *European Literature,* pp. 230 ff.

81. See Bate, *The Burden of the Past,* pp. 95-134.

82. In Richard Poirier, *The Performing Self: Compositions and Decompositions in the Languages of Contemporary Life* (New York: Oxford University Press, 1971).

83. Maurice Blanchot, *L'Espace littéraire* (Paris: Gallimard, 1955), p. 306.

84. Foucault, *Archeology of Knowledge,* p. 216.

85. Walter Benjamin, *Schriften,* ed. Th. W. Adorno, Gretel Adorno, and Frederich Podszus (Frankfurt: Suhrkamp Verlag, 1955), 2:464-65.

86. *The Autobiography of William Butler Yeats* (New York: Macmillan, 1938), p. 165.

87. June 19, 1896, Garnett, *Letters from Conrad,* p. 59.

88. Conrad, *Heart of Darkness,* in *Complete Works* 16:92-93.

89. Garnett, *Letters from Conrad,* p. 135.

90. See Harry Levin, *"The Wasteland" from Ur to Echt* (New York: New Directions, 1972).

91. T. E. Lawrence, *The Mint: Notes Made in the R.A.F. Depot Between August and December, 1922, and at Cadet College in 1925* (Garden City, N.Y.: Doubleday, 1957), p. 83.

92. Merleau-Ponty, *The Primacy of Perception and Other Essays on Phenomenological Psychology,* ed. James M. Edie (Evanston, Ill.: Northwestern University Press, 1964), p. 25.

93. Baudelaire, "L'Heautontimorouménos," in *Oeuvres Complètes,* ed. Y.-G. le Dantec and Claude Pichois (Paris: Gallimard, 1968), p. 74.

94. Mallarmé, "Variations sur un sujet," in *Oeuvres Complètes,* p. 368.

Notes

95. Wilde, *The Artist as Critic,* pp. 290-91.

96. Baudelaire, annotations to *La Double vie* in *Oeuvres Complètes,* p. 664.

97. Proust, *Contre Sainte Beuve,* ed. Pierre Clarac and André Fevré (Paris: Gallimard, 1971), p. 273.

98. T. E. Lawrence, *The Seven Pillars of Wisdom,* p. 549.

99. Rilke, *Sonnets to Orpheus,* trans. M. D. Herder Norton (New York: Norton, 1942), pp. 60-61.

100. Merleau-Ponty, *Sense and Non-Sense* (Evanston, Ill.: Northwestern University Press, 1964), pp. 9-19.

101. Marcel Proust, *A la recherche du temps perdu* (Paris: Gallimard, 1954), 3:1041.

102. Mallarmé, "Variations sur un subjet," in *Oeuvres Complètes,* p. 368.

103. Ibid., p. 378.

104. Renato Poggioli, *The Theory of the Avant-Garde,* trans. Gerald Fitzgerald (Cambridge: Harvard University Press, 1968), p. 182.

105. Mallarmé, "Quant au livre," in *Oeuvres Complètes,* p. 378.

106. Proust, *A la recherche,* 3:1042.

107. Ibid., p. 1047.

108. See, for example, Leo Bersani, *Marcel Proust: The Fictions of Life and Art* (New York: Oxford University Press, 1965).

109. Ibid., p. 239.

110. Proust, *Contre Saint Beuve,* p. 224.

111. Ibid., p. 295.

112. Ibid., p. 309.

113. Proust, *A la recherche,* 1: 557.

114. Ibid., 2: 326-27.

115. Ibid., 3: 871.

116. Ibid., p. 870.

117. Ibid., p. 899.

118. Ibid.

119. Blanchot, *L'Espace littéraire,* p. 308.

120. Proust, *A la recherche,* 3: 629.

121. Ibid., 3: 682.

122. Ibid., 3: 848.

123. Ibid.

124. Ibid., 3: 874-75.

125. Ibid., 3: 886.

126. Ibid., 3: 887.

127. Ibid.

128. Ibid., 3: 889.

129. Ibid., 3: 904.

130. Benjamin, *Illuminations,* trans. Harry Zohn (New York: Harcourt, Brace, 1968), p. 212.

131. Poggioli, *Theory of the Avant-Garde,* p. 66.

132. "The Next Time," in *The Novels and Tales of Henry James* (New York: Scribner's, 1909), 15: 215.

133. Wilde, *The Artist as Critic,* p. 242.

134. Husserl, *Logical Investigations,* trans. J. N. Findlay (London: Routledge, 1970), 1: pp. 230 ff.

135. Blanchot, *L'Espace littéraire,* pp. 48-49.

136. Ibid., p. 72.

137. Ibid., p. 86.

138. Ibid., pp. 92-93.

139. Merleau-Ponty, *Resumé de cours: Collège de France, 1952-1960* (Paris: Gallimard, 1968), p. 23.

140. Joyce, *Letters,* ed. Stuart Gilbert (New York: Viking, 1957), pp. 128-29.

141. See R. P. Blackmur, *Anni Mirabiles, 1921-1925: Reason in the Madness of Letters* (Washington, D.C.: Library of Congress, 1956).

142. Blanchot, *L'Espace littéraire,* p. 97.

143. See, for example, Michael Riffaterre, *Essais de stylistique structurale* (Paris: Flammarion, 1971).

144. *The Journals and Papers of Gerard Manley Hopkins,* ed. Humphry House and Graham Storey (London: Oxford University Press, 1959), p. 289.

145. Benveniste, *Problems in General Linguistics,* pp. 206-7.

146. Ibid., p. 227.

147. Hopkins, *Journals,* pp. 149 ff.

148. Benveniste, *Problems,* p. 227.

149. Foucault, *Archeology of Knowledge,* pp. 126 ff.

150. T. S. Eliot, *Collected Poems, 1909-1962* (New York: Harcourt, Brace & World, 1963), pp. 85-86.

151. *The Poems of Gerard Manley Hopkins,* 4th ed., ed. W. H. Gardner and N. H. Mackenzie (London: Oxford University Press, 1967), p. 107.

152. Ibid., p. 101.

153. For a discussion of this, see Edward W. Said, "Swift's Tory Anarchy," *Eighteenth Century Studies* 3, No. 1 (Fall 1969); pp. 64 ff.

154. Yeats, *Collected Poems,* p. 299.

155. Compare with Saussure's discoveries, discussed by Starobinski, *Les Mots sous les mots,* pp. 19-20.

156. Giacomo Leopardi, *Selected Prose and Poetry,* trans. and ed. Iris Origo and John Heath-Stubbs (New York: New American Library, 1967), p. 28.

157. Norman O. Brown, *Closing Time* (New York: Random House, 1973).

158. Hopkins, *Poems,* p. 48.

159. *The Letters of Gerard Manley Hopkins to Robert Bridges,* ed. Claude Colleer Abbott (London: Oxford University Press, 1935), p. 52.

160. Hopkins, *Poems,* p. 60.

161. Ibid., p. 63.

162. *Sermons and Devotional Writings of Gerard Manley Hopkins,* ed. Christopher Devlin (London: Oxford University Press, 1959), p. 123.

163. Hopkins, *Poems,* p. 70.

164. *The Correspondence of Gerard Manley Hopkins and Richard Watson Dixon,* ed. Claude Colleer Abbott (London: Oxford University Press, 1935), p. 133.

165. Hopkins, *Sermons,* p. 197.

166. Ibid.

167. Ibid., pp. 197-98.

168. Ibid., p. 200.

169. Ibid., pp. 200-201.

170. Ibid., p. 202.

171. Hopkins, *Poems,* p. 90.

172. Ibid., p. 101.

173. January 12, 1888, *Letters of Hopkins to Bridges,* p. 270.

174. Hopkins, *Poems,* p. 107.

175. Ibid., p. 108.

CHAPTER FIVE

1. Samuel Johnson, "The Life of Milton," in *The Lives of the Poets, The Works of Samuel Johnson* (London: Luke Hansard, 1806), 9: 150.

2. Ibid., p. 147.

Notes

3. See D. C. Allen, "Some Theories of the Growth and Origin of Language in Milton's Age," *Philological Quarterly* 27, no. 1 (January 1949): 5-16.

4. Michel Foucault, *The Order of Things,* p. 278.

5. Roland Barthes, *Critical Essays,* p. 164.

6. Foucault, *The Order of Things,* p. xxi.

7. Ibid., p. 298.

8. Ibid.

9. Ibid., p. xi. This is from Foucault's own foreword to the English translation.

10. Ibid., p. 168.

11. Steven Marcus, "In Praise of Folly," *New York Review of Books,* November 3, 1966, p. 8.

12. Foucault, *The Order of Things,* p. 208.

13. The last being *La Naissance de la clinique: Une Archéologie du regard médical* (Paris: Presses Universitaires de France, 1963).

14. Foucault, *The Order of Things,* p. 240.

15. Ibid., pp. 318 ff.

16. Ibid., pp. 328 ff.

17. Ibid., p. 366.

18. Ibid., p. 357.

19. Ibid., pp. 364-65.

20. Ibid., p. 382.

21. Ibid., p. 367.

22. Ibid., p. 364.

23. Barthes, *La Tour Eiffel* (Lausanne: Delpire, 1964), p. 82.

24. Conrad, *Heart of Darkness,* pp. 112-13.

25. Claude Lévi-Strauss, *The Savage Mind,* p. 252.

26. "Les Intellectuels et le pouvoir: Entretien Michel Foucault-Gilles Deleuze," *L'Arc,* No. 49 (1972): 6.

27. On the later Foucault, see Edward W. Said, "An Ethics of Language," *Diacritics* 4, no. 2 (Summer 1974): 28-37.

28. Foucault, "Nietzsche, la généalogie, l'histoire," in *Hommage à Jean Hyppolite* (Paris: Presses Universitaires de France, 1971), p. 159.

29. Deleuze, "Un Nouvel Archiviste," *Critique* 274 (March 1970): 198-200. In general, it is worth comparing Deleuze's essay on Foucault with Raymond Aron's attack on Foucault in *D'Une Sainte Famille à l'autre: Essais sur les marxismes imaginaires* (Paris: Gallimard, 1969).

30. Foucault, "Réponse au Cercle d'épistémologie," *Cahiers pour l'Analyse* 9 (Summer 1968): 19.

31. The literature on the loss of the subject is enormously varied in English. Two recent statements of note are Lionel Trilling's *Sincerity and Authenticity,* (Cambridge: Harvard University Press, 1972) especially "Authenticity and the Modern Unconscious," and Wylie Sypher's *Loss of the Self in Modern Literature and Art* (New York: Vintage, 1962). In French, Lévi-Strauss's *Savage Mind* and *The Raw and the Cooked,* Lacan's *Ecrits,* and Barthes's works all told are also of importance. In addition to such arguments as these, there is Foucault's objection that the subject does not do justice to, and analytically cannot cope with, the complexity of discourse. See *The Order of Things,* p. xiii.

32. Foucault, "Theatrum Philosophicum," *Critique* 282 (November 1970): 885-90.

33. Georges Canguihelm, "Mort de l'homme, ou épuisement du Cogito?" *Critique* 242 (July 1967): 611.

34. Other critics who have drawn attention to this process of "creative" dissociation are Barthes in *Critical Essays* (see Chapter 1, note 5, of the present work) and elsewhere; Richard Poirier, *The Performing Self;* Morse Peckham, *Man's Rage for Chaos: Biology, Behavior, and the Arts* (Philadelphia: Chilton, 1965); and Blanchot in *L'Espace littéraire.*

No contemporary writer has made more of the notions of creative dissociation, waste, and transgression than Georges Bataille; see his *Sur Nietzsche: Volonté de chance* (Paris: Gallimard, 1945) and *La Littérature et le mal* (Paris: Gallimard, 1957).

35. Foucault, "Nietzsche, la génealogie," p. 172.

36. Foucault, *L'Ordre du discours* (Paris: Gallimard, 1971), pp. 60, 61. *L'Ordre du discours* is the French original of *The Discourse on Language,* printed as an appendix to *The Archeology of Knowledge.* I have not used the published English translation because in the main it is both inaccurate and misleading.

37. Ibid., p. 61.

38. Ibid., pp. 49-53.

39. This work should be read in conjunction with Foucault's "entretien" with Deleuze, "Les intellectuels et le pouvoir: Entretien Michel Foucault-Gilles Deleuze," the two works providing a program of aggressive intellectual activity.

40. Foucault's word is *renversement*—literally, "overturning." However, in my translation I have chosen *reversibility* because it contains the idea of reversing and with it the suggestion of a continually practiced action. *L'Ordre du discours,* p. 54.

41. Some of the adumbrations of *discours* are to be found in Edmund Ortigues, *Le Discours et le symbole* (Paris: Aubier, 1962); Benveniste, *Problems in General Linguistics*; Barthes, "To Write: An Intransitive Verb?"; and Gerard Genette, "Frontières du recit," in *Figures II* (Paris: Editions du Seuil, 1969), pp. 49-69. *Discours* is linked also to conceptions of *écritures,* for which Barthes's work is preeminently important, as is Brice Parain's *Recherches sur la nature et les fonctions du langage* (Paris: Gallimard, 1942). Later developments in the theory of *écriture*—found in the works of Philippe Sollers, Julia Kristeva, and the *Tel Quel* group—are sketched in Leon Roudiez, "Les Tendances actuelles de l'écriture: Présentation et bibliographie," *French Review* 45 (December 1971): 321-32.

42. Emile Benveniste, *Problems in General Linguistics,* pp. 206-7.

43. Ibid., pp. 208-9.

44. Lacan *Ecrits,* p. 249. See also his *présentation* to a new French translation by Paul Duquenne of Schreber's memoirs in *Cahiers pour l'Analyse* 5 (November-December 1966): 69-72.

45. Foucault, *L'Ordre du discours,* pp. 19-21.

46. *Naissance de la clinique* is a detailed examination of the development and formation of clinical discourse from the middle of the eighteenth century to about the 1820s.

47. Foucault, *L'Ordre du discours,* pp. 54-55.

48. This is true of Foucault especially after 1968.

49. Foucault, "Theatrum Philosophicum," p. 899.

50. Foucault, "Le Langage à l'infini," p. 53. For another reflection on some of Borges's ideas of literature, the library, and language, see Gerard Genette, *Figures I* (Paris: Editions du Seuil, 1966), pp. 123-32.

51. See Foucault's account of Deleuze in "Theatrum Philosophicum," and also Gilles Deleuze, *Différence et répétition.* There is an important correspondence between the idea of interdiscursive repetition in Foucault and Deleuze and the attention paid in rather recent criticism (e.g., in the work of Northrop Frye and Hugh Kenner) to the echoic character of modernist writing.

52. Foucault, "Réponse à une question," p. 859.

53. Foucault, *The Order of Things,* pp. 306-7.

54. It is worth mentioning that after 1968 in Foucault's own discourse the archive replaces the *épistémè* as a focus of interest.

55. Foucault, "Nietzsche, la généalogie," p. 156.

56. Foucault, "Le Langage à l'infini," p. 44.

57. Ibid., pp. 45-46.

58. Foucault, "Le Langage de l'éspace," *Critique* 203 (April 1964): 378.

59. Ibid.

60. Foucault, "Le *Non* du père," *Critique* 178 (March 1972): 199.

61. Foucault, "Nietzsche, Marx, Freud," p. 189.

62. Ibid., pp. 184-85.

63. Ibid., p. 183.

64. Foucault, "Theatrum Philosophicum," p. 901.

65. Foucault, *L'Ordre du discours,* p. 55. Here, too, there is a large body of modern writing on the way in which discourse cannot be easily resolved into such concepts as "author" or "subject." For alternative arguments on the very active but circumscribed role played by the concept of "author," see Pierre Macherey, *Pour une théorie de la production littéraire* (Paris: François Maspèro, 1966); Walter Benjamin, "Der Autor als Produzent," in *Versuche über Brecht* (Frankfurt: Suhrkamp Verlag, 1966), pp. 95-116; and Barthes, "Writers and Authors," in *Critical Essays.*

66. Foucault, *The Order of Things,* p. 209.

67. Ibid.

68. Ibid., pp. 305-6.

69. Foucault begins *L'Ordre du discours* with a quotation from Beckett's *Molloy* as well: the point always seems to be to kill man the author.

70. Foucault, "Qu'est-ce qu'un auteur?" *passim.*

71. Foucault, *L'Ordre du discours,* pp. 11-21.

72. See the foreword especially written by Foucault for *The Order of Things,* p. xi: "What I would like to do, however, is to reveal a *positive unconscious* of knowledge."

73. In *L'Ordre du discours* Foucault makes it clear that all these are questions he has raised without as yet having answered them.

74. Foucault, "Theatrum Philosophicum," p. 893.

75. Ibid.

76. Ibid., p. 906.

77. Deleuze, "Un Nouvel archiviste," p. 208.

78. Foucault, *L'Ordre du discours,* p. 55. In this connection, see the investigative attitudes and the findings of the Soviet psychologist A. R. Luria in his *The Mind of a Mnemonist,* trans. Lynn Solotaroff (New York: Basic Books, 1968).

79. Foucault, "La Pensée du dehors," *Critique* 229 (June 1966): pp. 525-27.

80. Ibid., p. 525.

81. See note 44, above.

82. Canguihelm, "Mort de l'homme," p. 607.

83. Foucault, "Réponse au cercle d'épistémologie," p. 40.

84. The same complexity, tending to diffuseness, is true in structuralist methodological definitions and classifications. This is an important issue requiring full analysis, but suffice it here to say that the almost bewildering profusion of rules and definitions is linked more to methodological self-classification—and "scientific" discipline—than to application.

85. The problems of what is a "model" and what is "human" are, of course, very involved. I use both *human* (or *inhuman*) and *model* here in a very simpleminded way—which does not, however, necessarily reflect either Foucault's attitudes or his interests, especially since, on the basis of *The Order of Things,* he has been identified as the philosopher of the "death of man."

86. See "Qu'est-ce qu'un auteur?" pp. 92-93, for specific differences that Foucault draws between *rediscovery, reactualization,* and *return.*

87. Throughout this discussion of Foucault I have intended *imaginative* not in the sense of vague invention, but rather in the sense of representing, reconceiving. I imply reflection and originality together, but kept within the material of discourse, as Foucault describes it.

88. Foucault, *Raymond Roussel* (Paris: Gallimard, 1963), p. 210.

89. See the call to action articulated in the interview with Deleuze, as well as the

recently published study *Moi, Pierre Rivière, ayant egorgé ma mère, ma soeur, et mon frere* (Paris: Gallimard/Julliard, 1973).

90. See Chapter 2, note 7, and, in Chapter 4, the discussion of transformations of the notion of a text.

91. Wilhelm von Humboldt was one of the first to point this out. See his posthumous work of 1836, *Uber die Verschiedenheit des Menschlichen Sprachbaues und ihren Einfluss auf die geistige Entwicklung des Menschengeschlechts,* in *Gesammelte schriften,* ed. Albert Leitzmann (Berlin: Prussian Academy, 1907), 7: 253.

92. Benveniste, *Problems in General Linguistics,* p. 61.

93. Foucault, *The Order of Things,* pp. 217 ff.

94. Barthes, *Critical Essays,* p. 267.

95. Blanchot, "L'Homme au point zéro," *La Nouvelle Revue Française,* no. 40 (April 1966): 689.

96. See Georges Charbonnier, *Entretiens avec Claude Lévi-Strauss* (Paris: Plon, 1961), pp. 30, 31, 32 et passim; also Lévi-Strauss, "Introduction à l'oeuvre de Marcel Mauss," in *Sociologie et anthropologie* by Marcel Mauss (Paris: Presses Universitaires de France, 1950), p. LIX.

97. Lévi-Strauss, "The Disappearance of Man," *New York Review of Books,* July 28, 1966, p. 7.

98. Barthes, *Critical Essays,* p. 276.

99. Lévi-Strauss, *The Raw and the Cooked,* pp. 17-18.

100. Charbonnier, *Entretiens avec Lévi-Strauss,* p. 33.

101. Barthes, "Les Sciences humaines et l'oeuvre de Lévi-Strauss," *Annales* no. 6 (November-December 1964): 1085-86.

102. Barthes, *Michelet par lui-même* (Paris: Editions du Seuil, 1965), page facing frontispiece.

103. Barthes, *Critique et verité,* p. 71.

104. Ferdinand de Saussure, *Course in General Linguistics,* p. 6.

105. Ibid., p. 8.

106. Ibid., p. 9.

107. Ibid., pp. 65 ff.

108. Ibid., p. 67.

109. Edmund Leach, "The Legitimacy of Solomon: Some Structural Aspects of Old Testament History," *Archives Européenes de Sociologie* 3 (1962): 70.

110. Barthes, "Eléments de semiologie," *Communications,* no. 4 (1965): 132-33.

111. Lévi-Strauss, "Réponses à quelques questions," *Esprit,* no. 11 (November 1963): 630.

112. Barthes, *Critical Essays,* pp. 215-17.

113. Girard, *Deceit, Desire, and the Novel,* pp. 2-3.

114. This is the thesis of Louis Althusser's *Pour Marx* (Paris: François Maspèro, 1965).

115. Lévi-Strauss, "Introduction à l'oeuvre de Mauss," p. xxvii.

116. Lévi-Strauss, "Réponses à quelques questions," p. 644.

117. Barthes, "Rhétorique de l'image," *Communications,* no. 4 (1965); 43.

118. Barthes, *Critical Essays,* p. 215.

119. Ibid., p. 170.

120. Lévi-Strauss, "Vingt Ans aprés," *Les Temps Modernes,* no. 256 (September 1967); 386.

121. Genette, *Figures I,* pp. 201-2.

122. Barthes, *Critical Essays,* p. 269.

123. Lacan, *Ecrits,* p. 522.

124. Ibid., pp. 93-100. See also Edward W. Said, "Linguistics and the Archeology of Mind," *International Philosophical Quarterly,* 11, No. 1 (March 1970): 104-34.

125. Althusser, *Pour Marx,* p. 61.

126. Ibid., p. 238.

Notes

127. J. L. Austin, *How to Do Things with Words* (Cambridge: Harvard University Press, 1962).

128. Barthes, "Rhétorique de l'image," p. 48.

129. Lévi-Strauss, *The Savage Mind,* pp. 16 ff.

130. Genette, *Les Chemins actuels de la critique,* ed. Georges Poulet (Paris: Plon, 1967), p. 258.

131. Genette, *Figures I,* p. 155.

132. Lévi-Strauss, *Tristes tropiques,* trans. John Russell (New York: Atheneum, 1964), p. 398.

133. Benveniste, *Problems in General Linguistics,* pp. 217-22.

134. Genette, *Figures I,* p. 153.

135. Levin, *Contexts of Criticism* (Cambridge: Harvard University Press, 1957), p. 253.

136. Barthes, *Critical Essays,* p. 216.

137. Lévi-Strauss, "The Disappearance of Man," p. 6.

138. Lévi-Strauss, "La Notion de structure en ethnologie," in *Sens et usages du terme structure* (The Hague: Mouton, 1962), pp. 44-45.

139. Lévi-Strauss, *Totemism,* trans. Rodney Needham (Boston: Beacon Press, 1963), p. 103.

140. Lévi-Strauss, *The Savage Mind,* pp. 135 ff.

141. See Chapter 3, note 110.

142. Lévi-Strauss, *Totemism,* p. 31.

143. Jean Starobinski, "Remarques sur le structuralisme," in *Ideen und Formen: Festschrift für Hugo Friedrich* (Frankfurt: Vittorio Klosterman, 1964), p. 277.

144. See Barthes's essay "To Write: an Intransitive Verb?"

145. Barthes, *Le Degré zéro de l'écriture* (Paris: Gonthier, 1964), p. 39.

146. This applies explicitly to Derrida's early work: see, in particular, Jacques Derrida, *L'Ecriture et la différence* and *De la grammatologie.*

147. See Derrida's essay "La Différence," in *Marges de la philosophie* (Paris: Editions de Minuit, 1972), pp. 3-29.

148. Derrida, *De la grammatologie,* p. 39.

149. Derrida, *L'Ecriture et la différence,* p. 411.

150. Ibid., p. 417.

151. Ibid., p. 421.

152. Ibid., p. 427.

CHAPTER SIX

1. Vico, *The New Science.* For the sake of convenience, Vico's paragraph numbers appear in parentheses following quotations. These numbers also correspond to paragraph numbers in the Nicolini edition of Vico's Italian and both the paperback and hard-cover editions of the Bergin-Fisch translation.

2. See the important and excellent article on Vico's complex relationships with Cartesian philosophy by Yvon Belaval, "Vico and Anti-Cartesianism," in *Giambattista Vico: An International Symposium,* ed. Giorgio Tagliacozzo and Hayden V. White (Baltimore: Johns Hopkins University Press, 1969), pp. 77-92.

3. For an interesting study of Vico's "atheism," see J. Chaix-Ruy, *J.-B. Vico et l'illuminisme athée* (Paris: Editions Mondiales, 1968). See also Fausto Nicolini, *La Religiosità di Giambattista Vico: Quatro saggi* (Bari: Laterza, 1949).

4. Samuel Butler, *Erewhon* (New York: Dutton, 1965), p. 132.

5. Vico, in *Opere,* ed. Nicolini, p. 919.

6. Friedrich Hölderlin, "Brod und Wein" in *Poems and Fragments,* trans. Michael Hamburger (Ann Arbor: University of Michigan Press, 1967), p. 247.

7. *The Autobiography of Giambattista Vico,* trans. Max Harold Fisch and Thomas Goddard Bergin (Ithaca, N.Y.: Cornell University Press, 1944), p. 136.

8. Benedetto Croce, *The Philosophy of Giambattista Vico,* trans. R. G. Collingwood (London: Howard Latimer, 1913). The point is made throughout the book.

9. Vico, *Autobiography,* p. 149.

10. Vico, "De Antequissima Italorum Sapientae ex Linguae Latinae Originibus Eruenda," in *Opera Latina,* ed. Guiseppe Ferrari (Milan, 1854), 1: 63.

11. Croce, *Philosophy of Vico,* p. 141; H. P. Adams, *The Life and Writings of Giambattista Vico* (London: Allen & Unwin, 1935), p. 123.

12. Vico, *Opera Latina,* p. 66.

13. Samuel Taylor Coleridge, *Biographia Literaria,* in *Selected Poetry and Prose of Coleridge,* ed. Donald Stauffer (New York: Modern Library, 1951), p. 263.

14. Croce, *Philosophy of Vico,* p. 266.

15. Erich Auerbach, *Literary Language and its Public,* p. 37.

16. Vico, *On the Study Methods of Our Time,* trans. Elio Gianturco (New York: Library of Liberal Arts, 1965), p. 78.

17. Ibid., p. 79. Cf. Vico's remark in the *Autobiography* that his works were "so many noble acts of vengeance against his detractors" (p. 200).

18. In Vico, *Opere,* pp. 118-19.

19. For a clear description of *invention* as "finding" see Belaval, "Vico and Anti-Cartesianism," p. 79.

20. Vico, *Autobiography,* p. 144.

21. Ibid., p. 146. See also the essay by Elizabeth Sewell, "Bacon, Vico, and Coleridge and the Poetic Method," in Tagliacozzo and White, *Vico: An International Symposium,* pp. 125-36.

22. Jean-Jacques Rousseau, *Oeuvres Complètes,* ed. Bernard Gagnebin and Marcel Raymond (Paris: Gallimard, 1969), 4: 252.

23. Ibid., p. 468.

24. Ibid., p. 586.

25. Ibid., pp. 568-69.

26. Ibid., p. 550.

27. Ibid., pp. 346 ff.

28. Ibid., p. 570. On the general relationship between Vico and Rousseau, see Fausto Nicolini, *Vico e Rousseau* (Naples: Giannini, 1949), and Edmund Leach, "Vico and Lévi-Strauss on the Origins of Humanity" in Tagliacozzo and White, *Vico: An International Symposium,* especially pp. 309-11.

29. This is an aspect of the rise of the New Philology and/or New Linguistics discussed by Schwab in *La Renaissance orientale* and in a more restricted way by Hans Aarslef, *The Study of Language in England, 1780-1860* (Princeton: Princeton University Press, 1967).

30. Lionel Trilling, *Mind in the Modern World* (New York: Viking, 1972).

31. Paul de Man, "What is Modern?" *New York Review of Books,* August 26, 1965, p. 11.

32. For criticism of this surface phenomenon, see Edward W. Said, "Eclecticism and Orthodoxy in Criticism," *Diacritics* 2, no. 1 (Spring 1972), 2-8.

33. See Gilles Deleuze, *Différence et répétition,* pp. 89-90.

34. See Angus Fletcher, "Utopian History and the Anatomy of Criticism," in *Northrop Frye in Modern Criticism,* ed. Murray Krieger (New York: Columbia University Press, 1966), pp. 31-73.

35. Frye, *Anatomy of Criticism: Four Essays* (Princeton: Princeton University Press, 1957), p. 354.

36. Ibid., p. 351.

37. See Claude Lévi-Strauss, "Overture," in *The Raw and the Cooked.*

38. Deleuze, *Différence et répétition,* pp. 89-90;

NOTES

39. Ibid., pp. 164-65.

40. "Les Intellectuels et le pouvoir: Entretien Michel Foucault-Gilles Deleuze," *L'Arc* no. 49 (1972): 4.

41. Ibid., p. 5.

42. Ibid., p. 8.

43. Noam Chomsky, *American Power and the New Mandarins* (New York: Pantheon, 1969), p. 28.

44. Ibid., p. 321.

45. Pierre Thevenaz, *What Is Phenomenology?* p. 96.

INDEX

Index

genealogical sequence *(continued)*
158; vs. adjacency, 357; *see also* time
Gênet, Jean, 24, 74
Génette, Gerard, 328, 331, 334
German Ideology, The (Marx and Engel), 90
Girard, René, 141, 325
Gissing, George, 139
Göethe, Johann Wolfgang von, 95-96, 334
Goldmann, Lucien, 330; study of Pascal and Racine, 330
Good Soldier, The (Ford), 151
Gospels, 141, 210-13; Renan's stages of development of, 216-17; *see also* New Testament
Grainger, Gilles Gaston, 335
Great Expectations (Dickens), 222; cycle of birth and death in, 97-98; Pip's authority, 94, 95, 99; Pip's lack of beginnings, 93, 96, 99; Pip's lack of freedom in, 90, 97-98; significance of Little Pip in, 145
Great Transformation, The (Polanyi), 55-56
Green, W. H.: Old Testament as delivered by God, 214-15
Gulliver's Travels (Swift): reversibility in, 30-31

Hampshire, Stuart, 12-13
Hardy, Thomas, 138; rejection of hierarchical time by, 137-41
Hartmann, Anton, 214
Heart of Darkness (Conrad), 11, 84-85, 128, 287-88; reflection on beginnings in, 232-33; use of narrative in, 151
Hegel, Georg Wilhelm Friedrich, 42
Heidegger, Martin, 43, 44, 323; and intransitive beginnings, 73
Higher Criticism of the Pentateuch (Green), 214
Higher Critics, 206-209, 214-15, 222
Histoire de la folie à l'âge classique (Foucault), 73-74, 284
history, 347; gentile or secular, 11, 92, 349-50, 353; language in, appearance of, 43, 280, 316, 351; Nietzsche and Foucault's view of, 290, 301; sacred, 92, 142, 349-50; text as obstruction to, 203; Vico's description of, 91-92, 262, 349-50, 353, 354
"History of the Psychoanalytic Movement" (Freud), 180, 181

History and Class Consciousness (Lukacs), 41
History of Classical Scholarship (Sandys), 198
Hölderlin, Friedrich, 305, 312
Homer, 198; Nietzsche's view of, as man and as an aesthetic judgment, 56-58; poems of, as key to periods of history, 198
Hooker, Richard, 8
Hopkins, Gerald Manley, 138, 233, 240; biology parallels writing, 267-69; at end of career, 259-60, 272-75; on innovation and repetition, 255-57; self-sacrifice of the writer, 270-71; sexual parallels between divine and human author, 265-67; on writer's life, 237
Housman, A. E., 206, 208, 209
Huizinga, John, 35-36, 322
humanism vs. supranaturalism, 373-80; *see also* predeterminism vs. free will
Humboldt, Wilhelm von, 18
Husserl, Edmund, 41, 69; philosophy of, in relation to beginnings, 48-49, 72, 73, 78
Hyppolite, Jean, 291

Ibsen, Henrik; author as father of his text, 263
Importance of Being Earnest (Wilde), 238
intention, 59-60, 70, 192; definition of, 5, 11-13, 47-48, 63; in dream analysis, 165; Hopkins's temporality of, 268; Structuralist's control of, by system, 319-20, 338; for Vico, 361-62
Interpretation of Dreams (Freud), 160-73, 229; determinism of psychical events, 164, 173; as inaugural text, 179-80; intention of, 165-66; lack of final text of, 166; not a conventional scientific text, 163; paralleled in *Doctor Faustus,* 187-88; presence and absence in, 177
Islamic culture: novel, as inimical to, 81; spoken tradition in, 199-200; *see also* Koran

James, Henry, 84, 85, 95, 135, 222, 233, 253; interpretation of fiction, 162; use of narrative by, 151
Jaspers, Karl, 222
Jesus, *see* Gospels; New Testament; *Vie de Jésus* (Renan)